# THE TRIBE OF DINA

## A JEWISH WOMEN'S ANTHOLOGY

Edited by
Melanie Kaye/Kantrowitz and Irena Klepfisz

Associate Editor
Esther F. Hyneman

Beacon Press    Boston

*For our mothers*
*Rose Perczykow Klepfisz*
*Violette Wolfgang Kaye*

Beacon Press
25 Beacon Street
Boston, Massachusetts 02108

Beacon Press books
are published under the auspices of
the Unitarian Universalist Association of Congregations.

96   95   94   93   92   91   90   89      8   7   6   5   4   3   2   1

*Library of Congress Cataloging-in-Publication Data*
The Tribe of Dina: a Jewish women's anthology/edited by Melanie
Kaye/Kantrowitz and Irena Klepfisz.
      p.  cm.
   "Most of the material in this volume originally appeared in nos.
29/30 of the journal Sinister Wisdom (1986)"—T.p. verso.
   Includes bibliographies.
   ISBN 0-8070-3605-6
   1. Jewish literature.   2. Women, Jewish—Literary collections.
3. Women—Israel.   I. Kaye/Kantrowitz, Melanie.   II. Klepfisz,
Irena.   III. Title: Jewish women's anthology.
PN6071.J6T7   1989
810'.8'08924—dc19      88-43319

## Genesis 34:

*"....And Dinah the daughter of Leah whom she had borne unto Jacob, went out to see the daughters of the land [Canaan]. And Shechem the son of Hamor the Hivite, the prince of the land saw her; and he took her, and lay with her, and humbled her. And his soul did cleave unto Dinah the daughter of Jacob, and he loved the damsel and spoke comfortingly unto the damsel. And Shechem spoke unto his father Hamor, saying: 'Get me this damsel to wife.' Now Jacob heard that he had defiled Dinah his daughter. . .And the sons of Jacob answered Shechem and Hamor his father with guile, and spoke, because he had defiled Dinah their sister, and said unto them: 'We cannot do this thing, to give our sister to one that is uncircumcised; for that were a reproach unto us. Only on this condition will we consent unto you: if ye will be as we are, that every male of you be circumcised. . .' and every male was circumcised. . .And it came to pass on the third day, when they were in pain, that two of the sons of Jacob, Simeon and Levi, Dinah's brethren, took each man his sword, and came upon the city unawares, and slew all the males. And they slew Hamor and Shechem his son with the edge of the sword, and took Dinah out of Shechem's house, and went forth. . . ."*

## Dina

Dina, the daughter of Leah and Jacob, the sister of the founders of the twelve tribes of Israel. And she went out of her father's house seeking other women. What did she want? What did she want to give? Did she ever reach them before Shechem the Hivite took her? Did he seduce her? Attract her? Did he rape her? Did *her* soul cleave unto *him*? And when the brothers found out, what did she feel?

No words, no hints. Only what the men felt and thought: *his woman, his wife; their sister defiled, their honor sullied.* Only what the men did and wanted to be done: *taking. force. violence.*

And the women: Did Dina ever speak to the women? Did they gather secretly? Comfort each other? Weep over the blood? Did they tell each other stories? Did they want something for themselves?

And Dina: Did she want something away from the father, away from the brothers? Did she need her mother? Did she long for sisters, for daughters to gather a Tribe of Dina?

# Contents

## 3.  I Am the Present Generation

## 4.  Lot's Wife Revisited

## 5.  *Kol Haisha:* Israeli Women Speak

## 6. Bread and Roses

Writing this update to the introduction two and a half years after *The Tribe of Dina* was first published, we find that the work contained in that first edition is as relevant today as it was in 1986. Readers' responses to the book have repeatedly confirmed our belief that *Dina* revealed Jewish women's participation in Jewish life, affirmed the value of that participation, gave strength for feminist struggle to continue in the Jewish community. With the rise of Jewish stereotyping (particularly on American campuses in the form of baiting of Jewish women as Jewish American Princesses), *Dina,* we hope, will continue to be a tool of empowerment.

Nothing has been deleted from the original edition except for *Sinister Wisdom* magazine paraphernalia and a book review. We have added material, guided by current events as well as by reactions to the anthology. Most obvious is the continuing and intensifying political crisis in Israel. As Israel's invasion of Lebanon in 1982 shaped much of the Israeli material in the first edition, so the Israeli section in this second edition has been updated in response to the *Intifada*—the Palestinian uprising in the Gaza Strip and on the West Bank—that began in December 1987. We have also included more poetry by Israeli women. In addition, the experience of Sephardic women (in Israel and in the United States) is better represented, as is the experience of working-class Jews. We are pleased to be reprinting a story by a child survivor, which has been out of print for thirty years, material on Soviet Jewish women, and some additional artwork.

We are pleased with the reception of *Dina* over the past two years, for it has been a difficult self-publishing enterprise. The anthology was first printed as a special double issue of *Sinister Wisdom #29/30.* We distributed 9000 copies as small presses do: mostly without paid staff. Throughout the book's life, both editors have worked other jobs for a living.

The success of the book has been mirrored not only in the number of copies distributed but in its adoption by women's-studies and Jewish-studies courses, by study groups ranging from Hadassah to New Jewish Agenda. Political and Jewish consciousness-raising groups have singled out as particularly useful the handbook *"In gerangl/*In Struggle." This response to *Dina* has been extremely gratifying.

We have always been commited to keeping *The Tribe of Dina* in print. The decision not to republish the book ourselves was a difficult one. In the end, we simply could not fathom coming up with either the money or the time required for production, promotion, and distribution. Because of this, we were delighted that Beacon Press offered to reissue the collection in the expanded version you now hold, as the first offering in their new Jewish feminist line. We know that this edition will reach an even wider audience than the first and are grateful to Deborah Chasman, our editor at Beacon, for her commitment, openness, and, above all, her patience.

Many other women deserve thanks and appreciation for all sorts of help and support. Lil Moed again coordinated the Israeli contingent, sending us poetry by Israeli women and updates on interviews and resources. Associate editor Esther Hyneman shlepped, promoted, and sold with unflagging zest. Linda Vance was pressed into constant and varied service, from lifting boxes and packing books to designing ads and putting out bulk mailings, and—along with Esther and Judy Waterman—to womanning the book table at many of the readings, conferences, and events at which *Dina* and her public became acquainted. Rose Perczykow Klepfisz was a one-woman support team, persuading her many connections to pay attention to "this wonderful book about all kinds of Jewish women," selling copies not only from her Bronx apartment but also at two successive Jewish Book Fairs. For their labor and faith we are especially thankful.

Evelyn Torton Beck, Ellen Cannon, Janet Freedman, and Lee Knefelkamp helped promote *Dina* in very concrete ways, as did many other members of the National Women's Studies Association Jewish Caucus, especially the indefatigable Mindy Shapiro. Mindy probably is single-handedly responsible for the first Jewish Women's Plenary Session at NWSA in 1986, at which we both spoke, and which did much to bring *Dina* to the attention of academic feminists. Cindy Lanane, Priscilla Lynch, Laurie Todd, Laura Philips, and Chana Pollack all helped by organizing fundraising events, as did contributors Jyl Felman, Tryna Hope, Ellen Gruber Garvey, Elana Dykewomon, Teya Schaffer, Judy Freespirit, Sandra Butler, and the late Barbara Rosenblum. We want to thank Edythia Selman, our agent, for believing in *Dina* and helping us in the transition from self-publishing to commercial publishing.

Finally, our greatest debt is to the contributors of *The Tribe of Dina: A Jewish Women's Anthology*. We know this debt is shared by thousands of Jewish women for making us, our history, our breadth of experience, and our depth of creativity visible, audible, and tangible.

Melanie Kaye/Kantrowitz
Irena Klepfisz

# Introduction to the First Edition

If we began at the beginning—this being the year 5746—it would take a long time. So we begin at our meeting, with an event that marked a starting point for many Jewish feminists, the publication in April 1982 of Evelyn T. Beck's *Nice Jewish Girls: A Lesbian Anthology*; because we were both contributors to that collection, because we became friends and co-workers in a series of events connected with *NJG*.

For a number of years Jewish feminists had been challenging anti-Semitism and sexism in the women's and Jewish communities; *NJG* made this work and these issues more visible, inspired and mobilized Jewish feminists. In addition, it announced, perhaps for the first time, the existence of lesbian Jews unwilling to be excluded from our home tradition.

Although *NJG* was subtitled "A Lesbian Anthology," heterosexual Jewish feminists responded strongly to the proud female Jewish consciousness; and Jewish lesbians gave it to their parents as the one book, perhaps, that their family could relate to. We were aware that *NJG* represented an awakening of enormous creative and intellectual energy among Jewish women. And we were eager to continue the momentum. As writers, we wanted to gather an anthology in which a great variety of fine creative and theoretical writing would abound. That was our original impulse.

But the impulse became considerably more complicated. June 1982 witnessed the Israeli invasion of Lebanon, an event which had a profound effect on American Jews, as on Israelis. And it had its impact on the women's movement as well, fueling anti-Semitism and dividing Jewish opinion.

Jewish feminists and lesbians are of a diverse sort. In many ways they represent a microcosm of the Jewish community, for they stem from every corner of it—orthodox, secular, atheist, Zionist, anti-Zionist, cultural, communist, Sephardic, Ashkenazi. The result is that much of the debate mirrors that of the larger Jewish community. Disagreements are fierce; denouncements not uncommon.

At the time, we were both members of *Di Vilde Chayes*,\* a group that tried to formulate responses to the ever-worsening situation in the Middle East and to the increasing anti-Semitism in general and in the women's movement. The work was extremely difficult. Though *Di Vilde Chayes'* statements forced many women—Jews and gentiles—to think for the first time about the Middle East and Jewish political issues, we ourselves were confused about how to counter anti-Semitism without stifling opposition to the Israeli government. After the group disbanded, the two of us, aware that Israelis themselves were engaged in debate, recognized that, as feminists and as Jews, we needed to know more about these struggles. We wanted to support Israelis who were working on issues we were committed to and who were not receiving much encouragement or even acknowledgement in this country. We wanted to strengthen ties between American Jewish and Israeli feminists.

---

\* Other members were: Evelyn T. Beck, Nancy Bereano, Bernice Mennis, and Adrienne Rich.

We concluded that we wanted to hear directly from Israeli women and give them voice in the anthology. A generous grant from the Basser Arts Foundation made possible our trip to Israel in December 1984 to gather information, interviews, art, etc. That trip drastically changed how we viewed *The Tribe of Dina*.

We were already engaged in the anthology when Susannah Heschel's *On Being a Jewish Feminist: A Reader* was published in 1983, a book which contained important material for Jewish women. But the title which promised to include us, Jewish feminists, did not. In fact, the book focused entirely on the relationship between feminists and Judaism, the religion. And we are secular Jews. We realized that secular and cultural Jews needed representation and expression.

Our belief was reinforced by work we did in the movement. Trying to counter anti-Semitism, we conducted many workshops, wrote letters, analyses, and responses. And what we found was: this work was incredibly depleting. It was only fighting a negative: nothing in it made us feel good, only less horrible. We found ourselves perpetually at the edge of a peculiar void and other Jewish women—especially secular ones—at the edge with us. The question kept recurring: Is there a way of being Jewish outside of fighting anti-Semitism? Do we need to be Jewish after anti-Semitism abates? And the critical question: How?

We recognized this as a historical pattern, in the US anyway. In times of persecution, danger and discrimination, the Jewish community gathers to create solidarity. In between these times—solidarity flounders.

We concluded that the other side of fighting the negative, the hatred of Jews, was to build the positive, Jewish identity; that our task as Jews in the US in the late 20th century was to identify assimilation as a grave concern and then try to work against it by reclaiming our culture and history. That too emerged as an important force in shaping our conception of the anthology.

But still another realization was prompted by our work against anti-Semitism. Frequently we found bitter disagreement among Jewish women as to what was and wasn't anti-Semitic. We knew that some of this stemmed from the slippery nature of anti-Semitism itself. But some, we came to understand, stemmed from the diversity of the Jewish women in the movement and their complete ignorance about each others' Jewish experience. So another purpose of this anthology: to express the wide range of Jewish experience and culture, and to develop more empathy and *support* for Jewish identities which we do not share.

To an outsider, we, the editors, might seem the same—Ashkenazi, secular Jews, leftists, NYC raised, English majors, graduate work in literature, feminist/lesbians, in our 40's, writers. In fact, we come from diverse backgrounds and experience. Irena is an immigrant; Melanie was born in Brooklyn. Irena was raised in the Jewish Labor Bund, schooled in Yiddish. Melanie took her Jewishness for granted, spent her late adolescence in the civil rights movement. Irena's feminism was expressed through literary and publishing activities; Melanie was an organizer, especially around violence against women. Irena's writing has always been centered in Jewish themes; Melanie came to this more gradually.

We are sometimes perceived in terms that reflect a too-limited view of the possibilities of Jewish identity. It's as if Irena knowing Yiddish means she has no political awareness; or Melanie as an activist would not be committed to Jewish culture. There were those who would make one of us the better or the worse Jew: the real Jew, the assimilated Jew, the ghettoized Jew, the *goyishe* Jew, the conservative Jew, the radical Jew. What has made our collaboration successful was our recognition that the other—far from being bad or good—represented different perspectives on Jewish experience. Committed to our Jewishness, to women, to justice, equality, freedom, dignity. . .we have brought different experiences and emphases to these commitments. Our differences—and our mutual respect for these differences—have been sources of strength, means of expanding our own individual perspectives. Together we believe we have created a far fuller, more complex *Tribe of Dina* than either of us could have done alone.

As feminists, we are acutely aware of the sexism in Jewish, as in all known, cultures, a sexism which does not exclude women from participating—indeed, women's contributions to Jewish material and cultural survival are vast (as are women's contributions to all people's survival)—but prevents our contributions from being named, recorded, honored, so that a tradition gets passed along which tries, as much as possible, to pretend women had nothing to do with it. Certainly a major impetus for this anthology—from the very outset—was to present Jewish experience in which Jewish women are central.

We are conscious of limitations and goals not met. We had hoped the anthology would be international in scope and not just express the identity of Jews in the US. In this we have been only partly successful. Though Jews from a variety of places are represented and the voices of Israeli women are strong, we deeply regret not having included Jews from the Soviet Union, as well as Jews living in many other countries. Clearly this is a critical next step in developing an international Jewish women's perspective, one that probably has already begun as a result of the International Women's Conference in Nairobi.

We conceived of the anthology in 1982, almost 4 years ago. At that time we sent out a flyer soliciting work, setting a deadline that seemed a long time away, a deadline we have extended again and again: because some of the work we were seeking was hard to come by, especially work from abroad; because we both work for a living, sometimes several jobs at once; because we lived hundreds of miles apart. For these delays we apologize, especially to those who sent us work and waited patiently to hear from us.

Nor had we originally planned the anthology as a special issue of *Sinister Wisdom*. In May 1984, Melanie Kaye/Kantrowitz assumed sole editorship of the magazine. By fall of '84 it clearly made sense to merge the two projects, partly because of the work load—editing one project seemed hard enough, without attempting two at once; partly because as an issue of *SW*, the anthology could come out exactly as we wanted it, limited only by our own resources.

Our own resources, let us add, have been limited. We are aware that had there

11

been money sufficient to travel to Europe, Central and South America, the Soviet Union, or even to pay for international phone calls, Jewish women in these places could also have been represented more fully.

So far the expenses incurred have been covered in part by an overwhelming response to an appeal for advance orders and donations (many from contributors), and by loans from the editors. Needless to say, no one has gotten paid for her work—neither the editors, nor the contributors (except in copies of *Dina*).

But beyond money, people gave generously of themselves, their time, their energy. We want to thank first of all the women who came to our workshops, classes, readings. They continued to remind us that this work mattered, and they directly and indirectly offered us information about what needs *Dina* should address. Women in New York, Philadelphia, New Jersey, Minnesota, California, Maine, Albany, Washington DC taught us over and over that Jewish women in the US need to develop our Jewish identity. These women—and *Dina*'s contributors—taught us that Jewish identity is not just bagels and lox or a prayer shawl: it is activist, feminist, cultural, ethical, delightful, groping, ancient, Sephardic, Ashkenazi, radical, lesbian, international, religious, funny, courageous, loyal, eager, proud.

Next, we are deeply indebted to Esther F. Hyneman, our associate editor, who took on much of the editing labor last spring, consulted, advised, checked resources, proofread and—above all—convinced us that the project could be completed at a time when we were no longer sure. Without her energy and fresh perspective, completion would have been delayed still further. Judy Waterman read work and gave us feedback and conversation over the past three years; she transcribed tapes, retyped manuscripts, proofread, sorted, worked on the glossary. Linda Vance shared the burdens, including days of editing, proofreading, xeroxing, transcribing, source checking, leaflet design, advice and hours of hard criticism. More than anything, Esther, Judy and Linda gave moral support through the emotional upheaval these projects create in our lives.

Rose Perczykow Klepfisz checked sources, located photographs at the ILGWU archives, supplied us with lists of Jewish resources, and proofread. Fauna Yarrow saw *Dina* through her early stages as SW office manager, and Morgan Gray through these last several months, as the new office manager. Tania Kravath's original design for the cover speaks for itself; less evident is her remarkable ability to respond to our suggestions with what seemed infinite inventiveness. Violette Kaye and Roni Natov helped proofread. Bernice Mennis advised and consulted with us whenever we had a problem. Amy Kesselman dug up books for source checking, and Laura Kelleher located quotes. Jan Mailhotte and Georgia Fitzgerald transcribed and typed several pieces. Marianne Milton spent hours organizing the office. Edie Morang, incredibly accurate typesetter, and Helga Manning, creative and patient with layout and design, both labored under the most pressured and confusing conditions.

We are also grateful to individuals and institutions who willingly answered our questions and helped locate sources: Steven Levy who helped us with Judezmo (Ladino); the late Ahrne Thorne who discussed with us Jewish anarchism in the United States; Adrienne Cooper for locating photographs and helping with Hebrew transliteration; Sonia Pinkusowitz for help with glossary, transliteration and general feedback. We are indebted to YIVO Institute for Jewish Research and its staff for making available many of the photographs found in this anthology: to Hannah Fryshdorf and Itzik Gottesman; special thanks to Dina Abramowicz, head librarian, who answered endless questions and remarkably could always locate whatever we needed; and to Marek Web, head of the YIVO Archives, for his willingness to supply us with visual material. We are also grateful to Ettie Goldwasser, oral historian, at the ILGWU Archives, who helped in sorting through appropriate photographs; to the Rosenberg Era Art Project and Rob Okun, its director, for providing us with a photograph of Ethel Rosenberg.

Finally we want to thank the Israeli women who welcomed, housed, fed, and made connections for us, especially Pnina Putterman Ben-Horin and Chaya Shalom.We want to acknowledge the late Naomi Kies for her help; and Pnina, Galia Golan and Lil Moed for their assistance in gathering material about Naomi for our tribute. Lil Moed also gave hours—days—of back-up service in Israel, reviewing interview material, collecting photographs, and generally completing tasks which could not be completed from the US. We want to thank all the 23 women we interviewed, only four of whom appear here. It was their openness, hospitality and eagerness for communication and understanding between American Jewish and Israeli women which made our trip fruitful.

*In khaverteshaft*/In sisterhood,

Melanie Kaye/Kantrowitz        5746        Irena Klepfisz

# 1. My Ancestors Speak

*Esther Roditti de Cordovero in her eighties,
Argentina.*      Courtesy of Rita Arditti

YIVO Archives

*Student member of the Jewish Labor Bund. Swislocz, Poland 1908.*

*Rita Arditti*

# To be a *Hanu* *

I was born in Buenos Aires, Argentina, the second of three daughters of a Jewish Sephardic[1] family. My parents had left Turkey in the 1920's when it had gotten "bad for the Jews." They met and got married in Buenos Aires.

The Jewish community in Turkey traced its origins to Jews who had been expelled from Spain and Portugal by the Inquisition of the 15th century. The Turkish Empire had welcomed the Jews, who lived and prospered there for almost 4 centuries. But during 1912-1913, the Balkan war against the Turks resulted in extreme poverty for the Jewish communities. Turkish nationalism emerged as a powerful force, and the Jews and other ethnic and racial minorities were persecuted.

I grew up hearing stories of Jews in the army being treated like animals, of forced labor and heavy punishments. One story still stands out in my mind: a friend of my father's family, a middle-aged Jewish man, was ordered to move a piano uphill by himself. He tried but could not move it. He was beaten and sent to jail with a long sentence for "refusing to obey orders." As a result of such treatment, Jews started to leave Turkey and emigrate to the Americas.

As a young man, my father, Jacques, went to Argentina to join his older brother in the import-export textile business, a common Sephardic occupation in Turkey and Argentina. He had had very little formal education, maybe a couple of years after elementary school, and some accounting and business courses. He never read anything but the newspaper, but like many other Sephardim he spoke Spanish, Ladino[2], Turkish, French, Hebrew and some Greek.

My mother, Rosa Cordovero, came from a large family, but she had not grown up with her parents. As a young child she had been sent to live with and take care of her grandmother Rachel, after whom I was named. In the custom of her times, my great-grandmother smoked Turkish cigarettes, played cards and entertained friends around small tables where Turkish coffee and sweets were served. My mother was trained to

* Ladino word meaning "good-looking woman."

16

clean house and serve her grandmother. She also lacked formal education, but she spoke Spanish, Ladino, and French. Every month she read the Spanish edition of *Readers' Digest* — she had the complete collection bound in leather — and she liked women's romantic magazines and novels. Searching in her night table, I once found a clearly handled copy of *Forever Amber*, a book with graphic sexual descriptions. A few years later, I discovered a copy of *The Second Sex* by Simone de Beauvoir in the same place. This one, though, looked like it had hardly been touched.

Both my parents had received some instruction from the Alliance Israelite Universelle, an educational institution that tried to modernize the education available to young Jews in Turkey. They often spoke French between themselves and called their friends and acquaintances "*Madame*" or "*Monsieur.*" They used to switch to French when they did not want us daughters to understand what they were talking about. "*Pas devant les petites*" ("not in front of the little ones") became the subject of many jokes and a symbol of the way our family related. Serious topics, like money matters, illnesses or death, were never discussed in front of us.

All the women on both sides of the family were housewives and mothers; only one of them worked out of the home. My aunt Daisy, one of my mother's sisters (who married "very late" according to my family — in her middle thirties), worked in a bank and then in the perfume trade. For us, the daughters, it was expected that we would be *hanum*. We had to look pretty and have good manners; we had to be nice and helpful to the family and obedient to our father. Clothes and looks were very important. But in the right style. To look like a "gypsy" or flashy was not right. Most important, our looks had to elicit respect and admiration. Elegant, but with style. As for our education, we were not expected to continue after high school. We might work in an office or a bank until we got married. Men would take care of us. The boys we met and went out with were carefully scrutinized as to their potential earning ability. First of all, they had to be Jewish; the next questions were, "What does his father do? What is he planning to do for a living?" If the boy planned to join his father in his business, the anxiety diminished; if he was attempting a new venture, or a career of his own, there were wrinkles in my parents' faces.

We celebrated the Jewish holidays by gathering with my father's family. He and his brother had brought my widowed aunt Selma and her three daughters from Turkey. They supported her financially and acted as surrogate fathers for the daughters. No important decision was taken without consulting the "uncles." My aunt adored them. The celebrations would take place in her small apartment. She lived very modestly, making clothes for herself, her elderly mother-in-law and her daughters. The men would first go to the temple while we gathered and waited in her dining room for them. When they returned they read in Hebrew and Ladino. We fasted on Yom Kippur and celebrated Rosh Hashanah, Purim, and *Pesakh*. We the children, all female, had fits of laughter at the men reading the religious books with their hats on. We helped prepare some of our favorite Sephardic dishes that our mothers had planned days in advance: *huevos haminados* (hardboiled eggs cooked in water, oil and coffee, so that they become brown), *borekas* (pastry filled with eggplant or potato and cheese), *boyos* (spinach pies), *bamia con tomato* (okra with tomatoes), rose petal preserve. My favorite sweet was (and still is) *moustachudos*, made with walnuts, almonds, honey and cinnamon.*

My mother would go to synagogue every few weeks and light candles on the Sabbath before the pictures of her dead relatives. One of her sisters, Matilde, had disappeared from France, where she had been living during the Nazi occupation. For years my mother would visit international relief agencies, Jewish groups, foreign embassies trying to find traces of my aunt. After the war we learned that she had been deported

---

* The recipe for *moustachudos* and many other Sephardic dishes can be found in *The Sephardic Cooks*, compiled and published by Congregation Or Veshalom Sisterhood, Atlanta, GA, 1977.

*My sister Edith and I (on right) at the beach in Piriapolis, Uruguay 1938.*

*My mother, Rosa Cordovero at age 20. Turkey, 1925.*

*My father, my mother, my two sisters and I (my father's hand is on my shoulder) on the boat that took me and my mother on my first trip to the US. Buenos Aires 1951.*

18

and had died in Auschwitz. My mother raised money for Jewish organizations (the *Histadruth*, the Sephardic Home for the Aged, orphanages), and I would watch her transformation: her voice changed and she would not take "no" for an answer. She asked my father's friends for money to support the "birth of the state of Israel," and she cried with joy when the state of Israel was finally born. Her greatest wish was to visit Israel some day. And she did: in her early sixties, she went with a tour group, the only time she travelled without another member of the family. After that, she said, she was ready to die. My mother believed that in spite of all the suffering, Jews were indeed the "chosen people" and that justice would prevail in the end.

My father gave money to the Jewish charities reluctantly; but he was not interested in visiting Israel. He loved going to a club of Sephardic families which gathered to play cards, hear Oriental music and meet other Sephardim. Parties, weddings and social gatherings at the club, just a few blocks from our house, were his way of being active in the community.

Until I went to school I did not know that the rest of the world was not Jewish. Except for the maids, no Christians had been in our home. In elementary school we had "Religion" classes, which meant Catholic. After a while I was exempted from them, and, with another Jewish girl, I was given "Moral" classes. We had to read books that said that in spite of the fact that the Jews had killed Jesus, they could become moral beings if they cultivated the right qualities: obedience, forgiveness, selflessness. During the "Moral" classes we were left alone. At the end of the hour the "Religion" teacher would appear and throw some questions at us: "What were primary sins and secondary sins?" "Name five virtues!" There were never more than one or two Jews in my classes and never a Sephardic. The Ashkenazi children did not believe that I was a Jew; I did not understand Yiddish, and my parents were from Turkey. I convinced them by showing my knowledge of episodes from the Old Testament. Moses and the Ten Commandments. David and Goliath.

Though what was going on at school was clearly anti-Semitic, I did not recognize it. I was among the best students in my class, and I did not feel that I was being discriminated against. I was allowed to carry the Argentine flag in national holidays, a privilege reserved for outstanding students. Once, in a ceremony in honor of General San Martin (a leader of Argentinian independence), I was standing with the flag in the first row, close to the national authorities. My heart almost stopped beating when Evita Peron touched my head. She had red hair and wore a fur coat, and I did not say anything to my parents because I knew they did not like her. They thought she was an adventuress and mistrusted her involvement in politics.

My first direct experience with anti-Semitism came when I was about 9 years old. I used to go to a friend's house to do homework. When she and I were working in her room, I heard her mother say in the next room, "Dirty, noisy Jews." My face got very hot and my breath stopped. These people liked me and welcomed me in their home. I realized they did not see me as a Jew. Like many other Sephardics, my Italian name and Mediterranean appearance "disguised" my Jewishness. They were not talking about "us"; they were talking about the Yiddish-speaking Jews.

A constant theme in my life has been not to be seen as a Jew. My looks, my family background, my name: it all fit together. I could not be Jewish! Being separated from those "noisy Jews," being seen as different by the Ashkenazi Jews, created a scenario in which it was tempting to "pass" as a Christian. It seemed simpler. It was tiring to go through the long explanation about my background and then to face blank looks. Elias Canetti's autobiography *The Tongue Set Free: Remembrance of a European Childhood* is the only work I know that describes some of the complexities and ambivalences in the development of a Sephardic Jewish identity.* I could recognize some of the feelings of "difference" and questions that I have struggled with for most of my adult life. His work has encouraged me to take a look at my situation as a woman with a Sephardic background. I was excited to read that his mother, a Sephardic Jew from Bulgaria, was originally named Arditti.

I chose a high school that was the only coed school in Buenos Aires, a school supported by the small English-speaking community. I boarded there for 3 years, and I met Protestants, whom I had only read about in books and articles. I found them more tolerant than the Catholics, and I attended Sunday school services where we sang and prayed "each one to its own Lord." I liked their openness and toyed with the idea of conversion. To their credit, they were not at all interested in proselytizing, and my conversion fantasies did not find fertile ground. And I learned that there were other religious groups than Catholics and Jews, *and* that some Christians did not see Jews primarily as the "killers of Jesus."

During high school I met young people with Zionist ideas. I heard about their plans to live in Israel and work on the land. They were all, like myself, children of Jews who lived in Buenos Aires and did not know much about life in the country. At first I found their ideas attractive; they spoke of equality, of collective living, of "*kibbutz.*" Socialism was an integral part of their ideology. And indeed many of them lived up to their ideals. Though much smaller than the North American Jewish community, the Argentine community sent more settlers to Israel between 1948 and 1967. Because I could not imagine myself moving to Israel and working on the land, I decided that I was not a Zionist and parted company with them. However, I was glad that somebody was actually going to go and keep Israel alive. My attitude was naturally regarded with suspicion by my Zionist friends, who were very disappointed in me. After that, I was never sure that I would ever be welcome in Israel. At 15, I felt I had already ruined my chances.

During the Peron years (1946-1955) the Jews in Argentina, including my family, were concerned because Peron openly admired the Italian Fascist Mussolini. On one hand, Peron praised the new Jewish state, but then abstained in the United Nations vote to establish the state. He expressed sympathy for Jewish refugees, but limited Jewish immigration. He praised the Jew for his humility:

---

* In 1982 a Sephardic feminist told me that as a child she had wanted to learn Yiddish to be part of what she then thought were the "real Jews." This, in spite of the fact that she was born in Israel of a Sephardic family that had been there for centuries.

20

My father, like many other businessmen, joined the Peronista party as a protection
against anti-Semitism. We watched events in the Jewish business district of Once. If
windows were broken and anti-Semitic slogans painted on the walls, we would know
through word of mouth. Newspapers did not publish news of this kind — — in a city of
8 million people!

All the women in my family, except my oldest sister, married Ashkenazi Jews. We
all married in our early twenties, as expected, and we all tried to be *hanum*. I moved
to Italy where my husband was continuing his studies in physics. His family was
cultured; his father was a book publisher, they had books and paintings in their home,
and they supported my interest in books and ideas. I was dazzled; my father had
always been suspicious of people who had more education than he, and I felt that I had
now found my true home. In Rome, where I lived for 7 years, being Jewish became a
memory. I visited the synagogue a few times but couldn't distinguish the Jews of Rome
from the Romans. And indeed, the Jews of Rome have been there since the 2nd century
BCE, and our histories have very little in common.

I left my husband after 6 years, lived in Naples for 3 years, and came to the U.S. in
1965 with my 5-year-old son. I had also become a scientist, a biologist, and I went to
do research first at Brandeis, then at Harvard Medical School. Though I met many
Jews in the scientific world, they rarely spoke about their Jewishness, and I was silent
too. Somehow it seemed that now that we were all scientists, our backgrounds no
longer mattered. As I became involved in the women's movement in the late 60's and
began to look at the forces that shaped my life, I realized that being born in a Jewish
Sephardic home in a Catholic country had been a very important factor in my experiences. I was a member of an "invisible" minority and could not identify with the
experiences of many North American Jewish women, who belong to a visible and well-
identified minority. In the U.S. out of almost 6 million Jews, about 150,000 are
Sephardic (including not only the Ladino-speaking Jews but also the Oriental Jews).
Meeting another Sephardic feminist 3 years ago felt familiar and wonderful. With her, I
began reading Sephardic history and realized that we Sephardic women need to speak
for ourselves.

## Some Sephardic History

Though my family had frequently alluded to the splendid past of the Jews in Spain,
I still resisted accepting how important Sephardic culture had been in many different
areas. The work of Sephardic scholars was responsible for introducing science and
philosophy into Europe; they translated Hebrew and Arabic into the more accessible
Latin. During the Golden Era (900-1100) the Jews excelled in intellectual endeavors
such as medicine, mathematics, philosophy, poetry, ethics, and mysticism. At the same
time they strove to be "statesmen-scholars," to unite in their persons the holy and the
secular, the intellectual and the mundane, Maimonides being the foremost example. A

21

physician, rabbi, mathematician, astronomer, he anticipated ideas in theoretical mathematics and the atomicity of time. Practical contributions in medicine, astronomy and logic made Sephardic Jews famous all over Europe. The "Alfonsine Tables" (lists of the planetary movements compiled in the reign of Alfonso II of Spain, 1252-1284) were prepared by two Jews from Toledo. The voyage of Columbus was made possible by the almanac prepared by the Talmudist Rabbi Abraham Zacut. Indeed, there are grounds for believing that Columbus himself was a member of a *Converso* family.

The Sephardim were known for their love of music, and they have left an amazingly rich folklore of secular and religious songs. The secular songs, with themes from daily life and aspects of the life cycle (birth, childhood, courting, marriage, death) give a vivid picture of Sephardic life. Luckily, many of these songs are being revived.* They provide one of the best ways to learn about the Sephardic experience.

The Kabbala, the mystical body of Judaism, flourished in Spain and was later developed by Sephardic Rabbis in Palestine. Its influence spread back to Europe, where it led indirectly to the founding of the Hassidic movement in Poland. The Kabbala affirms the power of the subconscious mind, maintaining, for instance, that when a person carries out a good deed, s/he not only improves her or his own character and does good for society in general but also brings light and blessing into worlds which are hidden from our direct perception. Conversely, an evil act will not only cause specific harm, but create bad emanations which will influence these invisible worlds. As a feminist, I find it exciting that the Kabbala is one of the few sources of Judaism that acknowledges the power of the female. According to the Kabbala, one of the causes of the pain of present existence is the alienation of the masculine from the feminine in God, the alienation of God and the *Shekhinah* (the feminine aspect of God). The world will not be whole until this split is healed. Reunification of God and the *Shekhinah*, which the Kabbala encourages us to dedicate our efforts to, is the precondition for the end of alienation.[4]

In 1492, when the edict of expulsion was enacted, 200,000 Spaniards — men, women and children, rich and poor, aged and young, sick and healthy — were driven out of Spain. Many went to Portugal, where 5 years later the same tragedy took place. Many Jews became Christians outwardly but continued to practice Judaism in secret. Known as "New Christians," "*Marranos*"** or "*Conversos*," they were under constant scrutiny of the Inquisition. Women comprised the vast majority of those few who maintained their Judaism and died the deaths of martyrs. According to Cecil Roth, women became the spiritual leaders of the *Conversos* groups.[5]

Of the Jews who left Spain and Portugal, many were sold as slaves by the captains of the same ships that were supposed to rescue them; many died of illnesses and exhaustion during their escape. Those who survived spread through the Mediterranean and Northern Europe.

---

* See attached list of resources.
**The word *Marrano* means "pig." I use the word *Converso* in this article, for obvious reasons.

According to my father, our ancestors stopped in Livorno, Italy for a couple of generations — which explains our Italian name — and then settled in Turkey, where the Sultan Bayazid II was eager to accept the Jews. Jews brought invaluable commercial skills and knowledge of various languages and sciences. Many had risen to high military ranks in the Spanish army, and the Sultan wanted them to teach advanced military science to his officers. They introduced the use of gunpowder and the manufacture of cannon into Turkey. The Sephardim formed communities that kept their language, customs and traditions.

As in other Jewish communities there were clear roles for women and men. The women had no direct say in community affairs; their husbands ran the businesses and studied the Talmud. But the survival of the community depended heavily on the women fulfulling their roles in the home. Lighting Sabbath candles and keeping a kosher kitchen ensured the continuity of Jewish life in the new land well before the community organized itself in a more formal way.

Of the many women who achieved notoriety in Europe and the Ottoman Empire for their philanthropic and business activities, none has captured my imagination and curiosity more than Doña Gracia Nasi (1510-1569), also known by her Christian name, Beatrice de Luna.[6-7] A woman of incredible vision, intelligence and strength, Dona Gracia was born to a very prosperous *Converso* family in Portugal. Her brother was physician to the king. At 18, she married Francisco Mendes, also from a *Converso* family, and a successful dealer in precious stones, spices and international trade. The position of the *Conversos* was very tenuous in Lisbon; for in 1515 the king had applied to Rome for the introduction of the Inquisition. The Mendes family began plans to emigrate and to transfer the family business to Antwerp, where they could practice their religion openly. But in 1536, the same year that a papal brief ordered the establishment in Portugal of a Holy Office of the Inquisition, Francisco Mendes died and Gracia was left a widow at 26 with a small child, Reyna. Determined to accomplish the plan herself, she obtained permission to leave Lisbon by pretending that she intended to return, and made her way with her child, her sister, and her brother's son first to England and then to Antwerp, where, in 1537, she joined her brother-in-law. With him she attempted to convince the Pope to stop the Inquisition in Portugal while she helped many other *Conversos* to flee.

In Antwerp Doña Gracia was in touch with royalty, accepted in high circles. But fearing reprisals because she denied a Catholic nobleman's request for her daughter's hand, she left Antwerp in 1544 and went to Venice. There her own sister denounced her as a Jew, and she was imprisoned until pressure from Sultan Suleiman the Magnificent resulted in her release. From Venice she went to Ferrara, where she openly and proudly proclaimed herself a Jew and organized a true "underground railroad" to help Jews fleeing the Inquisition, using her agents and representatives as "stations." She became a patron of letters: the famous Ferrara Bible, published in Spanish by two *Conversos*, is dedicated to her. This bible was essential to sustain the faith of many *Conversos* who wanted to return to Judaism but understood only Spanish. In 1552, Doña Gracia left Ferrara and settled in Constantinople, where she helped the poor and established houses of prayer, schools, and Talmudic academies.

While living in Turkey she embarked on two projects that established her as a woman of foresight, well beyond her times. In 1556, Pope Paul IV persecuted the *Conversos* of Ancona; 24 of them were strangled and then burned. Doña Gracia organized a boycott of the city by the Jewish merchants in Turkey, who used Ancona as their point of entry for goods shipped to Europe. She planned to ruin Ancona and cut into papal revenues by substituting Pesaro as the point of entry: a woman against the Pope. Unfortunately the boycott was abandoned after a few months for lack of support from influential Jews like Rabbi Soncino, who opposed her.

Her other project was a plan for the resettlement of Palestine. Aware that a successful community must have a sound economic base, that agriculture, manufacturing and trade must be developed, she chose Tiberias as the site for resettlement because of its fertile land, potential fish industry, and rich historical past. Envisioning a refuge for the persecuted Jews of the world, she had mulberry trees planted for a silk industry, had homes restored, and created an environment where people could prosper. She herself had a mansion built near the hot baths, planning to settle there in 1566. But there is no record of her reaching Tiberias, and so we do not know if she fulfilled her desire. The chronicler Samuel Usque called her "the heart of her People," that being "the principal and noblest organ of the human body, feeling most readily the pain suffered by any other part."[7]

In the United States the history of the Jewish community *began* with the arrival of 23 Sephardic Jews, refugees from Recife, Brazil, who founded the congregation Shearith Israel in New Amsterdam in 1654. Another early settlement of Sephardim took place in Newport, Rhode Island, where a synagogue, dedicated in 1763, still stands; the oldest synagogue building in the United States, its simplicity and its beauty touched me deeply. Located on a quiet street, the synagogue stands diagonally on its small plot so that the worshippers standing in prayer before the Holy Ark face east, toward Jerusalem.

* * * * *

For me, learning the history of the Sephardim has been a strong and validating experience. Realizing that I belong to a minority within a minority has helped me understand my feelings of separatedness and isolation from Ashkenazi Jews. By creating and disseminating distorted images about Jews, anti-Semitism has also contributed to the invisibility of the Sephardim.

When people ask me why I identify as a Sephardic Jew (and not simply as a Jew), I explain that the Sephardim are invisible in this culture, that we are almost unknown by the majority of the Jews here, and that we have a long and proud history. Indeed, Sephardic history is a history of incredible survival through Inquisition, Diaspora and the Holocaust. I felt a mixture of anger and relief when I learned that in December of 1968 Spain formally lifted its expulsion order against the Jews. Though long abolished in practice, the decree was still officially in effect!

My raised consciousness as a Sephardic woman has also led me to take a clearer stand on the issue of Judaism and women. Traditional Judaism, which legitimates a hierarchical relationship between the sexes and devaluates female power, clearly did not deter Doña Gracia. More than once I have whispered to myself in a seemingly hopeless and oppressive situation: "You can be like Doña Gracia, too!"

## Notes

[1]Sephardic Jews are Jews of Spanish and Portuguese descent. The term comes from *Sepharad* - the Hebrew name for Spain. Ashkenazi Jews are German and Eastern European Jews.

[2]*Ladino*, the language of the Sephardim, Spanish from the 15th century, also known as *Judezmo*, Judeo-Spanish.

[3]Robert Weisbrot, *The Jews of Argentina* (Phila.: The Jewish Publication Society of America, 1979).

[4]Rita M. Gross, "Female God Language in a Jewish Context," in *Womanspirit Rising*, edited by Carol P. Christ and Judith Plaskow (NY: Harper and Row, 1979).

[5]Cecil Roth, *A History of the Marranos* (NY: Schocken Books, 1974).

[6]Sondra Henry and Emily Taitz, *Written Out of History* (NY: Block Pub. Co., 1978); a hidden legacy of Jewish women revealed through their writings and letters.

[7]Cecil Roth, *Dòna Gracia of the House of Nasi* (Phila.: The Jewish Publication Society of America, 1977).

──────────── **Resources on the Sephardim** ────────────

## Books

Angel, D. Marc. **La America: The Sephardic Experience in the United States.** Phila.: The Jewish Publication Society of America, 1982. An extremely interesting account of the Sephardim of New York between 1910 and 1925 through the eyes of Moise Gadol and the newspaper he edited, *La America*.

Angel, D. Marc. **The Jews of Rhodes: The History of a Sephardic Community.** 1978. Sepher-Hermon Press, Inc. and the Union of Sephardic Congregations, 8 W. 70th St., NY 10023. A history of the Sephardic community of Rhodes established in 1523 by Jews expelled from Spain and destroyed by the Nazis in 1944. A microcosm of Sephardic life in the Ottoman Empire. A chapter on "The role of women" with some interesting information.

Angel, D. Marc. **The Sephardim of the United States: An Exploratory Study.** 1974. Union of Sephardic Congregations. A very informative article on the history and characteristics of the Sephardim in the U.S. Data on four communities: Atlanta, New York, Seattle and Portland, OR.

Barnett, Richard, ed. **The Sephardi Heritage.** KTAV Publishing House, 1971. Essays on the history and cultural contribution of the Jews of Spain and Portugal. Articles on Hebrew poetry in Spain, illuminated manuscripts of Medieval Hebrew Spain, Romances and Songs of the Sephardim. Articles in Spanish, French, Hebrew and English. "The Spiritual Heritage of the Sephardim" by Solomon David Sassoon gives an excellent overview of Sephardic history and culture.

Beton, Sol, ed. **Sephardim and a History of Congregation Or VeShalom.** 1981. Congregation Or VeShalom, 1681 N. Druid Hills Rd., NE, Atlanta, GA 30319. Many excellent articles on the Sephardim and photographs and articles on the Atlanta community.

Birmingham, S. **The Grandees.** NY: Harper, 1971. Discusses the colonial Sephardic community and its descendants. Elitist.

Canetti, Elias. **The Tongue Set Free: Remembrance of a European Childhood.** Continuum Books/Seabury Press. The 1981 Nobel Prize winner for Literature describes his childhood in a Sephardic community in Bulgaria. Vivid picture of his mother, a strong Sephardic woman.

Henry, Sondra and Emily Taitz. **Written out of History.** NY: Block Pub. Co., 1978. Biographies of Jewish women, a number of them Sephardic.

**Lavender, D. Abraham,** ed. *A Coat of Many Colors: Jewish Subcommunities in the United States.* Westport, CT: Greenwood Press, 1977. Articles on small-town Jews, Southern Jews, poor Jews, Hasidic Jews, Black Jews, Jewish women, and Sephardic Jews. Worth reading.

**Laredo, Victor.** *Sephardic Spain.* Editorial Mensaje, 125 Queen St., Staten Island, NY, 10314. Laredo, himself a Sephardic Jew, has taken pictures of the monuments and the cities where Spanish Jews lived prior to their exile in 1492. Also chapters on Sephardic history.

**Patai, Raphael.** *The Vanished Worlds of Jewry.* NY: MacMillan Pub. Co., 1980. Text and pictures of extinguished Jewish communities with a section on Sephardic Jews from the Netherlands, Yugoslavia and Greece.

**Roth, Cecil.** *A History of the Marranos.* Phila: The Jewish Publication Society of America, 1932. A history of the "secret Jews" in Europe from the Middle Ages till 1834, when the Inquisition was finally abolished. The epilogue "The Marranos of Today" gives information about Jewish life in Portugal and Spain at the beginning of the XXth century.

**Roth, Cecil.** *Dona Gracia of the House of Nasi.* Phila.: The Jewish Publication Society of America, 1977. A fascinating topic, the biography of an extraordinary woman of the 16th century. The writing, however, is rather dry.

**The Sephardic Cooks.** A wonderful collection of Sephardic recipes compiled and published by Congregation Or VeShalom Sisterhood, Atlanta, Georgia (see Beton for address).

## Articles

**Angel, D. Marc.** "Ruminations about Sephardic Identity," *Midstream* 18. (March, 1972). The beginning of this article reads: "I am Jewish. I am Sephardic. For many years I did not know what either of these things really meant. I did not know who I was." A Sephardic rabbi describes what it feels like to be invisible as a Sephardic Jew.

**Angel D. Marc.** "A Sephardic Approach to Halakhah, *Midstream* 21. (Aug.-Sept.,1975). Rabbi Angel argues that Sephardic rabbis adhered to the quality of *hesed* (kindness) and tended to be lenient while Ashkenasim manifested the quality of *geburah* (heroism) and tended to be strict. The Sephardic culture is seen as practical and accepting of the pleasures and joys of this world.

## General Information

**American Sephardi: Journal of the Sephardic Studies Program of Yeshiva University,** NY.

**Sephardi World.** World Sephardi Federation, World Zionist Organization, Sephardi Dept., Box 92, Jerusalem, Israel.

**Sephardic House Newsletter.** Shearith Israel, 8 W. 70th St., NY 10023.

## Records and Songbooks

**Castel, Nico.** *The Nico Castel Ladino Song Book.* Cedarhurst, NY: Tara Pub., 1981.

**Castel, Nico.** *Sefarad - The Sephardic Tradition in Ladino Song.* Tambur Records. 590.

**Jagoda, Flory.** *Kantikas di mi nona.* Sung in Ladino. Altarasa Records. 1001. 6307 Beachway Dr., Falls Church, VA 22044.

**Jagoda, Flory.** *Memories of Sarajevo.* Altarasa Records. 1002.

**Voice of the Turtle.** *A Coat of Many Colors: Songs of the Sephardim,* vol. 1. Mnemosyne Records, Div. of Titanic Records, 43 Rice St., Cambridge, MA 02140. For info., write 189 Upland Rd., Cambridge, MA 02140.

**Voice of the Turtle.** *The Flowers Appear on the Earth: Songs of the Sephardim,* vol. IV. Mnemosyne Records.

**Voice of the Turtle.** *Small Miracles: Songs of the Sephardim,* vol. III. Mnemosyne Records.

**Voice of the Turtle.** *The Time of Singing Is Come: Songs of the Sephardim,* vol. I. Mnemosyne Records.

## Films

**Song of the Sephardi.** Jewish Welfare Board of New York. 75 min.

*Judith Wachs*

# The Heart of Her People

Doña Gracia de Nasi was a heroine—a Sephardic woman of the 16th century—a spiritual and tactical leader of the Jewish people during the perilous times of the Spanish Inquisition. She led her people across Europe, keeping a travelling "community in exile" together, while negotiating with, and resisting the continual oppression of, the Pope, Princes, Kings, and Sultans. She was celebrated as "the heart of her people." Yet she is virtually unknown, even in the Jewish community.

For at least five centuries, from the time of the.expulsion in 1492, many Sephardic women were heroines, performing the same functions as Doña Gracia in a very different, but no less significant realm. They preserved a monumental treasure: music and poetry of their Hebrew and Spanish heritage. And by these arts, they were able to unite and inspire their communities in exile. Yet they, too, have been invisible.

I have often read that the Rabbi had exhorted "the people" to sing at the time of expulsion, recognizing, of course, the value of music to a suffering community. I have recently discovered the source of that statement, and was interested to learn that the request was directed to "*las mujeres y mancebos*"—the women and the young men.[1]

The error is significant. Although the women are directly addressed, that fact has been virtually ignored. The women are made invisible—a phenomenon (persistent in Jewish as in non-Jewish historical methodology) which greatly affects their daughters and granddaughters. Since it is not acknowledged that women have made critical contributions, that there were extraordinary women other than Biblical figures, Jewish women are denied the variety of role models to which they are entitled.

There is no question that for at least 500 years, Sephardic women were largely responsible for the preservation, by oral transmission, of a very special genre of Spanish poetry. These were the *romançeros*, the epic ballads.[2] The subjects reflected their Hebrew heritage (as in *"Par'ó era estrellero"*), their Spanish heritage (*"La doncella guerrera"*), and their exilic heritage (*"Sol la saddika"*). Women sang them as lullabies, holiday songs, wedding songs, and whenever people gathered.

These ballads served a very important social and psychological function. By keeping the complex history alive and vital, people were able to acknowledge and to incorporate the trauma of exile and separation together, as a community. Amazingly, they preserved the integrity of the oldest ballads while creating new ones, expanding and vitalizing the tradition. And it was only in this century that scholars of Spanish music, literature and history discovered that an incredible wealth of unknown material existed intact on the lips and in the hearts of the Sephardic exiles in North Africa, the Ottoman Empire, and in the Middle East in the old language *Judeo-Español*, with the pronunciation of pre-expulsion Spain!

Unfortunately, but certainly not surprisingly, folklore does not treat women well; there are too many *romanças* whose"leading ladies"are vengeful murderesses, seductresses, "unfortunate wives," adultresses, or just plain victims. In a *romança* called *"El robo de Dina"* ("The Rape of Dina"), not only is Jacob's unfortunate daughter a victim, but her plight is depersonalized by her father's curious response—he sends for the matchmaker![3]

## El Robo de Dina

*Se pasean las 12 flores,   'entre 'en medyyo 'una konǧá.*
*Dišo la konǧá 'a las flores:   —'Oyy 'es dí'a de pasear.*
*Se pase'a la linda Dĭnāh   por los kampos del rey Hămôr.*
*'A favor de sus 12 'ermanos   kaminava sin temor.*
*5 Arimóse 'a 'una tyenda,   pensando ke non ayy varón.*
*Visto la 'uvyera visto   Šĕkem 'ižo del rey Hămôr.*
*Ayegóse para 'elyya, tres palavrikas le avló:*
*—Linda soš, la linda Dĭnāh,   sin afeyte 'i sin kolor.*
*Lindos son vu'estros 'ermanos;   la flor vos yevateš vos.*
*10 —Si son lindos 'i non son lindos,   a mí ke me los guadre 'el Dyyo.*

*Ayegóse más 'a 'elyya,   'izo lo ke non 'es razón.*
*Se 'esparte la linda Dĭnāh;   se va para ande su se[nyyor],*
*'a solombra del težado   ke non la 'enpanyyara 'el sol.*
*Su padre deske la vido,   'a resivirla salyyó:*
*15 —¿Kyén vos demudó la kara   'i kén vos demudó la kolor?*
*'O vola demudó 'el ayyre,   'o vola 'enpanyyó 'el sol.*
*—Ni me la demudó 'el ayyre,   ni me la 'enpanyyó 'el sol.*
*Me la demudó 'un muǧaǧiko,   Šĕkem, 'ižo del rey Hămôr.*
*19 'Estas palavras dizyendo,   kazamenteros le mandó.*

## The Rape of Dina

The twelve flowers go walking, in their midst walks a rose. Said the rose to the flowers: "Today is a day for walking." The beautiful Dinah walks through the fields of King Hamor. Because of the fear inspired by her twelve brothers, she walked without fear. (5) She approached a tent, thinking there was no man within. Shechem had seen her, the son of King Hamor. He drew near to her and spoke a few words: "Beautiful Dinah, you are beautiful without adornment and without rouge. Your brothers are handsome, but you take the flower." (10) "Be they handsome or not, may God protect them." He drew nearer to her and did what was not right. The beautiful Dinah departs; she returns to her father's house, in the shadow of the eaves, so that the sun would not tarnish her. As soon as her father saw her, he went out to receive her: (15) "What has happened to your complexion? Who has changed it so? Either the wind has changed it or the sun has tarnished it." "Neither the wind has changed it, nor has the sun tarnished it. A youth has changed it, Shechem, the son of King Hamor." (19) As she spoke these words, he sent matchmakers to her.

There are, however, a few ballads which do have strong images of women. In "The Warrior Maiden" the heroine is the youngest daughter who saves her aging father by disguising herself as a man, and going into battle for him, since he has no sons.[4] She is victorious in battle! But the "punch line" is that the king's son discovers her, and falls in love with her.

## La doncella guerrera

Pregonadas son las guerras,   las guerras del rey León.
Todo el que a ella no fuere,   su cuerpo estará en prisión.
Sea conde, sea duque,   sea cualquiera nación.
—¡Rematada sea Isalda,   por mitad del corazón!
Siete hijas que paritis,   entre ellas ningún varón.
¿Cómo haré de mí, mesquino,   cano y viejo y pecador?
Ni puedo cabalgar mula,   ni tampoco en bohón.—
Todas callan a una boca,   ninguna que respondió,
sino fuera la chiquita,   que en el buen día nació:
—No se os dé nada, mi padre   [. . . . . . . . .].
Dadme armas y caballos,   vestimenta de varón.
Os escaparé, mi padre,   de las guerras del León.
—Tu cuerpecito, la niña,   de hembra y no de varón.
—Con el juboncito, padre,   me los tapía yo.
—Tus pechecitos, la niña,   de hembra y no de varón.
—Con la chaqueta, mi padre,   me los tapía yo.
—Tu cabecita, la niña,   de hembra y no de varón.
—Con el sombrero, mi padre,   me la tapía yo.—
Ya cabalgaba la niña,   ya cabalgaba el bohor.
A la primera batalla,   la niña muy bien ganó.
A la segunda batalla,   el sombrero se la cayó.
Un hijo del rey la viera,   que de ella se enamoró.

## The Warrior Maiden

The wars of the King Leon are announced
Those who cannot go will be imprisoned
Whether Count or Duke or any nation
Cursed be my wife, may she die twice!
For I have seven daughters, and not one son,
What will become of me, grey old sinner?
Neither can I ride a mule, or even be a peddlar
All were quiet—none answered
Except for the youngest, born on a lucky day
Don't give up, father
Give me arms and a horse, and the clothes of a man
You will escape, my father, from the wars of Leon.
—Your body, little daughter, it is female not a man

29

—I'll cover it with a doublet, my father
—Your breasts. . . .
—with a jacket. . .
—Your head. . .
—with a hat. . .
She has already ridden away
In the first battle, the youngest is victorious
In the second battle, her hat falls off
The son of the king saw her and fell in love with her.

From Morocco (19th century), the ballad of Sol Hatchuel — "Sol la saddika" ("Sol The Righteous") tells of the young girl who chooses martyrdom rather than accept the order of the Sultan not only to become part of his harem but to convert to Islam. Her story was so affecting (despite the last lines of the poem) that both Muslims and Jews honored her by visitations to her grave for more than 100 years.

## Sol the Righteous

### Sol la saddika

Cuando Tara levantó el enredo,
sentenciaron a la hermosa Sol.
La hicieron juramento falso,
en presencia del gobernador.
El gobernador la manda
a una cárcel para seducirla.
Y allí mismo la declara,
si no es mora, la quita la vida.
—Adiós, padres y hermana,
que me voy presa delante del rey.
Aunque jure y perfecte otra ley,
hebrea tengo que morir.—
Y el verdugo desvaina su alfaje,
sin consuelo y sin piedad,
y la dice si quiere ser mora:
—Piénsalo pronto, que aún tiene lugar.
Cuando Sol vio su sangre vertida,
dio un suspiro que al cielo encloró
y le dijo: —No quiero ser mora.
Sigue tu fin, infame y traidor.
Por el mundo se extiende mi historia.
Las doncellas se cobren valor.
No fíase de ninguna mora,
para verse como se vio Sol.

When Tara bore false witness
The beautiful Sol was sentenced
Forced to swear falsely
In the presence of the governor
The governor sent her
To prison in order to seduce her
And there declared
That if she would not become a Moor
   she would die.
—Adios, my parents and sister
I have become the prey of the king
But although I may swear allegiance to
   another law
I will die a Jewess.
And the executioner unsheathed his sword
Without comfort or pity
And asked her if she would be a Moor
—Think quickly while you still have time.
When Sol saw his cold-blooded demeanor
She sent a sigh up to heaven
And said to him—I refuse to become a
   Moor.
Do your job, traitorous scoundrel.
For the world will know my story.
Maidens will be courageous.
Do not trust any Moorish maiden
For you will suffer the same fate as Sol.

In a *romança* sung at Passover, we find the rarely-told story of the *comadres*, the heroic midwives who performed a highly significant act of resistance: they disobeyed the charge by Pharoah to kill all the Jewish male children, and, thus, were responsible for saving the life of Moses.

## Par'ó era 'strellero

*Par'ó era 'strellero*
*Salió una noche al sereno*
*Vido una 'strella divina*
*Tenía que nacer Moxé*

*Mandó llamó a las comadres*
*Cuantas en Aífto son*
*A todas las aconjuró*
*Que no recivan a judió*

*Las comadres eran judías*
*Del Dió eran queridas*
*Arrecivían y fuivan*
*Emperó nació Moxé*

## When Pharoah gazed at the Stars

One night Pharoah went out into the night air
And gazing at the stars
He saw a divine star
Which foretold the birth of Moses.

He sent for the midwives
As many as were in Egypt
And made them conspire
Not to deliver Jewish males.

The midwives were Jewesses
Beloved of God
They disobeyed, and by their resistance
Moses was born. . .

By performing and publishing these songs and stories of Sephardic women, and by celebrating their dynamic role in Jewish history, we honor these "valiant women."

---

**Notes**

[1] Menendez Pidal, "El Romancero Sefardi," in *The Sephardi Heritage*, Richard Barnett, ed. (KTAV Pub., 1971), p. 522.

[2] Given the nature of oral transmission, the dates and places of origin for these *romanceros* are often unclear.

[3] *"El robo de Dina,"* text and translation from *The Judeo-Spanish Ballad Chapbooks of Yacob Abraham Yoná*, S. G. Armistead and J. H. Silverman, eds. (Berkeley-LA:Univ.of Calif.,1971), pp. 116-117.

[4] *"La doncella guerrera,"* text from *Romances judeo-españoles de Tanger*, collected by Zarita Nahón, S. G. Armistead and J. H. Silverman, eds. (Madrid: Catedra-Seminario Menendez Pidal, 1977), p. 179. Translation by Judith Wachs.

[5] *"Sol la saddika,"* text from *Romances judeo-españoles de Tanger*. Translation by Rita Arditti and Judith Wachs.

[6] *"Par'ó era 'strellero,"* text from *Liturgia Judeo-Española*, Isaac Levy, ed. with collaboration of the Division of Culture of the Office of Education and Culture, Jerusalem, Volume III. Translation by Judith Wachs.

*Irena Klepfisz*

# Secular Jewish Identity: *Yidishkayt* in America

...the present generation stands in a shockingly new relation to Jewish history. It is we who have come after the cataclysm. We, and all the generations to follow are, and will continue to be into eternity, witness generations to the Jewish loss. What was lost in the European cataclysm was not only the Jewish past—the whole life of a civilization—but also a major share of the Jewish future. . . .It was not only the intellect of a people in its prime that was excised, but the treasure of a people in its potential.

—Cynthia Ozick, "Notes Toward Finding the Right Question"

## I. *Di yidishe svive*: The Yiddish Environment

All my life I have defined myself as a secular Jew. It is how I was raised and taught to think about myself in relation to Jewishness. I was taught that there is no God. I was taught that capitalism oppresses the working masses and all poor people, that it has to be smashed, and that we are to work towards building a classless society. I was taught that Jews have a right to be anywhere and everywhere, that they are not necessarily destined to return to their ancient homeland. And I was taught that Yiddish is *mame-loshn*, mother tongue, the language of the Jews, the medium through which Jewish culture and politics are to be transmitted. *Mame-loshn* was the language that gave all the tenets which I'd been taught form and substance. I internalized all this and fought fiercely with anyone who disputed these "facts."

My upbringing was not unusual if seen in its proper context. I was born to parents

32

who were members of *der algemeyner yidisher arbeter bund*, Jewish Labor Bund. Founded in 1897, the Bund was a socialist revolutionary *bavegung*, movement, whose primary influence was among the urban Jewish working class in Eastern Europe, particularly Poland and Russia. *Di bavegung* swept those regions, becoming a kind of religion itself, claiming thousands upon thousands of adherents in less than 20 years. Many were from the religious community, and their "conversion" to socialism and the Bund often meant a painful break with family and tradition. My grandfather, Yakov Klepfisz, was among them.

On closer inspection, however, my upbringing was full of contradictions. Born in 1941 in occupied Poland, I came to the United States at the age of 8. I did not, therefore, learn about the Bund and its brand of *sotsyalizm* in the context and environment which shaped it and helped it flourish. I was learning a Jewish politics which was uprooted. That was the first contradiction, one which I never heard articulated. The second, also unarticulated, was that our presence in the US testified to the fact that Jews *did not* have the right to be anywhere and everywhere. Poland had proven fatally hostile to us during and after the war,[1] and most Jews who survived left the country which for centuries had been their home and immigrated to the US or Israel. As frequently as I heard anti-Zionist* sentiments, I also heard that in the face of a common enemy, anti-Semitism had triumphed; Jews and Poles had fought almost entirely separate battles. Many *khaverim*, comrades, in fact, felt so strongly about the Poles' collaboration with the Germans that they vowed never to speak Polish again. And they kept that vow.

The third contradiction: Yiddish was not my *mame-loshn*. Because I was born during the war and my mother and I were passing as Poles, Polish became my first language. I began hearing Yiddish only later in Lodz, though in the first kindergarten I attended, I began to write Polish. In 1946, my mother and I immigrated to Sweden, where we lived for the next three years. I attended school and learned to read, write, and speak Swedish. At home, I continued speaking Polish though I heard and understood the Yiddish of the other DPs living in our communal house. And then we came to America. I began speaking English and ever so slowly, over the years, started to think, to dream in English. Eventually, English was the language I spoke with my mother.

My awareness (if I had any) of the contradictions must have been on the subconscious level, for as I grew up I continued articulating without hesitation the Bund's basic atheistic, anti-Zionist, socialist tenets and accepted Yiddish as *mame-loshn*. In fact, in the '50s from a child's perspective, the contradictions were very difficult, if not impossible, to perceive. A very large number of the *lebn-geblibene*, survivors, lived in the same cooperative houses in which my mother and I lived, all within a few blocks of each other—a small, tight group in the midst of a Jewish, American-born, working-class neighborhood. For years, I thought every Yiddish-speaking adult was to be addressed as *khaver* or *khaverte* (m. and f. of comrade).[2] I simply did not know the Yid-

---

*The Bund's anti-Zionism was formulated before the founding of the State of Israel and, indeed, long before World War II. A complex ideology, it opposed nationalism while maintaining that Jews were a distinct people and that socialism would eventually eradicate anti-Semitism. The Bund, of course, supported Yiddish as the language of Eastern European Jews in contrast to the Zionist adoption of Hebrew.

dish equivalent of a plain "Mr." or "Mrs." And if I wasn't fluent in Yiddish, it seemed everyone around me was. I heard Yiddish constantly—in our home, in the homes of other *khaverim* and Yiddishists, on the street, in the stores. *Der tog, Der forverts, Unzer tsait* seemed to be flourishing. Yiddish books were everywhere. And besides I was attending the *Arbeter ring shule*, the Workmen's Circle secular school, five afternoons a week and later its *mitl-shul*, high school, on week-ends. I certainly knew more Yiddish than most of my American-born peers. I could read, write and even speak—though very stiffly and self-consciously. Still I loved the *lider un poezye*, songs and poetry, which I learned there, and today—thirty-five years later—still recite much of it by heart; poetry about poverty and the sweatshops; about the *khurbn* (destruction, i.e., Holocaust), songs and poetry about Purim, Hanukkah, and *pesakh*. We read the stories of Sholem Aleykhem—*Motl Peysi dem khazns* (Motl Peyse the cantor's son)—and I.L. Peretz—*Bontshe shvayg* (Bontshe the silent); the poems of Avrom Reisen, Morris Rosenfeld; sang songs by Gebirtig, recited poems by Leivik and Itzik Manger. It was in this *yidishe svive*, Yiddish environment, that I developed a passion for literature.

*Unzere svive* was naturally focused on "*der khurbn*." The Yiddish word was important for, unlike the term Holocaust, it resonated with *yidishe geshikhte*, Jewish history, linking the events of World War II with *der ershter un tsveyter khurbn*, the First and Second Destruction (of the Temple). Every April 19th (following the Christian calendar), my mother and I would attend *akademyes*, memorial meetings, commemorating the anniversary of the *varshever geto oyfshtand*, Warsaw Ghetto Uprising. *Di akademyes* emphasized the Bund's role in organized *vidershtand*, resistance, and the heroism of *poshete mentshn*, common people. And they were always very somber, painful events. When a speaker or singer finished, there would be total silence, no applause. People wept openly as they listened again to the details of the camps and ghettos.

As a child I naturally found *di akademyes* frightening and upsetting. At the same time, they instilled in me an enormous sense of pride in Jews, most of whom, under the worst circumstances, showed humaneness and heroism. *Poshete mentshn* were capable of extraordinary things. Repeatedly I heard Sutzkever's poem "*Di lererin Mire*," about the teacher Mira Bernstein from Vilna; Hirsh Glik's "*Shtil di nakht*" (Still the night), a song about the partisan Vitka Kempner (living now in Israel) and her heroism; and the song "*Papirosn,*" about a boy trying to sell cigarettes in the rain; and finally, "*Der partizaner him,*" the hymn of the partisans, "*Zog nit keyn mol*" (Never say), which taught me "*dos lid geshribn iz mit blut un nit mit blay*" (this song is written with blood and not with lead). All this seeped into my consciousness and left me with an unshakable belief that Jews were not to blame, that they had not gone to the ovens and gas chambers like sheep. I have never in my life experienced a moment's doubt.

*Di akademyes* also provided me with a sense of peoplehood. It was there that I heard tributes to Arthur Zygielbaum, the Bundist leader sent to London and the Polish government-in-exile to mobilize help for the dying Jews of Poland. Unsuccessful in his mission, he committed suicide when he learned of the Warsaw Ghetto's final destruction. Selections from his suicide letters were frequently read at *di akademyes*:

> *Ikh ken nisht shvaygn -Ikh ken nisht lebn*—I cannot be silent—I cannot live—while the remnants of the Jewish people of Poland, of whom I am representative, are perishing. My comrades in the Warsaw ghetto took weapons in their hands on the last heroic impulse. It was not my destiny to die there together with them, but I belong to them, and to their mass graves. . . .
>
> I know how little human life is worth today, but as I was unable to do anything during my life, perhaps by my death I shall contribute to breaking down the indifference of those who may now—at the last moment—rescue the few Polish Jews still alive, from certain annihilation. My life belongs to the Jewish people of Poland and I therefore give it to them.[3]

Those words shaped my consciousness and helped me formulate my relationship to other Jews, made me conscious that a Jew didn't separate herself from her people—even when she could.

Though *di akademyes* and the constant contact with *lebn-geblibene* emphasized what had been lost—political and cultural institutions, libraries, sports organizations, summer camps, schools, old age homes, unions, etc.—there was a way in which the loss was difficult to absorb. *Di svive* around me seemed to be thriving. Yiddish was alive. Chaim Grade, the poet and novelist lived a few blocks away. He once visited us and on Purim presented me with a scroll of *megiles Ester* (the Book of Esther). Avrom Reisen visited my *shule*. Itzik Manger came to the *mitl-shul* which I attended for four years every Saturday and Sunday. He wore leather "arty" sandals and was probably the first bohemian I encountered. I was impressed. Yiddish was on the radio. I heard records by Dzigan and Shumakher, the comedians. One particular routine involved two Jewish soldiers in enemy armies facing each other during World War I. It was the first time that I became aware of the complexities of Jewish dispersion.

It wasn't even so much that Yiddish was alive. A small part of Poland seemed to be alive. Bolek and Anya. Vladka. Brukha and Monye. Rivka and Lolek. Khana. Bernard. Khevka and Lutek. All *lebn-geblibene*. So for all the talk *vegn khurbn*, for all of my awareness of an absent father, aunts, and grandmothers, when I sat down at Brukha and Monye's *dritn seder*, third seder, and heard the words *"ver es iz hungerik,zol kumen un esn; ver es neytikt zikh, zol haltn mit undz pesakh"* (whoever is hungry, let them come and eat; whoever is in need, let them celebrate *pesakh* with us) and looked around me and saw our whole community; or when I went to an *akademye* and saw an auditorium completely filled; or when I looked at a newsstand and saw the big, bold letters of *Der forverts*—it was hard for me to conceive that an entire world had been destroyed.

But more—my entire intellectual growth was bound up in this world and in Yiddish. It was only in this *yidishe svive* that I heard ideas discussed—the arguments between the *tsiyonistn, komunistn, un sotsyalistn*. It was in this *yidishe svive* that I puzzled and then agonized over the issue of *fargitigung*—it would be years before I learned the English word "restitution"—and whether Jews should accept restitution from Germany. Finally, most of my political, ethical thinking was done here. *Di yidishe svive* seemed, was very much alive.

A child, of course, assumes that her world is the whole world. To me *di yidishe velt*, the Jewish world, was all of Jewishness. I don't think I ever thought that a *lebngeblibene* and a *khaverte* might not be one and the same. Survivor and comrade. Wasn't everyone that?

Nothing around me ever supported my Jewish generalizations. But the American environment was so empty it made no impression on me. The American world, as I saw it, was only a source of pain—a place where I was completely aliented, different, the greenhorn, the survivor. *Di yidishe velt* was where intellectual arguments took place, where I received a sense of identity, history, of the struggles of the world. My early American education was never intellectually stimulating; the required readings were deadly and meaningless. I read "Evangeline" but remember nothing of it; and I had to memorize long sections of "The Ancient Mariner," whose language completely eluded me ("Eftsoons his hand droppeth he"—??)

In fact, for years I suffered over my inability to use English effectively and, throughout public school and most of high school, English remained my worst subject. I realize now that until the age of 16 or 17, I really had no language in which I was completely rooted. Limited to our three-room apartment, my Polish did not develop and by my mid-teens was childish and ungrammatical. English seemed alien and lacked both intellectual and emotional resonance. And though Yiddish had the emotional and cultural substance, it simply didn't feel natural.

But eventually something changed. Towards the end of high school, I moved from reading mindless historical novels and romances towards world literature—Dostoyevsky, Shakespeare, Hugo, Melville, McCullers. English words started to have some meaning. My English prose would remain problematic for years, but I began experimenting with poetry. And perhaps because it was private and had never been labelled with an "F" for grammar—writing poetry enabled me to discover possibilities in the English language, possibilities which were supported by my reading. It was an important breakthrough for me, but one which simultaneously seemed to doom the role of Yiddish in my life.

Like other children I tended to assume everything is forever and took everything for granted. What appeared to me a very solid self-sustaining world, *di yidishe velt*, was in reality extremely fragile, barely holding. Its fragility lay partly, I believe, in its isolation and its inability to establish a coherent attitude towards and connection to the American environment. Though the students in my public school were probably 95% Jewish, *not once* between the second and eighth grades do I remember a single teacher—Jew or gentile—discuss a Jewish topic or issue, holiday, leader. All things Jewish belonged outside of the walls of P.S. 95. And with the parents' consent.

This also affected those children who came from religious homes. But the religious establishment in America was on a more solid footing—its institutions not dependent on a language or specific culture. For the secular Jew, the situation was more difficult. The Yiddish school, Yiddish books, theater, etc. were critical, and if these weren't maintained, the type of secular identity in which Yiddish played a central role was bound to become very precarious.

During my growing up years, there was no interaction between the American world and the *yidishe svive* and no demand that there should be. The '50s were a period of severe reaction, of having to prove oneself a good American. I can understand that survivors many with socialist and communist backgrounds,who had arrived four or six years earlier, might feel reluctant to challenge the school system when they were still threatened with deportation. The name of Ellis Island hung over us as a constant threat.

I did have one experience in which I was immersed in an ostensibly completely insulated *yidishe svive*. That experience proved, if anything, that this world was slowly losing ground. Established in the '20s, Camp Boiberik was a Yiddish, essentially secular camp (it maintained a ritual for *shabes* and kept a kosher kitchen). Many parents who were already assimilated were sending their children to Boiberik to acquire the *yidishkayt* they could not provide for them at home. When I worked there in the summers of '58 and '59, however, Yiddish was no longer being used. What remained of Yiddish were terms, individual words, and a great deal of heartfelt sentiment. Activities (*shvimen, shiflen*—swimming, boating), buildings (*der es tsimer*—the dining room), designations of campers(*di eltste-eltste*—the seniors) were used by everyone and easily incorporated into English. And in addition to the usual "specialists," there was a Yiddish counsellor who taught campers *dem alef-beys*, the alphabet, traditional stories and songs.

Actually songs punctuated camp life and provided the strongest medium for passing on Yiddish. Every child knew the camp song "*In boyberik iz lebedik, / In boyberik iz freylekh, / Ver es kumt tsu boyberik,/Lebt er vi a meylekh!*" [sic] (In Boiberik it's lively, In Boiberik it's joyous, Whoever comes to Boiberik, Lives like a king!). At night when the flag was lowered, we sang: "*Ven der tog vert mid, farmatert, / Aylt zikh tsu zayn sof. . .*" (When the day grows tired, weary, hurries to its end. . .). On Friday nights we dressed in white and lit *shabes* candles in the dining room and sang again. And the whole summer season culminated in *a felker yom tov*, a folk festival. Campers were grouped into countries and gave a grand performance in which each country danced and sang about *sholem un brudershaft* [sic], peace and brotherhood.

In other respects, the camp was like any other. There were regular sports activities, competitions with Camp Kindering, and performances of American plays. Though there were attempts to promote Yiddish and Yiddish culture as a norm, these inevitably were limited. I know of only one Yiddish performance, a dramatization of Sholem Aleykhem's "*Dos meserl*" (The knife). It was a unique event since most campers did not speak Yiddish.

But there was another part to Camp Boiberik, a "guest side," a modest summer colony of wooden bungalows. It was not all that inexpensive; on the other hand it wasn't Grossinger's either. The guest side also provided the usual summer activities—shuffle board, boating, nature walks—but unlike the children's side, Yiddish was very much in use. Not that everyone spoke it. Still, Yiddish newspapers, magazines were always in view. And almost every day, there was an event *untern boym*, under the tree: *a referat, a diskusye, a retsitatsye*. Lectures, discussions, readings provided the basis for intellectual, political and artistic arguments and were very popular.

In addition there was a small theater. A number of staff members in both parts of the camp were members of *Di folks bine*, the Yiddish theater, and performances were frequent. I was always eager to see them and felt quite disgruntled if I had to be on *vakh*, night watch. The most memorable performance that I saw there was one by the well-known actor Joseph Buloff. In Boiberik, Buloff's Yiddish material consisted of dramatic monologues, stories and poems drawn from Yiddish and Russian writers. On that particular evening, Buloff transformed himself into *a tepele zup*, a pot of soup—a metaphor for life, for Jewish life and all its turbulence. Buloff was brilliant as he became and gave voice succeedingly to every piece of *marevke, kartofl, bubele*—carrot, potato, bean—which an unidentified, but omnipotent hand dropped into the pot. As the story/poem progressed, Buloff's motions and speech became increasingly agitated as he tried to keep up with the pot's ever-growing chaos. But the soup just boiled more and more furiously and the chaos grew greater and greater.[4]

Though some of the adults were already themselves feeling deprived by assimilation, the difference between the two sides of the camp was quite clear. Few counsellors came to the events on the "guest side." And certainly there was no attempt to bring material from the adults to the children. Though some Yiddish must have been understood by many children because they heard it at home, a rich, adult Yiddish would have been incomprehensible to the majority. The white wooden fence that marked the boundary between the two camps was also a boundary line that delineated two different cultural territories.

I must have been somewhat aware of these issues, though I don't ever remember discussing them. I was aware enough at least to try and build bridges between *di yidishe svive* and the American because I became involved in writing and directing a musical comedy about the Jews of Khelm. I felt proud because I perceived it as a purely Jewish (which to me in those days was synonymous with Yiddish) product, even though the Khelemites spoke pure English. Camp Director Leybush Lehrer, a staunch Yiddishist, felt otherwise and openly expressed his dissatifaction. I would not admit to my own inadequacy, felt stung that my attempt to create "Yiddish" material was not appreciated and responded glibly, as only someone that age can: *"Di shprakh iz nit di gantse zakh!"* I told him. Indeed, language may not be everything, but I had yet to learn that it is a great deal.

At this time, I was already a student at City College (CCNY), a predominantly Jewish school with thousands of students coming from Eastern European backgrounds—most of whom I am sure had heard Yiddish spoken at home, many of whom probably even spoke it. Yet at the time there was no Yiddish course, no Jewish studies program of any sort.[5] Just as in public school, nothing encouraged us to look to our homes and backgrounds for cultural resources worthy of preservation. The message was just the opposite: we were to erase all traces of who we were and where we came from. Higher education continued the process of making us "become" something new.

Nothing symbolized this more than CCNY's four required semesters of speech which were in a large part devoted to divesting us of our working-class Jewish Bronx and Brooklyn accents. A speech test was required of all entering students and those who failed were placed in what amounts to remedial speech. In the regular classes we were taped and retaped in a desperate effort to get rid of our crude vowel distortions, glottal stops, etc. What were we supposed to think after such lessons when we returned to the Bronx and to our parents with their Yiddish intonations, heavy accents, misplaced adverbs and prepositions? Were we supposed to be proud?

But this "new" cultured individual which we were becoming was supposed to also speak another language—and for my friends and me, that language was French, a real curiosity when you consider that so many of us were expecting to be teaching Puerto Rican children. But parents and school officials presented French as the language of a culture of the highest order, while Spanish was deemed far below—the lowliness of its condition reflected by its alleged "easy" grammar.

There was, I know, real racism in this condescension towards Spanish cultures. But I don't think that's all it was about. I think, for example, that if most Jewish parents had valued Yiddish as a language, as a medium for a culture they wanted to preserve, had been able to envision it "in the world," they might have viewed Spanish somewhat differently. Certainly what the two had in common was that they were both immigrant languages. But immigrant languages were not valued in 1958. An Italian girl who studied Italian was usually characterized as looking for "easy" high grades. So why should a serious student study Spanish when Spanish-speaking children were being encouraged to forget Spanish as quickly as possible?

Despite this total indifference of the environment, some time in my sophomore year, I decided to study Yiddish literature. So a friend and I approached Prof. Max Weinreich who was teaching in the German Department. I was very lucky; Weinreich was perhaps the most distinguished living Yiddish linguist and historian and had been a founder of YIVO Institute for Jewish Research in Vilna in 1925. Just meeting him was a privilege, but I was unaware of it. He, of course, was delighted with our interest, took us to a Chinese lunch, and quickly agreed to make the necessary arrangements. We, in turn, rounded up a handful of students and the course became official.[6]

I cannot claim we were devoted students. The atmosphere was unpressured and completely unrelated to the rest of our more normal, but very anxiety-ridden academic lives. Certainly it was one of those "easy" three credits and we enjoyed the material and Weinreich, which I'm sure made the course academically suspect. Still, at the end of the semester, I wanted to do independent work and take honors in Yiddish.

I read the plays of H. Leivik (whom I legitimized to English-major friends as the Yiddish Shakespeare) and the poetry of Chaim Grade. I was particularly moved by Grade's writings about his mother, a poor, illiterate, pious woman who sold apples in the street while her son studied, oblivious to her struggle for survival. In one poem, Grade describes his mother's desperate effort to get everything done before sunset and ends with her blessing the candles while tears stream down her face because she *hot farshpetikt dem shabes*, was late for *shabes*. The irony, poverty, anger at religion's rigidity and his own youthful callousness made a deep impression on me. The power of that literature was enormous.

And yet—I didn't turn towards it. I had one struggle which represented my conflict. At the same time I was working in Honors Yiddish, I had been accepted into Honors English—an elaborate and long-established program, i.e., "the real thing." My struggle: Should I write my thesis on three American-Jewish writers—Bellow, Roth, Malamud—or on Herman Melville, whose work I loved? I was deeply interested in Jewish issues, but I was terrified of showing that publicly. This was not as contradictory with my studying Yiddish as might seem. The Yiddish course was safe; after all, it was off to the side. Who knew what I was doing there? But in the framework of an English Department (even though that department had many Jewish teachers and students), to reveal interest in Jewish matters, to reveal that I *cared* about Jewish matters—seemed inappropriate. We were supposed to be above that. And so I chose Melville.

When I graduated from CCNY with Honors in Yiddish and English, Brukha and Monye Patt gave me a two-volume set of the complete works of H. Leivik. Inside they had written: *"Tsum shpits barg heyb oyf dayne oygn."* Lift your eyes to the mountain top. I paid no attention. I was looking straight ahead.

I realize now that I simply did not know how to be an *active* Jew in the world. Neither my American education nor my Jewish education had prepared me for it. If I had been shown a strong connection between the two worlds in which I lived, if they had been supportive of each other, if bi-culturalism and bi-lingualism had been encouraged in my American school, if English had not been perceived only as an enemy by the Yiddish world—then Yiddish would have lived on naturally in my life. As it was, the older and more independent I became and the further I moved into the American world, the more English took over my intellectual life—the more it seemed the two worlds I had been living in were mutually exclusive.

I never formulated any of this. I was not pre-occupied with my identity. I took it for granted, much as I did the Yiddish world. Chaim Grade would always write. *Der forverts* would appear every day. So would *Di freie arbeiter shtime, Der tog.* Prof. Weinreich would be there to answer questions. Camp Boiberik would be there for the next generation. So would my *shule. Di yidishe svive,* I assumed, would be waiting for me whenever I got home, whenever I needed it. At the age of 21, it never occurred to me that *it* might need my support to ensure its survival. I never thought that as a secular Jew who defined herself through Yiddish culture, my sense of self was inextricably bound up in its existence, that when *it* was in jeopardy, *my own identity* was in jeopardy. I never realized that it was the mirror that made me visible to myself as a Jew.

## II. The American Environment

Writing this essay in 1985, I take stock of the *yidishe svive* in which I grew up: Chaim Grade has died. Monye Patt is dead and the *driter seder,* the third seder, which I always attended at his house, no longer takes place. *Der forverts* appears only once a week. *Der tog* and *Di freie arbeiter shtime* have stopped publishing all together. Max

Weinreich and his son Uriel, himself a great Yiddish linguist and scholar, have also died. So have many *khaverim*. Camp Boiberik is closed. So is Camp Hemshekh.[7] So is my former *shule* in the Bronx.

Generations pass. Institutions die. This is part of a natural evolution and cycle. But for a culture to survive, its losses must be replaced. And though there has been some replacement, I have become increasingly aware that in the Yiddish world each death, each closing of an institution represents a far greater loss than that of the individual. In 1985, I see that over the years *di svive* has become smaller and smaller and more precarious.

In the decade that followed my entering graduate school, a parallel process was occurring within me. It couldn't have been otherwise, since I took no care to protect against it. In 1963 I left for the University of Chicago and graduate work in English literature, and became completely immersed in an American environment. That is not to say I left my Jewishness behind me. The consciousness of Jewish history, the role of the *khurbn* in my life, and the politics which I had absorbed, I carried with me. *Sotsyalizm* was easily translated and I found no difficulty in applying everything I had been taught politically to the contemporary scene: the devastation created by urban "renewal" in Hyde Park, Chicago; the civil rights movement; or the war in Viet Nam.

But certain things resist translation. Bundist philosophy as I received it was not only socialism; rather it was a whole way of life in which Yiddish acted as the cement that bound the Jewish community together on a socialist foundation. What language we spoke was critical. It reflected our identity, our loyalty, our distinctness not only from the gentile environment, but from other Jews as well. The use of Yiddish was an expression of not only love of a language, but pride in ourselves as a people; it was an acknowledgement of a historical and cultural *yerishe*, heritage, a link to generations of Jews who came before and to the political activists of Eastern Europe. Above all it was the symbol of resistance to assimilation, an insistence on remaining who we were.

Though I could share *sotsyalizm* with American-born Jews and gentiles, there was no way I could share Yiddish and all that it represented. As a result, the language and culture themselves became more and more isolated and apart in my life. Decrease in on-going contact and exchanges, decrease in my facility with the language that had bound us together in an alien environment, that had acted as the borders which defined our cultural territory, that had defined us as a distinct Jewish group—inevitably loosened my ties to the *svive*. The less I was able to communicate with it in its own language and identify with its concerns over culture and survival, the more I became an outsider—the American Jew.

My awareness of how Yiddish and its role in my life had slipped came abruptly in 1975 when, almost by accident, I was plunged back in the *svive* and found myself teaching beginners Yiddish. I believe I was a good teacher. Still, in that class, over a period of three summers, I began to perceive what I had lost by not continuing studying; and even more painful, what I had lost from disuse. I was stunned at how much I had forgotten—not only of language, but of history and literature as well. As a result, the most difficult thing I had to face was that for all the intensity of my upbringing, for

41

all of my love of *di kultur*, I had returned to a country which had grown frighteningly alien.

I also became acutely conscious of the extreme effort, the commitment required to keep a language and culture alive in an environment that, at best, is indifferent. I was particularly stung by the disrespect with which Yiddish is treated by Jews. Historically, of course, this was nothing new. I had always heard stories of the clashes, some of them violent, between the Bund and the *komunistn* who advocated "normalcy" and assimilation or with the *tsiyonistn* who pressed for a Jewish homeland and Hebrew as the national language. And in 1963, when I had visited Israel, I myself heard the scorn with which most Israelis regarded Yiddish. To them, Yiddish meant *shtetl*, and *shtetl* meant the Holocaust. Never again. We're a new breed here. A different kind of Jew. I consciously thought them anti-Semitic, felt enraged at their lack of understanding and caring. Israel was one place where Yiddish culture might have survived. (The Soviet Union was the other.) But Eastern European Zionists were determined to wipe out the past of *all* Jews who came to Israel—not unlike the melting pot philosophy in America—and eliminating Yiddish among the Ashkenazi was one of the steps towards achieving that goal. The old antagonisms with which I had been raised in relation to Zionism seemed completely justified during that trip.

Here in the States, the story was not all that different, though until World War II there was a thriving Yiddish-American culture. At the turn of the century, German Jews considered Yiddish an embarrassment and couldn't wait to "clean up" and Americanize their Eastern European brothers and sisters who came after them. Philanthropic institutions like the Free Hebrew Schools and the Educational Alliance were vehement against Yiddish; the Philanthropist Jacob Schiff was purported to have given explicit orders that none of his contributions be used to support Yiddish or Yiddish culture.[8]

These early attitudes, the post-World War II push towards assimilation and American Jewry's increased involvement and identification with Israel have made their mark on the present generation. When I would tell people that I was teaching Yiddish, most—especially Jews—were amused. Over and over again, I heard: "How cute!" I would counter that Yiddish is a language like any other. Generations of Jews in Western and Eastern Europe spoke it and wrote it, just like any other people in any other language. But here in America what had been *mame-loshn* to millions of Ashkenazi Jews, what had been a medium through which Jewish history, culture, politics, ethics were transmitted—had become a joke, a joke usually made by Jews, a joke now so Americanized it has become the property of the gentile mainstream. What is funnier than a Yiddish accent? And what is funnier than a Yiddish inflection? Yiddish is after all nothing more than a bunch of words like *kvetsh, shmate, shpil, mishigas, shnorer, shayster, shlep, yidene*. What's to teach? What's to learn?

Given these attitudes and the commonness with which certain Yiddish words and phrases are used in English, I have found it difficult to convince others that we, secular Yiddishists, are on the edge of tragedy. Because the view of Yiddish is so limited (really puny) and because there is basically no knowledge of Yiddish culture as it developed in Europe and in the States, others, I sense, think I am fabricating a drama when I draw attention to the crisis.

During this period in which I was developing a sharper sense of the crisis surrounding *yidishe kultur* in my life, I was also becoming increasingly involved in a non-Jewish environment, i.e., the feminist and lesbian/feminist movement. (Needless to say, many of the feminists and lesbians I worked with were Jews; but our focus was never on Jewish issues.) The absorption of feminism into my politics, the recognition of gay oppression represented a major shift in my perspective, one that would permanently transform how I viewed the world. It was the first such shift in my political thinking since I had been taught socialism and *yidishkayt* as a child.

So towards the end of the '70s, I found myself in much the same situation as I had been as a child. My life was once again split between two worlds, and I moved from one to the other without feeling any connection or ties. My Yiddish activities were barely noted by feminist and lesbian friends, or evoked only mild curiosity. And most Yiddishists with whom I had contact knew nothing of my life in the lesbian community; it was the late '70s and the subject of lesbians and gays remained virtually unspoken in the Jewish world.[9]

Unlike 15 years earlier, the crisis I experienced over this split was conscious and my decision deliberate. I knew the kind of complete commitment continued involvement in Yiddish demands; I knew that by temperament I was not a scholar, but a poet; I knew that a complete commitment required a total immersion in the *yidishe svive*; and I knew I did not want to lead two separate lives. So I made a decision based on an "all-or-nothing" principle. Once again I left *di yidishe svive* and hoped that I could take with me and hold on to what remained.

The decision was excruciating. I did not want to feel alien in my own home. I did not want to be a stranger. But I saw no way out of the dilemma, no way to build bridges. I felt I had to choose and did.

Because I was born during the war, I have always had a keen sense of how Jewish history has shaped my life. And at this time, history stepped in again; for just as I was withdrawing from the *yidishe svive*, the women's movement began to take notice of Jewish issues. Evelyn T. Beck's *Nice Jewish Girls: A Lesbian Anthology*, published in April 1982, sold 10,000 copies over the next 10 months and made an enormous impact on the women's community. And in June 1982, Israel invaded Lebanon, an event which forced many Jews—including lesbians and feminists—to examine their Jewishness and their relationship to Israel. As a writer and publisher who had been very visible as a Jew, I became caught up in the turmoil and began leading workshops on anti-Semitism and Jewish identity.

It was the latter that ultimately absorbed me most because it was what I was struggling with myself. I began to see that whatever loss I was experiencing was but a fraction of what others felt. In workshops at various feminist and lesbian conferences, I met Jewish women whose last contact with Jewishness had been in early childhood with grandparents; women who had never been to a seder; women who knew no Jewish history or culture. Still, they yearned: How can I be Jewish? Is being Jewish more than just *feeling* Jewish? What should I study? What should I do? Where should I go? Like me, many of them were not drawn to religion or ritual; they were looking for *secular* answers.

I was full of these questions when in July 1983—37 years after having left—I returned to Poland with my mother on the occasion of the 40th anniversary of the *varshever geto oyfshtand*, Warsaw Ghetto Uprising. Though I had been raised in almost a *khurbn kultur*, a Holocaust culture, I was totally unprepared for the experience. In Poland I saw the *shadows* of Jewish-Polish culture and was able to infer from them the magnitude of what had taken place. It was like stepping into a negative rather than a photograph. I was overcome by the sudden realization of the scale of the loss.

A year before my return to Poland, I was finalizing the manuscript of *Keeper of Accounts* and struggling with the last section of "Solitary Acts," the concluding poem. Rejecting dreams that can never be realized, I ended the poem with the following lines:

This night  I want only
to sleep    a dark  rich  dreamless sleep.
to shelter   in me  what is left
to strengthen myself  for what is needed.

Twelve months later, walking through the mammoth, overgrown, vandalized cemeteries of Warsaw and Lodz; standing in front of their crumbling and abandoned Jewish memorials; making my way among the hundreds of sculpted rocks that served as anonymous markers for those who died at Treblinka, I kept repeating the words *to shelter in me what is left, to shelter what is left, to shelter*. During those seven days, I knew that I would never take Yiddish culture for granted, never abandon it again.

## III. *Di tsukunft/* The Future

In looking back, I wonder why something so basic as *di yidishe kultur,*so intimately connected to my life has been so difficult to maintain, to be actively loyal to. Why have I experienced so many setbacks? The difficulty cannot simply stem from my own particular circumstances. Too many other Eastern European Jews of different orientation and ideology and focus have also found themselves distanced from that culture. The problem stems from American society, which does not tolerate cultures outside the mainstream and does everything, materially and psychologically, to weaken them. Whether to Spanish-speaking or Chinese-speaking or Yiddish-speaking children, the message is monotonously the same: Change your name. Americanize. Forget the past. Forget your people.

But to stop there is not to articulate the entire problem. We must also look to the Jewish community which seems to have taken two polarized views of itself. Some Jews express an intense ambivalence about our relationship to the American mainstream, an ambivalence manifested outwardly in a movement toward complete assimilation and internally in guilt and yearning for the very things it has given up. Other Jews verbalize an ideology for holding on to our culture, an ideology whose necessary fierceness has often hardened into a narrowness and a refusal to recognize any positive values outside of itself. These Jews ask us to sacrifice everything for Jewishness, and consider anyone who does not do so suspect.

What I have come to realize is that if I am to maintain a strong relationship to Yiddish culture I cannot afford the luxury of an "all-or-nothing" attitude. Nor can *di yidishe velt*. Such a purist attitude is destructive, alienating the vast majority of Jews of Eastern European backgrounds, diminishing our ranks, making *di yidishe kultur* available only to a few. This attitude turns Yiddish into a kind of *loshn-koydesh*, holy language; makes *yidishe kultur* a religion in which only *di groyse gelernte*, great scholars, can practice. "Do you know Yiddish?" someone asks my friend, a woman deeply committed to Jewish causes, to peace in the Middle East, a woman who is trying to educate herself about Jewish history, to teach herself the *alef-beys*. "No," she replies, ashamed. "*A goy*," she is told.

This is perhaps the worst side of the *yidishe velt*, the Yiddish world—one which other Jewish communities share. We are all *goyim* to each other. In the *yidishe svive*, I have found provincialism, exclusivity, isolationism, a refusal to honor Jewish difference, a stubborn insistence that our *yidishe kultur* is *di gantse velt*, the whole Jewish world: a narrowness that has frequently looked down upon and denied the richness of Sephardic culture; that has mourned the destruction of Vilna, but forgotten that Salonika is also no more. A narrowness that dismisses the hard, sincere struggle of many American Jews to make up for what history and previous generations withheld from them. *Goyim*—anyone and everyone who is not completely immersed in *yidishe kultur* and/or fluent in the language. It is an attitude that drives many Jews away, that isolates Yiddish culture from the modern sphere, that keeps it from rejuvenating itself.

Yet Yiddish was never the exclusive property of *groyse gelernte*. It was a language of a people of different ideologies, education, commitment, as much the language of gangsters and shopkeepers as that of poets and intellectuals. Never was it a private cult.

And for a language to remain alive it must be used. Yiddish is *mame-loshn* to fewer and fewer secular Jews. But a passive knowledge of Yiddish is still quite strong and interest in Yiddish culture and Eastern European Jewry is on the rise. YIVO Institute for Jewish Research (NYC) continues critical research and its general Yiddish studies and language programs draw Jewish scholars and students, many of them committed to Yiddish and Yiddish culture. Courses in Yiddish are now given at many universities, Y's, Hillels, community centers. Though most do not extend beyond the first year, they represent an interest and concern that should not be minimized.[10] And there is enormous interest in Jewish music. The sudden emergence and popularity of *klezmer* bands must reflect the hunger of American Jews for *yidishe kultur*.

Perhaps nothing better embodies the contradictory interpretations we could make concerning the present status of *yidishe kultur* than the growing prominence of the National Yiddish Book Center, a new institution in Amherst, Mass. devoted to saving *yidishe bikher*, Yiddish books. In the past 5 years, the Center has collected (sometimes from city dumpsters) over a quarter of a million *yidishe bikher* which would otherwise have been abandoned and destroyed. *Zol ikh veynen oder freyen zikh*? Should I weep or rejoice? And what about some of its *zamlers*, collectors, Jews who cannot read the alien alphabet of the very books they're committed to saving? Are they *goyim* or *tsadikim*, saints?

Neither. They represent a totally new phenomenon, Yiddishists without knowledge of Yiddish language but deeply committed to the survival of Yiddish culture. A paradox, but a reality that should not be dismissed or mocked. For if Yiddish culture is to survive, the Yiddish world must include those who care about the culture, whose property it is; it can no longer limit itself and define itself by language alone.

The survival of Yiddish and its culture does not rest on our ability to find the right term for "corn flakes" or "jet lag"; but rather on our ability to find a proper place for *yidishe kultur* in our lives, a place among other commitments; on our ability to infuse it with our contemporary values and politics learned outside of its boundaries. For example, feminism: women were co-creators and conveyors of Yiddish culture. This fact should be reflected in cultural history, as in contemporary Yiddish institutions and events. Contemporary Jewish feminists have much to contribute and their perspectives should be sought out. The Jews who would say "we don't need *them*" should think again about history, about the size of the Jewish community. I believe we need each other.

I know that some Yiddishists will perceive my call for greater inclusion as a dilution; will hear my own admission of other commitments as a reflection of my being a dilettente. I believe otherwise. I want my Yiddish involvement to be rooted in my life, in the present, want it to be infused with my contemporary politics and concerns, with the special quality of Jewish American experience. *Di yidishe svive* in the American environment. One world, not two. That's what will keep Yiddish alive for me.

To those outside the Yiddish world, my commitment to Yiddish will seem narrow. How can it compare to the "larger" struggles of the Middle East, Central America, South Africa, nuclear extinction—struggles to which I too am committed. Spiritual concerns are easily classified as secondary. Yet I am convinced, particularly because the world is such as it is, that the survival of cultures is critical and that the effort to save cultures is one of the healthiest signs of our desire to survive as a species. That as a Jew I have a personal stake in the survival of *yidishe kultur* is not something I am ashamed of. I *do* want *di yidishe kultur* to survive and intend to contribute towards that end.

This commitment broadens my perspective, not narrows it. I believe that only when we ourselves are firmly rooted in our own cultural soil do we understand the commitment of others to their cultures: the binds of loyalty, the benefits of community. Furthermore, maintaining *yidishe kultur* supports Jewish diversity, and it is diversity which feeds me, which continues to make life interesting. My recognition of Sephardic culture, for example, caused an expansion of my own perspective on people in general and specifically on the extraordinary breadth of Judaism and the Jewish experience.

I was conscious of this last summer when I did a reading with the Chicana poet Gloria Anzaldúa at Old Wives' Tales, a women's bookstore in San Francisco. I read my bilingual Yiddish/English poetry and translations from Yiddish women writers. Gloria, Chicana from Texas, read her own material in Spanish and English. Our audience was a mix from our ethnic communities and from the general women's community. It was an experience that enlarged all of us, readers as well as listeners, offering both humor and pain, and breaking down the barrier that ignorance often creates. During the reading we bridged a number of worlds, Jewish and Chicana, lesbian and heterosexual, Yiddish and Spanish, Jews and gentiles. Diversity of commitments proved to be broadening, not limiting.

And as the Yiddish world needs to open to feminism, the feminist world needs to be open to Jewish cultures, including Yiddish. Women need to know of the powerful, brave, creative women from my culture, just as I and other Jewish women need this knowledge.

For example: the political activists, the Bundist women in Poland and Russia, *di yidishe froyen*, the Jewish women, who fought for workers' rights and human conditions, for Jewish respect in hostile environments; *di yidishe froyen* who led and participated in strikes, self-defense groups, workers' educational circles; *di yidishe froyen* who took endless risks for justice, for Jewish survival, for socialism, and who died for them. I linger over their photographs and brief captions in *Der Bund in Bilder* (The Bund in pictures). Here are a few:

> Esther Lipshitz—Member of Lodz committee of Bund. Arrested March 14, 1903, tortured in Pitrokow prison. Died June 28, 1903.
>
> Anna Lipshitz—Active in Wilno, Lodz, Odessa, Copenhagen, Riga. Orator and writer. Famed for speeches delivered to revolutionary sailors during uprising on cruiser "Potiomkin" in Odessa.

*YIVO Archives*

*Women members of the Bund. Gabin, Poland, 1907.*

Julia Abramowitch—Active in Warsaw, Siedletz, Kalish, Moscow, St. Petersburg, Caucasia. Wounded in both legs from a bomb splinter in Bialystok (1905). Spent long period in prisons of Siedletz and Kalish. Transported arms and illegal literature.

Nadia Kenigshatz-Grinfeld—Active in Kishinew, Odessa, Kiev, St. Petersburg, Paris. Was many times arrested and exiled. In 1905 belonged to Bundist Self-Defense Group in Odessa, was wounded by Tsarist bullet. Early in 1918 Rumanian security police drowned her in Dniester while expelling her from the country.

Gina Klepfisz—Was active in work of snatching Jewish leaders out of railroad cars which were taking them to death in Treblinka.

Patti Kremer—Murdered September 1943 when German occupying power led last Jews out of Wilno. The 77-year-old woman gathered a group of women Bundists around her and said to them: "We will join hands and together sing the Bundist 'Oath' ('Shevueh'), then death won't be so terrible."[11]

I turn to Fradel Schtok and know that another woman writer experienced similar conflicts over *mame-loshn*. I read her stories of the *shtetl* and America and see the two worlds between which she was caught. I turn to Kadia Molodowsky, predominantly known for her poetry, but whose stories minutely depict assimilation in America as she witnessed it in the '40s and '50s. All these Jewish women—Julia, Nadia, Patti, Gina, Fradel, Kadia—are my ancestors. They are *mayne bobes, mumes, shvester*, my grandmothers, aunts, sisters. *Mir darfn zikh bakenen.* We need to become acquainted.

But I do not want to live in the past. I need to move on and build. I want to contribute towards a literature which is rooted in my experience, which reflects the special place Yiddish has had in my life. So I have begun experimenting to see if I could reflect in my writing the two linguistic and cultural worlds to which I am committed. So far I have only finished two poems in which Yiddish plays a major part.[12] Neither quite escapes from intellectual formulation into the active imaginative expression of poetic form. This can only happen with repeated experimentation and feeling more *heymish*, comfortable, with the idea. I need time and patience.

But I have no illusions. What I am using is not the *mame-loshn* I would have used had I been born into a different Poland. It is not even the anglicized Yiddish of American Jews. It is a somewhat schooled, timid, sometimes fragmented Yiddish, insecure and embarrassed by its formality, by its present starkness.

But history has frequently forced Jews to cope with fragments and, as a result, we have learned how to create new contexts, new structures, new wholes—this process as in the case of Yiddish itself sometimes taking centuries. It is, I think, part of our resilience, part of our great capacity to transform when we have the will.

And so perhaps this Yiddish of mine, this fragmentary language, this echo of a European era and culture in which I never lived and about which I have only heard second-hand like a family story, this *mame-loshn* might prove worth salvaging and sheltering. I have no way of knowing what function, if any, it will have for me or for others. I do know that when I have presented my poems at readings, when I have formed the sounds, said the words out loud, those who had assumed Yiddish was a language of the past only, suddenly felt it had been revived. As my tongue, mouth, lips, throat, lungs, physically pushed Yiddish into the world—as I, a Jew, spoke a Jewish language to other Jews, Yiddish was very much alive. Not unlike a *lebn-geblibene*, a survivor, of an overwhelming catastrophe, it seemed to be saying *'khbin nisht vos ikh bin amol geven.* I am not what I once was. *Ober 'khbin nisht geshtorbn. ikh leb.* But I did not die. I live.

I am indebted to discussion and debate on language and culture with Melanie Kaye/Kantrowitz, Judy Waterman, Esther Hyneman, Gloria Anzaldúa, Sonia Pinkusowitz, and Linda Vance, and editorial assistance from Melanie, Judy and Linda. Of course, I take full responsibility for the ideas and opinions expressed.

## Notes

[1] After Poland's liberation, some Poles staged pogroms against Jews who had survived camps and ghettos and were returning to their homes. The largest took place in Kielce, where 40 Jewish survivors were murdered. Many Jews who were considering staying in Poland left.

[2] In Yiddish, *khaverte* is used for both married and unmarried women.

[3] Aviva Ravel, *Faithful Unto Death: The Story of Arthur Zygielbaum* (Montreal: Workmen's Circle, 1980), pp. 178-79. Zygielbaum wrote two letters, in Polish to the Polish government and in Yiddish to the Bund. The passage cited is from the Polish letter; at the *akademyes*, I heard it in Yiddish.

[4] Buloff was frequently typecast as a bungling Russian and is probably best known for his appearance in *Silk Stockings*.

[5] Some courses on Jewish topics and Hebrew did exist, but only in standard departments, i.e., history, religion, modern languages.

[6] I have frequently wondered what Max Weinreich felt about CCNY. Surrounded by a vast, young Jewish population of Eastern European background, he taught only German and linguistics.

[7] In 1959, the Bund opened Camp Hemshekh. It was Yiddish speaking and became a life-long influence on those children who were lucky enough to attend it over the next 20 years.

[8] Jacob Milner, "Yiddish and the Intellectuals," *Perspectives* (Winter 1964), p. 24.

[9] It's a relief to see that the Jewish media has finally broken this silence. *The Jewish Week, The Reconstructionist, Jewish Currents, Moment, The Book Peddler* have all written about or made positive references to lesbians and gays. And organizations like New Jewish Agenda and the National Council of Jewish Women have included lesbians and gays in their programs and outreach.

[10] Rakhmiel Peltz, "Who's Speaking Yiddish Today?" *Jewish Currents* (Dec. 1985), p. 31.

[11] J. S. Hertz, *Der Bund in Bilder/The Jewish Labor Bund: A Pictorial History 1897-1957* (New York: Farlag Unser Tsait, 1958), pp. 50, 158, 154.

[12] *"Etlekhe verter. . ./*A few words. . ." (p. 79) and *"Di rayze aheym/*The journey home (p. 51).

### Resources
**Books**

Chagall, Bella. *First Encounter.* New York: Schocken, 1983.

Dubnow, Simon. *History of the Jews in Russia and Poland: From the Earliest Times Until the Present Day.* Philadelphia: Jewish Publication Society, 1916.

Dobroszycki, Lucjan and Kirshenblatt-Gimblett, Barbara. *Image Before My Eyes: A Photographic History of Jewish Life in Poland 1864-1939.* New York: Schocken and YIVO, 1977.

Hertz, J.S. *The Jewish Labor Bund: A Pictorial History 1897-1957*. New York: Farlag Unser Tsait, 1958.

Howe, Irving and Greenberg, Eliezer, eds. *A Treasury of Yiddish Poetry*. New York: Holt, Rinehart and Winston, 1969.

Mlotek, Eleanor Gordon. *The New Book of Yiddish Songs*. New York: Workmen's Circle, 1972.

Pratt, Norma Fain. "Culture and Radical Politics: Yiddish Women Writers 1890-1940." *American Jewish History*, LXX (1981), 68-90.

Rubin, Ruth. *Voices of a People: The Story of Yiddish Folksong*. Philadelphia: Jewish Publication Society, 1979.

Tobias, Henry J. *The Jewish Bund in Russia: From Its Origins to 1905*. Palo Alto, CA: Stanford University Press, 1972.

Weinberg, Sydney Stahl. *The World of Our Mothers: The Lives of Jewish Immigrant Women*.Chapel Hill: University of North Carolina Press, 1988.

Weinreich, Uriel. *College Yiddish: An Introduction to the Yiddish Language and to Jewish Life and Culture*. New York: YIVO Institute, 1949.

_____. *Modern English-Yiddish Yiddish-English Dictionary*. New York: YIVO, 1968.

Whitman, Ruth, ed. *An Anthology of Modern Yiddish Poetry*, New York: Workmen's Circle, 1979.

## Institutions

**The Association for the Promotion of Jewish Secularism, Inc.**, Room 601, 22 E. 17th St., NYC 10003. The English monthly, *Jewish Currents*, regularly includes articles on Yiddish culture and Jewish communities around the world.

**Der forverts/Jewish Daily Forward**, 45 E. 33rd St., NYC 10016. The original daily newspaper, currently bi-lingual and weekly.

**National Yiddish Book Center**, Old East Street Road, POB 969, Amherst, MA 01004. Publishes catalog, sponsors Yiddish cultural events. Its quarterly English newsletter, *The Book Peddler*, includes translations.

**The Jewish Labor Bund Archives**, 25, E. 21st St., NYC 10010. Predominantly Yiddish material, but not all.

**The Workmen's Circle**, 45 E. 33rd St., NYC 10016. Has branches in major cities all over the United States. Publishes educational meterial for teaching Yiddish and Yiddish culture to children and adults. Lectures and courses. Catalog of books, tapes, etc. available.

**YIVO Institute for Jewish Research**, 1048 Fifth Avenue, NYC 10028. Sponsors the Max Weinreich Center for Advanced Jewish Studies and the Uriel Weinreich Summer Program in Yiddish Language, Literature and Culture (at Columbia University). Cultural events and lectures. Publishes scholarly work and a quarterly bilingual newsletter *Yedies/News of the YIVO*.

*Irena Klepfisz*

# *Di rayze aheym*/The Journey Home

### 1. *Der fentster*/ The window

She looks out the window.
All is present.
The shadows of the past
fall elsewhere.

This is the wilderness
she thinks.

And our tongues have become
dry  the wilderness has
dried out our tongues  and
we have forgotten speech.

She looks out the window.
All is present.

### 2. *Vider a mol*/ Once again

*Vider a mol*
she tries
to rise above circumstances.

Too much is at stake
this morning
*yedn frimorgn*
                 every morning
to see what can be wrenched
from the unconscious
crowded darkness
*fun ir zikorn*
                 of her memory.

It is there
*di gantse geshikhte*
*fun folk*
          the entire history
of the people.

*Vider a mol*
              she reaches out
and tries to hold on
clinging
         like a drowning
person
       to a flimsy plank.

*Ober der yam iz groys*
but the sea is vast
*un di velt*
            and the world
*afile greser*
               even larger
                           *afile greser.*

### 3. *Zi flit*/She flies

*Zi flit*
*vi a foygl*
      like a bird
*zi flit*
*ibern yam*
      over the sea
*iber di berg*
      over the mountains.

*Tsurik*
    *tsurik* back
      back

*zi flit*
    and settles
*oyf a boym*
      on a tree
*lebn a moyer*
      near a wall

*a moyer*
*fun a beys-oylem*
      a wall
      of a cemetery.

### 4. *A beys-oylem*/ A cemetery

*Der moyer*     the wall

*oyf der zayt*
      on this side
*un oyf der zayt*
      and on this side
*Oyf beyde zaytn*  on both sides.

*Oyf der zayt*
*a keyver*
      on this side
    a grave

*oyf der zayt*
*a vistenish*
    on this side

    a wasteland.

*Der moyer*
*a beys-oylem*
*oyf der zayt*
      *un oyf der zayt.*

### 5. *Kashes*/ Questions

*In velkhn yor?*
      in what year?
*Mit vemen?*
      with whom?
*Di sibes?*
      the causes?
*Der rezultat?*
      the outcome?
*di geshikhte*
      the history
*fun der milkhome*
      of the war
*fun dem sholem*
      of the peace
*fun di lebn geblibene*
      of the survivors

*tsvishn fremde*
      among strangers
*oyf der zayt*
      on this side

*tsvishn meysim*
      *oyf der zayt*
    among ghosts
    on this side.

6. *Zi shemt zikh/* She is ashamed

*Zi shemt zikh.*
          She has forgotten
              *alts fargesn*
forgotten it all.

          Whom can I speak to?
          she wonders.

| | |
|---|---|
| *di mame* | the mother |
| *der tate* | the father |
| *di bobe* | the grandmother |
| *der zeyde* | the grandfather |
| *di oves* | the ancestors |

*alts*
*alts fargesn*
forgotten it all

        *di gantse mishpokhe*
        the entire family

*dos folk*
the people

      *Mit vemen*
      *ken ikh redn?*
      Whom can I speak to?

*di meysim farshteyen*
*mir afile nit*
        even the ghosts
        do not understand me.

7. *In der fremd/* Among strangers

*Vi azoy?*   how
         she wonders
         should I speak?

        *Velkhe verter*
which words
should I use
*in der fremd*
        among strangers?

*Red*
*bloyz dem emes*
        speak
        only the truth
*kayn lign nit*
        no lies.

*Zi gedenkt*
She remembers
*di lektsies*
        the lessons
*di printsipn*
        the principles

        *un zi shvaygt*

and she remains

        silent.

8. *Di tsung/* The tongue

*Zi shvaygt.*

*Di verter feln ir*
she lacks the words
and all that she can force

is sound
unformed sound:

*a*
*der klang*
          the sound

*o*
*dos vort*
          the word

*u*
*di tsung*
          the tongue

*o*
*dos loshn*
          the language

*e*
*di trern*
          the tears.

9. *Di rayze aheym/* The journey home

*Zi flit*
      she flies
*vi a foygl*
        like a bird
*vi a mes*
        like a ghost

*Zi flit*
*iber di berg*
          over the mountains
*ibern yam*
        over the sea.

*Tsurik*
     *tsurik* back
             back

*In der fremd*
        among strangers
*iz ir heym*
      is her home.

          *Do*
here
*ot do*
       right here
*muz zi lebn*
      she must live.

*Ire zikhroynes*
       her memories
       will become monuments
*ire zikhroynes*
will cast shadows.

# 2. The Women in Our Family

*At night the women of our family*
*Come to me in dreams and say. . .*
— Kadia Molodowsky, "Women Poems"

*Irene Eber*

*Jayne Sorkin*

*Isabelle Maynard*

*Beatrice Lieberman*

*Jennifer Krebs*

*Ruth Whitman*

*Enid Dame*

# Lilith's Sestina

"For [Lilith's] first thought was *power*; she counted it slavery to be one with me, and bear children for Him who gave her being. . . . Vilest of God's creatures, she lives by the blood and lives and souls of men."

spoken by Adam, in George MacDonald's novel, *Lilith*


Sometimes I think I'll give up on men,
wash their smells out of my sheets and live by myself.
Look what they've done to the sky, how they live with their power.
(Look at the morning headlines and say I'm not right!)
Like other women, I've been in danger.
Like other women, I've had a bad press.


That's because women have never controlled the press.
Think of all those stories written by men
reviling the Female:  her treacherous mouths, her danger,
a dirty mirror reflecting a frightening self.
Like other women, I've been afraid they're right.
Like other women, I've never trusted my power.


True, I have known delight in sexual power:
the thrill of discovery, comforting press
of bodies in bed.  I've said, "This is right.
Nothing matters but merging of women and men,
the sensual sharing, dissolving the boundaries of self;
learning another country: its rituals, its dangers."


Since the beginning, I've been more or less an endangered
species. God's rough draft? Well, I've stood up to that power,
and my husband, who liked to name things.  I named myself,
lived by myself among others, seldom letting them press
in too closely with needs and commandments.  Men
crash through the world like proprietors, never doubting their right

to trample, to resurrect. But for me, wrong and right
blur like the sky's edge on ocean. Danger,
testing the limits of mind, is appealing to men:
forcing their enemies to acknowledge their power.
(One day, the planet won't start, and some expert will press
the wrong button, and that will be that, I warn myself.)


I still hear those voices shouting, "Give yourself
up to our god, to our cause, to our country! We know we're right!"
Faces distorted, blood-ripe, they press
all around me, their instruments gleaming. But I know the real danger
for me won't be physical. Power,
sisters, is frightening. Would you change places with men?


Sometimes I hope there's no danger that I'm right.
Like other women, I don't kid myself about power.
Like other women, I don't press my luck with men.

*Enid Dame*

# A Brief Interview on the _____
## _____ Subject of Women's History

Naomi came over last night. It was very important. She wanted to know was I a virgin when I got married. "Was I a virgin? Sure I was a virgin," I told her. "Everybody was a virgin then. In fact, I'm still a virgin. Three kids, I'm three times a virgin." I can't believe that girl. And Frances she calls me. Not Aunt Frances anymore, just Frances.

Was I a virgin. Oh, was I a virgin. Then and for three days afterwards. For a while I was afraid I'd never be anything but a virgin. Not that Sam and I didn't have a good marriage. Things moved slower in those days. We didn't know all about that stuff since we were fourteen like they do today.

No, they gotta know everything now. Like Naomi. "It's history," she says. "What history?" I told her. "If whether I was a virgin is history, I think instead I'll go shoot myself. Enough history for you," I told her, "is you knocked your front teeth out when you were six. You wanted to look older." "I fell off the jungle gym," she says. "You want history?" I told her. "George Washington. Abraham Lincoln. Mayor Wagner. What're you gonna do, write a book about my sex life?"

"It's family history," she says. "I want to interview the women in my family." "Women?" I told her. "Women? What do you think, you've got a family of all women? Whether I was a virgin," I said, "I didn't get three kids from the corner grocer. And to think, I used to say you were so bright. What is it, is this what you learned at Hunter?"

"What did you want to be when you were young?" she asked me. "You're changing the subject," I said. "I know," she says, "but tell me." "I used to think I'd want to be a schoolteacher," I said.

"So when you were young, you didn't think about getting married?" she asked me. "Sure I thought about getting married. Everyone thought about getting married. What else did a women do? Get married; be a teacher. In my spare time I thought I'd have babies."

"But what did you dream about?" she wants to know. "Dream," I said. "I used to dream of books, all laid out end to end, and a roast beef on rye to eat while I read each one; an apartment on Riverside Drive and no one to ask me questions. You make me nervous. Do you know that?"

"How'd you feel about the rest of your family? About Bea and Leah and David?" she wants to know. "You think I'll forget who's your mother," I told her, "because you call her Leah like she was someone you met just last week. But I saw you when she brought you home, so tiny you didn't have sense enough to cry. You slept in my bed till they got you a crib. I used to worry I'd roll over and crush you. I can't say I never had the chance, can I? But the crib," I told her, "you know where they got it, you with the family history? The junk man. Your father wore a yarmulke till he left home, and

59

he hid it in his pocket when he went off the block. Don't you forget where you come from."

"I don't want to forget where I come from," she said. "I'm trying to find out. You never told me that before, Frances. No one ever told me that."

"We're not a family to complain," I told her. "Not that you didn't have everything any of us could get for you. More than made sense for one kid, I used to say. But you were the first, and I didn't have any better sense than the rest of them, I have to admit it.

"You were the cutest thing. Bright. You talked at a year. Your mother used to call to tell me the things you'd said. And your Dad — he was a good father to you. I don't know why you turned out the way you did. We all thought you'd be something special. And when you went to college, Naomi," I told her, "I don't think I was more proud of my own kids. And what've you made of your life? Three unpublished books and enough poems to fill the holes in the linoleum. And now you want family history. My luck this one you'll publish. That's good. The whole neighborhood's been wanting to know was I a virgin when I got married. The super's wife, you know, she asked me just last week. Have you ever thought maybe you should get married. You're an attractive girl still when you comb your hair."

"I comb my hair, Frances," she said. "You never pushed me to get married, did you? You or Mom?"

"You were smart," I said. "A girl gets married she wastes herself. Legally dead. Nothing happens after that."

"But what about you?" she wants to know. "And Mom and Bea? You were smart."

"I fell in love," I said. "And then, you never knew your grandparents. Your Mom was bright enough and Bea was all right, though to tell you the truth she's no genius. But we were to marry. David, he was to be the scholar."

"You must have felt really bad about that," she said.

"You learn to live with things," I told her. But the truth — what bothers me. That's a terrible thing for a mother to say. I tell her I'm more proud of her than of my own kids and she goes on like it was nothing. She's had that all her life. Me, her mother, always there, always thinking she was something. She doesn't even know it. She thinks that's just how life is.

*Ellen Hawley*

# Food of Love

A woman drags a shopping cart up the 181st Street hill, looking furtively over her shoulder. She is sixty-five, wears a kerchief, the hem of her coat is undone in the back. Another woman appears with a cart. After a hurried conversation a parcel is transferred from the first cart to the second.

This is not a dope drop. The first woman is my mother who, after evading my father's questions with the excuse that she is going shopping, has secretly entrusted ten pounds of phyllo dough to her friend who will store it *sub rosa* in her refrigerator. My father does not like Mother to engage in extra-marital culinary activities. With the same subterfuge she might employ to meet a lover, she sneaks out to bake delicacies for the organization of which she is president. Because she has interests outside the home my retired father calls her a part-time wife. "Why don't you throw me out like a dog?" he says whenever she pleads an important committee meeting.

A tigress to her board members, my mother is too timid to go to a box office and buy theater tickets; though she has arranged gala functions for hundreds of people at the best hotels, she cannot bring herself to enter a public library for fear that she will not know how to ask for a library card.

However, within the confines of the synagogue where her organization has its office, she is — as Isabella was Queen of all the Americas — queen of all Sephardic womanhood.

She is forced to work with a vice-president who lacks authenticity. A descendant of Revolutionary War generals, the woman is made to feel like an outcast. She was elected because her name is embroidered on seat cushions and inscribed on the Declaration of Independence. Mother gives her useful work to do, stuffing envelopes. What can she know of Sephardic culture, a woman who cooks with safflower oil ?

The event for which Mother is preparing is a fund-raising luncheon to be held in the synagogue community room. The entertainment will consist of a Sephardic sing-along and a short lecture with slides on Our Unique Heritage, designed to wring some money out of our brethren, particularly the Sephardim from Salonika, many of whom are regarded as moguls of the garment business. Their wives cook with olive oil and have been discouraged from aiding in the kitchen by the faction from Izmir.

This is an orthodox synagogue, though half the members travel on the Sabbath to attend services. Mother cooks with a grain of salt and, in her fantasy, with a little unconsecrated cheese, which she sprinkles onto the spinach pastries when no one is looking. Hawkeyed, the rabbi's wife watches to see that all is kosher. She comes from Rhodes where (Mother says) they speak an inferior Ladino, the now archaic Spanish we carried with us after the Expulsion.

Long before the luncheon takes place I know I will be approached to attend. Except for me, daughters always attend their mothers' functions, however dull. For years I was successful in avoiding them, but this time it will be difficult. It is Mother's show and she will receive a plaque.

Knowing she will never ask me outright, I wait. Campaigning starts early.

Invited for lunch at my apartment one Saturday two months before the event, she arrives bearing her usual food parcel. She has never come to my house and eaten my food. Perhaps some bread and coffee, but in between she is her own caterer. She wants to spare me the trouble.

"Umm, isn't this good," she says, licking her fingers. It could be sawdust for the effort it takes me to swallow.

She has brought a new dress to show me. Do I think it suitable for the luncheon? "What luncheon?" I ask.

*The* luncheon. She expects two hundred people. There is already a waiting list. They have hired Aryeh the accordionist and his international band. Did I know they made a recording recently?

"A lot of people make recordings."

"You and I could make one. You have such a lovely voice. I know so many songs. Soon our music will die out if young people like you don't preserve it."

To parricide and fratricide we now add culturicide, with myself the first offender.

I crumple up her tinfoil wrappings and stuff them into the trash can which is overfull.

"Relax," Mother says, "I'll clean up, you rest." This is a woman who always insists upon carrying the fifty-pound grocery load on the grounds that I look tired.

Now she is hovering over my new electric typewriter. "Does it give you shocks?" she asks, standing back a respectful foot and a half.

"Sometimes." All those xxxx'd-out lines.

Watching her reach out to touch the keys I can't help remembering the time I demonstrated to her the instant cash apparatus found at many banks, the kind where you insert your special bank card, push a few buttons and receive cash.

We were short of money one day while shopping on Fifth Avenue. I found a bank and she watched me set the process in motion. When the computer screen said, *Hello, is there anything I can do?* she shrieked with wonder. When it asked if I wished to proceed in English or Spanish, she clutched her throat and said, *Que maravilla!* Reading over my shoulder she said that the computer was more polite than the bank tellers she dealt with. I invited her to take the money from the open cylinder, but to be quick about it at the risk of having her hand clamped in its turning maw.

"Do you know," she said when the transaction was completed, "an ignorant person might think there was a devil in there. I mean someone superstitious." Then she uttered an imprecation in Arabic to the effect that the evil eye should keep its distance from us and our loved ones.

Her campaign to get me to the luncheon is spread over several weeks. "Did I tell you that Professor Asher Halifa will be addressing us?" I had once made the error of saying that I had read an article of his in *Commentary*.

Another time: "You have a beautiful print dress. You don't wear it enough." Translation: "Wear it to the luncheon." I say nothing.

And finally: "I have a ticket reserved for you. It's a nice table, all young people." I consult my calendar, playing for time. The date is filled. "But Mother, I'm seeing a matinee that Sunday."

"Do you have to go?"

"I don't *have* to go, I *want*—"

"No problem then. They'll exchange the ticket. You have plenty of time."

Trying to salvage some pride I offer to pay my way to the luncheon, but she won't allow it. It's for a good cause. "Relax," she says. It is her battle cry.

The day before the luncheon takes place, she calls me. Do I have a tape recorder?

"I have a cassette, but the sound is not very good."

"You know we have Aryeh and his accordion. If you feel like taping the music—"

"Mother," I say, "I will not *feel* like taping. If you want me to, just say so and I'll be glad to do it. I'll go and buy some tape—".

"No, why should you, all that bother. It's too complicated."

"It's not complicated. If you want it, I'll do it. Really, Mom."

"No, no, forget about it. It's all right."

It's not all right. I should have volunteered of course. Another black mark against this unnatural daughter.

At the luncheon I am embraced by people who knew me when I was a little girl, handsome men and beautiful women with names like Diamante, Joya, Fortunée. "Will you sing for us?" "You have such a lovely voice." As a teenager I sang here a few times, accompanying myself with primitive guitar chords. I sang, with my American accent, songs that brought tears to their eyes. It was a phase, folksinging. I haven't been in this building for years.

Mother makes a welcoming speech thanking her vice-president and conveying regrets from the distinguished professor Asher Halifa who was to have addressed us today. The main drawing card as far as I was concerned. No wonder she was afraid to tell me.

Mother's speech is concise and charming. She worries needlessly about her English. My father is watching her as though he has just fallen in love with her. They met forty years ago after a fortune teller predicted that a dark stranger from Turkey would carry her off from Alexandria. She was twenty-three then, teaching French in an Arabic school, working to support her family while her brothers were at the university. Her father, a dapper gentleman who wore spats and a boutonniere, was a gambler. My grandmother had learned to read, rare for a woman in those days in Egypt. Even now, my mother talks wistfully about taking college courses, but is afraid people will laugh at her. She has always been interested in literature and can recite entire scenes from Racine and Corneille. She used to do it often—at home, in supermarkets and especially in front of my friends. If she weren't worried about my father catching her, she would watch the advanced Italian course given at seven in the morning on television.

The rabbi makes a speech. In spite of his degrees and erudition, his public relations manner and his Sephardic wife, he is barely tolerated as a man of the somewhat worn cloth. An Ashkenazi presiding over a Sephardic congregation. *He* doesn't need to tell *us* how unique we are, as he invites us to go from strength to strength.

Mother is everywhere as people begin to eat. I invite her to sit, but she says she doesn't have to eat. Aryeh is playing tunes from a popular Yiddish-American musical on his accordion and Mother is incensed. She whispers something to him and he switches in mid-chord to a Greek song. Five women, all in their sixties, walk up to the stage and begin to dance. There is a *soupçon* of belly dance movements, but not enough to cause embarrassment. Though the Greek song is about a whore, the rabbi is beaming. One of the women puts a coin on her forehead and throws her head back, arching her whole body. The others make a circle around her. The rest of the audience is clapping in time. A man leaps onto the stage—he must be at least seventy-two—and, whips out a handkerchief. The woman with the coin takes hold of a corner of the handkerchief, the man is down on one knee. The music becomes faster and faster and, at the last chord, Mother takes the microphone and announces that dessert is being served.

Now it is time for the plaque. The vice-president, in perfect Vassar English, thanks the lady who has given so much of herself. Mother is blowing her nose. I notice a run in her stocking; one shoe has been slipped off. I know she would like nothing better than to loosen her girdle.

The ovation forces Mother back up to the mike. No more speeches,she promises,and suggests we get on with the sing-along. She wants only to say how happy she is that her daughter could be here today to honor her, and they all know how much joy her daughter used to give them with her beautiful voice but "she said, 'Mother, please don't ask me to sing' and so I won't ask her—"

Pandemonium—my name shouted from every corner of the room, spoons tinkling against the demitasses. The accordion starts up, sounding like the bark of a mad dog. Mother smiles, shrugs—it is out of her hands—.

People push me out of my seat and up to the stage. "Only if you sing with me," I say, trying not to cry out. They have song sheets, but they don't need them. The accordion helps, Mother helps, I sing. I'll get them, I'll get her, they'll be eating out of the palm of my hand. People put down their cups, their baklava, lean back, sigh, sing with me in Ladino, songs about their countries, the almond tree, the sea that brings no letters, the daughters in exile, the smoldering mountains....Why have I waited so long to do this? Looking at her, my mother, I understand for the first time what it is to have a "maternal language." I feel that I am singing in tongues, astonishing myself with those archaic syllables, these Moorish melodies. I could swear I smell jasmine blossoms.

"Isn't she grand?" Mother says to the audience at last. While she is making her financial report, I escape to the ladies room and wash my shaking hands with the kosher soap.

I return to hear Aryeh play a flourish and the start of a lively Arabic song. The curtain, which was drawn across the stage, now parts, revealing my mother transformed into a *houri*, a harem woman clad in gold embroidered silk pantaloons, a silk blouse and vest, pointed velvet slippers with coins jingling at their tips, a silk kerchief at her hair with a fringe of coins over her forehead, finger cymbals in her hands. I stand up. I have never seen this outfit. Where does she keep it? Why did she never show it to me? It must be at least a hundred and fifty years old. It belongs in the Metropolitan Museum or on me. She shakes her shoulders and starts to sing in Arabic and people go mad with delight. She leans into the microphone, still shaking her shoulders in rhythm. "Sing, everyone.... You like it?" Roars, whistles, pounding on the tables, "It's to make up for my lack of voice. We want to give you your money's worth...."

A woman with a face like a gnarled pomegranate stretches out her hands to my mother, then makes her way to me and kisses me on both cheeks as though to confer upon me the Legion d'Honneur which I deserve today.

"The truth," Mother says on the phone later that night. "From you I want the truth."

"Really, you were great."

"Honest?" She giggles.

"Would I lie?"

"Not you. You always speak your mind. You are direct, like me."

I shuffle papers around on my desk while she talks. I had just been contemplating writing her an irate and formal note about her treachery to me at the microphone. Instead I ask if she was nervous. To get up on stage, all those people.

She has to confess to a little "reinforcement." Before leaving home, without my father seeing, she poured a thimblefull of scotch into an empty aspirin bottle.

I'm shocked. A nip before lunch? She should have offered me some. I catapult a paper clip across the room. She continues to question me — about the food, the seating arrangements, the color of the napkins....

What is this sheet of paper on my desk with words typed on it? I did not type them. Now I remember my mother hanging around the typewriter, gingerly touching the keys.

The words on the paper are: "Amérique. America. Maman I am here."

# Isabelle Maynard

# Stories

*I grew up in Tientsin, China in the midst of a segregated Russian-Jewish community. We were there not by choice but by circumstances of history, remnants of the Russian Revolution, and diligently suppressed in our own minds the fact that we were in a foreign land by accentuating the internal ties of the community. We had our own school, our own club, our own organizations and businesses. As Russian-Jews in China we were thrice aliens. We were alienated from the Russian community, with whom we share a language and culture, by virtue of a long history of pogroms and generational hostilities. We were snubbed by the more prosperous and self-proclaimed high status Americans, English, Germans and French, who not only were financially more secure, but most important, had passports and a country to go back to. We had booklets with "STATELESS" stamped on them, and no country wanted us. We alienated ourselves from the Chinese people by choice, snubbing them as we ourselves were snubbed. I never had a Chinese friend while growing up. Perched precariously on this foreign and strange soil, we put no roots down, bought no homes and seldom learned the Chinese language.*

*The various European communities, each with its territorial "concession," rarely mixed with one another, although all were united in looking down on the Chinese. The psychological and geographic lines between groups were clear-cut but not blatantly offensive. Life was often easy and gracious as we focused on the pleasures and details of the day.*

*Victoria Road, Tientsin's main avenue,ran through the European sections, linking the ethnic districts like beads on a string. Here we walked and gossiped, sat in cafés, met friends and enjoyed the park where a hand-painted sign read "No Chinese or Dogs Allowed." The sluggish Hi Ho canal at the end of town reminded us all that we lived in a seaport and that beyond it lay the China Sea and the world. Every few years the Hi Ho would rumble and spill its filthy brackish waters into the town. The sandbags put up by all the communities against the flood were equally ineffective.*

— from "Private Lessons"

## Mimosas Provide Shade

One hot shimmering day in August, I was barred from entering the convent of St. Mary Magdalene. I would have welcomed the cool tiled corridors and the dim interior. The convent was on the outskirts of the European part of Tientsin settled decades before by Carmelite nuns whose aim it was to educate and convert the Chinese. In the summer of 1941, when I was eleven, I arrived weekly for my French lessons, sitting on the cross-bar of my father's bicycle and hearing his labored breathing behind me as he pushed uphill on Davenport Road towards the convent. (Taking lessons was a way of life in our community — we took everything — piano, French, violin, ballet, painting. Parents madly exposed their children to "culture" as if to avoid the unseemly realities of life.) We rode past the International Swimming Pool where later in the day, after the lessons, I would submerge myself in the deliciously cool but highly chlorinated water, past the Min-Yuan soccer grounds — now deserted — and past the red-tiled pagodas in Victoria Park. During the summer *fu-tiens* (fierce heat) my father protected himself from the blazing sun by wearing a handkerchief on his head. He tied the four corners into knots, making it look like a little stocking cap. I never wore a hat. You'll never get a sunstroke, my mother said, you were born here, so you're a native and immune.

My parents had settled in Tientsin after the Russian revolution and my entry into this world was assisted by the Carmelite nuns who also ran the local, and the best (according to my mother) hospital in town. The difficult Caesarean birth was attended by the highly skilled but remote nuns who were not too sympathetic to my young mother's cries. The hospital, like St. Mary Magdalene, was surrounded by high walls.

To the north the convent looked on Davenport Road in the English concession. Its southern gates spilled into Rue St. Louis in the French concession. Thus it straddled two worlds with its massive grey structure. The streets were empty this August day, except for some Chinese servants squatting on their haunches in doorways or under dusty mimosa trees, fanning themselves with wide bamboo fans. They sipped hot tea from porcelain cups, the steam from their cups mingling with the afternoon haze.

My father dropped me off at the gate of the convent and said he would be back in an hour to pick me up. I watched his bicycle disappear in the glimmering haze, and walked into the small front garden. As I stood at the black carved door, I felt my red seer sucker dress clinging in wet spots to my thighs and midriff and I ached for the coolness inside.

The door was opened by an unfamiliar nun who towered over me. She held the door, barely ajar, with one hand, and looked down at me.

"Yes," she said. It was not an affirmative yes or a question; it was almost sung. "Y..e....ss."

"It's Tuesday," I said. "I'm here for my French lesson."

"Ah."

I looked up at her. The folds of her long black habit were shiny in spots. Across her forehead the white bandeau was starched and spotless. There was not a spot of sweat on her face. Mine was damp and down my back I could feel a trickle of perspiration.

"It's four o'clock. I usually come at four."

"Ye...ess," she said again in that undecipherable tone. She looked so cool and remote, so distant. I could not understand why she was not letting me in. I could feel the sun beating on my back.

It occurred to me that perhaps I was early, and looking at my newly acquired wristwatch I realized it was indeed ten minutes to four.

67

"I'm ten minutes early. Can I come in to wait for Sister Mathilde?"

She stared at me silently. I noticed her eyes were bright blue, almost purple. "Turn around," she said in a soft but commanding voice.

"Turn around?"

"Yes."

I turned around, slowly pivoting on my feet and realized with embarrassment that she would see the streaks of sweat on my back. I wondered how many layers of clothing she wore underneath her habit and how she managed to keep cool.

After examining me for what seemed a full five minutes, she said, "You can't come in today."

"Can't come in! Why not?"

"Your dress has no back. And no sleeves."

"But I always wear this kind of dress in the summer. They're halter dresses, you know. To keep cool in the summer."

"You cannot come into the house of the Lord dressed this way. It's disrespectful."

"Sister Mathilde let me in last week. And the week before."

She was silent for a while, and for the first time looked away from me. "Sister Mathilde is a novice."

"But where will I wait? My father won't pick me up for another hour." I panicked at the thought of sitting in the sun without any shade, for a whole hour.

"Find something to do. Go over your lessons."

I looked at her helplessly. She still had her hand on the door. There seemed nothing more inviting at this moment than the thought of the cool checkered tiles under my blistering feet.

"*Qui est là?*" I heard a voice from the interior.

"*C'est la petite Juive pour sa leçon,*" said the nun. She started closing the door.

"But, there is no shade outside," I said.

"Yes." Again that enigmatic tone. "We *will* be planting mimosa next year." She turned around and started to walk away. I took a step forward, about to ask her what she meant, but she closed the door and I found myself alone on the steps.

I looked around the unfamiliar garden, realizing I had never spent any time here before. There were no trees—just a few dusty shrubs with grey leaves. A clump of enormous sunflowers in a corner provided a spot of color but no shade. I sat on the steps and fashioned a visor (to protect myself from the sun) out of a piece of paper from my notebook and clipped it on my hair with two hairpins. I tried reviewing my homework but found myself losing interest. "*La petite Juive, la petite Juive,*" ran in my head over and over again. The disembodied voice from the convent's interior had not been a harsh one, but the words made me shiver even as the sun beat down on me. Listlessly I wandered around the cramped garden, kicking small round stones in the dust and hoping my father would come soon, but knowing his punctuality I knew he would arrive exactly on the hour. A giant spider, exposed by one overturned stone, scuttled for safety, its body quivering under a layer of dust. A Chinese servant came out from the convent and began to sweep the stairs, but soon gave up this endeavor, as the puffs of dust hung briefly in the thick air and then settled back on the steps.

At exactly five o'clock my father waved to me through the garden gate without getting off his bicycle and I ran to meet him. I climbed on the cross-bar and we rode silently, as we often did, through the quiet streets, the sun still beating relentlessly on our backs. When we got home my mother inquired how the lesson was. "I never had a lesson." I told her I hadn't been allowed inside the convent because of my halter dress. "My new red seersucker dress," I pointed out, "the pretty one."

My mother was puzzled. "Didn't you go in that dress last week?"

"Yes," I said, "but today she wouldn't let me in, the tall nun. She said Sister Mathilde had let me in because she is a novice. What's a novice?"

"A novice is someone new and inexperienced. Sister Mathilde probably is new at the convent and doesn't know the rules." My mother sat tapping her forehead with her fingers as she often did when making a decision. "We'll just have to think of something to get around this problem. I'll come up with something," she said cheerily.

Just before dinner my mother said she had come up with a marvellous idea. She told me we would sew little capes on my halter dresses which I would wear on the days of my lessons, thus covering my back and arms. I looked at her to see if she was joking, but there was not even a quiver of a smile on her face.

"Why do I have to do that?"

"Because it's their house and their rules. You have to be proper when you go there and not offend anyone. Besides, it's the best place to learn French. You know that, so don't put up a fuss."

"Why?" I persisted.

"You have to learn to accommodate, to put up with certain things. You'll understand when you're older."

My mother went on to tell me how tomorrow we would go to see Mrs. Feldman who had sewn the original backless dresses and order some "little cute capes" for them.

"I hate capes," I said. "Fania Stoffman wears them and she's a hunchback." I often saw Fania in the streets, head bent low as if trying to blend in, wearing orthopedic shoes and caped dresses.

"Hush," my mother said, and the subject was closed.

Next day my mother and I went to see Mrs. Feldman. We went in the evening when it was cooler. Mrs. Feldman lived in an alley and her two small rooms were littered with bolts of materials, old *Vogue* magazines, and Montgomery Ward catalogs from the United States. A sister in Pasadena sent them regularly to her before the war and it was out of these magazines, some months back, that I had chosen the halter dresses for summer. Darting around the room, Mrs. Feldman showed us various kinds of cloth and suggested a cape of contrasting material. She said she could have the cape fasten on little hooks, so it could easily come off as needed. Draping several pieces of cloth around her shoulder, and with her mouth full of pins, Mrs. Feldman danced around me, explaining to my mother how it would all work. "We'll start a new trend, a new fashion," she sang.

I felt gloomy and tired when we left Mrs. Feldman. "I'm going to look just like Fania," I kept muttering to my mother. "I could just wear my other dresses—the ones with sleeves."

"They're too hot for summer wear. This way, you wear the cape only on Tuesdays, for one hour. Once you leave the convent, you can whip it off and you'll be in your fashionable halter dress."

"But why can't you talk to the nuns and ask them to let me wear what I want?"

My mother stopped suddenly in the middle of the street and released my hand, which she had been holding. There was a puzzled look on her face and she squeezed her eyebrows as if in pain. "I can't talk to the nuns," she said, "I even pay them by mail."

"But why? Why can't you talk to them?"

"They're Catholic. It's a different world. They live in their world, and we in ours. Someday you'll understand. Come on. How about an ice-cream cone at Keesling Café?"

I did not understand at all and things seemed to be getting more and more bewildering all the time. *"La petite Juive, la petite Juive."* The phrase kept repeating itself in my head, as if the needle was stuck in the groove.

We walked silently the two blocks to Keesling's, where I had my favorite ice-cream. I ordered Keesling's special, called the *kuchka* — a cool mound of chocolate and wafers — but somehow it didn't taste as delicious as usual. I must have been sitting glumly, because my mother suggested we go see a movie, an activity usually reserved only for Saturday afternoons. I declined, saying I was tired and wanted to go home.

My mother brought home two little capes during the next week. Both she and my father oohed and aahed over them, saying what a genius Mrs. Feldman was. They were reversible, so actually I had four capes, and they flowed from my shoulders like wings. "I'm sure the nuns will approve," they both exclaimed.

My father deposited me on the doorsteps of St. Mary Magdalene the next week at the usual time. Just before we got to the gate, he got off the bicycle and helped me fasten the cape to my dress. "It's really quite attractive," he said.

I looked at my tall handsome father, leaning against the bicycle. "Why," I said. "Why can't I wear what I want?"

My father sighed, patted me on the head and said. "Cheer up." Then he started laughing, leaned towards me and whispered into my ear. "The cape makes you look like an angel. They look like wings sprouting from your back. Now you'll really fit in, the little Jewish angel." I thought of the fat little angels in the pictures and sculptures in the convent and began to laugh. We both roared.

"There now, feel better?" he said.

"Yes," I said, even though the cape was scratching my wet skin. I walked towards the convent door and it was Sister Mathilde who answered it. I hesitated, wondering if she would ask me to turn around.

"Come in, come on in," she said, and waved me inside.

I walked behind her, down the long dim corridor with the cool tiled floor, past the white alabaster statues gleaming in the dark. At the end of the corridor I could see the anguished statue of Christ and as usual I averted my eyes when we came close to the half-naked figure, wondering how come it was all right for him to be naked while I had to be fully dressed, cape and all. Sister Mathilde bent one knee in front of the statue, her black dress spreading like a fan behind her. I waited while she performed her ceremony, feeling slightly nauseous, and glad when she was through and we could go upstairs, along another dim hallway to the classroom. There we sat at our usual place by the window and Sister Mathilde told me to start reading the second chapter of *Les Misérables*.

A fly was buzzing in the corner of the room as I read out loud. The afternoon heat parched my throat and I asked Sister Mathilde if I could get a drink of water. As I got up, I gently swayed the wings of my "nifty" cape, hoping that she would notice and give me a sign of approval. I glanced back at her as I was leaving the room. She was looking out the window, her head tilted slightly to the right, her alabaster white finger stroking her lip. Without turning her head, she muttered dreamily, "The *fu-tiens* will soon be over. And we *will* be planting mimosa. In a few years they will provide shade for us." I stopped in the doorway wondering if she would say more. She must know about last week, I thought to myself. But Sister Mathilde continued to look out the window and was quiet. My head was aching from the heat and I welcomed the cool water from the fountain as it slithered down my parched throat.

# "We must return the hospitality"

Looking at me with her serious brown eyes, beneath the brows that formed a single line across her forehead, she said, "No, we can't have Shirley Canberry in our house for the afternoon." We were sitting, my mother and I, on the second-floor veranda of grandmother's house—a house we shared with my aunt and uncle and several other families, each renting a room and all keeping a communal kitchen—and I was rhythmically kicking the leg of the bamboo chair as I listened to her. She was wearing my favorite dress—the yellow cotton with black polka dots and the sewn-in black cummerbund that circled her tiny waist—a waist that I yearned to have someday but mine now was at the dumpy pre-adolescent 12-year-old stage.

It was May, but the air was still gritty with left-over Gobi Desert March dust, and I could feel the sand in my mouth as I licked my dry lips. Through the veranda railing I could see Cook, tall with bulging biceps ("unusual build for a North Chinese," my mother often said) throwing out the evening garbage into the two huge metal bins by the kitchen. Sui, the houseboy, was leaning against a tree, smoking a cigarette, drawing in the smoke in great gulps and then slowly emitting it in delicate rings. The rickshaw boy, Woo, was squatting on the ground and eating his rice from a bowl. He looked up and waved and I waved back. I could hear his voice as he talked with Sui and Cook but I could only understand a few words. I did not speak Chinese. I spoke Russian at home and English at the Tientsin American School where I met Shirley.

"But why can't Shirley come to the house?" I insisted.

My mother sighed and looked past me. There was a long silence as she gazed off into the distance. I kicked the chair, unravelling the rattan cords that bound the leg, leaving them in a wiry puddle on the floor.

"Because we don't have a house like the Canberry's. Shirley would be uncomfortable here. She's an embassy child. We have only one bathroom upstairs and there are . . ." Mother counted to herself, "at least eight people on the second floor sharing it."

"Shirley doesn't care about bathrooms," I said.

"Well, how many do the Canberry's have?"

I looked at her. This was ridiculous. But she really was serious and expected an answer. "They have four."

"You see," said my mother triumphantly. "I tell you it won't work to have her here. We'll take her to Victoria Cafe for tea." She leaned back into her high-backed rattan chair, plumped the slippery blue chintz pillows behind her and began to read a book.

The thought of spending an afternoon at Victoria Cafe, dressed to the teeth, having to mind my manners and listen to the quartet of four elderly German-Jewish refugees playing old-fashioned Viennese waltzes made me squirm with embarrassment.

"Let's forget the whole thing. Shirley's going to hate the Victoria. She only likes going to the Country Club. Says it's 'posh' there."

My mother continued reading her book. She wasn't paying any attention to me. I felt a surge of feistiness and pressed on.

"Why don't we ever go to the Country Club?"

"Because the membership is too expensive. Besides, it's mainly for Americans and the British. Very few Jewish folks. We have our own club, remember."

She ruffled my hair and I could feel her long fingernails scratching my scalp. "Don't look so woebegone. It's going to be fun at the Victoria."

I knew Shirley would hate it. She hated being cooped inside and getting dressed up. Shirley and I had discovered the joys of taking long walks and were often absent for hours from the Canberry household, wandering through the Chinese quarters—a fact I kept from my parents who had always warned me never to leave the European "concessions." But Mrs. Canberry didn't seem to mind at all and actually encouraged us to "discover" the world. She often told me how lucky I was to be living here, and how she hoped Shirley would "absorb" all the wonders of China before they had to go back to the States on home leave. Shirley and I liked to go down Victoria Road, across the bridge to the Italian concession and then find ourselves in the Chinese part of town, where the streets were narrow and jammed with merchants, each one in his own canvas-topped stall. Wash hung from the balconies and little children ran around in pants with wide slits, front and back, so they could urinate and defecate in the gutter. The smell of unwashed linens, feces and cooked rice, the bustle of people milling around excited and frightened me at the same time. I often wanted to go back before Shirley was ready, feeling overwhelmed by the sights and sounds.

"Can't figure you out," Shirley would say. "You're so uncomfortable here. I *love* being in the States." I was usually silent, since I could not explain my discomfort and envied her cocky sureness, her matter-of-factness, while I floundered in my uncertainty. Did I love my homeland, did I hate it? I didn't really know. All I knew was that I adored Shirley and wanted to be just like her.

My mother interrupted my thoughts. "We have to do it—because we have to return the hospitality. You keep going over to the Canberrys' all the time, and we have never entertained Shirley."

"But I know she doesn't like going to cafés."

"Well, it will be a new experience for her."

"Why can't I just bring something to the Canberrys? To return the hospitality, I mean. Something for Mrs. Canberry."

My mother perked up at this idea and I could see her giving it some thought. I watched her as she wrinkled her nose as she concentrated. "No, I don't think that would work," she finally said. "If you gave something to Mrs. Canberry, she would then have to give you something in return and then we would have to—No. I don't think it would work."

"But you exchange gifts with the Dridens."

"That's different."

"Why?"

"Because it is. Let's not argue. Invite Shirley. We'll go to the Victoria for ice-cream and cake. Saturday at four o'clock."

"Well, at least they have adequate bathroom facilities there," I said as I flounced out of my chair, giving the bamboo chair a swift kick, and ran downstairs into the garden.

The garden was overgrown with weeds. I sat underneath my favorite weeping willow tree and stared up at my mother who was reading her book. She looked cool and lemony in her yellow dress and I felt hot and itchy. I heard the veranda door creak and saw my aunt come out and join her. I could hear them laughing together.

I pressed my back into the trunk of the willow as I squatted at its base, picking up a few daisies and making a chain out of them. "Don't lean against the tree, you'll tear your dress," I heard my mother say as she leaned on the veranda rail and looked down at me. I pressed even deeper into the bark, squashing my white linen blouse against it, and hoping it would leave huge unwashable stains down the back. "Come in, come in, it's getting dark," I heard her say and her voice seemed as if coming from a great distance as the sun set and evening breezes cooled the dusty garden.

On Monday morning Shirley and I met outside the school yard, where we always waited for each other to share the events of the weekend. We had a favorite elm tree with a bench built around its huge trunk. I couldn't figure out a way to tell Shirley about the Victoria Cafe plan in a diplomatic manner, so I just blurted it out.

"We're going to the Victoria for ice-cream and cake. You and me and my mother."

Shirley stared at me with her protruding blue eyes beneath the fashionably cut bangs and didn't say anything.

"Just you and me and Mother," I repeated furiously.

"I hate the Victoria," said Shirley. "You know how I hate getting dressed up. Besides, none of the embassy people ever go there."

"My mother says we have to return the hospitality. I'm always going over to your house."

"So what. My mother likes having you over."

"I know. But it's uneven. Me always going to your place."

"Why do you always have to compare? Let's just have fun."

I looked at Shirley who was drawing pictures on the dusty ground with a branch, weaving an intricate pattern of circles and crosses. Shirley was always talking about having fun and chastising me for being too serious. I wondered if one had to be born American to "have fun." Such thoughts led me to despair. I knew I could never achieve that delicious state of "fun" that Shirley was always talking about.

"I think you should come to Victoria Cafe. Otherwise my mother will keep after me. Or she might even not let me go to your house anymore."

Shirley rolled her eyes with an expression that said "grown-ups—they are impossible" and agreed to meet us on Saturday.

"How will you get there?" I asked.

"I'll have the chauffeur drive me—it's too far to walk and I'm sure Daddy will let me use the embassy car on a week-end if I ask him."

We didn't speak of the impending Saturday date during the next week, although we saw each other daily at school. On Thursday, as we did every week during the warm months, we "camped" in the Canberry backyard, sleeping under a tent that was set up by the Chinese servants the night before, and lying on sleeping bags that the family had brought from the States. Shirley always told me stories of how the family spent summers in the Colorado Rockies, Grand Canyon, and Yosemite, and my mind would whirl with visions of giant waterfalls, soaring snow-capped mountains, and prowling bears. "Sleeping on the ground," as my mother called camping, was considered a strange American aberration, leading to colds and backaches, but with much pleading from me, I was allowed to indulge in this pastime with Shirley.

That evening we sat in front of the tent by a small campfire that had been lit for us and roasted marshmallows on a branch cut to size by the Canberrys' number one houseboy, Liu. "I like sleeping under the stars, don't you?" said Shirley. She started counting the stars in the sky, naming constellations and stars I had never heard of before. I envied her knowledge. Then she said something that really surprised me. "I can't wait to get back to the States and do some real camping. Maybe you could come and visit. Do you think your parents would let you? It would be such fun."

74

"Sure, Shirl," I said, knowing full well that none of this would come to pass. "Sure I'll come and visit."

"Super," said Shirley as we snuggled into our sleeping bags and went to sleep.

I lay on the hard ground and listened to Shirley's regular breathing. She had fallen asleep. I watched the lights go off in the master bedroom. Shirley's voice, as I had heard it earlier, sifted through my half-dreams. "Bring the hot cocoa in the blue thermos jug," she had ordered the servants. I marvelled at her ability to know exactly what she wanted. I fell asleep and dreamt of floating amidst a sea of red balloons.

Saturday morning I woke early and heard the chattering of the servants outside my window. Under the hallway that connected the house to the kitchen I saw Cook sitting on the barber's chair. His bald shiny head was being scrubbed vigorously by the travelling barber who came around every few weeks. Cook's wife squatted on the ground eating her morning bowl of noodles, and his two children threw smooth shiny pebbles into a can.

"We're going to the Victoria today. Remember?" sang my mother's cheery voice, as she poked her head into my door. She bustled around me all morning, made sure I washed my hair and set it in curlers. She had my yellow dress ironed by Cook's wife and rummaged around in my chest of drawers trying to find just the exact shade of socks to match the dress. She even had my hair ribbon ironed and starched.

"Why this preparation? Shirley will probably come in her overalls—the ones she just got from the States."

"You know that everyone dresses for the Victoria."

"Everyone except Shirley. She hates the Victoria."

"I'm sure her mother will have her wear a dress."

"Her parents are away this weekend. There's just her older sister and Kent, her brother."

Throughout the day I wandered around the house feeling restless. I went downstairs to watch Cook prepare for the midday meal. He was chopping vegetables with the big cleaver, and a cigarette dangled in his mouth. I watched as the ash collected on the butt and hung over the carrots and onions. Just as it was about to fall, he flicked it off with a powerful jerk. Cook's children were squatting on the ground drawing pictures on the sand and I squatted down with them for a few minutes but they seemed uninterested in me and I walked back to my room and lay down on the bed. I must have dozed off because all of a sudden I heard my mother say, "It's time. Hurry up. We have to get dressed for the Victoria."

At three-thirty, I, in my yellow dress with socks to match, and she in a blue silk dress with puffy sleeves and shoes to match were on our way. We rushed through the streets not stopping to talk to anyone, just saying, "Hello—We're on our way to the Victoria," to the people we passed.

"She's here already and we've made her wait," grumbled my mother as we turned the corner of Davenport and Victoria Road. Shirley was leaning casually against the front door of the Victoria, both hands on her hips and looking around with a bored expression. She was dressed in an elegant sailor-suit outfit popular that year. My mother said, "I told you she would get dressed up." I didn't answer her.

"The ice-cream is great here," I whispered to Shirley as my mother herded us in. I felt a surge of love for Shirley. For my mother. For everyone in the cafe. Perhaps, after all, this would be a fun afternoon.

Inside the Victoria I smelled the freshly baked goods that were arranged on white doilies in the shiny glass counters. Presiding over the bakery was the owner of the Victoria, a lady as round and fresh as her crescent breads with beady raisin-black eyes. She greeted us in a husky voice. From the homey domain of the bakery we moved on into the bowels of the Victoria, the cafe itself, where everything was somber and heavy. There were no windows and the big room was lit from wall sconces and hanging chandeliers. I felt oppressed by the brocaded wall coverings, the black leathery booths lining the walls and the thick carpet. There were several scattered tables with shiny tablecloths in the middle of the room. As my eyes began to get used to the dimness, the quartet of musicians swam into my vision. We sat down at a table close to them. They began to play the Danube Waltz. My mother settled with a contented sigh into her chair and Shirley looked at me and rolled her eyes. She looked at the quartet and began to giggle. She kicked my foot under the table. I kicked her back and we both started giggling. My mother said, "Hush, act grownup," which sent us even further into peals of uncontrollable laughter.

A waiter appeared and we gave our order. Shirley couldn't decide what to get. My mother spent a long time going over the menu with her. Finally a decision was made to have an "American Sundae," a concoction of ice-creams, bananas, and chocolate cookies topped by whipped cream and mandarin oranges that was always a favorite of mine.

When we were served, the quartet broke into "Vienna Woods" and my mother swayed with the music, tapping her feet to the one-two-three. She waved to Mr. Berman the violinist who nodded to her without missing a beat. My mother said that he used to play with the Berlin Philharmonic. I watched Shirley as she dug into her "American Sundae," picking out the cookies and laying them aside as prizes to be eaten later. My mother was asking Shirley about the States and Shirley was answering politely and even with enthusiasm. I saw Shirley in a new light as she talked with pride about her home town in Illinois.

"Do you miss the States?" said my mother.

"Very much. But we're going back. At the end of the summer. Because my sister is entering Stanford University. We're all going back."

"I didn't know you were leaving. You never told me," I said. Hot tears stung my eyes and I looked away.

Shirley shrugged her shoulders casually and said, "I forgot. I was going to tell you soon. Honest. Anyway, we still have the whole summer ahead."

The quartet was playing a medley of Russian songs. My mother was deep in an animated conversation with Shirley. I poked my spoon into my totally disarrayed melted sundae. The Victoria began to fill with people, and I thought about life without

Shirley. Shirley ordered an iced tea and it was brought to her in a tall glass with a long spoon sticking out of it. As the waiter was about to set the glass on the table, Shirley's shoulder got in the way. The glass fell and spilled its contents onto her lap. The remains of the "American Sundae" landed in her lap too.

For a moment no one moved as we stared at the mess of ice cubes, chocolate cookies and three shades of ice-cream on Shirley's sailor-suit skirt. Then Shirley jumped up and screamed, "I hate the Victoria!"

She ran into the bathroom. My mother ran after her. I sat, stunned, while the quartet played "March Militaire."

After a while my mother and Shirley returned, looking tired and distant, as if they had come back from a long journey and had now decided that travelling together was not for them. Shirley looked at her Mickey Mouse watch and said she was sure the chauffeur was waiting for her. She didn't sit down but stood by the table and expressed her thanks for a "lovely afternoon" in a clipped manner. She walked over to me and said, "See ya Monday," and walked out of the cafe swinging her bright red purse on its brass chain. I got up and ran after her. She was standing by the door waiting for the chauffeur to bring the car around.

"Why are you leaving?" I said. "We can order another sundae."

"I hate the Victoria. I never did want to come here. It's a bore."

"Don't be mad, Shirl. I want us to be friends."

"You're so serious all the time. And so *sensitive*. My mother's always telling me to be careful of your feelings. She says all Jewish people are super-sensitive. All I want is to have fun."

I stared at Shirley. This was the first time we had ever discussed my Jewishness and I didn't know how to talk about it.

"I want to have fun too," I said. "I really do."

"Well, you certainly don't act like it."

The black embassy car drove up and Shirley ran towards it with a swing of her bright red bag. "Ta, ta," she threw over her shoulder.

I walked back into the Victoria. My mother was finishing her sundae and seemed to be really enjoying herself. She was swaying with the music and nodding to various people.

"Shirley took it quite well—the accident, I mean," said my mother. "Didn't make a fuss."

"She was just being polite. She hated it here."

"Well, there's nothing wrong in being polite."

"I want to go home," I said.

"We will—soon." She looked at me and patted my hand. "And we did return the hospitality. Now you can go to the Canberrys' with a clear conscience."

"I'll probably never get invited again. Besides, they're leaving town soon—you heard Shirley say so."

On Monday morning Shirley and I met outside the school yard. Shirley was late. The bell rang just as she was about to sit down, so we had to rush to class. She was sick the next two days and on Thursday she told me that her parents were having a big embassy party and we had to cancel our weekly camp-out. In the next few weeks she began to see a lot of Marianne Webster, another embassy "kid." I saw them at our elm tree before the morning bell, and I began to take a new route to school.

"How's Shirley?" my mother asked.

"She has a new friend."

"Well, we did return the hospitality. You'll probably be friends again," my mother tried to reassure me.

"I don't think so. She never speaks to me now."

My mother hugged me. "I know. It's hard."

I didn't see much of Shirley that summer. In August I got an invitation to her going-away costume party.

I came as a gypsy. Shirley was dressed up as Marie Antoinette. The quartet from the Victoria was there, playing a waltz.

"I thought you hated getting dressed up. And quartets. I thought you only liked camping," I said.

Shirley shrugged her shoulders, her huge white wig tilting to one side. "Well, I've changed my mind. These past few months Marianne and I have been dressing up lots. And I kinda like the quartet. They're cute."

I looked at Mr. Berman dressed in his smoking jacket and tie. He did not look cute to me. He looked tired and uncomfortable. I saw him slap a mosquito and brush off sweat as he bowed his violin.

"I don't think they're cute. They're just trying to make a living . . . and you've changed. You used to hate all this."

Shirley looked at me and sighed. "That's the trouble with you. You're too serious. So I've changed. 'You got to go with the times!' That's what my mother says. Come on, have some fun!"

I hated the party and sat in a corner feeling miserable, watching all the embassy kids dancing and giggling. I decided that my mother was probably right and Shirley would have been uncomfortable in our house with only one bathroom.

I didn't say goodbye to either Shirley or the Canberrys. I left just as the quartet started playing "Virginia Reel" and the whole backyard became a whirling kaleidoscope of color. Shirley's brother Kent was standing outside their house and he looked bored and asked if I was leaving and I said yes I was and he said "Bye" and that was all.

Then the war broke out and I never heard from Shirley again.

*Irena Klepfisz*

## Etlekhe verter oyf mame-loshn/
## A few words in the mother tongue

עטלעכע ווערטער אויף מאַמע-לשון

*lemoshl*: for example

*di kurve* the whore
a woman who acknowledges her passions

*di yidene* the Jewess the Jewish woman
ignorant overbearing
let's face it: every woman is one

*di yente* the gossip the busybody
who knows what's what
and is never caught off guard

*di lezbianke* the one with
a roommate though we never used
the word

*dos vaybl* the wife
or the little woman

\* \* \*

*in der heym* at home
where she does everything to keep
*yidishkayt* alive

*yidishkayt* a way of being
Jewish always arguable

*in mark* where she buys
*di kartofl un khalah*
(yes, potatoes and challah)

*di kartofl* the material counter-
part of *yidishkayt*

*mit tsibeles* with onions
that bring *trern tsu di oygn*
tears to her eyes when she sees
how little it all is
*veyniker un veyniker*
less and less

*di khalah* braided
*vi ihr hor far der khasene*
like her hair before the wedding
when she was *aza sheyn meydl*
such a pretty girl

*di lange shvartse hor*
the long black hair
*di lange shvartse hor*

\* \* \*

a *froy kholmt*   a woman
dreams *ihr ort oyf der velt*
her place in this world
*un zi hot moyre*   and she is afraid
so afraid of the words
*kurve*
*yidene*
*yente*
*lezbianke*
*vaybl*

די קורװע

*zi kholmt*   she dreams
*un zi hot moyre*   and she is afraid
*ihr ort*
*di velt*
*di heym*
*der mark*

די יידענע

די יענטע

די לעזביאַנקע

*a meydl kholmt*
*a kurve kholmt*
*a yidene kholmt*
*a yente kholmt*
*a lezbianke kholmt*

דאָס װײַבל

אַ מײדל

אַ פֿרוי

*a vaybl kholmt*
*di kartofl*
*di khalah*

*yidishkayt*

*zi kholmt*
*di hor*
*di lange shvartse hor*

זי חלומט

*zi kholmt*
*zi kholmt*
*zi kholmt*

זי חלומט

זי חלומט

*Vera Williams*

## *from* My Mother, Leah, and George Sand

At least I don't live alone. I share a place with my mother. We made this move a year ago when she was eighty-one. After my father had been dead a year and a half. She was getting too thin eating by herself; I was fed up with eating by myself. . . . But this is not the place to give my whole history and how I still required, in mid-life, only one chair at my breakfast table. This is a story about my mother, Leah, George Sand and how many years might be left to our planet. . . . Things that matter.

So my mother gave up her apartment. I gave up my apartment and we moved together into this project where my mother's oldest friend Leah lives.

Our first meal among the boxes in the kitchen my mother said, Reeva, this is it. From here I move out feet first. Thanks for something Leah said. I thought you would try every apartment in the city Rose. My mother had been changing residences her whole life, starting with crossing the ocean from Poland as a girl on which voyage her littlest brother fell into the opened ship's hold and was killed so that the family arrived bewildered, excited and tearing their clothes in mourning.

But now I must learn, if I'm going to go on living with my mother, not to confuse myself with her. She says herself sometimes on Saturday nights (she'll probably say it tonight which I don't look forward to). . . . But you're young yet, Reeva honey. You don't need to sit home with an old lady like me. I'm not dying and if I did nothing else my whole life, I learned to enjoy a good book, I made a few friends. . . So go out. Have a good time.

I want living with my mother to be, if not terrific, at least nice. Yet often I feel, though she's been a lifelong radical, that the St. Andreas fault lies between her consciousness and mine. So I'm careful. I don't lie to her but I don't bring certain experiences to her attention. And it's not sex I keep from her as you might think, but disappointments. And pessimism.

One evening she was fixing her hair at the bathroom mirror. I was sitting on the toilet, tampax in hand, and she tells her own face in the mirror, Rosie, you were born, can you imagine, before sanitary napkins even. We just used rags then. Before airplanes, before. . . . Who even could imagine what at that time.

If you could have imagined, I said, the first world war, the second world war, Dachau, Hiroshima. . . . You would have turned around and crawled right back in.

That was blasphemy to her. Reeva! Don't say a thing like that.

But she straightened it out with her face in the mirror. You wouldn't have Roseleh would you? After all, what is the big adventure of life but to see the future; to make the future. At least it was till now. Now the future is in question like never before in my life. Still, what a crazy thing that an old person like me; look how thin my hair is getting . . . even piled up like this it looks so thin . . . should have more hope than you at forty-three. Dope! You're in the midst of life.

Is that why I live with her; to nurse on hope from old dugs? It came up at our CR group; living with mothers. What I am doing, I said, is taking the chance to apprentice to her before she dies. L., who's tough, said No No No. Yes but No. Forget it. That was the time of your childhood. So, I admit in this area I'm retarded. But at that session I said something I hadn't even known I knew. . . . I couldn't do it when I was growing up because then I was my father's girl and *only* his. I had no respect for mothers. But now he's dead and his hold on me is loosened. I'm ready to learn what I can learn of her through love and admiration; a loving admiration. Then, to keep from howling, I made a slightly formal declaration of gratitude. Sisters, I saluted, I want to thank you for your part in giving my mother back to me.

This evening, walking from the subway to the apartment, everyone seemed to be walking the other way and in couples. I saw the truth in L's diagnosis. It's a shelter for me. I was looking to supper with my mother and Leah to keep me from the blues. Leah especially gets a laugh out of me. Leah still has her husband Bernie but on nights he goes to the trotters she eats with us. When I come in she's sitting beside my mother. The TV is turning out its images soundlessly. My mother is wiping her eyes.

It was so moving Reeva, she tells me as I bend over to kiss her. She rests her head against my coat. If you'd just gotten here an hour earlier. . . though what you're doing here at all on a Saturday night. . .

A half hour, Leah says. A half hour would have been enough Rose. And Reeva is a grown woman. Saturday night. . . Wednesday night. . . Let her decide for herself.

Ooo Don't be so strict Leah. I only asked her from concern.

It's alright,I tell my mother. I let her wind the thread of a loose button on my coat. I play with her hair. . .

A half hour, an hour, Reeva . . . you would have seen the most moving show; a really great work. Are you acquainted with George Sand?

Is she acquainted with George Sand? Would your daughter, Rotsky's daughter, and a history teacher to boot not know a George Sand? A woman who was so much in the forefront of her time even Bella needs to run to catch up with her. Though Rotsky, and I myself for that matter, would not have agreed with Sand on the Paris Commune.

Leah! Still the Paris Commune. Forget the Paris Commune.

Forget the Paris Commune. This would be like forget you're a human being.

Oh Leah. I put my hand on her wrist while my mother brings me up to date.

Listen Reeva. It was about George Sand and Chopin we were watching. As you know from college probably . . . and by the way, Channel 13 is doing a lot for the education of the older people who never got the chance to go to college . . . Chopin died of TB and this episode showed so well the disease progressing and the way it affects the love between them. But it was subtle; not one of those tearjerkers that just play on your sympathy.

In plain language Rose; the man is dying.

Of course he's dying Leah . . . honey. Everyone dies. But Chopin is a magician. One of those great individuals who turns suffering into music. Reeva, I wish you could have seen him at one of those old grand pianos playing his new work for her. They're

in Spain and she's managed to get a piano there for him. They have such difficulties. . .
But what faces. . . Reeva, Leah, such fine human faces on those people.
And what of Sand's children Rose? Leah turns to me. Reeva, your mother the great
child lover, left out about the kids. She's so starry eyed about the love element. But
this Sand, really a crazy person in certain ways we have to admit, packs up the whole
family and drags them off to Spain. Ahh. Rosie, wasn't it wonderful to see them in the
carriage going over those old dirt roads. You could see the lamps on the carriage.
That's the beauty of TV. History comes to life in the living room. In spite of the lies
and capitalist propaganda it really shows the life of that time. What a way to travel.
Nowadays we just get on a plane. . .
Which is not socialism, my mother reminds. . .
But it is progress, Leah completes.
I, who have trouble with friendships, have noticed that one reason my mother and
Leah have remained such good friends is that their power is roughly equal. Their
knowledge and confidence is evenly distributed. Leah mocks, but long ago, perhaps
when I was born, she accepted her friend as authority on upbringing. Now my mother
gives her opinion.
But about the children I admit you're right Leah. First she spoiled them, then she
neglected them. And what did they really need to show the children for anyway.
Wasn't the drama between Sand and Chopin actually?
Ohoh Rosie! I'm surprised at you. They should kill off the children for the sake of
the drama? And people today, even the radical young people, don't neglect the
children?
People today neglect. And she neglected. What do I tell you? History works itself
out on the backs of the children.
She produces one of her examples; Leah's cousin the flaming anarchist who, like
Emma Goldman, was a nurse because as I've been taught that was a way a woman
could become independent in those days.
Reeva, you remember her. . .?
I've never met Leah's cousin but like me my mother forgets where her life stops
and mine begins. . .
You remember Clara the flaming anarchist? Well we know for a fact her poor
sisters didn't thank her for stealing them. . .
Rose, you exaggerate.
Alright; bribing them from the family home to dump them right into her wild
bohemian life in Greenwich Village. And what did they learn; to hate her and to hate
men. They were victims of those times.
Now Leah is patient. My cousin Clara I can't defend; how she is so crazy now with
her theories of fasting for every ill of the society. . . But you know as well as I, Rose; it
was to save those girls from their orthodox father and his medieval ignorance. Marriages he wanted for them like deaths while their minds were just begging for education, for adventure. . .
But Leah, even a radical has to have some sense of proportion. To get back to Sand;

I wouldn't have taken those children to Spain with a man coughing like that. And it was a man who wasn't even their father . . . even if it was Chopin; *even* if it had been Beethoven. Children need stability. Your father could never understand that Reeva. . .

So what's wrong with Reeva? She turned out a hundred percent. Leah turns to me . . .a hundred and one percent even. We exchange smiles. She's an old supporter. She used to call me Stringbean and she let me call her Leah-Funnyface. And Rose, be realistic. What else could Sand have done with the children; put them in daycare to the nuns for a few months? So it's again the struggle of the mother; what you're always talking to me about. It's not just one of your pretty love stories.

But Leah, Leah. In life there's more than one kind of love. You see Reeva, Sand is really a mother to all of them. She takes Chopin to Spain for the sun so he'll have an easier time with the TB. But she finds those old houses have such cold floors made of stone. He coughs all the time. Didn't it look chilly in that bare room though, Leah. Yet that was the south. It reminded me of that one time I went to Florida and the oranges all froze.

I see her regard her living room with satisfaction. She is at last very much at home in the project.

But that was just the Spanish Grandee style Rose. I'll save my sympathy for the old people in this city right now sitting by the cold radiators. . . .

Leah, it's only October. Please. I'm trying to tell Reeva about Sand, Chopin. It was very sad Reeva and at the same time very beautiful.

Now you talk about beauty. Rosie . . . my romantic friend. But do you realize that TB then, and when we were kids too, which in terms of history is not so long after Sand. . .

She died in 1876, Leah.

1876 and I was born in 1893. In 1901 my brother Abraham was already 14 years old. Remember? That was the year he went to America. Then we came the year after. TB then was like cancer now. The people were dying like flies in those slums from TB. We lived then on Attorney Street. That's way downtown Reeva. . . .

Leah is still teaching me the geography of the Lower East Side; it was both her kindergarten and then her university.

Everyone was coughing up blood then. Our own union's health study showed TB alone was one of the biggest killers of the girls in the industry. There's no beauty in TB Rosie; in Black Lung either. But there's money in it for a few.

Leah! Do me a favor. Take your propaganda to the coal companies. It's Chopin's music, not his sick lungs I found so beautiful. And Sand's strength in the midst of everything. We see how she can't be torn from her own writing yet we also know she was involved in the political situation around her in a revolutionary time. This was not a true artist Leah? This did not move you? This is not what we struggle for?. . . Let there be at least a few minutes in this life for the heart Leah.

My mother holds on to my hand. She hums one of Chopin's nocturnes. . . .A siren fourteen floors below dies away among the streets. I stand beside them still in my coat. I feel that if I move out of the room, down the hall, open the closet door, I will disturb something rare and fine in the room; the long friendship of my mother and Leah in full bloom.

Reeva, Leah says, how come you're still in your coat? Take off your coat, my mother says. Make yourself comfortable. This isn't your home? I'll make us some tea.

I hang my coat in the closet and join them at the table by the living room window. We look out now at the lights all around and below us.

Doesn't our project look nice in the evening, comrades, my mother says.

You can't even tell there's a garbage strike, I say.

But allowing a few minutes for the heart has reminded Leah of yet another aspect of George Sand. Leah has always been tenacious whether in organizing or in discussion. Wasn't Sand a beautiful woman Rose, she says now.

I was thinking this myself, my mother says. And I wanted to point out to Reeva that, though by today's standards Sand might not be considered beautiful. . .

Ma, I've seen portraits of her. By anyone's standards she wasn't beautiful. She had a face like a horse. Maybe for the series they thought it would be good to glamorize her.

No Reeva, no. Channel 13. They are, I would say, 95 percent true to life. But I'm surprised at you! A girl who has no use for makeup, for nice dresses (an argument of many years now). However it's of no importance whether a person has a face like a horse. She had dignity, strength. . .

Not *just* strength Rose. Strength alone can be ugly even. We know that for a fact. You remember Tanya? Leah snorts.

In the legends of Leah and my mother; and these legends are like the I Ching, an educational entertainment, Tanya stands for what is good but then by overstatement turns negative. She came from Russia before the revolution with only her sandals and a stone bowl for her porridge. An early nut and grain enthusiast, this Tanya boarded with my mother's family at the time Leah and my mother had their first jobs, addressing envelopes and packing underwear. Tanya had a secret love for the young anarchist Alexander Berkman who was in prison for the shooting of the steel magnate Frick. (A politically naive act, my father later instructed me, still, a deed of principle. And let us not like the Social Democrats make the error of confusing Berkman with the *real* enemy!) And all the time Berkman was imprisoned, this Tanya refused to consider marriage, even go out with men or dance.

Tanya! What are you talking about Tanya for? Tanya was like a cement post. She was a tremendous big woman Reeva. Asking her for the rent your grandmother looked like a little peanut. Leah, you remember her great big underpants on the line that place on Allen Street, how we used to laugh?

Do I remember? Of course I remember. . . .

I was learning, since I moved in with my mother, the far reaches; no, the limitlessness, of memory and yet its precision in use. Leah and my mother sharpened up each other's memory; one the knife, the other the hone. And turn about. They kept their memories at the ready like the thirty years old paring knife my mother cut vegetables with. (That little knife was one of the unexpected bonuses of being in her kitchen

85

again, along with the green glass lemon squeezer, a flat perforated pan-like device for broiling eggplants and peppers on top of the stove and a three sided waterless potato baker.)

. . . her big underpants I remember, which was funny, and her face I also remember. Like you said; a concrete post. You hit the nail on the head for once Rosie.

Leah turns now to me. You see, Reeva. It's not this kind of wasted, turned inside out strength, a George Sand has. A fire. . . an intelligence . . . is what George Sand had. Right? A strength to struggle; not just to sit like a statue for twenty years and hold her legs together so no man can get in.

Leah! It was only that she surprised me. In my own childhood legends, Leah is actually a figure as stony as Tanya. It doesn't matter that she's married to the camel-hair coated Bernie, a druggist by trade but a gambler for real, and that she rhapsodizes over the ballet. (She prefers the Soviet ballet but she'll wait in line for any ballet.) I see her as a purist. Before she became an apostle of the molded space shoe that grounds her now as she trudges from meeting to meeting, she wore a sturdy oxford. She used to refer to it; "The Coward Shoe," something as crucial and precise as "The Marxist's Use Value."

The everyday things of Leah's life are unvaryingly served up with the lemon and salt of principle. My mother says in certain ways I could be Leah's daughter. She cites my Birkenstock sandals, my dislike for makeup, my thrift-shop clothing, my "extreme" feminist positions, my "unrealistic" educational theories. . . my daily swimming and my unmarried-ness.

She analyzes that neither Leah nor I have had any children to break our hearts and teach us certain things; that talk and life are different, for instance. (Leah and my father could talk sometimes on Sunday afternoons until my mother, no silent-sister herself as she points out, would run from the apartment with me even on bitter cold days to escape their voices. . . like machine guns rat a tat, rat a tat, right inside your forehead. It drives a person crazy. Can *this* change the world? she would demand of me and the empty park benches.)

Leah is shrewd about people too. Sometimes, when I'm feeling particularly despairing about a lovelife of any kind; man, woman, child . . . even cat, I'll catch Leah's one brown eye and one green eye right on me. And she'll address an ironic remark to the single condition or the nature of men. Yet if there's something to be learned in any quarter, she'll keep at it. . . . Now she goes on . . . but to say of Sand that she was merely intelligent is not enough; not nearly enough to describe the companion of Liszt, of Chopin, of Flaubert, of Victor Hugo. George Sand was brilliant. Brilliant. And *that's* what makes a woman attractive and beautiful. Right, Reeva?

Leah had been a powerful soapbox orator. It was her true metier. Now with a hand on her hip she's turned to me as though to ask who could disagree.

That's what made Sand beautiful? You're trying to tell me that the attentions of men is what makes a woman beautiful! Maybe you should write a piece on this discovery for Playboy or Esquire.

Ree-va! Is women's liberation just invented by your generation? Before we were even teaching you where to make your pee pee I was going to lectures by those giants among women, Sanger and Goldman. The point I'm making here . . . and I've made it before . . . and I'll make it again in cases such as these. . . It was Sand's own brilliance those genius men gathered round like bees around nectar.

This was the theory of beauty my mother and father taught. Take care of your mind, along with frequent bathing of course, and beauty will take care of itself. It kept me from spending my allowance in the 5 & 10 on the lipsticks, eyeshadows and creams my schoolmates in P.S. 42 were already sniffing into. I can still see, without even shutting my eyes, a certain Barbara in a trance; her nose buried in a perfume bottle. But I stood among perhaps two hundred graduates of grade eight, the only girl without lipstick.

But what was once represented to me as demeaning for a radical girl in the vanguard of the people, a smart girl who wanted to go to college; now that I am 43 and without a man and the revolution is not just around the corner . . . is no longer so suspect to my mother.

She pleads with me when I'm getting dressed to go out. . . Darling, don't emulate Leah. Leah overdoes the plainness. These things are just style; a little lipstick, a little auburn highlight in the hair just helps nature. And Henna is after all nothing new. I see they're featuring it in the Health Food stores now. Well, that's *their* idea of a revolution.

Because I want my mother to live forever now that I've "found" her again, I've been sending her into those stores for bran and brown rice and vitamin C. But the prices and the millenial tone put her off. Instead she brings me beauty aids from the drugstore.

Reeva, you have such beautiful eyes. She said this to me in the bedroom just last week; a small bottle in her hand. . . . Your father's eyes . . . I never noticed. You should use a little kohl to bring them out. She traced over my eyebrows with her finger prepared to apply the kohl around my "beautiful" eyes.

I was embarrassed; touched and furious that it had taken her forty-three years to notice these eyes, green hazel . . . my secret pride. I ducked my face into my hands.

Oh you! Are you 43 or 7 years old? Every time we tried to take your picture when you were a kid you made a face. Like another kid she tried to pull my hands from my face.

But with Leah and me now she does her thing of becoming suddenly very serious. Now you listen to me. Whether a person is or is not ugly is not the point. And anyway who is ugly? Are any babies ugly? But what I see in George Sand . . . is Reeva, Leah . . . you say what you like . . . is devotion to ideals; above all to ideals. What a strong letter she writes Chopin when he leaves her. Wasn't that a scene; Sand sitting on a little chair with her skirts spread around her and her back bent over and her hair up in one of the chignons like we used to wear writing by her candle way into the night. . .

And Leah adds appreciatively . . . with one of those old fashioned pens made from a long feather Reeva. . .

. . . even with a ballpoint, Leah, I would have been proud to have written such a letter. What it is, is dignity. Conviction. Yet she also forgives.

Rose! Does a radical tell only the touching things, the pretty parts? You said yourself here was no soap opera. Sand's daughter . . . what was her name, Solag. . . Solange? Well, she exhibits very bad character there in the end. True, Chopin was a weak person. But for a woman's own daughter to come between a mother and her beloved. . .

Again she had surprised me. I didn't remember her having any use for family relations. I have to get my mother to tell me more details from Leah's childhood. When I ask Leah she puts me off with "what does it matter" and "who can remember." I actually know only that her mother and her grandmother struggled along in the back of their hole-in-the-wall remnants shop. My mother says she always shivered to go in the basement there because Leah's father had hung himself from the steam pipe and the children were told to look out for the father's ghost if he came and tried to get them to go away with him. My mother remembers Leah's father was so kind to the children; an educated man whose heart was broken that in "the land of the free" his children had to go out to work at twelve and thirteen instead of going on to high school.

But Leah, you want to rewrite history. Sand was devoted to that daughter, my mother points out. The TV showed that. She was a mother all the way. Once a mother, always a mother.

Yeh. . . Rose. . . Take this news to my old neighbor Bea there in the home of 106th Street. Her daughter, living not one hour away, gets herself to her mother's side not even once a week. Bea sits home alone night after night except when I come. I, the lousy leftist she wouldn't talk to anymore because of Israel. I shouldn't have to remind you Rose, at no point does the family escape the strains of this society. And Reeva, you listen to old Leah here. . .

I'm listening Leah. I'm listening.

I listen now the way my avocado plant drinks up water when it's dry.

Don't you let them make you regret your choice not to have any children. (My choice, she calls it! Ambivalence is not a word in Leah's vocabulary.) The world we see has enough children already and this way you have at least one less heartache.

This gets my mother out of her chair. She knocks over her teacup in the sudden thrust of her body across the table at Leah. She, whom I remember so often as the conciliator in the arguments between my father and Leah and herself, now "lays down the law" at Leah.

But Leah. You! You crazy. These heartaches *are* life. Without such struggle there *is* no life. This singsong from you we've heard enough now. Enough. If I had listened to you would we have our Reeva today? In 1936 it was not so easy to decide to have a child. . . .

Feeling like the adored daughter of two mothers I give them each a kiss. My mother relents a little . . . and anyway, where's the sense to speak like that now Leah. We're talking about George Sand and one thing George Sand was not, is afraid of life.

Well, this I have to admit Rose.

In argument Leah has a generosity of spirit. The Soviet Union broke up the friendship of my mother and her cousin Ray. Israel brought silence between Leah and her close neighbor Bea. But Leah . . . my mother discusses with me many nights, the love-killing twists and turns of history . . . But Leah has a larger heart, a larger mind than any of the women of our group. Leah has stature Reeva. You see it too, don't you darling? But why do you hide it dummy, she shouts sometimes at Leah, pushing her forehead affectionately.

I admit, Rose. You're twice correct here. I admit, so don't shoot me. And it's in Sand's letters to Flaubert that you really see this. That's where you get a true sense of her fearless intellect and her breadth of understanding. They discussed everything . . . anything. You should read them Reeva. For this series, I got the book from the library with their collected letters.

(Oh Leah. If her Bernie has ever written her a letter it was probably just to tell her where he had put the keys or to remind her to pay a bill.)

Leah what . . . Whaaat Flaubert? Why do you bring in Flaubert now when they won't even get to Flaubert till the week after next.

So what have we here, Rotsky's Rules? (She refers, as we used to, to my father's way of controlling a discussion.) By Rotsky's Rules the conversation must be limited to what we exactly saw today? Sez who? Am I a person whose knowledge is only what I see on TV? If we discuss Sand, naturally I bring up Flaubert. Despite his Royalist position.

I don't like to side with Leah because I always get farther in than I bargained for. But I see the justice. I'm in the kitchen studying the contents of the refrigerator and I call out, this isn't a meeting Ma. Let her say what she wants.

Let her! I'm not stopping her. Who could stop her anyway?

When I come back in they're both quiet. At first it's only my mother's pique that shuts them up. With Rose and Leah this is very rare. For a few short minutes the room is drained of conversation. The two women are silhouetted against the evening sky. Like grand and historical sculptures these, my forbears, my good guides appear to me; the Ramses figures in their stone chairs overlooking the Nile or Rodin's Balzac, imperious and full of intelligence. Self-hewn mothers of my life; on this October night with its wispy moon rising behind your heads here in our apartment on 24th Street. . . allow me a minute to adore you.

*Vera Williams*

*Beatrice Lieberman*

## Judas Tree

mother, the tree i planted
for you
sprouts this year—
the last time you walked
with me
in your thick yellow shoes,
i should have known,
as we paced among the weeds,
those ruined arab graves

you pulled seed pods from this tree,
in purple blossoms then,
spoke of war—our moving to hardness

mother, i found the seeds
after your death
in a jar
for you
this sameblossomed tree
will leaf now
the sky howl cloudful and gray

3/1/83

# In This Country, But in Another Language, My Aunt Refuses to Marry the Men Everyone Wants Her to ———————————————————————————

My grandmother sat in her chair. She said, When I lie down at night I can't rest, my bones push each other. When I wake up in the morning I say to myself, What? Did I sleep? My God, I'm still here. I'll be in this world forever.

My aunt was making the bed. Look, your grandmother, she doesn't sweat. Nothing has to be washed — her stockings, her underwear, the sheets. From this you wouldn't believe what a life she had. It wasn't life. It was torture.

Doesn't she love us? I asked.

Love you? my aunt said. What else is worth it? You children. Your cousin in Connecticut.

So. Doesn't that make her happy?

My aunt said, Ach, what she saw!

What? I asked. What did she see?

Someday I'll tell you. One thing I'll tell you right now. Don't carry the main flag. When you're bigger, you'll be in a demonstration or a strike or something. It doesn't have to be you, let someone else.

Because Russya carried the flag, that's why? I asked.

Because he was a wonderful boy, only seventeen. All by herself, your grandmother picked him up from the street—he was dead—she took him home in the wagon.

What else? I asked.

My father walked into the room. He said, At least *she* lived.

Didn't you live too? I asked my aunt.

Then my grandmother took her hand. Sonia. One reason I don't close my eyes at night is I think about you. You know it. What will be? You have no life.

Grandmother, I asked, what about us?

My aunt sighed. Little girl. Darling, let's take a nice walk.

At the supper table nobody spoke. So I asked her once more: Sonia, tell me no or yes. Do you have a life?

Ha! she said. If you really want to know, read Dostoevsky. Then they all laughed and laughed.

My mother brought tea and preserves.

My grandmother said to all our faces, Why do you laugh?

But my aunt said, Laugh!

*Tryna Hope*

# Riva  Story

My parents always used instant coffee. I don't think I realized that it wasn't really coffee until I was already thirty or more. Sometimes I wonder about flavoring as a child and not just with food and stuff like that, but with how you raised kids, or saw the rest of your life. There was really no experimentation, just rules, and the rules rarely changed. You grow up, get married, have kids, and die. I remember once, I even asked my Aunt Riva. She had two kids and was married to a kosher butcher. There's a story in the family that he never talked, not even to Riva or the kids, and he was a very, very religious man. But the story was that he swore vilely in his sleep. Can you imagine that? Instead of the *Shema* or *Borukh ato*, he's yelling Fuck or Cunt. I used to stare at him different after I heard that, a little embarrassed, but I'd stare anyway. I think I learned from that that people and things are not always as they appear to be, you know what I mean?

Anyway, once when just the first kid was born, Riva tried to leave Milton, they think for another man, a guy who traveled around selling stuff like *talises* and Torah covers to different shuls in the area. It was quite a scandal. My mother tells me Riva actually left Milton and came to Chicago but the traveler either never showed up or he left her or something. She didn't want to go back to Milton and she tried to make it on her own. This was about 40 years ago and here's this religious woman on her own for probably the first time in her life with a kid. And her father, a pious man, instructed the rest of the family not to help her out, not to give her money, or food or a place to stay. She *has* a place, he said, with her husband where she belongs. Her mother cried and carried on and pleaded with him, give her a chance, she's your daughter, she wasn't happy, but Zeyde wouldn't budge. Bube used to sneak behind Zeyde's back to give her a nickel here, a nickel there, but mainly everyone was scared of Zeyde or something and they listened.

I think my mother feels bad even still about it. Riva was so unhappy and Ma could have helped even if just a little. But that's in the past. So Riva went back to Milton. Had another kid. . . .a really rotten kid, who tore down curtains, put mustard all over everything, the walls, the floors, the television. And if she couldn't find mustard, it was stuff from the garbage, a real interior decorator that kid was. Riva had no control over that one. She couldn't take her anywhere because she was so wild. So there was Riva, stuck again in her own home with a little monster kid like that and a husband who swore in his sleep.

When she died, they found thousands of science fiction novels and magazines in her basement and all over her house, in her closets, under the beds, in the pantry right alongside the food. And pills, pills, pills, you wouldn't believe. Her brother worked in a pharmacy and he could get her all kinds of medicine and stuff. He thought he was helping her out, uppers, downers, diet pills, amphetamines, sleeping pills, depressants, anti-depressants. And it was all this big secret. No one would have ever known either but she died real suddenly. She went to Israel to visit her oldest daughter, Malka the Queen we used to call her when we were little. Malka was the good one, the beauty, so we made her pay for that one. We'd tease her and tease her but she was an OK kid. She stood it and gave it right back to us. Anyway, Riva went to Israel to visit her and never came back. All sorts of secrets and mystery about her death. No one thought she was really that sick, and then just before she was supposed to come back, she died.

Something about her dying really got to me though, I'll tell you. Whenever I thought about growing up and making a life for myself, I thought of Riva's life. I made a vow when I was a child to never grow up. I thought, OK, so you'll get married and have kids and die if that's all there is to life, but at least hold out on the growing up part and maybe, maybe, that'll make the difference.

And it did make the difference, you know. It's not that I didn't grow up. It's just that I did it out of order, *after* I got married and had the kids. Let's see, I had the kids and got divorced. . . .the boy's been with his father for ten years now, the girl's been on her own for five, and I ain't dead yet. And now me, I'm growing up. I brought some flavor into this life of mine after all. No instant coffee for me. It's funny how I can't stand the stuff. . .it's got to be my own blend.

*Tryna Hope and daughter Kyneret*

*Ruth Whitman*

## Bubba Esther, 1888

She was still upset,
she wanted to tell me,
she kept remembering
his terrible hands:

       how she came, a young girl
       of seventeen, a freckled
       fairskinned Jew from Kovno
       to Hamburg with her uncle
       and stayed in an old house
       and waited while he bought
       the steamship tickets
       so they could sail to America

       and how he came into her room
       sat down on the bed, touched
       her waist, took her by the
       breast, said for a kiss
       she could have her ticket,
       her skirts were rumpled, her
       petticoat torn, his teeth were
       broken, his breath full of
       onions, she was ashamed

still ashamed, lying
eighty years later
in the hospital bed,
trying to tell me,
trembling, weeping with anger

*Melanie Kaye/Kantrowitz*

# Jerusalem Shadow

*for we were strangers in exile*

imagine the desert   the cast of light
imagine the day breaks at sundown
imagine the thirst and the cool water

in the desert   imagine you never left
the village never burned   your voice
was never too loud     imagine

you never lugged children and bundles to the sea
for a boat   to anywhere
never entered blond neighborhoods
never timed by the sun     imagine

you   in the desert   dark
as your darkest cousin   everyone's hair
is coarse and wild   the oil on your skin

is good   for something
in the desert   imagine you never left
your people have been here for centuries
places are named for them

        * * *

                 so the plane sweeps down into the desert
imagine breaking open to hold
what the desert holds

but you're a stranger
the language blurs   like any unknown tongue
you feel stupid   straining your ear   for sense   you eat

cake   lots of cake   *uga*   and say
*tayeem meod*   very tasty   and it is   but then
you're silent     your vocabulary exhausted

and the people   familiar   not
strangers   but still
you have to meet them one by one

slow   imperfect
like any human encounter

             * * *

I sit drinking tea on the balcony of the house you were raised in
where evenings your grandparents  cousins sipped tea
told stories in Ladino  but you are named in Hebrew  *Chaya*
meaning *life*  the sun washes my skin
you talk of walks through East Jerusalem
of the lost backpack returned intact  with a gift of fresh *pitot*
these things changed you  opened you  you fill my cup again
it's morning on the *Rechov Nisim Bekhar* in West Jerusalem
Jewish Jerusalem
I am your guest  you are yourself
not a mirror  not a statistic

this might be my home  but is not
I was born all over the planet  this time in Brooklyn
I came here looking for the seas to part  and truth
to rise up  wet
and obvious

I sit on the pink-grey stone by the Damascas Gate  eating hummous
the sun is lavish  direct  you sit one step up  dressed in a black robe
a white headdress  beside you a boy  *my brother*, you tell me  later
after we catch each other's eyes  after we smile once
and again  until you pat the stone by you  motion for me
to come sit  your name is *Ma'ha*
you want the English word for my sunglasses
for the digital watch you wear with your black robe
you say, *you like hummous?*
I nod  smile  speak neither English *yes*  nor Hebrew *ken*
though I'm sure you know *ken*  I don't know *yes* in Arabic
I think you know I'm a Jew
your watch shows 12:01
it's noon by the Damascas Gate in East Jerusalem
Arab Jerusalem  I am your guest  you are yourself
not a victim  not a symbol

        * * *

*Yerushalayim*
waking on *Nisim Bekhar* in the golden city

if I walk the winding streets
in the clear gold light

if the past is written on pink-grey stone
tablets  the walls of the city
houses  polished in blood

if the future is billowing
formless

shall I count the windows in Kiryat Arba
and call them facts

or discount the nights in shelters at the Northern edge—
are these not facts?

and the Litani
and the desert's need—

are these not facts?

\* \* \*


*Yerushalayim shel zahav*

I came here looking for home  or exile
not both

I came here looking for women
but there are men in front

the Arabs  without their *kaffiyehs* would pass for Jews
the Jews  without their *kipot* would pass for Arabs

the *Hasidim* who walk to prayer when the day
dips into *shabat*

the Muslims washing their feet to enter
the Mosque  radiant over the city

and the Mosque was nearly blown up
like the Jewish bus  like the Arab bus

enter the market  they check my pack for bombs
this is a fact

                    * * *



I came here seeking a thread
and see a shadow  or is it a woman
or two women  shifting back and forth on the same spot
looking alike  though at first you
wouldn't see it  the hair  skin  language close
almost comprehensible  *shalom  salaam*
and which is the stranger
whose flesh was torn
who grabs whose sleeve
who eats dark bread and potatoes
whose teeth stain dark from the tea
whose tongue was formed abruptly in kitchens
in whispers  *quick  quick*
and which century do I mean
when does one woman become the other
when does the rooted one  who belongs  transform
into the one forced out
when does the one forced out  and out  and out
return  to force out
and when does the other return
and how

                    * * *


98

here are some facts:

    peace is not an absence

    victims are not ennobled

    home is the storm's eye
    unless the stranger   too   is welcome

    we were strangers in exile

    a people is bound in memory

    I thirst  for my people

        * * *

*borukh ato adenoy elohenu*

let my people in
to history

let me not wait outside

let me not freeze in the posture of victim

let me break open to hold
the *khet-raysh* sound
the goat-honey smell
the light on the stones of Jerusalem
where I lived on hummous  and sweet dark tea

let my people heal

*omeyn*

5745-5746

99

*Jennifer Krebs*

# Short Black Hair

My short black hair. My sister studying to be a hairdresser cuts it shorter still. Much to my parents' horror. My mother mumbles: you look like a man. You look like your great aunt Adele, my father tells me.

Wasn't she the poet? Aunt Adele.

No. She was a bookkeeper. Although she might have written a poem or two. Bad poems. Pure emotion. Rhymes without meter, rhythm.

Aunt Adele. Foremother I never met. Aunt Adele. I probably don't look a thing like her.

On my father's side of the family there were two unmarried women.

Grandma's sister Paula, the tailor. I met her twice. She sewed me a brown corduroy dog with floppy ears and a black button nose. I named her Cleo. I still have Cleo somewhere in my bedroom in my parents' house.

Grandpa's sister Adele. The poet.

My grandma kneads bread dough. Tells me about the world. Before. In Germany. Waltzes and polkas and farms and trips to Frankfurt. My father as a baby. Grandma's eleven sisters and brothers. Mainly sisters. Grandpa getting drafted in World War I. Grandma lost two brothers in that war. She met and married Grandpa after he came back.

All my grandpa's brothers and sisters married after the war. Except Adele.

Why?

A cousin tells me Adele fell in love with a Gentile poet or teacher. They wrote poems to each other. Her father Levi forbade her to intermarry.

My grandma doesn't understand the question. She just didn't marry.

My grandpa died before I had time to ask.

My father says my cousin is wrong. There was no poet. Where did she/I get such ideas? My father thinks the inquiry is pointless.

But I'm not getting married. I'm getting my hair cut. Short. These questions are vital. My aunt's life is vital. Her life is denied.

Germany killed her.

Except a poem. She wrote in Theresienstadt. A poem, I am told, about the winds. A poem. A prayer for the messiah.

My father wants to know why I want to be a writer. To contribute to magazines? Time, Commentary, National Geographic? Write about politics—after all I studied International Affairs.

No.

They shaved Adele's hair off to do brain surgery. Incised a cross in her skull to find out why she stopped walking. A cross in her skull right above her spine.

They opened her up. Saw her grey brain matter. Same as anyone's grey brain matter. Sewed her back up. Still didn't know why she couldn't walk anymore.

She couldn't walk. She couldn't go.

My cousin says I should be fair to the doctors at Marburg. It was a university hospital. Not a Nazi hospital. They were scholars, surgeons. Not Nazi quacks. But it was Nazi Germany. They cut a cross in her head. She wore a cross of scar tissue for the rest of her life.

She couldn't walk.

She stopped walking because they took her job away. They took her job away because she was a Jewish woman. And because it was 1933.

She couldn't go.

She went to the town school through the eighth grade. Then she went to a business high school. A bookkeeper. An accountant. She became the merchandise manager of the local chain of grocery stores. She was efficient. She was competition for any man.

They fired her. On the way home from work she collapsed in the street. She never walked again.

Or maybe she did. My father can't remember. Maybe she did walk a little bit now and again. Maybe.

The family got her a wheelchair.

I took care of a woman in a wheelchair for three years. Twice a week. I was a college student. I needed money. She asked me: can you push a wheelchair? I said I'd try. She had multiple sclerosis.

I spent two Christmases with her. Her family was far away. She spent Christmases with Jews. I got her up in the morning. Dressed her in her newest wraparound skirt. Took her to the toilet. Opened her Christmas presents. Spoonfed her turkey and cranberry sauce and pearl onions.

Tried to help. Aunt Adele. Help. Felt sick. Adele. Screamed. When I left.

In 1941, my grandpa secured visas for himself, his father, his wife, his children to the U.S. In 1941, they didn't let Adele out. Or they didn't want Adele in.

She couldn't walk. She couldn't go.

My grandpa, grandma, father, aunts, great-grandfather left. Adele.

Stayed behind in Germany. Short black hair. Wheelchair.

My father says she screamed. Short black hair. Alone. Screamed. Alone. When they left. They left.

They moved the rest of the Jews in town into her house. Her father Levi's house. My family's house. A woman came every day to take care of Adele.

A Gentile woman. Came every day for a year. She got Adele up in the morning. Cook-ed. Fed. Got Adele ready to celebrate Jewish Holidays. They didn't celebrate Jewish Holidays in 1941.

I fed her turkey and cranberry sauce and pearl onions.

My grandpa worked as a painter in New York City nine years before he and his brothers made enough money to buy a farm in upstate New York like the farm they had in Germany.

My grandma bakes bread. Feeds the cats. Sleeps under German quilts. Eats on linen tablecloths her mother embroidered.

My father is a mechanical engineer turned farmer. Returned to farmer. Like his father.

I write.

Aunt Adele wrote poetry.

They put her on a train to Theresienstadt with her wheelchair and the rest of the Jews. She wrote a letter to the woman who took care of her after my family left.

I got a letter last week from the woman with multiple sclerosis. She's got a new college student working for her. Who writes. Who wrote the letter for her. She's well. Except the bed sores. Except she can't move by herself.

I sent her a letter yesterday. I'm writing. I'll send her a story or a poem. Soon. Next letter.

Adele sent a poem to the woman who took care of her. She was a writer. Even in the concentration camp. She wrote. She wrote about the winds. She prayed for the messiah.

They tossed her body in an unmarked grave.

She had short black hair.

I'm getting my hair cut. Short.

## Todesahnen

by Adele Krebs

1894-4/25/1943

## Premonitions of Death

*Translated from German by*

*Lucie Weinstein and Jennifer Krebs*


*Es heult der Sturm, es pfeift der Wind*
*In Theresienstadt wir gefangen sind.*
*Karglich und arm ist unser Los,*
*Die Not wird taglich riesengross.*

*Meine Wangen verbleichen, meine Glieder*
*werden schwach*
*Wie lange werde ich trotzen diesem*
*Schmach?*
*Mein Herze blutet, mein Haar ergraut*
*Weil dieses Elend ich erschaut.*

*Und wenn Ihr druckt mir die Augen zu*
*So gonnet mir die ewige Ruh.*
*Gekampft gelebt, gehofft hatte ich*
*Doch trugerisch sich alles erwies.*

*Meine Lieben Ihr findet im fernen Land,*
*Grusst Sie und drucket still Ihnen die Hand.*
*Mein Sehnen, mein Trachten ging da hinaus*
*Zum Wiedersehen im Elternhaus.*

*Auch meine Heimat grusset von mir,*
*Mein Sehnen galt auch stets nur ihr,*
*Meine Berge, meine Walder und auch Hohn*
*Warum darf ich Euch nicht wiedersehn?*

*Und wenn Ihr blickt zu den Sternen empor,*
*Und seht einen Komet am Himmelstor,*
*So denkt ich sitze am ewigen Trone*
*Und dass ich beim himmlischen Vater*
*wohne.*

*Dort werde ich weilen immerzu*
*Und endlich haben ewige Ruh.*
*Ich sehe Euch wieder wenn der Messias*
*Kommt,*
*Die Zeit ist nicht fern, er kommt, er kommt.*

*Theresienstadt 2/16/1943*

The storm rages, the wind whistles
In Theresienstadt we are prisoners
Shabby, impoverished
Misery each day more gigantesque.

My cheeks pale, my limbs weaken
How long can I resist this disgrace?
My heart bleeds, my hair greys
In this life-consuming suffering.

When you close my eyes
Grant me at last eternal peace.
I fought, lived, aspired to be
But everything that was my life betrayed
me.

My loved ones you will find in far away
places
Send them my greetings, press their hands
solemnly
My yearning, my hope
Is for a reunion in our family home.

Send greetings to my hometown
My hopes also return there
To the mountains, the forests, the hills
The sights I'm forbidden to see.

When you look to the stars
See a comet at the heavenly gate
Imagine me sitting by the everlasting
throne
Living with the heavenly father.

There I shall be
Resting in everlasting peace
When the Messiah comes, again we'll meet
That time is soon: he will come, he will
come.

# Choices: Frankfurt, 1945

At night the conversations were always the same.

"Where are you going?"

"I'm not sure. Prague, maybe Pilsen. Or Austria. Linz."

"Are you crazy? Stay on the Russian side? Come with us. We're crossing over to the American zone."

"Ha, the American zone. And where will I get papers?"

"Never mind. We'll manage. Let's go to Munich. I hear the Americans really take care of refugees."

"I have to go to Radom. See if anybody's there."

"Sure. But better get out of here quickly. Go to the American zone."

"I wish a train would come. The waiting's killing me."

"Oh, stop complaining. It won't come until morning."

"Where are you going?"

The young man rolled over on his back, folded his arms under his head and looked up at the star-filled sky spread like a richly embroidered canopy above the railroad station. "If I could fly, I'd fly up there and rest my head on a star. No more Prague and Munich, no Russians, no borders, or waiting for trains." He began to hum a song and the others joined in.

Tight circles of people huddled up and down the platform of the little railroad station. Ukrainians, Poles, Czechs, Hungarians, Russians, Jews, each small group carefully separate from the other. They were returning. They were leaving. They were coming and they were going. All day long they moved restlessly from town to town, elbowing their way onto the trains and open railroad cars. At night they rested in small stations of nameless towns, waiting for dawn when trains would take them to yet another town.

The days were bright and sunny in the summer of 1945. Belching black smoke, the train rushed through the golden fields and green meadows of the Polish countryside. And every time it pulled to a stop, there were more people pushing and shoving to get on. One made friends easily on the trains and quickly lost them again at the next station. It didn't matter. At night, in another station, under the same star-studded, velvet sky, another group of young people shared bread, perhaps a slice of cheese. Another tight circle where someone asked, "Where are you going?" and another answered, "To the American zone."

We left Poland and came to Czechoslovakia. Now kindly faced peasants greeted us with large canisters of milk and cauldrons of soup.

"Eat," they said, "eat your fill. You must be hungry."

They took us to the water pump where we washed the black soot off our faces. We thanked them and wanted to shake their hands, but they embraced us and wished us

Godspeed. They stood on the platform and waved white handkerchiefs after the departing train.

Soon we would reach the American zone and some began to worry.

"When shall we cross the border, at night or by day? How will we find our way?"

"In daytime. The Russians can't stop us. We'll just walk across," said our self-appointed leader.

"And what if they do?"

"Stop worrying. We'll manage."

The Americans received us with DDT guns and bemused smiles. Perhaps they had never seen so many ragged and hungry young people. For our part, we had never seen such tall, handsome young men in clean, pressed uniforms and polished boots. Their un-soldierlike slouch conveyed a new meaning of freedom.


I came to Frankfurt because someone along the way — was it in Regensburg? — had pressed a small piece of paper with a scribbled name and address into my hand.

"Flora and Arthur will take care of you," the man had said, "they're comrades."

Later I discovered that Arthur was a German and well known leftist journalist, hence a "comrade," who had been imprisoned in a labor camp toward the end of war. He was a handsome man, perhaps in his forties, and he and his Jewish wife, Flora, were known to help everyone who came to their door. That summer the couple was busy preparing to publish a newspaper.

By the time I arrived, Sonya, Hanna, and Leah together with her mother were already there. Like myself, they had been given Arthur and Flora's names by someone along the way. Their house stood in what must have been an exclusive part of the city, but which, like the rest of Frankfurt, was mostly in ruin. It was an elegant house, with a wood-panelled foyer, marble bath tubs, and silk-covered walls. At first I felt uneasy in these surroundings and thought of moving on after a few days rest. But Arthur would not hear of it. There was plenty of room for everyone, he argued. His women, as he called us, needed to be taken care of.

After some days I found a place half way up the spiral staircase. There I sat for hours under the window, an open book on my lap, sometimes reading and sometimes simply brushing the red carpet back and forth with my open hand. The sunlight poured through the open window warming my head and shoulders, and my bony knees seemed a shade less purple. The weeks when I rode the trains, when the wind and sun caressed my face, when warm summer showers washed away the dirt, and when friends shared bread under the stars seemed already long ago. Yet, in this peaceful household I still sometimes heard like an echo the "chug, chug" of the train and the clanking of the cars and I was overcome by the unreality of both myself and this place.

In my corner, where the staircase turned to the second floor, I could hear Leah and her mother talking on the roof. They called it the sundeck, although it was actually the burned-out third story floor of the house. Below, Flora and Arthur were at work in the large room off the foyer. Arthur dictated while Flora typed. Although the front door was not in view, I could hear anyone coming and going. Sonya breezed in and out, often with David, the handsome American press officer; Hanna came for her daily visit since she did not sleep over, and Hans, the chauffeur without a car, arrived on his bicycle to deliver and pick up messages. His cheerful greeting boomed up the staircase, and later I heard his bicycle bell as he pedalled away.

I felt invisible in my corner—even Hanna and Leah didn't notice me when, deep in conversation, they came downstairs to prepare lunch. No one saw me, I thought, but I knew everything that was going on. Probably I first pretended being invisible when I was hiding during the war. Whenever I heard house searches nearby, I would burrow deeper into the straw, imagining myself become so small until I was no more than a fleck of dust. After the Germans left off searching, I often had to reassure myself of my actual size. I was a child then. Now I was fifteen and the war was over. I knew, as I sat in the corner of the red-carpeted staircase, that I need no longer think of disappearing. Why then, I brooded, do I feel as if I'm not altogether here in Frankfurt, in this once fine and now half-ruined house?

Arthur had given me Stefan Zweig's short stories which I was reading one rainy day under the open window. The smell of the damp, charred wood was unpleasant, and the constant sound of the rain made me feel undefinably sad. Leah and Hanna were downstairs in the kitchen, giggling over a dress Leah planned to alter into a blouse. Sonya, who didn't know the first thing about sewing, was apparently giving instructions. I could hear her mock-serious voice over Hanna's peals of laughter. David was in the large room with Flora and Arthur. They seemed to be having a friendly argument. I suddenly realized that this undefinable feeling must be loneliness.

"Loneliness," I silently formed the word. So that is how one's feeling of separateness should be called. Strange, I thought, that I had never known this loneliness while hiding. Perhaps I didn't know the word then. I knew fear, terror, bowels cramping; I had learned to listen sharply, my eyes being of no use in the perpetual twilight and darkness. I learned to distinguish the seasons by the sounds outside, by the air on my skin, catching the hastily whispered sentence when the Polish woman brought me food. But loneliness? I had not known what it was.

Loneliness is being up here on this staircase, listening to the steady drops of rain, feeling far away from the laughter of the girls and David and Arthur's conversation. Why does it come so easily to them? I wondered.

Had I ever laughed with my friends before the war? Of course, I did. My friend Toska and I talked about books we would write and places we would see once we were older. I must have forgotten how to laugh and speak while I was hidden. I remembered the strange and unfamiliar sound of my own voice when I first spoke aloud to the Polish woman; how hard it was to form words. I was conscious of having a tongue. But I need not be silent any longer, I said to myself, closing the book. My discovery of loneliness pleased me. I must ask Arthur for more books by Stefan Zweig. If I can understand the way I am, maybe I can learn to be like the others.

When I came down to the kitchen, the cut-up dress was all over the table and no one was sewing. Sonya was examining Hanna's hair.

"Nothing to worry about," she said cheerfully, "it's growing in beautifully. No bald spots either. Thick and strong all over."

"Ouch, don't pull out a single hair," protested Hanna. "I believe you. I worry because some people never get their hair back after they've had typhus, and sometimes they have bald spots all their lives."

"After I had typhus someone told me to wash my hair with urine," giggled Leah wrinkling her nose, "but I never could bring myself to do it." She passed her hand over her thick, brown hair that had already grown quite long.

"Why is your hair so much longer than mine?" asked Hanna. "Why can't mine grow as quickly as yours and Sonya's?"

"Because we didn't have typhus that recently, and by spring the Germans worried more about their heads than about our hair. Now, if you just let me pull out one hair, I'll show you how long it is."

"Don't you dare," shrieked Hanna dashing for the door, "not a single hair, not a one."

She stopped when she saw me at the door with the book in my hand. The three girls looked at me and I blushed self-consciously. I had long braids, my hair had not been cut in years, and I had heard Hanna describe how smooth her head had been, just like a baby's, she said, after she had typhus in April.

Hanna pulled me to the kitchen table. "Come here. Why not cut out a blouse for the little one? She never wears anything but these rags. Don't you think she needs some new clothes, Leah? We should pay more attention to her, find her a pretty dress or skirt." The girls turned back to the table and at once seemed to forget about me, their heads bent over the brightly colored material, pushing the pieces this way and that on the paper pattern.

I walked to the window, upset for being called little, and sat on the window sill. It had stopped raining and the air was still and heavy. There were no leaves on the stunted, half-dead trees that lined the street. No birds had built their nests. Had they escaped, I wondered, or were they killed when the bombs fell and the houses burned? I didn't like this ruined German city.

I felt clumsy when I was around the girls. They really were good looking, I thought, especially Sonya who had elegant striped and print dresses which clung to her slim body. In comparison, whenever I looked at myself in the large mirror upstairs, I saw a drab, square figure with dull hair and long, skinny legs like sticks. Flora had found me a pair of sandals which were too large and I shuffled about like an old woman. But no one ridiculed me; the girls accepted my silent presence and let me be, even when I carried my books down to the kitchen, or up to the sundeck. Leah's mother too only looked at me with her large frightened eyes and sighed deeply.

The girls were as different from one another as day and night and their friendship puzzled me. Although they talked and joked incessantly, they, at the same time, seemed to be distant from one another, as if each had a separate life that was inaccessible to the others, that had to be guarded, and each was careful not to encroach on that secret preserve. Of course, they hadn't known each other very long; still the three were about the same age, and it seemed to me that they would want to become close friends. Between Leah and her mother there was also this distance; not at all what I thought a mother and daughter should be like. A deep sadness clung to Leah's mother that yet did not invite comforting and seemed impenetrable. She walked slowly and silently from room to room, cleaning and dusting, and even when she busied herself in the kitchen, she moved pots quietly from stove to table to sink.

Leah did not turn to her when she needed advice, she rather asked Flora or Arthur who treated her almost like their daughter. They would urge her to rest when they thought she looked tired, and they remarked how little she ate and that she was too thin. Flora and Arthur were kind to all of us, but it was Leah they seemed to think needed protecting.

Not so with Sonya, who never asked for advice and whose every movement was purposeful and energetic. Her quick steps echoed through the house. Snatches of American songs she had learned from David wafted up the staircase. Her gray eyes sparkled in the sunburned face and her deep, melodious voice dominated every conversation.

"I'm off to America. They'll send large, white ships for us," she said confidently. "I'm through with Europe. I don't ever want to see it again. Never."

Sonya was in love with David and whenever she spoke of him her eyes became misty and her strong, determined face softened. Flora often frowned when Sonya wondered whether David was as much in love with her as she with him.

"Of course he loves me," she always concluded, "he told me so. He said he would do anything for me after what I've been through. He won't hurt me, and he'll never let anybody hurt me again. Don't worry, everything will be okay." She used the American word whenever possible. "Any day now, I'll get papers for America and then David and I will be happy for the rest of our lives." Her sunny smile returned, but she tried to keep her mouth closed. Sonya's teeth were badly decayed and some were broken off at the roots.

Once, however, Hanna made a strange comment. The girls were on the sundeck and I was in my customary place on the staircase when I heard Hanna interrupt.

"All that talk about love: he loves me, I love him. What are you talking about? David is a nice boy, he makes you feel good, you feel human while you are with him. He smells clean, he has good American soap. He gives you soap and now you also smell clean. You haven't smelled this good in years. That's all there is to it. Promises—love, America, no one will hurt you again—are all nonsense. David may mean what he says, but out there," I imagined her pointing at the ruins below, "out there is death and destruction, and promises that are in no one's power to keep."

How unlike Hanna, I thought, I have never heard her sound so harsh or, for that matter, so decisive. Hanna was usually vague, she didn't answer questions directly. Not that she was evasive, it was simply that when someone asked a question, it usually reminded her of something else. Instead of answering, she told whatever she was reminded of, and yet here she was telling Sonya that David might not keep his promise.

Hanna was very different from Sonya, who teased and laughed, or fragile Leah and her helpless and apologetic ways. With her black curly hair and her delicate pale face, Hanna could be a playful child one moment and withdrawn the next. She seemed then to be in another place and in another time. This happened frequently, especially when she talked about her little brother Yosel, her father the rabbi, or the camps she had been in. She appeared to retreat into the past then: to her mother's kitchen; to the train; she stood with thousands of women for roll call in the cold dawn; she was lying on the hard bunk in the barrack touching her shaven head.

Hanna relived the past in great detail, but with no sequence and no sense of time. One late afternoon—we were having tea on the sundeck—Arthur asked Hanna how she made her way from Bergen-Belsen to Frankfurt. At first she was lost in thought, as if trying to conjure up the pictures she was about to describe. Then she began slowly, her eyes far away.

"It was very cold. My mother made me put on several dresses and stockings the night before. I was big and heavy, almost as round as grandmother, and I wore my mother's shoes. In the morning, when the Germans came to drive us out of the house, my father gave me a small bundle of food to carry, telling me that was all we had and not to lose it. We went out of the house together, little Yosel with Mother, Esther with Haim-Yankel; Father let me help carry the bundle of bedding. We stood for a long time in the market place. There were many German soldiers with dogs. The soldiers went into the houses looking for people who had hidden. Those they found they drove out into the market place and shot at them. Not to kill at first. They wanted to see them run, hear them scream, make them bleed. So the Jews ran and the blood ran out of them. The soldiers laughed, aimed and fired; the dogs strained at the leashes and growled; and I stood very still next to Father, helping him hold the bundle as he told me to. Finally everyone started moving. We walked out of the market place, through the Polish part of town, past the church into the open country. I saw Aunt Rivke's daughters, I saw old Mordechai and Dvora, and I wanted Father to walk with them. But suddenly, when we were already in the fields, people began to scream and push this way and that. The soldiers were shooting again and Father tried to break out of the knot of people. I let go of the bundle. Mother disappeared, I ran and pushed. . . ." Her voice trailed off and she was lost in thought. "The cattle car was so full. I could not breathe or move, and I kept saying, Little Yosel, are you there? Yosel, where is *mame, tate. . .* are you there, Yosel?"

Her stories were always like that. They had neither beginning nor end, as if they were meant to go on today, tomorrow, next week, for years to come. Like a child, she seemed intent on reciting her lessons accurately, fearful of making a mistake.

In contrast, Sonya ticked off information like reading a list. Theresienstadt 1943; Auschwitz 1944; her family sent on transport, no doubt to Auschwitz. She shrugged her shoulders, her face hard. From Auschwitz to Ravensbruck, and then to a nearby factory where she was liberated. Sonya concluded with an eye to the future: "The moment the Germans ran away I said to myself, 'Sonya, no more Europe, no more Vienna; you're alive, go to America.' I walked out of the camp and, when someone told me to go to Frankfurt, I did. And now I'm here." Sonya bit into a slice of bread emphasizing that she was indeed here and, wherever else she would be thereafter, she'd be altogether solidly in that place.

Hanna had a friend, an American soldier. But she never talked about him the way Sonya did. Hanna did not mention love. Arthur and Flora often pressed her to let them meet her Bill; what did he do in the army, is he young, is he old, who is he? Hanna only smiled vaguely; once she handed Arthur a photograph as if it explained everything.

Sometimes in the evening, after Hanna had left, and we sat around the kitchen table eating sandwiches, Arthur and Flora questioned Leah. Did Leah know anything about this Bill, what did Hanna say about him?

Leah shook her head. "She rarely says anything. Bill gives her clothes, the beautiful white dress and the red hat are from Bill, so was the coffee and tea she brought us. But Hanna isn't in love with him. She isn't in love with anybody. She simply needed someone before she met us and Bill helped her. He found her the room where she lives now. Still, I don't think Hanna would care if he disappeared tomorrow."

"Poor Hanna," said Flora, and Arthur thoughtfully chewed on his cold pipe.

Leah's mother who was usually silent looked up. "Something strange is happening with Hanna. She told me the other day that her mother visits her. At night while she sleeps. Her mother looks very well, said Hanna, she is wearing the black *shabat* dress with the silk shawl and the string of pearls. Her mother has been visiting regularly for some weeks and she always comes alone, said Hanna, even though Hanna has been pleading to bring along her father and little Yosel. 'Later,' Hanna told me her mother said, 'later, after we have everything arranged and I've given you the present I'm preparing.'" Leah's mother shook her head, "I don't know what has come over Hanna."

There was a long silence broken at last by Sonya. "Such rubbish. The trouble with Hanna is that she looks to the past. She is childish and playful, like a butterfly in her white puffy dress, about to be blown away by the next wind. Goodness, she doesn't even know the name of the street where she lives. We should help Hanna face the present, look to the future. She should go to America. She should learn to love again."

How complicated living is, I thought, watching the serious faces around the kitchen table. What does it mean to love, to be in love, not to love? I must ask Arthur to give me a book about love. There is so much to learn. And how can people appear in dreams? I only have nightmares, I thought, about German soldiers finding my hiding place, about running away in the snow, being chased and shot down. I try to forget the nightmares in daytime. How can one remember what is said in dreams? And what if it isn't a dream at all, and Hanna's mother is alive and can only come at night? I shivered involuntarily. Sonya is right. This talk is rubbish. The dead are dead and gone. I caught Flora's concerned glance. She leaned over to pat my cold hands.

I was reading *Anna Karenina* when Kuba roared up the street on a black motorcycle and stopped in front of the house. Arthur looked approvingly at the handsome young man in his well-fitting flared slacks and casual shirt. "Working for the Americans," he told Arthur, slapping him on the back. Although Kuba had apparently come to see Leah—they had met in Regensburg when Leah was on her way to Frankfurt, she later told us—he was pleased to find the others. His loud voice and boisterous laughter filled the foyer and he gave everyone a firm handshake. "Ahma," Kuba said, as if the purpose of his visit was to search for other Jews.

The girls, Kuba, and I trooped up to the sundeck. Instead of sitting down, Kuba went to the edge of the roof. The late afternoon sun cast golden rays over the ruined city and its grotesquely shattered houses. Some rooms, their privacy exposed, were almost intact; a bedroom here, a bathroom there, even a dining room complete with table and overturned chairs, the walls covered with elegant striped wallpaper. Below, people silently picked through the rubble of the houses. They carried stones and bricks to one side, piling them up neatly. Sometimes they gathered in small groups to stare at a find.

"Look at this rubble and the Germans digging in their dirt," Kuba said. "How can you stand seeing this day after day?" He didn't wait for an answer. "Of course, this is German rubble, it has nothing to do with us, and I like to watch them slave. But you should be elsewhere. Some place beautiful, in the mountains, in green fields, forests, in cities with happy, laughing people."

"America," Sonya cried, "America, New York, where the buildings are taller than any we've seen. Where you can buy anything you want, stockings, perfume, dresses, chocolate cake. Where you order soup and fried chicken in restaurants."

Kuba laughed good-naturedly, like one does with a child, and pulled out a package of Camel cigarettes. "No, not America. Another country, a country that's ours, a country for Jews, where we now belong. I'm talking about the land of Israel. Tel Aviv, the Galilee, the Kinneret. The hills and valleys of Judea and Jerusalem, guarded by the Prophet Samuel. He turned to me, "You're a child. There are so few left your age. We'll send you to a kibbutz to be with other children. You'll work and learn to sing again, be a child once more."

To the three girls Kuba said that we, the remnant, must go and build the land. We must build vineyards and orchards. Drain the swamps. It's our duty to return to the soil. Had we done this sooner, there would have been no murder and no killing. We should not have become a nation of merchants and peddlers. But it's not too late. We're here and alive, we're young and healthy. And even though some of us think we're homeless, we have a home in Zion. We are expected in Zion. "The sights you'll see," said Kuba, "when the ship pulls into Haifa. The blue ocean and the yellow beach full of cheering people. And in the distance the Carmel."

Kuba talked for a long time, smoking his Camel cigarettes, and when he tried to show us the height of the Carmel and the expanse of the Kinneret, his large gold watch sparkled in the setting sun. Finally he finished and, leaning back in his chair, waited for our questions.

Sonya spoke up first. "It sounds great, but I still want to go to America. Any day now the Americans will send ships for us. A private cabin for everyone and as much food as we can eat. There'll be music for dinner and after dinner dancing. Where are the ships that will take us to Haifa? Have you heard the British say they'll let us in? Who are your contacts? Are you a Zionist?"

Kuba didn't answer and turned to Leah. Leah had that look about her that I had seen before, her helpless, defeated look, which said that all decisions about everything were equally futile. "I know you mean well," she said, "and what you have told us sounds beautiful. But I don't know whether I want to go anywhere, or do anything. So much of my life has been wasted, so many years are gone never to be lived again. It frightens me to think of going somewhere and doing something. I would have to decide and I can't decide anymore. For three years I decided—stand here, stand there, don't talk, work faster, look healthy, but not too healthy. . . ." She raised her hands in a gesture of despair.

Kuba's face showed disappointment. He had counted on her, he said, Leah had made a deep impression on him when they first met. That's the reason he sought her out now. "We need you," said Kuba, "don't let us down, we need you to reclaim the land, for all of us to live in peace." He leaned close, whispering conspiratorially, "I have connections in Bavaria, in Austria; there are Jews from Palestine in Italy, we have an organization. There's money and there'll be ships."

I felt sorry for Leah, but Kuba's enthusiasm almost persuaded me. Besides, he knew how to flatter, even if he called me a child. He didn't ignore me and from the start had included me in his audience. I didn't necessarily want to sing in the kibbutz; still, if there really was an organization to help Jews leave Germany, maybe Kuba had the solution. A time would come when I would have to leave this house, and I wasn't about to settle for a refugee camp. "What about schools? Will I be able to study and read?" I asked.

"For two thousand years we read books," said Kuba, "and look where it got us. To the gas chambers. To the crematoria. This isn't the time for sitting in musty rooms over books." He leaned forward and grabbed my hand, nearly pulling me out of the chair. "Look at these hands, good strong hands, made for work, for planting trees, for harvesting oranges. Why would a pretty girl like you want to read and study?"

Hanna had been very quiet. Lost in thought, she had not looked at Kuba. Now she raised her head and by the way she looked at each of us in turn, I knew she sensed the growing tension. "Now, now," she murmured, "some must work and some must read, even in the land of Israel. . . ."

Her sentence hung in the air and we waited for her to continue. "Everyone knows," she said slowly, "that the souls of the dead go to Zion. We too at one time or another will go there. Each Jew must. That's how it is. There are many ways, long and short, direct and round about. Sometimes Elijah helps. He throws his coat on the sea and it becomes a ship. Sometimes a person thinks he is ready to go, but his time hasn't come and the journey takes many years with stop-overs on the way. The souls of our dead will go sooner to Zion than usual because they suffered so much. They are ready to go, they needn't stop on the way. Of course, not all at the same time; even souls must wait their turn. Some are still lost and must be found. It will be some time before everyone gets there."

In the long silence even Kuba was lost for words and Leah suggested we go downstairs. She shivered in the cool night air.

"Maybe you'll change your minds," said Kuba in parting, "I'll be back. Our group is growing, you should be part of it." He shook his head. "Strange, after I talk to people, they usually want to know the quickest way to Italy. But you? Why talk about souls? It's the living that count, the young, not dead souls."

We stood in the dark street with its ghostlike ruins and watched the black motorcycle roar off into the night. Sonya said knowingly, "Did you see that watch? He is doing well on the black market. And that big machine — why do they so go for motorcycles? I wonder whether he's really in touch with the Palestinians, or whether he's just bragging? I don't trust him, Zion, sunshine, oranges, yellow beaches? That kind would sell his own mother for a profit. No," she added after a while, "I don't want to plant orchards."

After Kuba's visit everything seemed changed. Autumn had come and overnight the weather turned cold and rainy. The ruined city felt more desolate than ever under the gray skies. Inside the house water seeped through the burned-down third floor and molds appeared on the silk-covered walls. Flora had found a wood-burning stove which she put in the large room, pointing the chimney through the window so that the ruins across the street loomed surrealistically through the drifting swatches of smoke. The round table was moved near the stove and each day David, having grown bulky in layers of sweaters and army coat, carried his chair to the wood box. Flora watched gloomily as the pieces of wood and coal disappeared in the merrily burning fire. Fuel was hard to come by that winter.

Leah's mother had left for Bavaria where a relative from the Flossenburg camp had turned up. Leah developed a cough and slight fever and spent most of the time in bed. Flora brought large cups of tea, and Arthur, armfuls of books to her room. I too dropped in occasionally to chat with Leah and to put my cold feet under her warm quilts.

"How do you feel today?"

"Not bad," she answered cheerfully, her dark eyes feverish, "I don't mind staying in bed. Look how everyone is spoiling me."

"Don't you miss your mother? Don't you wish she were here?"

"Oh, mother. I don't know. She deserves a little happiness. Maybe she'll get married again. As long as I'm with Flora and Arthur she doesn't have to worry about me. I know we're lucky that the two of us are left, but I don't know how to explain it, it'll take time. . . yes, it'll take time. Of course, I miss her," she added brightly. "I'm sure she misses me too."

Strange, I thought, looking at her thin, oval face framed by thick, brown hair. Leah is perfectly content letting everything be as it is. She's neither happy nor unhappy, neither troubled nor untroubled. She seems to feel nothing at all, except gratitude to whoever does something for her.

Whereas Leah patiently succumbed to being ill, Sonya was more restless than ever. She left the house each day, intent on errands connected with her departure for America. One by one her summer dresses vanished. She brought home sweaters, wool skirts, and mufflers apparently acquired in a carefully organized trading operation. She spread the clothes on Leah's bed and urged her to get well in order to start alterations. Sonya was often impatient now and spent little time in the cold house.

It was too drafty on the staircase and I brought my books to the kitchen where tea water was kept hot on a low fire. Sometimes Hanna joined me when Leah was asleep. We sat on either side of the stove, she with her knitting, I with my book. Hanna had found some old sweaters which she carefully unravelled and re-knitted into strangely misshapen oblongs.

At first I felt content in the silent house, listening to the steady rain, the singing tea kettle, and the clicking of Hanna's needles. Hanna spoke little, she seemed deep in thought, sometimes humming quiet tunes that sounded like lullabyes. At times she told me stories about Yosel and the snow-covered forests and fields of her hometown. It was not too long, however, before the silence and the steady clicking and humming became oppressive. I can't sit here forever, reading books, I thought impatiently. I must decide to do something. Kuba's visit was still vivid: who is right, I asked myself, Sonya and her American dreams, or Kuba and his promise of Palestine? I am not like Hanna, content to remember the past, nor am I like Leah who has decided not to decide. But how can I know what to do? My father's image came to mind, why was he not here to tell me what to do? Alone, abandoned, alone, the words repeated themselves as they had earlier in summer. Why was it different now? What had changed? Why was the loneliness a source of pain now?

I made up my mind to find out more about America and Palestine, what sort of places they were, and the very next day I went in search of other refugees who I knew lived in a run-down hotel in the city. I was apprehensive, insecure, afraid of meeting new people. Would they be friendly? Would they ignore me? Would they make fun of my clumsiness? Maybe others were not as eager as I to leave Germany? But I needn't have worried. As soon as I arrived at the ramshackle hotel, a girl in a large man's coat spotted me and pulled me into what had once been a dining room. A dozen or so boys and girls in tattered clothing and shivering in the cold sat around a large table. Their noisy talk reverberated through the large room. The argument I thought they were having turned out to be a serious discussion.

"We can't stay much longer in this hotel," said a young man, raising his voice above the din. "The roof is leaking and about to cave in, the walls are crumbling, the hotel will either fall on top of us, or someone will throw us out. We won't go to a refugee camp, we'll not be behind barbed wire with guards telling us what to do. The Americans despise us, we saw that when we came over the border and they pointed their DDT guns at us. Where do we go from here? There was no place for us in Poland, we don't want to be in Germany. Do we have a place anywhere? We are here, we are alive, we are free, what do we do next?"

While he talked, the girl in the overcoat turned to me, "This is Poldek. He was a student at Warsaw University before the war. So was Stefan over there." She pointed at a pale young man leaning against a pillar, his pants held up by a rope. "They both studied philosophy; it comes in handy when you're trying to solve problems. We all met in Prague and decided to stay together." To the others she said, "I heard someone from Landsberg camp say that Ben Gurion's visit two weeks ago was like a miracle. Imagine, a real, live person from Palestine. That he came, that people could see him, touch him, gave everybody new hope. After he left, some of the younger people actually came alive, instead of just sitting dumbly and letting the Americans order them around."

Stefan nodded. "Fortunately, we don't need Ben Gurion to know that we must act. Poldek asked whether we have a place in this world," he smiled bitterly, "we the outcasts, the leftovers from the crematoria. Yes, we do, in two places: Palestine and America. Europe is out. Ben Gurion's visit proves that the Palestinians are interested in us; I've heard that men from the Jewish Brigade are in Italy. We should try to contact them. The Americans, we know, want to lock us into camps. But there are Jews in the American army, let's try to find them; we need to know whether Jews in America are willing to help us. We don't like camps, still we shouldn't isolate ourselves. Camps are useful contacts for finding people we knew. If the Zionists are organizing, it's in the camps."

Again a heated discussion began. Some were absolutely opposed to the camps; others suggested that the group make its way to Austria and from there to Italy. Someone proposed sending one person to Italy to find the Jewish Brigade and return for the others if he did. Several objected to, what they called, the imposition of the Zionist option. They should wait and see what the Americans would do. Go to a camp meanwhile, they said, after all, in the weeks we've been together we've already developed group discipline. A girl spoke passionately about democracy, freedom, the dignity of man, individualism, and collective responsibility. "We belong to a people," she cried, "whether rich or poor, educated or not, assimilated or religious, our fate in the concentration camps was the same. Now that we're free, we cannot set ourselves above the others in the camps. Let's go to a camp, no matter which, and organize."

Poldek reminded everyone that in Prague they had decided to abide by democratic principles. They must vote on the suggestions. I had listened intently, and was both bewildered and fascinated. Much of the discussion I didn't understand: human rights, democracy, these were new words to me. So that's what living in a group is like, I thought, everybody expressed an opinion and the views of all are respected.

For the next week I went each day to the hotel, and in the evenings I returned to the house, my face glowing, my head filled with new ideas. Arthur noticed the change and with a pleased smile questioned me about my new friends. No, I didn't think they were dealing on the black market. They didn't want to be in refugee camps and are therefore in the hotel, I told Arthur. Some had studied at the university. Did I want to study at the university? asked Arthur.

They didn't always talk about immediate problems, what to do next, where to go, and how to get there. Sometimes, in the gray, cold dusk of an early afternoon they sat around the large table in quiet discussion. However heated and practical the arguments in daytime about principles and actions, when the growing darkness hid their faces, they began to speak haltingly about their pain and their doubts and their shattered selves. Yet the somber mood never lasted long. Someone, usually Poldek, introduced a lighter note, and soon they would joke and laugh about the cold or the food.

Stefan was invariably serious. "Who are we? I don't recognize this person who is thinking, planning, deciding. How did he come to be here? Who is this person Stefan? Is he the same Stefan who had a family in Warsaw, who got up each morning, put on clean clothes, collected his books, sat in a classroom, listened to lectures on the Socratic method and Plato's *Republic*? Who was he and who is here now? Tell me, Poldek, am I real, and if I'm here and real, who am I?"

The question hung in the large, barren room, it refused to dissolve, it echoed in my ears: "who am I, who am I, am I real?" I too don't know who I am, and I barely remember the time when I laughed and played games with my friend Toska. What was it like then not to be alone? I asked myself.

Poldek broke the tense silence. "It's hard to explain, sounds sort of crazy. . . I know. But listen. Ever since we came to Germany and, well, although this isn't exactly a luxury hotel, we're no longer in danger, no one is going to kill us tonight or tomorrow. It often seems to me that when we're discussing the situation and working things out the way we're supposed to that I'm two people. This other Poldek comes and stands behind me — he is the old one — and applauds the second Poldek and praises him, 'You're doing great, you're managing marvellously.' And when I go out and organize some food from the Americans, there he is again, smiling, 'Bravo, you didn't think you could do it, but you can do amazing things, you'll see.' The old Poldek is very positive. I kind of like him."

A playful tone had crept into Poldek's voice and one of the girls at the end of the table remarked that she hoped the second Poldek wouldn't claim a portion of food. Everyone laughed and they sent Poldek out to look after dinner.

It was a strange week. It seemed long. A lifetime, but it passed much too quickly. Each day my new friends taught me something I hadn't known before. Slowly, cautiously I learned to move out of silence, groping for words of my own, trying to explain why it felt odd to be alive.

My heart was heavy when I opened the front door, closing it gently behind me. I had just said goodbye to my friends. They were evicted from the hotel when someone discovered the leaking roof and the unsteady walls. They were packing their belongings when I arrived, cheerfully holding up each worn sweater and threadbare shirt before discarding or packing it.

"We may meet again," Poldek had said, holding my cold hand in his, "we have something in common. We are here."

But I was doubtful. Being here was not enough and no meeting would ever be again like this. The persons we might have been, we never became. In time our new becoming would make us unrecognizable to each other. Perhaps even to ourselves. I had been sad on the way home.

The house was quiet and dark. Somewhere from within I heard loud sobbing. The light was on in the kitchen.

"What happened? Who is crying?" I asked Hanna and Leah, "Is Sonya ill? Is something wrong with Flora?"

Hanna looked up from her knitting. "You are so busy these days with your own affairs, you no longer know what's happening." Her mildly reproving tone made me feel guilty. I sat down next to her and patted her shoulder.

Leah smiled sadly. "We're all very upset. It's Sonya. We've tried everything to calm her, now she has locked herself in her room and won't talk to anyone. I'll tell you what happened. Last week David was put in quarantine with measles in the military hospital. Sonya went every day, even when she couldn't be in his room. Finally, this morning the nurse allowed her to sit next to David's bed. He was much better and his fever was down. David told her that the army is shipping him home in two or three days. And then David told her that he has a wife in America. We don't know what David may have promised her or what Sonya may have said. By the time she came home she was crying hysterically. After Flora got the story out of her, she ran into her room and locked the door. She has been crying ever since."

This is dreadful, I thought, neat, pleasant David in his ironed uniform with his shy smile, why didn't he tell Sonya sooner? Didn't he realize how she embellished and clung to her American dream because of him? I was angry. Lies, lies, he should have known that Sonya wanted to be done with lies. I remembered Hanna's words about love; maybe she was right. Still, here was Sonya crying her heart out. "What will happen now?" I asked.

The girls didn't answer. Hanna suddenly stopped knitting and looked at me. "I might as well tell you. You'll find out anyhow. I'm going to have a baby. Arthur and Flora are very angry with me. I told them this morning, before we knew about Sonya. Flora was beside herself. It was a bad day."

I was dumbfounded. "How can you have a baby when you're not married?" I blurted out and blushed.

"This is a special baby, some day I'll explain. Flora can't understand that I'm very happy. It will be born soon, maybe four or five months from now. Look, you can almost see it." She lifted her shapeless sweater and, indeed, her stomach was round and her skirt was held together with a safety pin.

Too much was happening at once. David had a wife and loved Sonya. Hanna was having a baby without a husband. And I had found friends and lost them all in one week. At least Leah seemed the same, as helpless as ever with that half-finished dress spread out on the table. "It won't even fit you after I'm done," she said.

The next day Hanna came to live with us. Flora was still upset and could be heard muttering something about irresponsible young people. Arthur wandered in and out of the kitchen for no apparent reason, chewing on his cold pipe and glancing worriedly at Hanna as if he expected her to have the baby any moment. Hanna continued to knit unperturbed and Leah stared at the unfinished dress. Behind her closed door Sonya sobbed.

Sonya's sorrow filtered into every part of the house. It made Arthur restless and Flora moody. Her sorrow hovered over the kitchen where Hanna was humming one sad tune after the other. Although she had withdrawn from us, I felt that Sonya included all of us in her grief. So great was her weeping that I thought she wept for Leah and her indecision, Hanna and the baby growing in her belly, and even for me. I listened to Sonya's weeping and wondered what it would be like to cry like this, to let tears flow with such abandon. Leah and Hanna might have been thinking the same as we sat dry-eyed at the kitchen table.

"She is grieving," said Flora, "she is grieving for her whole life, for her dead family, she is grieving for her wasted youth, for the dreams she had that will never come true. This is more than David, he only deceived her, though his deceit brought her to face the awful truth." Flora wiped her eyes. She too was crying.

Leah twisted the brightly colored materials between her fingers. "Well," she said slowly, "I don't know. You make a decision and it turns out well. Like when my mother went to Bavaria. Now she's no longer alone. Then again you make a decision and it doesn't turn out well. Every time you decide you take a chance. Winner to the right, loser to the left. Sonya took a chance and lost."

"It couldn't be all that serious," said Arthur, "a little affair that Sonya magnified out of all proportions. David acted irresponsibly, there's no excuse. But it isn't the end of the world."

"Sonya is a fool," said Hanna. "She's looking for love when she should have known that love turned to ashes and smoke. The smoke dispersed and the ashes were scattered. Sonya believed that falling in love and going to America would set things right. Nothing will ever be right, neither here nor there, nor anywhere. Even if she goes to the end of the world."

Only Sonya had nothing to say. She just cried.

At last Sonya stopped sobbing and left her room. She looked wretched and worn-out when she appeared in the kitchen to heat a pot of water. Her face was swollen and her beautiful black hair was in tangles. She asked Hanna to help wash her hair. Then she got dressed and went out without saying another word. Sonya returned in the evening; she opened the kitchen door, said that she was leaving for Munich the next day, and went to her room. Her face was like stone and no one dared ask her why, or how long she would be gone. Sonya left early the next morning — I knew when I heard the front door slam shut.

At once, the lethargy caused by Sonya's sobbing vanished. Not that Arthur and Flora or Leah were happy to see Sonya go. To the contrary, they worried, and each day hoped for news of her. Sonya's crying had simply immobilized everyone while we waited for her to stop. Now that she was gone, Arthur returned to his desk, Leah attacked the dress with renewed energy, and Flora turned her full attention to Hanna who, as before and during Sonya's sorrow, continued to knit.

Hanna must see a doctor without delay. Moreover, said Flora, we must find Bill, who is after all the baby's father. Hanna patiently explained that no one she had ever known saw a doctor while having a baby. She was perfectly fine, she felt very good. As

118

for Bill, said Hanna, she had told Flora before, he was sent back to America. No, she didn't know his address.

Flora clutched her head in exasperation. "Scandalous. He's the baby's father and he must assume responsibility for it. If we find him, we might persuade him to send for you. He may even marry you. It's his baby you are carrying."

"No," said Hanna quietly and firmly, "it's my baby. Mine alone. I don't want to go to America. I don't want to marry Bill. I just want to have my baby."

"Why, why," cried Flora, "why are you so obstinate? You need someone to take care of you and the baby. Why did this happen to you of all people."

Hanna stopped knitting. "Please don't be upset, Flora. You don't understand. I do, because my mother came to me and explained. There must be a kaddish, Mother said, it's my first responsibility. Everything else can wait. 'You've been a good daughter,' Mother told me, 'our eldest; once the kaddish is here we can start our journey.'"

Flora stared at Hanna. "All this because of a prayer for the dead? Hanna, why do you spin these fantasies? Your mother cannot come to you because she's not here. You went to bed with Bill and now you're pregnant. We must figure out what's best for you."

Hanna said patiently, "Dear Flora, their souls can't leave here until the kaddish is born. My mother said so. I'm telling you the truth. Bill was good to me, and that's all. This baby is mine. I'll do nothing without my mother's advice."

Flora groaned. I didn't know what to make of this strange conversation. Could there be something to what Hanna said? How did women get to have babies anyway? Where were these souls Hanna talked about? And what was death, aside from the terrible fear of it? I had seen people shot and beaten, their piercing screams finally stilled when they died. They just lay there, disfigured and bloody. The dead were dead. Were there perhaps mysteries Hanna knew and I couldn't understand?

"Hanna," Leah tried to sound reasonable, "you forget that the souls can go to Zion only when the Messiah comes. He'll lead them back. But the Messiah hasn't come yet."

Flora stood up. "I will not discuss Jewish theology nor Messiahs and souls and their comings and goings. Tomorrow we see the doctor."

Hanna did go to the doctor, winking mischievously behind Flora's back. Leah continued to alter dresses for Hanna, and Hans came each day to warm his hands at the kitchen stove and to inquire how Hanna felt. From his pockets he pulled special tidbits: some powdered eggs, dried milk, a wrinkled apple. I returned to my reading. Arthur had given me books by Upton Sinclair and Jack London. But the wonder of discovery of the summer was gone. I often thought of Poldek and Stefan. I thought of the long discussions in the hotel; they were right, we must leave. As long as we stay in Germany we'll be haunted, we'll never make a fresh start.

Arthur and Flora were too busy to listen to me. A new press officer had taken David's place, and the first issue of the newspaper was about to appear. I missed Sonya. Only after she was gone did I realize how much cheer and laughter she had brought us. I missed her optimism; the crazy American songs David had taught her; I missed her teasing whenever I watched the two girls — the one knitting, the other sewing — who seemed content with things as they were. Hanna no longer talked about her mother or souls, but she often described the baby she would have as if she had actually seen it. Leah listened patiently, nodding her head, her mouth full of pins.

I made up my mind to leave before the end of the year. Go to one of the Bavarian camps and then to America, or... I might look for Poldek and his friends. Arthur was at first opposed, suggesting I wait until the weather was warmer. In the end he realized that much had changed since summer.

"You're impatient like Sonya," he said, "but you're more careful. You've learned not to trust, which is a good thing for now. Some day, though, the world might again return to normal ways; people will trust one another, faith and love will exist as they should. Will you recognize that day when it comes? Sonya's problem was that she didn't understand that trust like love cannot flourish in these ruins."

One day, early in March, Leah's mother came to see me in the refugee camp in Munich. Although winter was nearly over, spring still seemed far away. There was no warmth in the pale sunshine and the mud puddles between the barracks were as deep as ever. The gray German army barracks smelled of mold and dirty laundry. I was glad to see a familiar face and marvelled at her transformation. Leah's mother was barely recognizable in her well-tailored suit and heels. Her hair was carefully waved. The hunted look had disappeared, she smiled gently at me behind a pair of new glasses. We sat on my bed, the straw sack faintly crackling, and she told me of the hard time she had finding me. Flora had written that I was in the Funkkaserne. Why didn't I let her know? she asked accusingly. Passover is next month, and do I want to spend the holiday with her and her new husband, the relative from Flossenburg?

"These barracks are terrible," said Leah's mother, glancing around the grimy, unheated room with its nine rough cots, "in our camp we live in apartments and in the hotel."

We talked about conditions in various camps; yes, life was especially hard for those who were assigned to German barracks, we agreed. I told her about the Ukrainian block leader who stole coffee and chocolate from our CARE packages. Leah's mother nodded sympathetically and said that I would be much better off with her. They had enough food and just received their first clothing shipment.

I agreed, "But I'm finally assigned to a children's transport to America, although all the children are twenty and twenty-five years old."

We laughed. Everybody we knew had taken off years on the new American papers, the years we had lost and now thought we could retrieve. I wanted to know about Frankfurt. What had happened with Sonya? Did Hanna have her baby? How was Leah feeling? Was she finally thinking of leaving Germany?

Leah's mother shook her head. "Not my Leah. She still can't make up her mind. She isn't strong, the poor child, always ailing with something or other. Arthur and Flora are spoiling her, but she deserves it. Once she is healthier, we'll all sit down together and decide where to go."

"Sonya is fine, although no one knows where she is right now. Flora told me what happened, it's a very strange story." Leah's mother shook her head. "Sometime in January, Sonya suddenly turned up with two young men. All three looked terrible: ragged, dirty overcoats, worn old shoes; especially Sonya, who was always so fastidious and had managed to look elegant when no one else did. Sonya no longer laughed the way she used to, and her eyes didn't sparkle. She was pale and had lost weight. Flora said that the first thing she did was to give them a bowl of hot soup which Sonya finished as if she hadn't eaten in days. Nobody was very talkative. Do you remember how Sonya loved to tease and joke? It was like the old Sonya had disappeared. She laughed only once, and that was when Hanna walked into the kitchen in one of those strange misshapen sweaters she has been knitting, with her big stomach sticking out in front. According to Flora, Sonya pointed at her and then, covering her mouth, she laughed and laughed until the tears ran down her cheeks. Poor Hanna was embarrassed when everyone stared at her. But Sonya seemed pleased about Hanna's baby. Even the two dour young men, Flora said, looked a little happier.

Anyway, Sonya said that she came to say goodbye. She was leaving Germany for good; she was on her way to Palestine. Flora was shocked. You remember how keen Sonya was on going to America? The stories she had about white ships and New York? It was, said Flora, as if that dream had never been. The new Sonya had cold eyes and a hard face. She didn't look backward, though she still looked to the future. What a future!" Leah's mother sighed deeply.

We were silent for a while. It was hard to believe that a person could change so much in so short a time. "Did all this happen because of David?" I asked.

"Good you remind me, I nearly forgot. David had written to Sonya before the Americans shipped him out and Leah had kept the letter. So Leah took Sonya to her room, and what do you think Sonya did? She tore up the letter without reading it. To Leah she said that she was working for the *Briha*, the organization that helps refugees cross borders in Europe on their way to Palestine. Her two companions are also in the *Briha*. Leah must not tell anyone because the organization is illegal. 'Are you then a Zionist?' Leah had asked, and Sonya said, yes, Jews should recognize that there is nothing except Zionism and Palestine. You know how sensitive Leah is, she didn't want to hurt Sonya's feelings, still she couldn't help asking whether a life of hard work is what Sonya really wanted. As Leah tells it, for a moment, for one brief moment, Sonya's face softened and a look of such pain came into her eyes Leah had to look away. 'You and I know,' she told Leah, 'that betrayal is death. The real murderer was the one who betrayed you. The Germans only finished the job. We both have seen traitors and those they betrayed. David betrayed. He is no better than a murderer.' Imagine, saying such a thing."

"Later Leah told this to Arthur," continued Leah's mother, "and Arthur being the wise man he is said that Sonya joined the *Briha* because she wanted someone to finish the job."

I wanted to ask Leah's mother whether she agreed with Arthur. How could Sonya, who had been so full of life, think this way? But Leah's mother didn't look at me. She had taken off her glasses and was wiping them vigorously. I thought I saw again that hunted look.

"And what about Hanna?" I pressed her.

Leah's mother looked at her watch. "That's such a long story, the poor girl. I'll tell you another time, otherwise I'll miss the train home."

"Let me walk you to the gate. I'm not allowed to leave the camp. We chopped up one of the beds for firewood and the Ukrainian denounced us. Tell me about Hanna on the way."

I put on my coat and muffler, and we slowly walked down the stairs. "It happened while I was visiting Leah at the beginning of February. I slept in Leah's room, and with Sonya gone, Hanna had a room to herself. One night I heard Hanna say something in a loud voice and I got up to check. The room was dark, apparently Hanna was talking in her sleep. She stopped as soon as I switched on the light. To make a long story short, when she opened her eyes, I saw that she was terribly frightened. I couldn't tell whether she was still dreaming, or whether she was awake. I couldn't tell whether she even knew where she was. In fact, I myself was also at first confused. Of course, I knew Hanna had had a dream, but when she told me it sounded as if it really had happened. In her dream, it seems, her mother had brought her father so that Hanna could tell him about the baby. Instead of being pleased, said Hanna, he was furious. 'This isn't a proper kaddish,' he yelled, and 'I'll send this false kaddish back.' Hanna and her mother pleaded with him, but he wouldn't listen, and in the end her mother too agreed to return the baby. 'They went away,' said Hanna, looking at me with dark, frightened eyes, 'he refused my kaddish.' She didn't cry, not a single tear did I see, she only put her hands over her stomach as if trying to protect the baby inside.

Hanna didn't get up the next morning. She just lay there, her eyes wide open, staring at the ceiling, holding her stomach. She refused all food and didn't speak to anyone. In the evening Flora called the doctor. He examined Hanna — she still hadn't moved — and said he thought that the baby was dead. We took her to the hospital, Arthur, Flora, Leah and I, and we stayed with her all night. She didn't close her eyes, though she looked at no one at all, and she never said a word, even when the doctors examined her. After they were through, she just lay there, her hands folded over her stomach. They operated the next day, and the doctor told us that it had been a boy." Leah's mother shook her head, "It was uncanny, I think Hanna knew exactly when the baby died."

We stood at the gate, saying goodbye. "Will Hanna be all right?"

Leah's mother shrugged her shoulder and kissed me on the cheek. She returned the pass to the guard and quickly crossed the street to board the tramcar. I watched her through the barbed wire fence, wanting to run after her to beg her to promise, as I used to beg mother when I was small and frightened, that everything would turn out well.

# Soviet Journeys

## The First Meeting

The only way to get there was by train. The full day's ride through the countryside of northern Russia, with its thick evergreen and birch forests, punctuated by villages and small train stations, was just what I needed to make the transition in time and place; it gave me time to think, to wrestle with varying emotions. The steady landscape outside the train window had a strangely soothing effect.

I was visiting the last remnant of my family in Europe, some cousins who had survived the Holocaust and returned to make a new life for themselves on the ashes of the old. I knew the stories of the others who had survived: The cousin who, in the post-war chaos of banditry and occasional pogroms, cursed the land and left for Israel. Or great-uncle Naum, returning from Soviet labor camps and service at the front to find his wife and three daughters dead, victims of the Nazis. I knew Naum best, for he had emigrated to the U.S. He and his second wife, Leah, survivor of five concentration camps, were my only direct connections to the world I was about to enter.

The train stopped at one of the larger stations, my destination. I gathered my things as quickly as I could. What would my cousins look like? Although Naum had corresponded with them, we had no pictures. I was one of a handful of passengers alighting, typically American with my big suitcase. A woman and a man approached tentatively. From a distance they looked like everyone else on the platform, she with her brightly colored kerchief and simple dress, he with his worker's cap and open-necked shirt. As she approached, I could see that she looked remarkably like my grandfather. "I am Mitzi," she said. "You must be Rachel."

The Soviet bureaucrat droned on. "Where were you born? How are you related? Why didn't you register when you first came here?" I looked over at my cousin, her hair covered with a scarf, her angular face so eerily reminiscent of my grandfather's. The Soviet bureaucrat droned on. "Why didn't you register when you first came here?"

What was it that drew me back to this Russian town twenty miles from where my grandparents were born? By what miracle had this small remnant of my family survived Nazi bestiality and returned to the old Pale, the land of the *shtetl*?

We were related, but our lives were so different. "My mother almost came to America," Mitzi told me. "She even had steamship tickets for August, 1914. But then the War began. She never left. Your grandfather and great-aunt came back in the 1930s to visit." (I never knew that; strange I had to come here to find out.) "We were so happy then; we sang Yiddish songs well into the night." My grandfather lived vividly in her mind as a great hero, an image so different from my memories of him smelling of shnapps, calling us *paskuniak*. (Only later did I learn that this meant "scoundrel and bastard.")

Bit by bit Mitzi's life unfolded. Her father was a socialist. On June 22, 1941, at the news of the Nazi invasion, they fled. Strafed by German planes, plundered by bandits, they lost what few possessions they carried. All she had left was one spoon and several faded pictures. Still, she and her family were lucky; they spent the war in Siberia. The Nazis moved with such lightning speed that another aunt, awaiting her daughter's return from an overnight visit to a nearby village, was trapped. Most of Mitzi's friends and relatives shared similar fates.

After the war, Mitzi met Sima. Orphaned by the Nazis, he had survived by joining a Jewish partisan band in the nearby forests. Now the couple lived in a two-room apartment, with a tiny kitchen the size of a small walk-in closet. They considered themselves fortunate, as their earlier home had consisted of one room in a large wooden house, with no running water and an outhouse. There they had lived with their two sons and Mitzi's parents. When I visited them the first time, Mitzi's father was dead; her mother had just emigrated to Israel. Mitzi herself had applied to emigrate; her request denied, she seemed resigned to staying put. She felt a bond to this land, she told me.

Indeed, right after the war, when they moved back, she had been an ardent Communist—the first in her town to join the party youth organization, the *Komsomol.* Disillusionment set in with Stalin's postwar repression, particularly its anti-Semitism. Her father, the old socialist, spent time in jail for having his grandson circumcized; years later, this same grandson was denied admission to a military academy because he was Jewish. Around them, Mitzi and Sima saw children of outlaw band members who had terrorized their area during and after the war now elevated to positions of power in their town and in the local party. Still, she proudly showed me around the town, recounting its past glories, pointing out an old synagogue that is now an electrical workshop, taking me to the local museum.

I stayed with Mitzi and Sima for seven days, long enough to walk around the town, to visit their friends, and to see some of the surrounding countryside. The town was so different from the large Soviet cities with their tall buildings and row after row of concrete slabs in the new sections. Here, reflecting their proximity to the forests and the fields, most people lived in wooden houses, neatly trimmed and fenced in. Inside, the houses were heated by wood from large kitchen stoves. Besides the kitchen, there were usually two or three small rooms. Weather permitting, life went on in the back yards, where one usually found a small garden plot, a well, the outhouse, and a chicken coop. By growing their own vegetables, foraging in the forests for wild mushrooms and berries, and occasionally hunting, people in this area supplemented the bland Soviet diet more successfully than did people in the cities.

I met many of the town's tiny group of Jews. When they greeted one another in Yiddish, the sound echoed in my ears. I imagined the ghosts of thousands of others, now mute, who once walked the narrow rutted side streets with the neat rows of wooden houses, the main square, the park, the empty pedestal where the statue of Stalin once stood.

Sima had a cousin who had joined the Red Army and survived the war. Roza, a short, stocky and very handsome woman, lived in one of the wooden houses with her husband, Igor, a Siberian *muzhik* (non-Jewish peasant man). They had met as soldiers. For Igor, as for many of his generation, the Great Fatherland War (the Soviet name for World War II),

124

was the key event of his life. He never tired of telling war stories, particularly about the valor of the Siberian troops called on to save Moscow when the Germans were at its gates. Profoundly attached to the land, he grew potatoes, carrots, and cabbage and cultivated his fruit trees organically, cursing chemical fertilizers and pesticides.

At home, the relationship between Roza and Igor stayed traditional. He farmed and kept the chickens; she cooked and canned. Whenever we came to visit, she set out an elaborate spread. In contrast to Igor, she talked little about the war. Sima told me that she had won a medal for heroism, as one of many female radio operators who played a key role in the Soviet war effort. Her family, too, had been murdered by the Nazis.

Like the great majority of Soviet women, Roza worked outside the home. I visited her once at the trade office she managed. It was an unpretentious wooden building, leading into a large courtyard, with warehouse and storage facilities. In the courtyard stood a row of horse-drawn carts, still the primary mode of transportation in this area. Near them gathered their peasant owners, there to trade wild mushrooms and game to European gourmet businesses for foreign currency. Everyone gained. The peasants exchanged their profits for Levis or other western jeans; the Soviet state got badly needed *valiuta* (western money, so-called hard currency), and the gourmets pleased their palates. Watching Roza working crisply and efficiently in this office was a pleasure. There was an easy sense of cameraderie, no visible resentment at having a woman boss, no self-consciousness or self-deprecation on Roza's part.

I visited Mitzi's job, too.She was a bookkeeper at the District Trade Commission. Downstairs was a small clothing shop with the usual range of drab scarves, even drabber rayon sweaters, and dreary dresses, the dregs of the dismal selection available to the average Soviet customer in the provinces. The salesclerk knew about me and immediately engaged me in conversation about the U.S.

"What kind of a house do you live in?" "How many rooms?" "Do you own a car?" "Is it true that there are no collective farms in your country?" "Are your cities overrun by gangsters?" Finally, she eyed me up and down and said, "You know, for someone from such a rich country, you don't dress very well."

Sima had a fourteen-year-old car. A gifted mechanic, he nurtured it so that it still ran perfectly. This car gave us quite a bit of freedom, and we traveled around the countryside whenever Sima could take time off. I saw the *shtetl* my grandmother came from, the *shtetl* of my grandfather and great-uncle Naum. Before the war, Naum ran a successful lumber business. His large wooden house, still standing, was now the village medical station. Most of the other houses in these *shtetlekh*, burned by the Nazis, had been rebuilt. As Mitzi and Sima told it, everything looked the same, except for one thing. All the Jews were gone. The scattered tombstones in a few cemeteries offered the only physical evidence of centuries of Jewish settlement here.

Senia had been born in this area and emigrated to the U.S. from Israel in the 1950s. His father managed to save Senia and his mother and sister through the war, only to be killed during a robbery in a New York grocery store. Senia, quiet and serious, sometimes visited us. On one of our short trips, Mitzi and Sima took me to see Ivan, the peasant who had hidden Senia and his family for three years.

Ivan and his family, several generations of them, lived in a small wooden house near a neighboring village. The house had three rooms plus a kitchen, and a dirt-floored room for the animals. There was electricity, represented by a bare light bulb in each room and a sewing machine in one corner. All the beds were covered, as is the custom, with large featherbeds and pillows. Under one, in the living room, lay a box of hatching chicks. Here Ivan lived with his wife Maria, their daughter Mila, a schoolteacher, and her two boys.

During the war, Ivan never revealed to his family that he was hiding Jews. The Nazis had decreed the death penalty for anyone helping Jews; the fewer who knew about these things the better. Senia and his family had lived in a pit not far from the house; he remembers the protective warmth of his father holding him close. Senia's older sister was not so lucky. Given to another peasant for safekeeping, she was turned in to the Nazis within a day.

Toward the end of my visit, Mitzi took me to a field near Pritzka, a large village. The car jolted and swayed as we lurched along the old cobblestone road. We stopped near a small monument capped by a red star. "This is where the Nazis shot all the Jews from these *shtetlekh*," she said. The monument read, *On this spot the barbaric Nazi fascists killed 2000 Soviet citizens.* I looked around. We were in a large cleared area, the forests in the distance. The nearby village, its squat wooden houses arranged around a market square, was a renowned talmudic center before the war, Sima told me. A man approached, riding a bicycle. He stopped at the monument and began chatting with Mitzi's husband. "The last Jew in Pritzka," she whispered to me.

Back at Mitzi's, she showed me some group photos taken at the monument. Every year, relatives and children of the massacred return to the monument and gather for a memorial and reunion. They rent a room in a nearby restaurant, reminisce, sing Yiddish songs. Sometimes it is easy to find a meeting place; sometimes all the banquet rooms are already reserved, and they are forced to crowd into someone's apartment. Hearing about the reunion, I am eager to go. Mitzi's descriptions of the 1930s and its vibrant Yiddish culture haunt me.

## The Reunion

Thirteen years later, I am able to plan a visit to coincide with the reunion on Victory Day, the annual celebration of the end of World War II. Familiar with the ways of the Soviet bureaucracy, I plan far in advance, get the necessary invitations and bring them to the Office for Foreigners. Then I wait. Several months go by. Each time I inquire, some new snag appears. Your relatives need to send another form, they say. But, I reply, they can only get the form from you, according to their visa office. Finally, this logjam is broken.

Then: "How are they related to you, and why do you want to go there anyway?" Naively, I think that my interest in this patriotic holiday will impress them, and I indicate that I want to see the positive side of Soviet life. I am wrong. A sympathetic office worker advises me to invoke the Helsinki accords, with their guarantee of unhampered travel to family members. I get a visa. My visit can begin the day *after* the holiday.

By the time I arrive, only a few celebrants are left. Fearing that Mitzi's apartment is bugged, they take me out to the woods. On the way, they tell about their lives then and now. All were partisans in these very woods, having escaped the nearby Nazi ghetto. All lost family members, buried in the field Mitzi had shown me.

Eager to regale me with tales of their partisan days, they never fail to emphasize the importance of Soviet military aid (and U.S. supplies) in their survival. Sima remembers fixing Studebaker trucks with crude parts fashioned from material found in the forest. Now Sima is a truck driver; his friend Misha drives a taxi in Moscow; Anna, like Mitzi, is a bookkeeper.

We stop and they take me to a small clearing. It is a beautiful sunny day; the white birch trees sway gently in the breeze. I take out my tape recorder and they begin singing Yiddish folk songs, partisan songs, the classic songs of the cigarette seller (*papirosn*), of the orphaned partisan, of the bagel hawker (*bubliki*). This culture, this heritage lives; lacking recognition by the Soviet state, it is transmitted orally, the old-fashioned way. They dedicate their songs to an old partisan comrade, now living in Brooklyn, and ask me to bring the tape to him.

## Death

Seven years had passed since my last visit. We had kept in touch by letters, and when I arrived in Moscow, I called. It is not easy to make long-distance calls, but after several attempts, I got through. Elena, Mitzi's daughter-in-law, answered the phone. "Mitzi is very sick," she said. "She just spent two months in a sanitorium; her heart is bad, and now her lungs are giving out."

Before I could get permission to visit, a telegram came. "Mitzi is dead. Funeral tomorrow." I went to the Office for Foreigners, expecting the usual stonewalling and delays. To my amazement, they had a visa for me in four hours! Although I was not permitted to fly (the nearest airport was in a city not stipulated on the visa), I could take the train (which went *through* that same city).

So once again I was on the train. The long overnight ride gave me time to ponder, to mourn. Mitzi was only 54. Periodically, she spent time in a sanitorium for chronic conditions of one sort or another. During my previous visit, she had shown me strange blotches on her leg and mentioned a heart condition. When I questioned doctor friends at home, they provided few clues. Despite her ailments, Mitzi seemed too young to die. Survivor of the war, of Stalinist excesses, how could she succumb now?

Anna, Mitzi's daughter-in-law, met me at the train station, along with Igor. Embracing me, she said softly, "We must hurry. They've held the funeral for you." The ride was a blur. I sat in the back seat, numb with grief and terror as Igor sped along the two-lane highway, passing cars with abandon. Anna filled in the details, her warm manner soothing my raw nerves.

A crowd of people had already gathered by the time we arrived. I bounded up the stairs to Mitzi's apartment. The door was open, and there in the living room, scene of so many lively gatherings, lay Mitzi in an open coffin, surrounded by Sima, their sons Grisha and Borya, and Borya's wife Elena. The three men were unshaven, their eyes red. I do not know how long they had been sitting there. We embraced and sat silently for a few minutes. Then several friends helped move the coffin, still open, down the stairs and onto a flatbed truck. Followed by a band, and the crowd of mourners, the truck moved slowly through the town, past Mitzi's office, past the park with the empty pedestal, past the marketplace. We walked about a mile before turning at the end of town up a dirt road to the cemetery.

It was the old Russian Orthodox cemetery, now a secular burial ground. A few crosses stood out, but for the most part the stone markers bore no religious symbols. The old Jewish cemetery lay in ruins at another end of town; no Jewish symbols were in evidence here. And this would not be a Jewish funeral; no one here would say Kaddish, at least openly. Instead, in a simple ceremony at the gravesite, two town representatives spoke of Mitzi as a hard worker and productive citizen. Then all who wished filed by to give her one last kiss, and the body was lowered into the ground. The grave was covered with wreaths, and the band played a last mournful song. In my grief at the time, I saw all the wreaths blended together. Only later, in a photo, did I see that the stars on one wreath were not five, but six-pointed.

*Jayne Sorkin*

# Ima

*Ima* (H) Mother

With blue mascara,
and cheeks too rouge,
and weird red hair,
and your planning of past and future meals,
and how velvet is your house,
and your tears over Rosie,
your beautiful Rosie,
living in sin with a drug drunken goy,
Ima you bore me.
Under how many layers of Estée Lauder
did you bury you?

Thirteen and hiding in the Polish forests,
with your mother who limped,
and with your four brothers,
two of whom fought in the underground
until they were hanged in full view
of the jeering peasants
out for a good time.
Do you recall crying,
mama, mama, I'm scared and hungry,
and your mother offering you
all the leaves in the forest,
a grand feast to choose from.
Remember fifteen in Stalin's factory
with the soft puffs of angora,
a warm fog that knotted you
to the sewing machines.
Ten years for being late;
twenty for missing a day
(must have been the same age
when movies, parties, and boys
released me from you).
You at sixteen, keeping vigil all night
at the prison fence
to finally steal a glimpse of him,
in striped pajamas, the only man
you ever loved, led at dawn to the
urinal in a row of thugs,

129

Bolsheviks, murderers, Jews,
politicals lacking proper papers.
And you,
pregnant, on your knees, pleading,
kissing the blond hand of the female
Russian guard:
you are a woman and you must understand
please let him go.
And a year later, there you were,
two teenagers on a frozen Georgian morning,
your feet wrapped in rags,
the only shoes you owned,
carrying your dead infant to the
snow-shrouded Christian cemetery
(was it at that age that I rid myself
of my virginity?)
And then pregnant again,
hollow-cheeked in the Austrian refugee camp,
alone in a tent with dozens of bickering
snoring others,
while he was off searching for his parents.
The Polish natives cried and cried.
Wringing their hands, they told how they
tried to help, how they offered to take
the old folks in at a great risk to their
own lives. All in vain,
the Nazis acted too fast.
What did you see in his face
when he returned?


I followed your dead, infant son,
were you disappointed?
You never let on.
You were there when I woke up,
a child from a bad dream,
snakes, lizards, and scorpions,
and other crawling things,
and you sang that Polish song I loved,
something about a tiny sparrow
nestling on a tall elm tree,
the melody of which I've long since forgotten.

I recall how you hugged me
and laughed,
that girlish laugh,
and how you looked in your long, cotton
flowered dress and auburn hair the time
I planted anemones on the untiled living room floor.
And I recall your voice
on a balmy spring night,
when the breeze from the Eucalyptus tree
could not chase the sands away,
late into the scorching night,
crying with your mother,
when you thought the children were no longer awake:
Mimma Channa, why didn't she run with us?
What beast would shoot an old woman in bed?
and Grandma saying,
in America they murdered the Rosenbergs last night.

Lady, lady with your diamond rings
and smooth mink coat,
American lady, with your blue Buick
and weekly trips to the health spa,
Lady, with your silk dresses
and high heeled shoes,
if only once before I die,
before you die,
I could hear that song once more,
in that now foreign tongue,
something about a tiny sparrow
nestling on a tall elm tree,
the melody of which I've long since forgotten.

# 3. I Am the Present Generation

*Where is America? Is there an America? What is this wilderness in which I'm lost?*

—Anzia Yezierska, "America and I"

*Aishe Berger*

# Nose is a country. . .I am the second generation

*for Emma Eckstein*

Emma Eckstein was a socialist and a writer before she became a patient of Freud's. He diagnosed her as an hysteric because she was prone to emotional outbursts and masturbated frequently. Freud turned Emma over to his colleague Dr. Fleiss, who believed operating on the nose would inhibit sexual desire. Fleiss broke Emma's nose and left a large wad of gauze inside her nasal passage. This "error" wasn't discovered until years later, long after Emma's physical and emotional health was ruined and she was left an invalid.

*"Such a nice girl, you have the map of Israel all over your face."*
*— Woman in fruitstore when I was thirteen*

## I. Rhinoplasty

Nose that hangs on my face like a locket
with a history inside   you kiss
on our once a week date like lovers
in their mid forties
or maybe just my mother who is a lover
in her mid forties who had a nose job
in her mid twenties
the bump
the bumpy roads that troubled my father
the trouble with my father
who liked *zoftig* women
all sides moldable
no bumps on the nose
map of Israel   on the face
map of Israel   on the map
a place on the edge of a deep blue
romantic sea   on the map
a place that keeps shuffling its feet
backward   shrinking
like her nose under gauze

under wraps
under hemorrhage that accidentally
happened when the doctor left
the operating room and didn't
return till the anesthesia was already
loosening to sound
like an avalanche
in preparation
her nose bleeding under that
temporary wrap
a change in the landscape
my mother passes me down
this nation
this unruly semitic landmass on my face

My teeth were always
complimented for their four years
of braces
the rumblings of my jaw as my face
continentally drifted and my nose
grew
not like my mother's which is
like a border with its bone gates
levelled neutral
a passive face my mother's
bumpless smile


## II. Hemorrhage

I think of Emma Eckstein
whose cartilage
was hammered out of her   the ancient
steppes on her face    the long view
of the world flooded
with large quantities of blood

Emma Eckstein who took her hands lovingly
inside her
who perhaps merely rubbed her legs together
in her seat and orgasmed
told she is hysterical

she wants too much in the final analysis
in the final analysis
the nose is inextricably linked
to the clitoris and the need to take hands
to yourself lovingly
is abnormal

Which was then a fresh new word
*abnormal*
the desire to treat oneself with kindness

*Take your hands and put them on your lap*

*Take your nose and put it on inside out*

On the ancient steps
up Emma Eckstein's nose
a man named Fleiss committed

strange unnatural acts in the name of
Psycho therapy
which was then a fresh new word

Emma
Levelled
Neutral
a passive face
a bumpless smile
her hands
jerk
at the thought
of herself
the hammer
reinforced
the hammer


III. Assimilation into the modern world


and the gauze
under my own eyes
black and blue staying
in my house for a week
like sitting *shiva*
fourteen years old
the most important days of my life

My mother promises me
a profile
like Greta Garbo

She used to tell me
my best friend Hilary
was prettier than me

The little Yeshiva boys yelled
that I took all their air up
when I walked down the hall

Then the boys at camp said
they'd kiss me if they could
ever find my lips

My dermatologist pierces
my ears
when I'm ten and advises me
to wear big earrings
it will distract people away
from my face

At eight I learn the word *rhinoplasty*
and it becomes a goal in my future
like becoming the first woman president
or flying to the moon

I am the second generation

Nose is a country where little wooden puppets
tell lies
where paintings of Shylock
are in every hotel lobby
Nose is a country where women have to
walk with their heads down
Where I await my new
modern look
assimilated
deconstructed

## IV. Bridges

The body doesn't let go
of bridges

they expose me to the world after seven days
I expect to be noseless  erased
but I am there    long and sloped
like a mountain after a fierce rain

I am there
the body knows

Mine stopped breathing at the crucial moment
the moment where they smash
bridges
the moment where the enemy
takes over

This time they couldn't finish
what they started
a part of me   revolted
against the gas    they had to
revive me before the last
bone was broken

The suspension of my long
winding bridge where my Jewish soul
still wanders over
the slightly altered terrain

the body knows

My desert nose  my sweet ripe nose    my kosher nose
my zoftig nose my mountain nose    my gentle nose
my moon of nose my sea of nose    my heart pumping
lungs stretching fire of nose    my full bodied
wine of nose    my acres of *sheyne*   *sheyne  meydele*
nose

that you kiss at night

Nose that I put my loving hands on.

# Jewish Food, Jewish Children

1. When you are around them your Jewishness becomes an obsession, a connection, but different from what it is when you are away: what sets you apart; your consciousness. When you are around them your eating becomes an act of hostility, appeasement. But never what it is when you are in your own home: pleasure; nourishment; a meal. Jewish was always on their lips—still is—yet they take it for granted, while you are always asking inside your brain like a tic *is she Jewish   is he Jewish   am I in doing/thinking/believing this just like a Jew?*

Which Jew?

And eating. Always they said in words gestures and just plain food stuck in front of you or cleared away: eat/don't eat   eat/don't eat   eat/don't eat. You have learned to do both when you choose in spite of them, but here in their home in the city half your learning slips off your shoulders like a sweater slung carelessly for momentary warmth. You feel it go and you think *o jesus*—you have lived away from Brooklyn too long.

2. And she is 63 this woman and her husband is ill, some would say senile, and the doctors say dying, never sick a day in his life except such bad colds daddy gets and then 5 years ago it started—blurred vision, forgetting—had the customer given him a 5 or a 10, had he added the tax on already, even the name of his high school—and *food*: crumpling dropping spilling dripping; and missing the toilet when he pees.

She cleans up. All her married life she has cleaned up. For her, for all of them, the future begins to be measured by, *how long does he have?* For him, the future has vanished, he knows and doesn't know, but he has stopped looking ahead, and besides he only ever planned for next season's buying and when to have sales, when to phone "the girls," he would say, the ones who owed on their charges. He would call and urge them to make "small but regular payments," and your whole life when you hear about cheap Jews and Shylock's throbbing pound of flesh, you will think of the blockprinting on 5 x 8 index cards, one for each customer, with the columns drawn in neatly with a ruler, and never a penny interest. He paid the bills promptly in cash, bought little, borrowed nothing, and saved, against old age and no pension he saved, building his future and hers and for the first 18 years of your life, yours, from Brownesville to Flatbush, and finally when you and your sister were long gone, built across the water to Manhattan, the Village, their dream. Where they live now. Where he is dying.

Where the mother is close to everything she loves, films galleries shops gourmet stores Sunday music in the Square, everything she had longed for and taught you to long for, CULTURE meaning Western Europe, highbrow, never the *shtetl*; never Brownesville. So what was the thread that joined him to her, Brownesville to Washington Square?

There was dancing which they both did with grace and in unison, what a couple they made; there was class tension and class attraction, he, to the lady, the pretty one, flashy; she to the one who knew it all, the handsome one, the socialist; but for you, born nearly two months after the camps were opened, one month to the day after Nagasaki, three years before Israel could give the Jews a home, what seemed to join them was pride and horror.

Pride: in the Jews. Einstein was a Jew; Eddie Cantor, Arthur Miller, Sam Levenson, and they talked of Adlai Stevenson in such tones that years later you insist to your soon-to-be ex-husband, *Stevenson was a Jew, wasn't he?* Pride: in the values of the Jews: family Jewish men don't drink (a lie but what did you know? he didn't) we don't bend our knee even to God (so what the gentiles did in church seemed servile). When you took dance classes for 6 months and never thought to mention that your teacher was Black, the mother felt she had achieved something, you didn't understand what. When you walked on your first march, ban the bomb—they told all their friends. And when you went to college, that was the real delight, to get As, to become an intellectual, as they had not, could not. You were their chance, and if you flubbed it when you ate and ate and ate, cut classes and slit your wrists, still you recovered and so did they.

**3.** But before you were young, they were young, there was the depression and there was the war, which these first generation spared American Jews waited out, in fear, in isolation—in Wilmington, Delaware to be exact, where she was pregnant and got screamed at on the bus for causing the war—*you people are so pushy*—and he worked in the shipyard hooking up electrical wire and breathing asbestos that would later cost his life. Was now costing his life.

And the war was the horror, the other thing they shared. You always knew, cannot remember learning. Always to know they killed the Jews. Always to picture bodies with no flesh on them. Always to imagine the thinnest possible soup with grease floating on top. Always to know Nazis were evil incarnate, worse than what Gentiles called the devil, and never to buy German, always to shun the sound of it, so different, they would insist, from Yiddish which the mother did not know and the father rarely spoke but in phrases, tender or humorous, *sheyne meydele, meshugene, yenems hintn iz gut tsu shmaysen* (someone else's behind is good to hit).

But growing up he was law, money, power, the boss, grouchy and pompous because outside the store he was no one but you didn't know that yet and you loved to go to the store with him Friday night, secular *shabes*, in Bay Ridge, selling to gentiles who bought like crazy at Christmas. You would sit on the high stool covered with bright orange vinyl, writing up sales receipts with the carbon paper placed just so. You belonged here with your aunts and cousins and he had to claim you; you were proud and stayed proud until after high school when you jumped class and learned to see him through the eyes of the class you were climbing into. He was no one.

And you were no one too, but from the mother, a vibrant wild girl whose energy and ambition run high in your veins, came the will to be somebody. She herself became the perfect salesgirl in the store—glamorous, gossipy, an eye for the latest thing—the perfect wife at home, though each Saturday when he was at work and she and the daughters were not, she wound up to a frenzy of shrieking, smacking, grabbing clotheshangers and hairbrush, beating you and your sister till the backs of your legs rose in welts and she broke into shame and sobbing, and you would say you were sorry for making her hit so you could get out and go to the movies.

And in between she would work clean and cook. But the food, the food: salmon croquettes, clam cakes, casseroles, cream puffs, sweet and sour meatballs, and then, through the years, as you and your sister left and money was looser, escalating in gourmet finesse, spinach crepes, sole amandine, souffles and vichysoisse and chiffon tarts. O the visits were filled with food.

**4.** And when you call to say you'll be late, driving ten hours down from Maine where you live with your lover in a log cabin, no electricity no running water, and once in a while you cook rice or cabbage soup—when you call to say you'll be late, her first words are *I'll wait dinner*. And when you say no, don't wait, she hedges, and you arrive to a perfect plate of chicken marinated in soy sauce with bean sprouts and corn kept warm and do you want herb dressing or roquefort and the red wine saved special.

Eat eat as fast as your little fork can move. The mother smokes, one after another. You can listen or you can talk. Talk. For him, the sick father who can only sometimes focus, you talk about a book you've been reading about—for a change—the Holocaust. "Daddy, it said at first no one knew, only Hitler and Himmler and a few others," and he comes alive arguing, "6 million Jews, how could they not know?" You try to explain—"But the killing came later, at first it was just hate but not killing, who could imagine such a thing?" Still he insists, "6 million, they knew." For the first time ever you don't try to prove you're right. Besides, he's right too. Keep talking: as long as it's Jewish, he'll stay alert, listening, interrupting, being a know-it-all, forgetting a word or a thread, spilling his coffee, but hanging on for life.

**5.** And the mother cooks and serves. This morning it's raisin bran, she tries to give you a bowl of it while you talk on the phone to your sister and she, jealous, bangs kettle and cups around the kitchen big enough for one. "I only give him half a cup of coffee," she's saying, "whatever I give him he doesn't finish, and he adds half & half like it was going out of style."

You hang up the phone feeling hateful, protective of the sick man referred to always as *he*, as you were never permitted to do, always say *mommy* and *daddy*, so that now you and your sister always, with the luscious taste of conspiracy ask *have you talked to them? what does she say? how is he?* And you wonder, is there a Jewish law you'll discover one day, a Talmudic commentary to explain this prohibition against parental pronouns, maybe a law for each prohibition, a few misplaced commandments preserved in genetic memory—then you would understand who they are, who you are, and why things were forbidden, like spending Sundays with friends instead of family, like eating supper with no potato, or, later, like taking pictures in the 4-for-a-quarter booth with your blouse unbuttoned to show your recently acquired stuffed with tissues bra, for which, when they found the pictures, you were severely smacked.

**6.** From the sofa where you sleep, where you should be clearing away bedding but instead sit lazy, reading yesterday's paper, slightly sick from the mother's cigarette smoke, you hear familiar tones: hers, anger simmering beneath forced sweetness; his, bossy, snappish, *get me my sweater, my coffee, my pills.*

Your guts rumble, stab of pain. In your life, in the cabin with an outhouse, at the campsite where you lived in a tent all summer, when you sleep in the truck pulled over to the side of some back road, you forget how many years you spent wrapped around pain in the sacred room, but here not 24 hours, it sets in and you head for the toilet. You enjoy sitting there—*is anyone in?* they will ask, over and over, him, her, your sister, maybe a guest, and the answer will be the same: *yes, yes.* Your childhood ploy: for comfort, privacy, and revenge, a weapon: against his bossy rules, his heavy worrying presence; a wall: against her tightness, control everything in its place at its time, now we get up now we dress now girls time for supper, she the clock; you, the clock watcher, clenched against compulsiveness learned in this house, the tightness you detest in yourself, you sit on the toilet reading the paper, gut cramping against knowledge you can't afford to feel yet: he is dying and will be in pain. She is rageful, deceitful, and in pain. You are their child.

You're reading an article, a reprint from a journalist who entered the camps in 1945, he talked to a Czech Jew named Helen. She said mothers had been given the choice of staying with their children and getting gassed, or going to work and leaving their children, who would get gassed either way. It got around to the six-year-olds, there were terrible scenes between children and their mothers. One child was so angry that even though her mother changed her mind and stayed, the child still wouldn't talk to her. You, in pain on the toilet, ponder the gesture of staying, the option of leaving; the force of the child's anger.

**7.** And a little while after they eat breakfast, you, having refused the raisin bran, are hungry, go poking around the refrigerator and come up with—pickled herring in cream—"ok if I eat this?" "It was for later," she says, "but ok—maybe I'll have some too, do you want some?" she asks the father, and there you are, the three of you, another meal, onion rolls, sliced tomato, it is delicious. "Honey, your napkin," she says to him, reaching across to straighten the napkin, automatically brushing crumbs from his lap.

She turns to you. "Did I tell you about my party?" she asks. "This summer I had such a party—for spite. Lois had a party and didn't invite us. The only ones she didn't invite. I was furious—not that I think much of her but everyone else was invited. Except us."

The mother lights a cigarette and looks sideways at the father. His head droops forward, he stares at something you can't see. You're angry. You can imagine people are inviting them less these days.

"So," she continues, "at the end of the summer I got an idea to have a party and I invited everyone, and I invited Lois. I got some zucchini artichokes pineapple pieshells mushrooms marzipan"—the list is mouthwatering, endless, but it ends. "And I was so relaxed," she says, "and everyone told me it was perfect, I should open a restaurant, everyone ate till their tongues swelled."

You remember marriage. Cooking. The perfect dinner party, passing the fresh-baked fruit bread again and again, urging everyone to have more, more, till Bob Weed with the glasses and thin dark hair to his shoulders said *no thanks* with an edge in his voice. *Mommy*, you think, *I no longer cook for men, I no longer eat till my tongue swells.*

She brings out coffee and cake, excellent coffee which you pass up—colitis—and Entemann's danish, only fair but you eat it anyway. There is more to the story of the party.

"So when Lois came to say goodbye, I told her, 'Lois, I know you didn't invite me to your party and I just wanted to say, I know it was an oversight and I have no bad feelings and I want you not to have any bad feelings either.' And Lois went 'heh heh'—she's such a jerk." The mother drags on her cigarette.

The father excuses himself and walks crookedly to the bathroom. The mother stands, follows him down the hall, tossing over her shoulder, "But, you know, I didn't want anyone to feel bad."

You sit, touched by her loyalty to him, embarrassed by her spitefulness, her pretense: to shame by being good. Something in this goodness shoves you, the daughter, into guilt: whatever anyone sacrifices, you must swallow. Her words come from your mouth with a certain inevitability as you fetch your lover her vitamins, make her tea, fuss and bother, care for her in that least personal sense of caring, do all this when you are angry because you are angry and then say "I only did it because you said you wanted it," or—better yet—"I made *you* tea even though you always make just for yourself"—don't look at what you earn in your own mind, points for endurance, the sense of worth this gives you: power of the victim, trapped into it, and here at the source where you learned it—

Crash from the bathroom. You run to see. He's pulled over the bathroom shelf, broken the stained glass tissue holder she made last summer, carefully piecing together the blues, the ambers. She's looking at the broken tissue box, not crying but with a thin shake to her voice: "I can make another," she says. Something grabs in your throat. She's locked up with him crashing into peeing on grinding food into disrupting her world, the apartment.

"Go on," you say, "I'll clean up the glass."

You fetch the broom and dust pan. You want your lover here to rock you to tears, release. You're remembering, just before you got in the car to drive down here you drank tea together, huddled close to the stove, and she told you about a man who had fought in the French Resistance, a friend of a friend's. The Nazis tortured his six-year-old daughter. It worked—he betrayed his comrades, the comrades were caught and killed, the fighter and the little girl released. Stunned, you asked, "What was their relationship like after that?" "He left," she tells you, "the daughter was raised by the mother, in England. He went to Barbados and lived alone, he saw no one." You agreed, how could he have stayed to watch her grow, asking, was she worth it, those lives, that betrayal? You had thought him brave not to kill himself, but now you wonder how he lived. Life seems suddenly fragile, like a glass precariously balanced, tumbling and crashing, at least let there be a daughter to sweep it up. Is this my gesture, so slight, fit for the century's last flutter? Daddy, mommy, did they betray themselves, was it for me?

8. And where, you think later, at dinner, was he during the party given to spite Lois? Enjoying the perfect food, the perfect spite? Did he sit in a comfortable chair and eat what she brought him, dripping sauce into his lap, staring vaguely at who knows what: Did he wander puzzled unfocused through the company, sometimes chatting, sometimes so off the wall people would get fidgety, not know how to respond, as for example right now, as the mother goes into rhapsodies about Judith Jamison's dance solo, the father interrupts knowingly—"Didn't I give her a sweater two years ago?"

But this is the last meal of the visit, fish baked with grapefruit and bananas, it is delicious. And time to leave, to drive north, get home by sunrise, but not before ice cream cake. The father puts spoonful after spoonful in his mouth, and so do you, slurping in delight, with two cups of tea, and some thanks that the mother puts the cake back in the freezer instead of leaving it melting on the table for you the daughter to poke at with a fork until there is nothing left.

## Kadia Molodow

קאַדיע מאַלאָדאָװסקי

The best known of all Yiddish women writers, Kadia Molodowsky (1894-1975) was born in Lithuania and spent her early life as a Yiddish teacher in Warsaw. She immigrated to the United States in 1935 and—except for an extended stay in Israel—lived in New York City for the remainder of her life.

As her reputation grew, she came to be called the "First Lady of Yiddish Poetry." Her volumes included Dzike gas (1933), Freydke (1935) and Likht fun dornboym (1965). Extremely versatile, she wrote children's literature, plays and fiction, much of which reflected her concern with 20th-century Jewish history. The play Nokhn got fun midbor (Toward the God of the desert, 1949) and the novel Baym toyer (At the gate, 1967) gave voice to her growing commitment to Zionism. Other fiction included the novel Fun Lublin biz New York (From Lublin to New York, 1942) and the collection A shtub mit zibn fenster (The house with seven windows, 1957).

The latter shows Kadia's awareness of the tensions in American Jewish life. "The Lost Shabes," for example, reflects her observations of assimilation and the abandonment of Yiddish. "Oys" (Gone) describes how the Holocaust profoundly affected American Jews' sense of identity. Other stories—"Di kvin" (The Queen)—depict the materialism of American Jews.

Her tendency was to romanticize European Jews who, she claims in the preface, didn't need interior decorators for their walls, just wanted to know which wall to face when praying. Still, her depiction of ordinary people is remarkable. Her characters never become bigger than life; rather they remain exactly who they are—ordinary and unaware of the large historical currents in which they are caught and which they shape.

—Irena Klepfisz

t Shabes                            דער פֿאַרלאָרענער שבת

*Translated by Irena Klepfisz*

Mrs. Haynes drops in on her neighbor Sore Shapiro at least twice a day. She does it out of the goodness of her heart. She is teaching Sore Shapiro, who is all of two years in the country (dragged herself through Siberia, Japan, and finally reached New York)—she is teaching her how to be a homemaker in America while keeping in mind the role of *vaytaminz*. She sticks her head in the door (she is wearing the red bow which she never removes from her hair) and without any preliminaries begins talking about *vaytaminz*. She speaks with gusto, with heart, as if she were keeping Sore Shapiro alive.

The little red bow in Mrs. Haynes' hair looks alive as if it had swallowed all the vitamins at one time and had become fiery hot.

Mrs. Haynes comes in with her six-year-old daughter Teresa Filipine. While her mother is busy with the theory of vitamins, Teresa Filipine hangs around the kitchen testing the faucets to see if water pours out when they are turned. Every so often Mrs. Haynes calls the child to her.

—Teresa Filipine!—And seeing the child is wet, adds—You good-for-nothing.

—Why call such a small child by such a long name, Mrs. Haynes?

—What's to be done? My mother's name was Toybe Faygl. And it's forbidden to give only half a name. If you do, they say the ghost is disappointed.

Sore Shapiro calls the child by her Yiddish name Toybe Faygele, gives her a prune to eat and teaches her a rhyme:

—Toybe Faygl a girl like a bagel.

The little one repeats the rhyme, nibbles on the prune and laughs.

Teresa Filipine's grandfather calls her Toybe Faygele. He visits them every Friday night and brings her a lollipop, and Teresa Filipine understands that her grandfather and the neighbor Mrs. Shapiro have some connection to Friday night and to her Yiddish name Toybe Faygele.

Sometimes the little one drops in on Mrs. Shapiro by herself without her mother. She knocks on her door, and before anyone asks who's there, she gives her Yiddish name: Toybe Faygele. Sore Shapiro gives her a piece of bread with butter and talks to her in Yiddish, just like her grandfather:

—Eat, Toybe Faygele! Eat! A trifle, all they feed her constantly are *vaytaminz*.

Teresa Filipine sits on a stool and eats simply and with great pleasure. The piece of bread with butter which she eats at Mrs. Shapiro's has also something to do with her Yiddish name, with her grandfather and with Friday nights when her grandfather brings her a lollipop. Teresa Filipine eats obediently and seriously with childlike self-importance.

When her mother looks around and sees that the child has disappeared, she calls

146

out through the open window down into the street:

—Teresa Filipine! *Kam hir*! Where are you, you good-for nothing?

Teresa Filipine hears "good-for-nothing" and knows that her mother is angry. With a sly smile, she places the piece of bread with butter on the table, stops being Toybe Faygele and immediately begins speaking English:

—*Am hir*!—and her small steps click rapidly through the stone corridor.

Mrs. Haynes asks Soreh Shapiro with a friendly reproach:

—*Pliz*, don't give Teresa Filipine bread and butter. What does she get from it? A little bit of *startsh*? The child needs protein.

But Teresa Filipine doesn't know what she needs. When her mother leaves her neighbor's house, the little one slips inside, in an instant reverts to being Toybe Faygele again and finishes eating the piece of bread and butter which she had left on the table. She eats with obedient earnestness down to the very last crumb, as if she were finishing praying.

Friday night Teresa Filipine's mother lights four candles. She puts on velvet slacks, sticks a red handkerchief in the pocket of her white blouse; in the light of the candles the red bow in her hair becomes a flaming yellow. Teresa Filipine stands, looks at her mother's fingers as she lights the candles. Soon her grandfather will come, will give her a lollipop, will call her Toybe Faygele—and that's *shabes*.

One Friday evening after her mother put on her velvet slacks and lit the candles, she told Teresa Filipine that her grandfather was not coming. He is sick and is in the hospital. Teresa Filipine became lonely: without her grandfather, without her grandfather's lollipop, and without her Yiddish name Toybe Faygele, she was left with half a *shabes*. She remembered their neighbor Mrs. Shapiro. She left and knocked on her door looking for the second half of *shabes*.

—Toybe Faygele—she announced even before anyone asked who was knocking.

There werc no candles on Mrs. Shapiro's table. She herself was dressed in a housecoat and not in velvet pants: it was like any othcr day.

—Oh, Toybe Faygele! Come in, Toybe Faygele!

Teresa Filipine stood in the middle of the room and looked around. She walked slowly into the kitchen, took a look at the table, turned around, and feeling dejected, walked towards the door.

What are you looking for, Toybe Faygele?—the neighbor asked her and followed her.

—*Nottink*—Teresa Filipine answered in English.

—So why did you come?

The child didn't answer, moved slowly closer to the exit.

From the other apartment Mrs. Haynes' voice echoed in the summer air:

—Teresa Filipine! *Ver ar u*?—and angrily threw the words good-for-nothing.

It was all like any other weekday.

This time Teresa Filipine did not run to her mother. Her small steps clicked slowly on the stone floor of the corridor. She went down to the floor below, sat down on a stone step and cried.

147

*Marilyn Zuckerman*

# The Melting Pot

Up the worn steps of the Gothic building on Jorolemon Street, covered with ivy like an etching out of the Brontes—clutching my father's hand which is slippery with sweat. An old brass plaque states it is a Female Seminary founded in 1840. Inside it is cool, dark and high-ceilinged. There is an ancient elevator cage, and girls with long blonde hair and wooden clogs fly down a wooden staircase so old the treads are grooved from almost a century of women's feet. At the head of the staircase, a portrait of a thin, elderly lady dressed in the fashion of Victoria's time. Later, I learn it is Harriet Packer, the foundress herself. In a wood-paneled room, carpeted with Persian rugs, a distinguished gentleman of middle years, who looks like a senator, judge or a movie actor made up to be president of the United States, waits for us. My father's hands tremble as we are motioned to stiff high-backed chairs covered with red plush like something I imagine from a church or funeral parlor. This is the first stage of a journey I will take out of the life I have lived for thirteen years. This interview is a test to see whether I can become one of five percent of Jewish girls chosen to move in paths light years away from immigrant grandparents and second generation parents who have never gone beyond the eighth grade. My father, who seemed tall and distinguished to me before, shrunk next to the headmaster, and the voice I waited for every evening and Saturday afternoons became high and thin, quavered, and the visible trembling of his body caused me to duck my head so I wouldn't have to look at him. If he was afraid, how was I to feel before the smooth grandeur of the majestic gentile?

"Remember to say we read *The New York Times*, not *The Daily News*," my father had coached me the night before. It was an unnecessary warning, for he always threw the *News* into the garbage whenever he saw it in the house. Sometimes the young woman who worked for us would bring it with her and leave it around on the kitchen table, and my father coming in for a glass of seltzer would snatch it up before I could glimpse lurid headlines that I would see in any case on the bus or subway, which I was now old enough to take alone. Captions like GIRL'S MANGLED BODY FOUND IN TRUNK or SENATOR'S LOVE NEST REVEALED stared me in the face at every news-stand or on street corners.

"You might also mention we take *The Herald Tribune* from time to time." He knew we couldn't hide the fact we were Democrats. Not keeping the *Tribune* gave that away and marked us as Jews and supporters of Franklin Roosevelt. At Packer I would learn for the first time how much rich *goyim* hated Roosevelt. They referred to him as Rosenfelt or Rosenberg. His wife Eleanor, too, was the butt of many jokes, and I soon began to see her with their eyes. Though I still admired her, I felt the same shame for her that I was now obliged to feel for my family. There she was on the Movietone News, descending into mine shafts or squeaking out in upper-class accents a speech about the poor, wearing a fox fur around her stork-like neck — her malocclusion a

148

setup for parody as the Japanese overbite would become several years later, after Pearl Harbor.

But I must have acquitted myself well on the day of the interview, for I was soon in an atmosphere so alien that every morning on the way to Chapel, which everyone was required to attend, I would try desperately to stem juices which would flow from me in a flood as though I were being punished by God for betraying the ancient Hebrew promise to worship no other before Him. Allergy-prone all my life, under stress I could count on a running nose, streaming eyes and sweaty armpits. Fortunately, as high school freshmen we sat upstairs among the younger girls of the elementary grades. All that first year I would sit in the back row, sniffling and red-eyed, hoping I didn't have body odor as well, mumbling words of hymns that everyone else but me knew by heart. And every time Christ was mentioned, my nose ran harder than ever, sometimes even bleeding, and I without a kleenex or hankie as though I never could remember this was going to happen every morning, surreptitiously using the back of my hand or the hem of my cardigan sweater, while down below, seniors and teachers in black academic gowns and mortar boards walked the aisle to processional and recessional, and Dr. Shaeffer, handsome and confident, stood at the lectern, sunlight pouring through stained glass windows on unruffled Anglo-Saxon features of the students, teachers and their guests, as though this chapel were set in a Jane Austen village. Even Catholic girls, Irish and Italian, daughters of politicians and Wall Street lawyers, looked English, and were more part of this scene than I. For every afternoon I would leave the quiet, mannerly streets of Brooklyn Heights with its brownstones and plane trees, sometimes glimpsing interiors foreign to my life in the house of a classmate or saw at one of Dr. Shaeffer's teas the ground floor kitchens and the dining room with glass doors leading to a lovely garden. Inside there were ferns, lace curtains and polished Georgian teasets. Then I would head home on the subway, which became on New Utrecht Avenue an elevated under which the steamy streets were overrun with pushcarts and gaberdined, ear-locked Hasids off to synagogue for evening prayer — to the ethnic neighborhood of my childhood, to Boro Park where I lived in a six-story apartment house. There children skated on the sidewalk and mothers leaned comfortably out window sills, gossiping or calling down:

"Pearl, come up now. Supper's on the table!"

"Ahh it's too early, Ma!"

"Come up already. Your papa has to go back to the store!"

Skate key swinging, Pearl would toss her braids and yell:

"Alright, throw me down the key!"

And I would go upstairs to the four room, fifth story apartment I shared with my parents, my sister and the maid. There the large kitchen was enlivened by a dumb-waiter through which mother would talk to her mother, who lived in the apartment above us with my grandfather. The two women would signal each other to open the door to this convenience by knocking on the iron pipe that brought steam heat from the basement; and then thrusting both their heads, one facing up and the other down, into the dark passage from which ropes hung, they would conduct the business of the day. And if it was Friday, I went upstairs to grandmother's for the Sabbath meal. Overcome by the smell of roasting chicken, livers frying in rendered chicken fat, I watched preparations for *gefülte* fish — pike and white fish ground in the heavy steel food mill attached to the kitchen counter — and saw potato *latkes* rolled out on the white enamel surface of the table. Later, sucking chicken bones in the shine of candlelight, I listened to adult voices talking in a mixture of Yiddish and English and felt my school life far away as though adrift on an ice floe or like a movie plot happening to someone else. Returning Monday morning on the subway, switching at De Kalb Avenue from the Boro Park train to one that brought from a fancier part of the world a Packer classmate, Patricia Dean, blonde and haughty, who, even though we once clung to the same pole in a rush-hour subway and were flung against each other over and over again, never looked at me but stared over my head at advertising posters, the ceiling fan and other passengers.

So I learned to slice my life in half; to become the archcritic of my family; to betray and disown them at every turn. Yet I was only continuing what had been done in a different way by my mother's father, who had gone from pushcart to world tours, from driving a brewer's wagon to seats at Metropolitan Opera, from *Der Forverts* (which he still read) to the Harvard Five Foot Shelf.

For me the process of joining the other side occurred in small stages until it was perfect, and I lived in my parents' house as if they were holding me for ransom. First I sang the hymns, learned the words, said the Lord's Prayer, listened with head high though shuddering inside when Dr. Schaeffer retold the Easter story — tuning out the meaning of the words until the only significance they had was that I was at last a member of an elite band. Then dressed in dyed brown Dr. Denton long johns with a night cap on my head, I sang Christmas carols on the balcony of the main branch of The Brooklyn Bank for Savings at Prospect Park, my voice ringing out with abandon, able to enjoy Christmas for the first time, remembering with resentment how once a little Christmas tree which the woman who worked for us tried to smuggle into our house found its way into the same garbage can where *The Daily News* had been flung.

Soon I was a member of a small gang. My friends had names I loved to taste on my tongue, Polly Prince, Maryanne Maguire, Molly Horton, and Grace Van Deverre. We ate lunch together, taught each other to jitterbug, went horseback riding and ice skating after school. And if I was never asked to the dances at Poly Prep, our brother school, I was happy to walk arm-in-arm with Maryanne around the garden blooming with magnolias in the spring and didn't try to push my luck.

One day after skating at the Brooklyn Ice Palace, I stopped for hot chocolate with a new acquaintance, an older girl for whom I felt a great deal of awe. At first I was proud she had chosen me for confidences which turned out to be petty gossip about her classmates — who had boy friends at Poly, who brown-nosed the teachers and got good marks. According to her only something sly won good academic standing. Finally she said:

"You think all those *yids* are so smart? They cheat. That's how come most are on the headmaster's list. You should see fat, pimply-faced, hook-nosed Barbara Weiss pull cribs out of her shirt sleeves." Then she turned to me, "You don't have any kike friends, do you?"

I thought fast. Was my face red? She was looking hard at me, and I wondered what she knew and what her question really meant. My father's father, who, God knows, looked like the orthodox Jew he was, had been assigned a neutral name at Ellis Island by an impatient immigration officer. However, at Packer the rumor-mongers were as thorough as the FBI, so perhaps she was testing me. My heart was beating hard and I was in the total panic that always took over at such moments leaving me unable to think. Finally a small "no" struggled out. It was slow in coming but it was said, and before she could see my hands shake, I got up hurriedly and in a voice that trembled, said, "I have got to go now."

A year later the whole family moved to Flatbush. Life was more decorous now. Gone were the Hasids, women shouting out windows, pushcarts and the thunderous el. What we received in exchange was a more neutral setting. Now everyone was cut off from a part of themselves — mother, father, grandfather, grandmother. But I, at least, was better off, for several of my friends from school lived nearby.

One night Molly and I were walking down the street bumping into each other, saying boys names aloud:

"Allen!" I said. Molly giggled.

She said, "Frank!" and I giggled.

When it was my turn again, I said, "George!" She looked at me with disdain, "Don't be ridiculous."

Then I saw them far down the street. My grandfather, the ex-brewer who had never learned to speak unaccented English, and she, an obviously Jewish old lady. He was ill now, bowed and slow, but still dapper, swinging an elegant malacca cane, tenderly steering the woman by her elbow. They swayed together and I tugged at Molly's arm.

"Quick," I shouted, "let's cross the street."

"What?"

"Come on!" I dragged her by the arm diving out of the way of a passing truck.

"What's the matter with you?" She was sullen and shaking.

"That sweater, see! Isn't it sweet!"

And as we stood in the semi-dark tiled lobby of the U-shaped store, safe from two pairs of mild blue eyes, I had a flash of memory: I was six and the old people, younger then, had taken me to the Ritz Carleton in Atlantic City for the holidays. I was staring into a silver teapot, saw my distorted face like a chipmunk's, tiny eyes topped by a huge polka dot bow over a sausage body encased in my black velvet dress with a white lace collar. My grandfather pinched my cheek gently, the light from chandeliers striking off his pince-nez. "*Sheyne meydele*," he said, " *sheyne meydele* , my beautiful girl."

151

*Elinor Spielberg*

# Tall and Proud as a Czarina

After wanting a horse for twenty-five years and finally getting one, I still keep having the Long Island nightmare of my childhood: Just as I jump onto a restless stallion to gallop away, he turns into a hamster.

When at last I convinced myself I was no longer five years old, that I lived in New England, and would not find myself squashing a bewitched rodent, I rode my horse down into the village.

I looked horsey enough, I figured. No one would know I was wearing Sandra's jodhpurs and Julia's old velvet hardhat and that my boots cost thirty dollars at a close-out sale from a petshop that had carried riding apparel in its better days. I didn't even pay for the boots. They were a birthday present.

The fancy saddle I sat on, worth 600 dollars, was donated by another friend. Her great grandmother, Elizabeth Downing Fitch (herself an excellent horsewoman in her day), bribed Caroline with the saddle in 1967 so she would not "run off with those hippies." Caroline gave me the saddle thirteen years later when she was pregnant with Saffron—her third.

My own great grandmother, Toba Lichtblau, had exactly one experience with horses. When she was a girl planting rye in someone else's field, the Austrian army came galloping through and Franz-Josef's mount kicked her in the head.

As I rode my horse into town, I realized how far my family had come: I was its first owner of a registered pleasure horse. If only my great grandmother could see me now, I thought: straight-backed, healthy, riding a stylish mare.

I imagined seeing her stooped little body stepping from the hedgerow, a hooked finger emerging from her shawl as she pointed at us with the delight of recognition. To my shock, as I turned onto Main Street near the Grange Hall, she did.

It was Anna Gittlestein, who, with her KGB nightmares and stomach trouble, comprises the entire Soviet Jewish population of the town.

"Yoo-hoo," she shouted, standing in the road and blocking my way.

"You have horse?"

"Yes."

"Vy not you tell me? Can I touch?"

"Sure."

"You don't have automobile?"

"You know I have a car, Anna, the yellow one."

"You have horse AND car? Vy is this?"

"My car is for work, and I ride the horse for, well—you know, pleasure."

"Pleasure! Oh, hoho! Oh you, in America, such pleasure," she teased, laughing and timidly stroking the mane.

"I should go now, Anna, she's chafing at the bit." I looked down at tiny Anna and felt, suddenly, that I didn't belong up there: that I was, somehow, a traitor. Hadn't I just that morning admired myself in my tight Napoleonic breeches? And as I had unwrapped the boots from their box, didn't these words come out of my mouth: "Oh, darling, I love these high black ones; they have a sort of cossack elegance, don't you think?"

"You not tell me you wery rich," Anna said.

"Because I'm not," I said. "I am *not*. You don't have to be—" How could I explain? Now she asked if she could touch the saddle and took out her eyeglasses.

How could I explain to her that she was kissing the hem of the garments on the wrong person? I could only wish that I had sewn tags with each donor's name onto my apparel and tack. She also was wearing hand-me-downs; not English breeches but a dated, flowery pantsuit, too large. Underneath, weren't our bodies the same type? Small, with strong backs made to bend for long periods of time; to reach the soil easily?

This is ridiculous, I told myself. You are third generation; you have as much a right to own a horse as anyone else. So your great grandmother suffered over a hundred years ago—you should sell your horse and move to the ghetto? Anna's obsequiousness repulsed me.

Then, stroking the smooth leather, she told me a story from her own girlhood that was almost identical with my great grandmother's story. She showed me the scar on her neck. It was not so very long ago.

Towering over her, tall and straight as a czarina, I desired, right then, that the earth would open up. I wished— even more— that the animal's hide would tremble and split, the sky darken, and my horse would turn into a hamster.

*Elinor Spielberg*

153

*Adrienne Cooper*

## About Anna Margolin

אַנאַ מאַרגאָלין

By the time Anna Margolin arrived in America to stay in 1914 at the age of 26, she had already moved from Brest-Litovsk to Konigsburg to Warsaw to Odessa, spent two years in America, returned to Warsaw, married, lived in the Palestine of 1908 and given birth to a child, whom she was forced to leave behind in Tel Aviv. This itinerary doesn't fit the cramped contours we associate with the lives of Jewish women at the turn of the century. But even though Anna Margolin was far from typical, her life and her writing tell us something about the restlessness and dislocation that marked her and many other Jewish women of her time.

She was born Rosa Lebensboim in Brest-Litovsk (Russia) in 1887, the only child of Menakhem, a one-time *hasid* turned Zionist, who worked as a minor government official, and Dvoreh-Leah, the daughter of a religious shopkeeper. Margolin's parents lived in different worlds. Dvoreh-Leah was ill-suited to the cosmopolitan way of life of Menakhem, and he was ashamed of the awkward, unassimilable wife who dressed badly, spoke only Yiddish and rarely left the house. The parents separated and later divorced. Margolin shuttled between them, but lived primarily in Warsaw with her father. He gave her a European education, hiring tutors in German, Hebrew and Russian, making of her the intellectual companion that his wife had not been.

When Margolin was 18, her father moved to break up a love affair by sending her to live with his sister in America. It was in New York that Margolin began writing, at first short stories published in the anarchist Yiddish paper *Freie Arbeiter Shtime* (The Free Voice of Labor). Returning to Warsaw a few years later she married Moshe Stavski, a young Hebrew writer, and left for Palestine, where she gave birth to a son. Unhappy with the taciturn Stavski, desperately lonely and isolated in bleak turn-of-the-century "Little Tel Aviv," she tried to leave Palestine with her child. When Stavski refused to let her take the boy with her, she left alone. She never saw her son again.

Now she returned to America, joined the staff of the Yiddish daily *Der Tog* (The Day) and wrote a weekly women's column. During this period Margolin also began writing the poetry which was published in 1929 in a volume entitled *Lider* (Poems).

Margolin wrote around what Tillie Olsen calls "hidden silences" or "one book silences," publishing journalism for years, then editing a volume of the poetry of others (*Dos yidishe lid in amerike* (The Yiddish Poem in America), 1923). Her own poetic voice emerged in the single volume *Lider*, published when she was 42, and even here the images tell of enforced silence, muffled cries, women mute as statues, "madness closing tenderly over [the] throat". Margolin actually felt the silence, writing desperately in letters of pressure in her throat, obstruction; imagining growths, tumors.

Three years after her book was published, Margolin sealed herself in silence, writing an epitaph that she made her husband promise to engrave on her tombstone:

> She with the cold marble breasts
> And the narrow bright hands
> She wasted her life
> On trash, on nothing.
>
> Maybe she looked for misfortune
> And lusted for the seven knives of pain
> And poured out her life
> On trash, on nothing.
>
> Now she lies with a shattered face.
> Her dishonored soul has quit the cage.
> Passerby, pity her and be still.
> Say nothing.

For the remaining 20 years of her life, Margolin rarely left the house and saw almost no one. She died in 1952 at the age of 65.

*Anna Margolin*

# Poems

*Translated by Adrienne Cooper*

## Full of Night and Weeping

A silence sudden and deep
between us two
like a confused letter
with a greeting of parting
like a sinking ship

A silence without a look
without a touch
full of night and weeping
between us two
as if we ourselves
had locked the gate
to an Eden

## My Ancestors Speak

My ancestors:
Men in satin and velvet
Long gentle pale faces    silk
Fainting, glowing lips,
Thin hands caress the yellowed books,
Deep in the night they speak with God.

And merchants from Leipzig and Danzig
Clean cuffs    the smoke of fine cigars
Gemora jokes    German manners
Their gaze is wise and opaque
Wise and sated.
Don Juans, merchants and seekers after God.
A drunkard,
A couple of converts in Kiev.

My ancestors:
Women like idols draped in diamonds,
Darkened red in Turkish shawls,
Heavy folds of Lyon satin.
But their bodies are weeping willows
and their fingers withered flowers
and in their faded veiled eyes
is dead desire.

And grand ladies in calico and linen,
Big boned and strong and agile
with snide little smiles
with quiet talk and strange silences
In the evenings they show themselves
at the window of the poor house
like statues
and in the dimming eyes
cruel desire.

And a couple
Of whom I am ashamed.

They are all my ancestors
Blood of my blood
And flame of my flame
Dead and living come together
Sorrowful grotesque and big
They go through me as through a darkened house
Go with prayers and curses and moans,
Shake my heart like a copper bell
My tongue beats in my mouth
I don't know my own voice
My ancestors speak.

## Mother earth, well worn, sun washed

Mother earth, well worn, sun washed
Both slave and mistress am I beloved
Out of me, the humble and dejected
You grow, you push your roots through me
And like the blazing stars, like the flame of the sun
In long blind silences I run
Through your roots, in your branches
And half awake and half in a dream
I seek the sky through you.

## Not happy

. . .And people look at me strangely
What am I supposed to do?
I am not happy with my *furnished room*,
I am not happy with anything.

Rocked myself today on the strap in the El
In time with the worn out Jews
The night was black, spirit enslaved.
I am not happy with these nights.

And the days are holy and yellow,
Like verses in an old *sidur*.
Maybe I wouldn't feel so bad
If I didn't dream poems.

*furnished room* is in English in the original

## The Proud Poem

דאָס שטאָלצע ליד

On golden thrones
In towering castles
Sit the queens of life.
Their eyes are hard diamonds,
Their lips ripe pomegranates
And with delicate white hands
They apportion among men
Cups of poison and cups of peace.

אויף גאָלדענע שטולן
אין הויכע פאַלאַצן
זיצן די קעניגינס פון לעבן.
זייערע אויגן זיינען האַרטע בריליאַנטן.
זייערע ליפן זיינען רייפע גראַנאַטן.
און מיט וויסע איידעלע הענט
טיילן זיי צווישן מענער
בעכערס מיט גיפט און בעכערס מיט גליק.

On the fifth floor
On a broken throne
I sit, the queen of words.
And with delicate white fingers
I create a race of men
and women and distracted children
And apportion among them
Cups of poison and cups of peace.

אויפן פינפטן שטאָק
אויף אַ צובראָכענעם שטול
זיץ איך, די קעניגין פון וואָרט.
און מיט וויסע איידעלע פינגער
שאַף איך אַ ראַסע פון מענער,
פון פרויען און פאַרטראַכטע קינדער,
און טייל צווישן זיי
בעכערס מיט גיפט און בעכערס מיט גליק.

## (Untitled)

Don't think that I have changed
Don't let the calm smile fool you
I am the tiger with the look of a dove
I am the dagger in the flower.
        Look out.

מיין ניט, איך האָב זיך געביטן.
דעם רואיקן שמייכל ניט גלויב.
איך בין אַ טיגערין מיטן בליק פון אַ טויב,
איך בין אַ קינזשאַל צווישן בליטן, —
זאָלסט זיך היטן.

The hour comes and is gone
with a smile, a knife, and a rose.
My lips will be sweet and red.
My hand will dance, will fly
and lie tender and big
on our dishonorable death.

אַ שעה קומט און באַלד איז זי אויס —
מיט אַ שמייכל, אַ מעסער, אַ רויז.
מיינע ליפן וועלן זיס זיין און רויט.
מיין האַנט וועט אַ טאַנץ טון, אַ פלי טון
און אויף אונזער שענדלאַכן טויט
ליינען זיך צערטלאַך און גרויס.

159

*Irena Klepfisz*

# Fradel Schtok

*Yiddish writer. B. 1890 in Skale, Galicia. Emigrated to New York in 1907. Became known when she introduced the sonnet form into Yiddish poetry. Author of* Erzeylungen *[Stories] (1919), a collection in Yiddish. Switched to English and published* For Musicians Only *(1927). Institutionalized and died in a sanitarium around 1930.*

> "Language is the only homeland."
> —Czeslow Milosz


They make it sound easy:  some disjointed
sentences  a few allusions  to
mankind.    But for me  it was not
so simple    more like  trying
to cover the distance    from here
to the corner    or between two sounds.

Think of it:  *heym* and  *home*  the meaning
the same   of course   exactly
but the shift   in vowel    was the ocean
in which I drowned.

I tried.  I did    try.
First held with Yiddish    but you
know  it's hard.   You write   *gas*
and  *street* echoes back.
No resonance.   And—let's face it—
memory falters.
You try to keep track of the difference
like *got* and *god*  or *hoyz* and *house*
but they blur    and you start using
*alley*  when you mean *gesele*  or *avenue*
when it's a *bulevar.*

160

And before you know it
you're on　some alien path
standing　before a brick house
the doorframe　slightly familiar.
Still　you can't place it
exactly.　Passers-by　stop.
Concerned　they speak　but you've
heard　all this　before　the vowels
shifting　up and down　the subtle
change　in the gutteral sounds
and now　it's nothing more
nothing　more　than babble.
And so　you accept it.
You're lost.　This time　you really
don't know　where you are.

Land or sea　the house floats before you.
Perhaps you once sat　at that window
and it was home　and looked out
on that *street* or *gesele*.　Perhaps
it was a dead end　perhaps a short cut.
Perhaps not.
A movement by the door.　They stand there
beckoning　mouths open and close:
*Come in! Come in!*　I understood　it was
a welcome.　*A dank! A dank!*
I said　till I heard the lock
snap　behind me.

161

*Nava Mizrahhi*

# In the "Unlimited Opportunity Land"

In the "unlimited opportunity land"
(I'm talking about the United States)
I find myself being asked so many different
Kind of questions, starting from:
"Does *Nava* mean you came from a Navaho tribe?"
To: "Is *Mizrahhi* your given name?"
Walking in Richmond, California
During the "hostage crisis" in Iran
The one-fourth Iranian blood in me
Stood out. In people's eyes
I could see blame and hatred.
Some of them also asked,
"Are you Iranian?" as if
They wanted to confirm their suspicion.
In the Mission in San Francisco
My Spanish blood stood out
And they talked to me in Spanish.
They got frustrated when I couldn't answer them.
They didn't know that my father
Never shared with me his Ladino culture.

Today I find myself playing puzzle
Trying to put my past together,
To figure out why am I so influenced by American/European culture
Even sometimes questioning myself
Why don't I look white like the others around me—
Forgetting what I look like. . .

# My Life Was Rich

I was born, almost, when this century.
We grew together in sheltered peace.
The key word was "Progress," the favorite
"Civilized." The wings for flying were barely tried.
Nothing really happened. The road was
Boring, straight and quiet ahead.
Everything exciting was only in the books.
I wanted historic times. I dreamed of heroic deeds.
I wanted my life to be rich.


So, the whirlwinds came, one after the other.
They snatched me, swept me, dropped me,
Lost me, — and mine.
I heard the roar of the mobs and the bombs,
The rumble of the guns and the stomach,
The shrieks of mothers, and the bark of hounds.
I knew the orange tongues of fire,
And the vivid red of blood.
The blue sorrow got me and the yellow fear,
The bottomless black, when nobody to find,
And tell to, the stored-up fierce tale.
I was choked-up full. My life was so rich.

Now I, and the century are growing old.
I am tired of all wild colors and noise.
I want in the pale violet quiet
Twilight of the years only news
Of a five-legged lamb, of a girl
Whose hair grew down to her knees,
Of soothsayers, royal romances,
Maybe a lover's suicide now and then,
Who recovers. Of poets, actresses,
Buddhists, nudists, pugilists,
Or a little earthquake, as it seems
It must be, but far-away.
BIG EAR! Now listen! I want newsless news.
History only in the books. I am not restless any more.
I want the straight road. My life is overflown.
No action, please. . .Peace.


(Of course, this serenity is a lie.
A mask in this masquerade
Fitting to mores, custom, etiquette
To wear at the "golden" age.
Why gold, instead of lead?
I really hate that
"Quiet, pale violet twilight,"
It is nothing, but a fading, greying,
Sorry shade of dusk.
Tired of trouble, yes! But no tombquiet either.
I am still alive. Don't tell. . .)

# Elza Frydrych Shatzkin

## 1936–1962

Elza Frydrych Shatzkin was born on December 14, 1936, in Warsaw, Poland. Her parents, Zygmunt and Cyla, were active in the Jewish Labor Bund. After the Warsaw Ghetto was established, the family hid on the Aryan side and ultimately decided to place Elza with a Polish family. Elza was then six and understood that she was a Jew but must always deny it. Until the end of the war, the Jewish underground moved Elza several times to ensure her safety. During one period she was placed in a Catholic orphanage in Prszemysl.

Zygmunt Frydrych was a member of the ZBO (Jewish Fighters Organization) and was the person assigned to go to Treblinka to confirm reports of mass exterminations—reports that many did not believe. He is credited with the verification that Treblinka was indeed an extermination camp. Cyla Frydrych was deported to a camp near Lublin and eventually died at Maidanek. Zygmunt survived the Warsaw Ghetto uprising but was later ambushed and killed along with other resistance fighters in Pludy. In 1945 their collective grave was identified and they were reburied in the Jewish cemetery in Warsaw.

After the war, friends of the Frydrychs reclaimed Elza. The Polish woman who was hiding her refused at first to give her up and Elza herself denied who she was, insisting she was the woman's daughter. The woman was finally bought off and Elza went to live with Drs. Ala and Marek Edelman in Lodz. Later she was sent to Sweden to other DPs who were awaiting visas to the United States. A Bundist couple in Peekskill, New York, agreed to adopt her, and in 1948 Elza left Sweden to live with Helen and Julek Shatzkin.

Outwardly, Elza seemed to adapt well to American life. An excellent student, she was named valedictorian of her high school class. She loved languages, translated Latin poetry into English, wrote her own poetry, and went on to major in American and British literature at Cornell University. The story "Prszemysl" was written during her senior year there and published in the university literary magazine.

But Elza was extremely conflicted about her Jewish identity and never came to terms with her early childhood and the loss of her parents. She committed suicide on October 16, 1962, two months before her 26th birthday.

—Irena Klepfisz

*Elza Frydrych Shatzkin*

# Przemysl—December 1942

Six o'clock. It's six o'clock again, because that bell is ringing. I hate that bell. I am six, and it is six o'clock. That's nice. I must see if Josephine is awake. She is only four. If she doesn't wake up, or if she wets her bed, they will beat me, and maybe her too. They beat everybody, especially if you're little. There is Sister Catherine. She wears that heavy brown dress, long to the floor, that they call a habit. She thinks I don't know that she has hair, just because her head is always covered. But I know. Once, when Josephine was asleep, I peeked behind Sister Catherine's screen. Sister Catherine has long brown hair, but it was wrong for me to see. She brushed it, so long and heavy and brown, and she smiled and looked in the mirror. That's wrong too. She shouldn't have hair, but if she has it, she shouldn't like it. Jesus didn't have long black hair. But if he had had it, he wouldn't smile and look in the mirror when he brushed it. But it was wrong to peek too. And I did another wrong thing. Nobody was anywhere, and I walked behind Sister Catherine's screen, quietly, quietly. Nobody there. Only Sister Catherine's white nighttable and her neat white bed. It was wrong to open a drawer. A green apple in the drawer. It's terrible to be hungry. One big bite, but then I had to slam the drawer and run.

Come, Josephine, now we will wash. Josephine didn't wet her bed again. She cuddles up to me, as if I were her mother. But I am too little. It is breakfast time. I want some more cereal, but I am not big enough. Big girls need lots of food to keep alive. But I thought little girls needed food to grow. Stephanie and Helen are big. They have long braids and they eat a lot. But I think Stephanie wet her bed once.That's silly for a big girl.She must have been very ashamed. She shouldn't get so much to eat.

Sister Margaret gave me more cereal, but I'm not big enough to have more cheese. The sisters are very nice, because they give us food. They have to walk about the city, with big baskets, and ask people to give them food for them and for us. It is called requisition. Some people call it begging, but that is not nice. Once I saw what they eat. They eat better food than we. I saw some jam, but I didn't put my finger in it, because Jesus would see. Besides, my fingers would freeze in the jam, and I would be a statue there, and Sister Agatha would see me.

Today is Saturday. Tonight we take baths, and we get clean shirts. It is not nice to be naked, and we have to keep our dirty shirts on when we take baths, and wash under the shirts.

I dress Josephine, and then it is time to dust the bannister. Then we go to church. We all have the same striped blue cotton church dress. The big girls say they are sacks. We look funny, because there are many of us, and we all wear the same dress. We all wear bangs, because they are easier to comb. I hate bangs.

Why is Sister Agatha mean? She is pretty, but she is mean. Jane had holes in her pants. We all stood in a row, and Jane had to take off her pants, and Sister Agatha beat her with the belt of her habit. Jane cried, because she was ashamed, and because it hurt.

Mother Superior is nice to me. She knows that I am Jewish, and that my name is not really Maria. My name is Hana Stern. It is bad to be Jewish, and I will never tell anybody. All the sisters would die, and I would be killed. I get very good marks in Religion, and I want to have my First Communion, but they won't let me. I hope Mother Superior didn't tell them I was Jewish. Jews use the blood of Christian children for matzohs. My Grandpa was a Jew. He had a long white beard, and he wore a kaftan, like Sister Catherine. He wore a striped shawl and he prayed to God all day. I don't think he would eat that kind of matzohs.

I wish I had my doll. My Daddy brought her. I don't know where they are now. She opened her eyes and said Mama. Once when I had measles, a long time ago, my Daddy came in with his friends. He was a Jew, too, I think. I didn't let them know I was awake, and I stretched and stretched so they could see I was big.

In the little yellow room last year it was dull. Nobody in the other building could know we were Jews. I cried too much, and Mr. Malinowski and my Mama stuffed my mouth with an awful gray handkerchief. He always played dominoes with me and read me stories. He was an old man with a red beard. My Mama said he was a hero.

My Daddy came to see us sometimes. He whistled the Pobudka, and he hugged me and bounced me to the ceiling. My Mama and Mr. Malinowski taught me prayers and to tie shoelaces and to scrape apples the right way. They taught me Our Father, and other special prayers. We say them in chapel every night. It is cold in chapel and I fall asleep. It is pretty. The red light always burns, and a little tiny part of Jesus is always there. When we polish the floor in front of the altar, we polish one side, then kneel, then we polish the other side. That is called genuflect.

I was alone yesterday, and I climbed the stairs higher than ever before. I went to a bathroom only for the Sisters.There was a window and I was high above the city. A train passed, and I heard the long whistle. It made me cry, because nobody loved me, and because there was nobody in the world. I want my Mama and my Daddy. But they are Jews. I hope they didn't die. Probably, if they are not dead, someone will come and take me back to them. It is cold, but I will sleep now. Jesus knows that I love him. He doesn't mind that I am Jewish.

*Teya Schaffer*

# With Love, Lena

Dear Sadie,

It's a long time already and it could be longer since last I wrote but as you can see by the crooked letters I am here again. The arthritis is as usual but better it is to write to Sadie than not, so behind my complaints let it be our secret that my joints uncurl for you.

Sadie, Sadie, am I crazy for writing? After so long what should I tell you? The government gives to the bank, the bank gives to the landlord, and the rent is paid for another month; something's going up in the lot, I don't know what, only that it requires a lot of noise; Mr. Issacson's wife was mugged not two blocks from the hardware and he had a heart attack from it. . .is this what you want to hear? As if you didn't know 9th street.

I got a letter from your Norma: everyone's fine, her Laura's baby is walking already, David is making *aliyah* to Israel this summer. You did well Sadie. Meanwhile life continues. I drink my tea, the Senior Citizens sends up a hot lunch, every bone hurts, you know how it is Sadie.

Sadie. I could write your name for a whole page. What did they say about names? My Joseph, may he rest in peace, would have known: "Lena, the sages tell us that the numbers of a name reveal the fate of its owner." But what did he know of names or numbers, names and numbers all that is left of those he named. Sadie, I don't cry any more for them. Now that you are gone there is no one to receive my tears.

Remember how we cried the first time we cried together like animals, like cows, as if our throats were not designed for emoting, the funny ugly sounds that finally made us laugh. And when we could talk I touched the place where Norma was growing in you and asked, "Sadie why did we never cry for our dead before?" and you said, "Because we refused to water the void." Sarah, my princess. . . .

I pick up the pen again. I am not in the habit of writing anymore and you, you are so finally gone after your bits-and-pieces departure. True the fat from your bones and the hair from your head flew quickly away as if from disaster but the rest. . .a slow dream-like quality to those days and then, suddenly, gone, to the home. . .and your letters, little notes of love encoded in the pages you dictated.

Sadie I am as foolish as you said I'd be. I never told you the truth about your apartment—it's been taken: a family, four of them, poor as poor, crucifix on the wall. I didn't want you to know that you were gone from 9th street. I didn't want to know that I was all that was left of you. One day the new woman put curtains in your window. When I saw them I felt faint like an undergarment had come undone and was sinking down in a pile around my feet — Sadie today nobody reads your mail — remember my princess the day we put up curtains. . .

. . .It was so hot, we stripped to our brassieres and still our breath was short. It was like a movie, wasn't it? The hot day a year before that when you met me on the stairway, my one sleeve rolled up and the other sleeve down, and you said "Excuse me," lightly touching the cloth over the numbers, "Excuse me but I think we can survive differently." And I learned to roll up both sleeves, the way you did, and a year later our bare arms touched hot and sticky with July and we rolled ourselves together — just like that.

It is two days since I've begun this letter. . .well, I won't make excuses, there is no rush. I know it wasn't "just like that" our loving, it had been coming and coming, but when it arrived—it seemed a gift from nowhere, Sadie Nowhere. Shall I call you that? but it is me who feels without a home while you are a spirit, or a scattered aura...or only my memory—SadieSadieSadie according to the teachings of the Mothers of the Dead as long as I can pen your name you will not leave this world, my Sadie, my Princess Sarah....

I'll tell you: in the morning, when I awake, sometimes I am disappointed, but at night before my eyes close I pray for the next day. Remember what we worried? that we would be discovered and shamed, that we would in old age regret and repent... well we outlived those fears. . .Sadie. . .Sadie: there is a reason I write to you. Do you notice my Sarah my gift that I am still here on 9th street? I mean my Sadie that I am still not dead, that I am once again left alive. . .there grows a fist in my throat, a hand squeezes tight about my heart.....I write this letter, I bind you to it with your names Sadie Sarah Princess my gift, I call and hold you by the writing of your names Sadie Sarah because my Princess, my gift, I refuse to water the void.

*Sandra Butler*                    *Barbara Rosenblum*

# Reverberations

We both thought that our joining would represent "coming home." A place to rest where we didn't have to explain everything, where we would be understood, where our samenesses would balance (somehow) our differences. But instead we found that our homes were furnished differently. I found myself living in overheated and overstuffed rooms filled with silent others and unfinished dreams. The mirrors that were to reflect us in each other are cloudy and scratched and we cannot always see where we are going and remember where we have been.

> *I know she will say it's like a mirror, like looking at yourself in a mirror. It is not that way for me. It is more like two diamonds each of which is spinning around. Maybe like a* dreydl *or dice, and I don't know which side will be up when it topples over. Sometimes, only sometimes, does my Jewish or lesbian side match her Jewish or lesbian side. More often, it is a mismatch; my lower class facet faces her maternal side or my spare, tight, conceptual academic side faces her dramatic, flamboyant, emotional side. The same rubbing against, the same reaching out and not connecting, the same as in all other relationships. Is it like coming home? Only sometimes.*

> *But when it is, it is powerful, rich, sustaining, fulfilling. It is a connection of a sort unlike any other. A* mekhaye! *When other girls were reading* Sweet Sixteen *and anticipating their seventeenth summer, I was reading* Mark Twain *and* Thomas Wolfe. *They had imprinted in me the stories of American injustice, the inherent wrongness of slavery and a passionate sense of the possibilities of human freedom. I had learned that*

*being a Jew meant seeing those injustices and doing something about them. My parents first sent me to Hebrew School but I rebelled at once. A year later I was sent to a Jewish cultural school (shule). The teacher was a progressive Jewish man, a survivor, making a living in America by teaching. How I hated it! The room was dark and smelled wet. Not enough electric lighting, one or two bare bulbs on the ceiling. We had to learn Jewish culture and some Yiddish songs. I could not bear the smell. Each day as I passed those I wanted to be my friends in the school playground, the girls laughing together watching the boys play football, I was dressed like a poor immigrant kid in hand-me-downs. We were then still very poor. I wore funny colored leggings and they pointed and laughed at me. That was to shape my sense of myself as an outsider. As marginal. A sense of myself that remains still central.*

It was different in my house. We were scrubbing to erase all traces of the *shtetl*. An elaborate training to be with "my own kind." A search that has taken nearly half my lifetime. Admonitions that still ring in my ears hissed nervously for fear/of fear. Don't holler out the window. Don't draw attention to yourself in a public place. Don't talk with your hands. (The irony now is that one daughter is a dancer and talks with her entire body.) But always it was a struggle to keep balance. Being Jewish but not "too Jewish." Everyone in my suburb was Jewish, of course. We were to go to school together, to temple together, to marry together. But it was all to be muted. Well-behaved. Not to be like those "others." Gangsters, entertainers, shysters, communists, troublemakers. Not our sort.

There was always emphasis on good manners and an admonition about passion of all sorts. Intellectual passion was unseemly for a girl since it might frighten off the smart boys. "It is hard enough to get a boyfriend without being too smart." Words my mother's mother had told her a generation before. The legacy handed down as truths from mother to daughter and again to daughter. Instead the skills valued were those of "drawing the other out." Listening, nodding, smiling, feigning interest in others. Not the impassioned and heated arguments about Poland, Stalin, Israel, the Bolsheviks that she remembers. Never. The rules were lengthy but consistent. Never to interrupt. Never to talk too loudly. Never to be too strident. Never to have a different opinion unless it was couched carefully in a warm smiling voice. Not to be Jewish (in the bad way). I did understand that there was something dangerous about being Jewish, but during the first dozen years of my life, except for muttered conversations abruptly ended when I entered the room about the "camps," I didn't know what it was.

*When I read* The Painted Bird, *I was not shocked. I was not even surprised. These horrendous grotesque stories straight out of the ignorance of the Middle Ages were familiar to me. Did I not grow up hearing about the dumb Polish villagers? My mother laughingly told me how she would ridicule their believing in the sanctified birth of Jesus Christ. "A bastid. They believe in a bastid," she would laugh. Her own syphillitic brother, in the state of paresis and fully delusional, used to roam the streets of the village, talking to ghosts. The villagers laughed at him, the town fool and idiot; they taunted her: "There she goes, the sister of the idiot." When he became unmanageable, my mother remembers, they locked him in the closet where he withered, shriveled and soon died.*

*Is this a story from the 20th century?*
*I remember now another story. When my mother was a girl in her village and someone got sick, you went to a witch, what we would probably call now an herbalist, perhaps a midwife or a barber. They would burn your back with bankes (hot cups), collect odd things and make potions. When I was a young girl and got sick, my back was badly burned with bankes. These were my growing up stories.*

When I was 13, I had a jukebox in our fully decorated "gameroom." I used to listen to the music of Nat "King" Cole and sway with (my boyfriend) a broom, preparing myself for the popularity and social success I hoped was awaiting me.

*When she was 13 and dancing to popular American music, I was 8 and still listening to the Yiddish radio. But I made it. Upward mobility was my way out. My parents wanted the job security of the civil service for me, a postal clerk I should become. But I went up through the City College system in New York, that free university that permitted thousands of first and second generation Jews to become professionals. I did it too.*

*Often the difference between us is expressed through food. I order fancy wines, exotic cuisines. It is a way of marking how far I have come. We ate poor. Jewish people's poor food: chicken feet stew, beef, lung and heart soup. And pitcha: calf's foot jelly smeared on rye bread with a piece of garlic and shmalts was often supper. Beef flanken soup packed with bones. When she is out of town on business, I buy a bag of bones in the supermarket and make soup. I call my mother and tell her I made soup. She seems pleased. I still remember the first time I had steak. I was eleven years old. It was a sign we were beginning to become more American. Beginning to assimilate. Steak.*

We did not eat with our fingers. We did not talk with our mouths full. We did not have "seconds" until all our "firsts" were eaten. We ate roast beef, steak, lamb chops and mashed potatoes. Every Sunday we went to the Abner Wheeler House for dinner after my mother finished listening to Milton Cross and the opera. I always ordered roast beef and popovers.

172

My brother had steak and mashed potatoes. My mother had breast of chicken, very well done and with the skin removed please. My father drank and nibbled at whatever was put before him. WASP food. A WASP restaurant. One Sunday my brother loudly told us about the woman at the adjoining table who had a noticeable moustache. Horrified, my mother muttered that now the entire restaurant was staring at us. We were drawing attention to ourselves. Now, thirty years later, I know that we were the only Jews in the restaurant all those Sundays. We sat and were careful not to spill, not to talk too loudly, not to make "them" stare at us. The outsiders. The unwelcome ones. I still don't know why we always went.

And smells — another admonition of my middle-class Jewish catechism. There was always airwick on the counter, fans spinning, windows open to remove "smells" of cooking. A house that smells of cooking is a poor house, I was repeatedly told. I remember my grandmother's apartment lobby and hallway being the best smelling place in the world to me. Welcoming, thickly textured smells all mingling: cabbage, beets, potted meat, baking bread. I didn't understand why fresh air was nearly as good. Oilcloth I didn't have to worry about spilling on. No lace cloths, no centerpieces unless you counted the bits and pieces of projects she was always beginning. Snippets of crepe paper, bits of wire, pots of paste all jumbled in a clutter that drew me. I remember once realizing delightedly that she probably never even dusted! And now when I step off the elevator to visit my lover's family who live on the 22nd floor (not in a private home), the smells surround me again. The same smell of my grandmother's lobby. The smell that welcomes. The house full of food and smells and the house that welcomes.

Entering her parents' house I see the walls filled with *shtetl* pictures, memories of the loss of a way of life. A home with history in it. Books about the Holocaust. Stories still to be repeated. To be remembered. For me, the Holocaust was an intellectual and emotional immersion into a period of my history that served as a guide for me in formulating my moral, ethical and political posture in the world. A way to understand what it is, what it means to be a Jew. What the nature of evil is. What the imminent dangers are. What my relationship to the state of Israel, that "sorry miracle," has become. It was an immersion that was both connection and warning. Work that led me directly to engage in the political issues of my own decades. School busing. Civil rights. Vietnam. A sense of the urgency of a principled life. It was a period of heightening the sense of myself as "other." As outsider. As hated Jew. (Not yet woman.) And understanding that even if the *goyim* saw me as a troublemaker, a

173

Zionist scourge, a dirty, aggressive, shrill kike. . . I began to see myself in community with other Jews and a sense of pride emerged. Those of us actively involved in political work during the 60's were the bearers of the torch of freedom and righteousness with other oppressed people. I was an oppressed person. It was a huge leap from the well-behaved, well-modulated young girl. My immersion in the Holocaust was the beginning of my bonding with all Jews.

> I know there are many ways to understand the Holocaust but they all come down to one of two ways: from the outside and from the inside. How come an American Jew like me looks at it (and feels justified to look at it) from the inside? It wasn't until I was in my 30's that I could look at it from the outside, in terms of scholarship, of genocide, or the origins of totalitarianism. Most of my life, I saw it from the inside, from my family, hearing the stories of those who had survived. In the early 50's, my mother spent almost all of her time in the courthouse, signing sworn statements about the character of all her relatives who were coming to America. One by one, I met them. Emaciated bodies, toothless mouths, metal teeth. I met each one as they came through our house. I went to the beach with them and saw their scarred bodies, Hitler's experiments. One uncle had no ribs on one side of his body. It was an experiment so the German doctors could see how someone might live without ribs. Another woman had no insides. They excavated the flesh of my living relatives. They wrote numbers on their arms. I met each one and learned their stories. Who among them did not almost die. And saw their families die?

> Each morning before leaving for school, I heard the announcements on the Yiddish radio. A man, Moishe Schwartz from the town of Czecknova, has just arrived. Does anyone remember him? Does anyone know someone from his village? Does he have any living relatives? If you know, please call the radio station. Can anyone please locate a lantsman for Mr. Schwartz? Tombstones of the living on the airwaves.

And together we go now to Sh'aar Za'av. A congregation in San Francisco for homosexual Jews. We attend the Rosh Hashonah services eagerly without knowing exactly what to expect. Only knowing that a conservative and traditional temple has no room for us. There is no place for us to pray together, to be in community with Jews together. We go hoping that this place will be another dimension of our coming home. And as we enter the basketball court of a community center where the services are to be held, there is good feeling. We see many we know. Separately and as a couple. We are greeted, hugged, we smile, nod, acknowledge, squeeze hands and lower ourselves into the folding chairs with a sense of possibility. Perhaps a resting place.

*After my grandmother died, I went to services every year but felt so alien in those elegant surroundings, velour seats, well-dressed congregations. I go now with eagerness. A place. The pulse of excitement animates the spare room. "How nice to see you here." "Take my new phone number." "Call me soon, so we can catch up." Shhh. Sha shtil. The service begins. I look around feeling something is wrong. This group is too young. Where are the old ones? The bobes and the zeydes, the tantes and uncles, the cousins? Where are the children shifting around impatiently? This is no shul. The illusion cannot be sustained. There are too many blondes. Too many goyim. Some even sit and watch as we rise for responsive reading. "Get out you goyim," I hiss to myself. "Get out. You don't belong here. I don't want you here." I ache with disappointment. Where do I go to say the prayer for my grandmother?*

I sit alongside her and hear the voice of my grandmother. "Give a little. Take a little. Before you know it, it all evens out." It is just what I need to do to find a place here. Our grandmothers are both so present. Not dear and departed, but alongside us in our lives. But my temple had an organ, a choir, maroon upholstered seats, donated prayer books with inscriptions "in the memory of" carefully typed inside. Not the poorly xeroxed sheets I hold in my hand. But was the congregation of Temple Ohabei Shalom "my own kind"? Are they in this room now? Why does it still all feel so alien? There are moments when I feel full of the possibility of this new experiment. But then the sense of marginality intrudes. A room full of 30ish queers and many with their gentile lovers. Do these people carry the ghosts of the murdered dead with the same urgency? I know that just beyond this small room is a world that hates us. Hates me. As a Jew. As a woman. As a queer. And I know that finally there is no safety except that which we provide for ourselves and each other. And the fragility of it overwhelms me in this moment.

*For me, I suppose, there has always been the loss. My mother thinks she is lucky because she lives in an apartment with indoor hot and cold running water. She never feels safe and has a recurring dream that she will have no place to sleep at night and awakens with the same terrified feeling she had as a girl. So there is nothing more to lose. Just to continue to regain. Recapture. Build. And always understand we live on the margin. Always.*

*And as we walk the streets of San Francisco together we see many of the same things. While we each come to this moment with so many differences, we see so much of the same thing. Hardships etched into a*

175

*face. A child looking frightened. A mother trembling with frustration. A window advertising Irish sweaters decorated with sacks of rotten potatoes. Bag ladies. Those who are alone. Marginal, lost, anxious, angry. We turn to each other and silently acknowledge that "Yes. I see. Yes. We are them too. Yes." It is a very big consolation in a very disorderly world.*

We have become mother, lover, friend, confidante, partner, playmate, it is too much. And yet, beyond each other is the danger. We use each other to represent our "own kind." There is always the sense of thin ice upon which we walk as confidently as we can, holdng tightly to each other's hand.

We ease the passage for each other now. I steer her through the labyrinth of social rules I have memorized since girlhood. She is patient with me in my intellectual hungers. We open doors for each other and allow our arms to circle the other's waist. Just for a moment. I am here with you. Don't worry. I'm on your side. It isn't finally coming home but making the home we always hungered for.

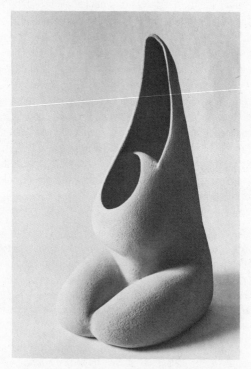

*Sculpture by Tania Kravath*     Photo by Yonah

# 4. Lot's Wife Revisited

Savina Teubal

Julie Greenberg

Judy Freespirit

Ellen Garvey

Jyl Felman with Janet Burstein

Bernice Mennis

Elana Dykewomon

*Sarika Talve dancing at granddaughter's wedding, 1983*

# Sarika

Sarika saved my life when I was a baby. I loved to ask my grandmother, "Tell me the story of when you saved my life," because she would always answer, "It was God who saved your life." Her humility and strong Jewish faith became a part of me at a very young age and shaped the life of the person that I would become.

Sarika had the most beautiful smooth olive skin one could imagine. Her first wrinkle didn't appear until after her seventieth birthday. Her granddaughters always wanted to know the secret of her beautiful skin. When she was in a serioud mood, and when she knew that we were serious, she would say it was because of the waters in her town outside Salonica, near Drama. My grandmother was a Sephardic woman, and she spoke of the well in her town and the crystal-clear pure water with which she began her life. Then she would look at us and say, "You know, all beginnings are important," as if to suggest that those waters were connected to her faith.

We would sit many hours in her apartment in Brooklyn fighting over whose turn it was to braid her long dark hair, and she would tell us story after story of her life before she came to this country. One of my favorite stories took place just before the sabbath in the small town near Drama. Sarika (a name that means "little Sara") and a bunch of her girlfriends were collecting flowers in the village square, when a handsome cavalier named Sabbatai came into town. All the girls were looking at him and he was looking at all the girls. Each young girl held out a flower for Sabbatai to smell. "Ah," she would say, and as she reenacted the scene the room would fill with fragrance. He smelled each one, throwing them aside until, of course, he reached Sarika, who held the sweetest of them all.

She took him home, and they celebrated *shabat* together. Even though he was a Turk and she a Greek, their common Sephardic heritage linked them. They married and their families were happy. They had a beautiful child called Reina, after Sarika's mother. But this was right before World War I and my grandfather was a merchant. He traveled around

179

o know that it was time to leave, so he gathered what he could and raised the ary fare to book passage for his young wife and their infant daughter to journey with any others to America. With a pain in her heart that I'm sure she never lost for leaving r mother and her sisters, Sarika boarded the boat with Sabbatai and arrived like hundreds of thousands of others at Ellis Island.

In America they got off the boat with their clothes and one pair of *shabat* candlesticks that they had managed not to trade for a little more shelter for their child, or a little more clean water to bathe with. They changed their names from Sarika and Sabbatai to Sara and Sam. They birthed seven children on the kitchen table, accumulated fifteen grandchildren and fourteen (we're still counting) great grandchildren. They were proud to be in America, but there was always that sadness in Sarika's stories because, looking back, she remembered that they were the only ones of their large extended families who survived World Wars I and II.

From Ellis Island and Eldridge Street on the Lower East Side they made the big move to Brooklyn. My grandmother lived in the same neighborhood for sixty years and never really had to learn English because her Ladino, the Spanish language of the Sephardic Jews, was always understood at the grocery store downstairs, even as the neighborhood changed from Sephardic to Puerto Rican to Cuban. You would enter her apartment and feel like you were in a different world. The smells were different. The music was different. The movement was different. Somehow her grandaughter, this Jewish girl from the suburbs of Westchester County, felt more at home in her grandmother's apartment than anywhere else.

I don't think my grandparents ever really understood my becoming a rabbi. I was, however, the only one of all the children and grandchildren that my grandmother would call every Friday night just before the sabbath would start. At the time I thought that this was because she knew it was also a sacred time for me, something that she and I shared. Now I think the real reason she called was to make sure that I didn't forget that it was *shabat*. I mean, I was a rabbi—wouldn't that be awful!

But the time she really tested me was when she was dying in a New York hospital. I lived across town. Every day I took the bus to bring her a kosher Sephardic meal because she wouldn't eat the hopital food: it was "poisoned." I cooked for her, brought her food, and fed her for more than a month. Then one night she was like a frail bird, so close to death. I really didn't want to leave. I stayed later than usual and then went home. Later the call came. "Come quickly, come quickly, she's asking for you." I ran all the way. I wanted to be with her. I wanted to hold her as she left this world. I wanted to say goodbye.

When I arrived she was sitting up in bed. All the doctors and nurses were standing around her with their mouths open in amazement. Sarika was putting red ribbons in her hair and giving orders just like the old "Nona" we all knew. "Ah, Suzika," (that's what she called me) "get me a rabbi."

I said, "Nona, I am a rabbi."

She laughed. You should have seen her. Red ribbons in her hair to keep the evil spirits away. Red, from the red of the earth of Lilith's hair.

She said, "Your grandfather, Sabbatai, he came to me during the night. Was he handsome! He was all dressed up. He said, 'Sara, I'm not ready for you yet. Get well. I'm having too good a time.'"

Whatever it was, my grandmother lived ten more years.

Just before my grandmother died, I brought my three-month-old daughter, Sarika, to meet her. They lay together side by side on a couch. My grandmother, losing her ability to move around but still with that glint in her eye, well past ninety, looked at this little Sarika lying next to her and said, "This is what I lived for." And then she said, "Remember Sara of the Bible? She was ninety when she had her child. This one is mine, anything is possible...."

I do all the life-cycle events in my family. It's just easier to call me for weddings, Bar/Bas Mitzvot, baby namings, whatever. They call me. I'm cheap. I do them. I know what to say, what not to say. It's easy. But when it came to my grandmother's funeral, they wanted a "real" rabbi to say Kaddish. The Kaddish prayer is a prayer we say for the dead. Traditionally a woman does not say the Kaddish prayer in public. (One reason given is that she might humiliate the men. If a woman is saying the Kaddish, you might think it's because no man is able to.)

My father insisted that I do the eulogy because no one knew my grandmother like I did. No one loved her quite the same way, and I think everyone knew that. But when it came to the Kaddish, they hired an orthodox rabbi to come and do what was really important. I gave the eulogy and stepped away for the Orthodox rabbi to come up and read the Kaddish prayer. Instead, I saw that he was standing there with tears in his eyes. He nodded to me to continue. His heart had been opened by a tradition that is meant to be loving and inclusive, a tradition that is meant to open hearts and minds, not close them. And both with tears in our eyes, for this woman who had pushed our tradition to its best, perhaps just for this moment, he followed as I led the Kaddish for Sara Aruest Talve, the daughter of Yitshak and Reina. A.id we cried together for this woman, who for just that moment changed the world a little bit.

Then her children, grandchildren, and great grandchildren—who really are more American than anything else, I must say—for that moment remembered not that they were the children of Sara and Sam but that they were the *people* of Sarika and Sabbatai. And for the very last time we all gathered around my grandmother and sang to her together her favorite lullaby...

*Duerme duerme mi alma donzella*
*Duerme duerme sin ansia y dolor*
*Duerme duerme sin ansia y dolor*

Sleep, sleep my sweet soul, sleep without worry or pain
Sleep now and be at peace.

*Enid Dame*

# Lot's Wife Revisited

It is said that Idith, Lot's wife, distressed at the fate of his . . . daughters, looked back to see whether they followed. Her body, a tall pillar of salt, still stands at Sodom. Though every day cattle lick the salt off until nothing is left but the feet, by night the pillar is always miraculously restored.

Robert Graves and Raphael Patai, *Hebrew Myths: the Book of Genesis*

Every morning
cows lick me
down to the nub.
Every night
I grow myself back

into shape.
I'm a starfish:
I can replace missing parts!
a talent I wish I'd developed
in that other world.

My oldest daughter
was killed by the State
for feeding a hungry man.
That was a city of rules.
Every rule
had a knife thrust behind it.
Every stranger carried
an enemy's face.

Now
an overgrown girl visits me,
stringy-haired and distraught,
dirty tears stuck to her face.
She carries a sticky child.
"Please forgive me," she sobs,
and, "Give me a message."

I've got no message.
I'm not a prophet.
I'm simply a woman
who slid
away from the world of men:

their night sweats, their rules,
their contradictory lusts.
their problematical gods.
Their rituals
of mating and torture

mean nothing at all
to a rock.

Every morning
cows scrub me down
with damp washrag tongues.
I reappear
in thousands of buckets of milk,
in the bones
of thousands of years of children.

This
is immortality: a gift
I never prayed to achieve.
Yet I know
I carry it off
rather well.

*Enid Dame*

# Ms. Lot Makes a Political Statement

I saw
a city eaten by fire: first
the shower of searing rain,
people crowding the pools
for a last taste of water, of blood,
or dying choked in their bathtubs;   then
the explosion of flowers,
promiscuous
lilies and orchids  speckled
multiplying like cancers,
littering doorways;
finally ashes
a scar on the desert.

That's when
I stopped fooling myself
about men and their gods.

A city of stories chopped
off in the middle,
the characters stand in my mind
like tableaux in a wax museum:
that dreamy young girl
pulling the fingers off daisies
will never find out if "he" loved her,
that mother
will never meet
the person her son might grow into;
that bitter old woman
casting a spell on her landlord
won't know
if it worked.

That city
was stupid and ugly
and hard on its women  but
it cradled my world  many worlds
as a basin of water
holds millions of lives
in each drop.

Today,
I don't get around much.
I'm not political.  Yet
all about me
technology mumbles.
I know what I know.

That was
a city.
This is
a planet.
I can't say I care much for progress.

Having outlived
husband and daughters and neighbors
I've got
little to say.  Soon
I'll know the ending
to everyone's story.

*Enid Dame*

# Vildeh Chaya

The day before her hairdresser appointment, my mother says, "By now I must look like a *Vildeh Chaya*. Neither of us knows that this Yiddish phrase means "wild animal." I imagine it is the name of a woman: wild Chaya. I imagine her in various incarnations.

1.

Vildeh Chaya
in the woods   on the edge
of the shtetl   she hides
mud-splattered   dress torn
barefoot   she won't
peel potatoes   get married
cut her hair off   have children
keep the milk dishes
separate
from the meat dishes.

Instead, she
climbs trees   talks to animals
naked   sings half-crazy
songs to the moon.

2.

Vildeh Chaya
in New York
in the sexual 'sixties
lives in a tenement
toilet in hall
wallposters   cats   dirty sheets
learns to say "Fuck"
sleeps with men   she meets
at peace demonstrations

later, she
cuts off her hair
sleeps with women
writes poetry

3.

Vildeh Chaya
in the suburbs   lives alone
on Social Security
afraid of
her floor-length drapes
her glass-topped tables
the color television

her daughter's married
an Orthodox Jew
her son's hitch-hiked
off the edge of the world

she hides when
the mailman knocks
keeps missing
hairdresser appointments

at night, she creeps
around the development
avoiding swimming pools
the glare of headlights

she's starting to worry
she's starting to
like her smells

# Manna from Heaven

It came to me. I was wandering and it came to me. It fell from the sky. I was hungry. Go on, show me a Jew who denies being hungry for safety and rest and I'll show you a liar. Show me a woman, show me — well, that's not the point.

I was wandering, as I said, but not quite as alone as I like to think. There were hundreds of us. Sometimes I could not see them. Sometimes we were separated for months. It's a long time in the desert. And we did not all enter the journey equal. Not every one of us was a slave mixing mortar in the heat. Some of us were — were what? Were supported by the labor of others. Someone was Moses, someone else a priest, and someone else a priest's daughter. Maybe. It's hard to remember Egypt. Hard to want to.

We've been out here in the wilderness such a long time, traveling in circles. It seems.

So. I was trying to tell you. I did know where everyone was, I just didn't want to be with them. Everyone was so hungry, discouraged, cranky and hot. I just wanted to be alone. My friend wanted me to stay with her, she was sick and frightened. But I said, "There are others here, ask them." I went off on my own. I knew I had hurt her, that maybe we would not be friends anymore, but I was so hot and tired of everyone complaining, of everyone needing something they didn't have. Tired of my own complaints as well. I said, "I don't care," and I left.

But I did care. I was alone and I was wandering. I stopped on a rock that jutted out from the path and looked over a dry canyon. It was just before sunset and my cheeks were burning from exertion, heat and pain.

It was against my cheek I felt it. As if a bird had brushed me. But there were no birds. I moved to touch it — it was a kind of sticky substance clinging to my fingers — and suddenly there was a breeze. The breeze was full of this substance, like a pollen, but there no flowers. I tasted it, and it was sweet. I ate it until I was full. I had pockets in my robe and I threw out all my rocks and stuffed my pockets.

I would like to say I went back — at least to my friend — and shared what was in my pockets with her. But I used it to stay away three more nights.

And you would like to believe that at that moment the manna came to everyone, as it came to me. But it didn't.

It came to us all about a year later, and I never could tell anyone I had tasted it before.

1984

*Ellen Gruber Garvey*

# How Is This Week Different?

## New York City Transit Strike: Spring, 1980

Everyone is hoping to leave the office early: in a rush to get home for the Passover holiday, or just anticipating heavy traffic as the transit strike begins. The office manager paces along the rows of desks and whips around corners, checking to see that we're all still at our typewriters.

We'll never get done in time to leave early anyway; they've given us twice as many letters to type, though the office is out of white-out and carbon paper. And besides, we're in the middle of our break. We haven't even finished eating.

Behold the danish of our affliction, which our foremothers bought every morning at the coffee cart to solace themselves when they had been pulled too soon from their beds, their first-born dreams taken from them and drowned in the second of the ritual four cups of coffee.

The office manager listens to the radio news, scratching his scalp. He's worried that we'll be marooned here by the transit strike, sleeping on the floor under our desks like wild animals. Then he'd be stuck here too, with the city dark all around and nothing to drink but the washroom's rusty red tap water.

The elevator brings corporate officers to our floor to drive us from our work stations. Management now doubts that the air conditioning system will keep out locusts.

"Out," the office manager rasps. He has a frog in his throat. "Please leave now. We're closing up." We can't be sure whether to believe him. The decision is terrifying: if we go now, we may never be able to return. But if we delay, we may never be able to leave.

We approach the red-carpeted reception area. The strike starts. We are safe across. The office door shuts behind us.

But their hearts have been hardened. The office manager calls us at home from work. "How are you getting in?" he asks. "Can we put you in a car pool? Do you have a bicycle? When will you be in?"

We won't be. With a mighty hand and an outstretched arm we are freed from the house of bondage. The horse and his rider, rider and subway car, bus and railroad car have been thrown into the sea. _____

186

# On Health and Being Jewish

There is a Jewish saying that goes: Your health comes first, you can always hang yourself later.

One of my earliest memories as a child is sneezing and having my mother say, *"Zay gezunt,"* which means "You should be healthy." I didn't know that's what it meant. I just knew that was what you said to someone every time they sneezed. I'm still unable, under most circumstances, to refrain from shouting *"Zay gezunt"* in public places. When you're trying to "pass" it can be a dead giveaway.

My mother, may she live and be well, would often say, "Listen, it doesn't matter if you're rich, as long as you're healthy," or "If you haven't got your health nothing else matters."

I've been thinking about health lately. I've had a few rough years in the health department and I think about it a lot. I also think a lot about being Jewish and being poor. And about what it means to be sick and Jewish and poor. Or sick and poor and anything else for that matter.

If you're sick and you're too poor to go to a doctor, you might get better all by yourself. On the other hand you could die for lack of treatment. On the other hand if you could afford to go to a doctor, you might get treatment that would kill you. Occasionally you can even get cured by medical treatment. So there it is—a risky business. Lots of uncertainty. Health, like being Jewish, is a very uncertain condition. That's why we use the phrase "on the other hand." Do you think it's a coincidence that it was a Jew who refined the theory of dialectics? Maybe Marx would have thought in those terms if he weren't a Jew, but who knows for sure?

So I ask myself, "How are issues of health and being Jewish linked? Is it healthy to be Jewish?" And I answer, "Sometimes it is and sometimes it isn't." For example, it's healthy to be happy and to laugh. It's a Jewish tradition to dance, to sing, to laugh and to celebrate. We celebrate births, circumcisions, *bar mitzvahs, bas mitzvahs*, weddings, anniversaries, birthdays, escaping from Egypt, the beginning of spring, the end of the old year, and every week we celebrate the Sabbath. This is happy and, therefore, one can only assume, healthy.

On the other hand we also suffer a lot. We suffer on our own account and we suffer over the pain of others. Maybe it's because of our history. Who can say? But one thing I can say for sure, we are a people who have suffered. We have suffered social ostracism, religious persecution, poverty, imprisonment, murder, slavery, genocide. . .I could go on and on. Still, as a people we persist—we somehow survive despite the suffering. Despite the illness of the world we still manage to survive.

Some people might say that since we suffer so much and since we manage to survive nonetheless, suffering creates strength and is therefore a positive thing. I think that's false logic. If I had the choice, I'd choose less suffering and take my chances that it would make me less healthy in the long run.

This subject is beginning to make me sick. What good does it do to be asking all these questions about health and being Jewish? And how can it help me to think about suffering? And certainly it's not likely to be healthy to be writing about such things. Ten years from now someone could come across this and hold it against me. Anyway, worrying has got to be bad for your health.

But I also think it's not healthy to ignore the issues. If we forget our suffering, if we ignore the suffering of others, how can we be on guard to protect ourselves the next time? How can we stop there being a next time? If we don't stop suffering where we see it, aren't we responsible for it continuing?

Oy, all this is muddling up my head. But listen, don't worry. Everything will work out, as long as you're healthy. And if not, you can always take the advice Molly Goldberg gave her husband when he came home one cold winter's evening. "Jake," she said, "go take off your coat and hang yourself in the closet."

*Bernice Mennis*

# The Miracle

Each year you say that maybe
next year you won't bother
anymore to make the old foods.
The price of fish exorbitant
the $4 a pound becoming 5
two days before the holiday
women bunched together shouting
and then the chopping  grating  mixing.
Hard work for an old woman.
And nowadays  they say  the package
is almost as good  and cheaper even.

Yet each year
there on that clean ironed white heavy cloth
with its delicate stitches of leaf green
        and yellow red—
I hadn't noticed how small the stitch
how intricate the pattern—
the food there again.
Not simple or quick or fancy
but hours of careful shaping.
It is nothing like packaged food.
Nothing.

This year I was
to make *tsimes* for another seder.
We worked together  my mother and I
in her kitchen of forty-five years
where the water drips cold
and the hot water never gets
really hot  where the oven
must be watched and the refrigerator strapped closed.
I was to grate 20 carrots.
And I  the jogger basketball athlete
invested in my woman's body strength
grated 6 carrots with great
difficulty  my arm exhausted
my fingers grated.
And you  my 4'll''
74 year old mother
grated 14 carrots
without stopping
evenly
not easily or quickly
but calmly
silently
providing again
the dark coarse uneven ground.

189

## Fradel Schtok

פֿראַדעל שטאָק

There is scant biographical information about Fradel Schtok, who was born in Galicia in 1890, immigrated to the United States in 1907, and died in a mental institution probably in 1930. Though she commanded attention by being the first Yiddish poet to use the sonnet form, Fradel's primary energy seemed to have gone into fiction. Her immigration must have had severe consequences on her writing and she obviously experienced language conflicts: Erzeylungen (Stories) appeared in 1919 and then an English novel, For Musicians Only in 1927. Both received poor reviews.

Erzeylungen was set in Eastern Europe and in America. Some stories, humorous and satiric, depict Jewish society at critical moments: "Der ershter ban" (The first train) in a small shtetl or "Der ershter patsyent" (The first patient) of a young dentist in America. Other stories are more somber and describe the conflict between inner longings and social (i.e. Jewish) norms. Trapped by social and religious mores, Fradel's characters often cloak their feelings in "appropriate" behavior.

*This is certainly true of "Opgeshnitene hor" (The shorn head), a story of a 19-year-old widow in pre-World War I Poland under Austrian rule. Ignorant of feminist issues and deliberately kept illiterate, she instinctively rebels against the sexism of the* shaytl *tradition—the requirement that Orthodox married women crop their hair and wear wigs. The only story of 38 to bear a dedication—"To My Aunt Tsipora"—it suggests historical sources and a dissatisfaction among women in the* shtetlekh *which they could not express directly, but which Fradel Schtok articulated for them. Though awkward in many of its transitions and use of internal monologue, the story effectively evokes the inner tension of Jewish women in a society which ignored their individuality and artistic aspirations.*

*—Irena Klepfisz*

---

## The Shorn Head

(A gift for my Aunt Tsipora)

אָבגעשניטענע האָר

(מיין מוהמע צפּורה אַ מתנה)

### *Translated by Irena Klepfisz*

Her mother braided her hair till she was eighteen years old. And how it grew—God protect her!—by leaps and bounds. Black and thick and long—down, down past her waist.

Even when she was still very small, Sheyndl was already a wonderful little homemaker. Her dress carried her scent and seemed to grow right along with her. Her darning, her embroidery were passed around, miracles to behold. Was there anything she couldn't do? She could imitate a bird as it flew.

Her pious mother hadn't allowed her to go to school on account of Nekhe, who would never have written little love notes to the inspector if she hadn't learned to write.

But what Sheyndl understood with her own common sense her mother could not take away from her. And Sheyndl had common sense. Ah, that at nineteen they had married her off to a sick widower and three months later he died—that was a piece of luck. The misfortune was that in that very same year both her father and mother died too—her devoted mother. And Sheyndl was set adrift.

Sheyndl cried and cried. She herself didn't know what made her cry more, her shorn braids—which always reminded her of her bound head—or her devoted mother. All that remained for her now was the little room, her inheritance. The little tiny room with not even a piece of bread.

Sheyndl had nothing to eat. Her brothers were poor folk themselves and claimed it was nice enough of them to let her live in the apartment.

When her mother was alive, Sheyndl would buy a *graytser*'s worth of pumpkin seeds, wash them down with a drink of cold water and feel revived. But now, when she didn't even have a *graytser* she couldn't indulge herself.

Hungry, she'd run to the cemetery and undam a river of tears. And if it hadn't

191

been for Esther, God only knows what would have become of her by now.

Esther was, in fact, a respectable child. But since people have mouths, they dreamed up that she liked to talk with the *klezmer* boy. Sheyndl knew there was nothing to it. If only everyone had Esther's character—the way she sat and worked at the machine and contributed at home.

Esther wanted Sheyndl for a friend because Sheyndl had a reputation as a virtuous girl. And Sheyndl latched on to her. She knew Esther was smart and decent, despite what people said about her. But she never told Esther she was hungry. She was ashamed. It seemed to her it was a great crime that she was hungry. But how was she to blame?

Gradually Sheyndl learned to sew, and after that she earned a *manger* a day, a whole *manger*, a *graytser* and a half. And so she wasn't so aimless anymore.

And when gradually she began to sew on her own and suddenly saw a whole *ranish* before her eyes, she felt she was becoming prosperous. Soon a red satin apron came into being, a pair of gold slippers with little ornaments, and a bordeaux peasant blouse trimmed with lambskin. And the blouse had a scent.

People said: Sheyndl is right as the world. And so decent.

But she: inside her heart cried. Every time she looked at her *shaytele* with the bangs in front, her heart would twinge. . .her head was already bound.

At night she would stroke her shorn head, back and forth, back and forth and her hair actually grew, quickly, beautifully. Yet it seemed to her that her two braids would never grow back. But when they finally did? Wouldn't she have to cut them off? Cut them off again? No! No? A Jewish woman—a wife? Woe is me! My poor heart! But no! God forbid! Who says she has to walk around with her hair exposed. Let it stay under the *shaytl*—like that. Her head is already bound. And for what reason? And for how long, *gotenyu*? She hadn't even known her husband, and he'd already been sick before he married her. And her own hair? God protect her! What kind of sin was it? A terrible, an enormous sin.

But if only her braids would grow back, she'd feel easier for a little while. She won't cut them till they've grown as long as they used to be.

Her little house sparkled with cleanliness. During the day, she would sit and work, and at night clean the little house till it sparkled.

But she was miserable and cried about her misery. Esther was indeed a friend, but a friend is not as deeply rooted in one's heart as one's misery, as one's grief. More than once her heart became more embittered as she looked at Esther's head of hair; more than once she wished herself an old maid, wished the town were gossiping about her, wished her head were not still bound.

Her brothers turned themselves inside out trying to convince her to remarry, especially when they saw how well she conducted herself. They'd wander over to their sister's house, sip a glass of warm tea, and by the by drop a few words: How will all this end? And how long can someone be alone? A person is obliged to marry—that's the way of the world. The oldest brother, the pious one, claimed a person is obliged to bequeath another generation. . .

Sheyndl would remember her growing hair and feel as if they were after her life, that they resented that her hair had grown back.

So she would concentrate on her sewing and not answer.

Only when she was left alone did she feel the depth of her unhappiness and cry and think: Oh, if only one could recapture those years. . .those young years. . .Old age brings a person troubles. Troubles make a person—make her old and gray before her time. Already little by little and thirty years old. So what good is it when you can't get those years back? And to be like you once were, as if this time had never even passed, is also impossible.

But things could be different. Perhaps even better? Better. Not for the sake of others, but for your own sake. Inside you feel quiet, peaceful, joyful; you don't eat yourself up. And so you yourself want to become more and more decent. And as you become more decent, you feel as if you were always dressed in a clean, new garment.

In the sparkling little house there was a large mirror and Sheyndl polished it with her golden hands, always polished it so the mirror was clear as water. There in the mirror she saw another sparkling little house, with another proper wife who polished another mirror. And the wife looks at her *shaytele* and her heart aches because her head was bound when she was so young and her years cut short.

The glassware stood on the polished table; two Majolica plates were in a green rack; and a blue vessel sparkled on the wall. A Turkish spread already covered the bed and an expensive dress sewn by Moyshe the Tailor hung in the closet.

When they got longer, Sheyndl began to steal a few of her own hairs and to mingle and entwine them in the *shaytl*. And when she stepped out on the street for the first time, her heart pounded for fear someone might see. The next week she snuck out more hair and her heart pounded again. In this way, little by little, she smuggled out more and more hair, and with her heart pounding, trembling, she waited to see if she'd be discovered. After each time she exposed herself in this way, dared, a new joy grew inside her and she hoped that things would become better, even better.

Once after *pesakh*, the sun shone into the sparkling house with such devotion that tears of joy welled up in her. She looked out of the clear windowpanes and rejoiced without reason. On that day, she took all her hair from the front of her head and covered the *shaytele*.

With a joyous heart she went to Esther's. On the way, she met Itshe-Mayer's wife who took one look and clapped her hands:

—Oh my God! You're out with your own hair?

Sheyndl stood still and didn't know what to say. But her heart beat like a criminal's. And seeing how frightened Sheyndl had become, Itshe-Mayer's wife intensified her wrath.

—What can this mean! A Jewish woman—and with such a pious mother!

And she went on and on thundering at her.

Sheyndl wept on her way home. The day was bright and this caused her even more pain.

*Julie Greenberg*

# Seeking a Feminist Judaism

What does it mean to be a Jew and a woman, and particularly a religious Jewish feminist? On one side, non-Jews and non-religious women in the feminist movement often condemn any organized religion as patriarchal and sometimes especially Judaism for having "murdered the goddess." This camp perceives Jewish feminists as having by definition sold out. On the other side the Jewish male-dominated establishment, ranging from ultra-Orthodox to egalitarian-style liberal, often condemns feminist Jewish experience as abandoning and endangering the Jewish community. Its adherents are seen as "not really Jewish," caring more about feminism than about Judaism.

Despite the skepticism of the Jewish establishment, there is a growing body of feminist Jews who care deeply and mutually about being both Jews and women. We are not willing to compromise on either identity and are equally commited to fighting anti-Semitism among feminists and sexism among Jews. In the life of a Jewish women, there is not a Jewish self separate from a female self. Being a Jewish woman or a female Jew is a totality and all experience is filtered through that integrated reality. We look at Judaism and feminism in terms of what makes sense to Jewish feminists. As full participants in Judaism and in feminism, we recognize that what is good for Jewish feminists is also good for Judaism and feminism, and that what is bad for Jewish feminists is also damaging to both. The subjective position of Jewish feminists becomes a starting point for ethical decision-making, in an attempt not to legislate for anyone else but to organize our own lives as Jewish feminists.

\* \* \* \* \*

What are some issues of concern to Jewish feminists? Why should Jewish women stay actively Jewish? How can we relate to what has come down to us as Jewish tradition? What does our own expression of Judaism look like? What *is* Judaism anyway?\*

A feminist approach to Judaism involves a shift in viewpoint. The first step in this shift might be to ask: why have women been excluded from certain rituals? A second step might be to wonder, how dare men claim the prerogative to define Judaism for us all? And a third step might be to redefine Judaism from a pro-woman point of view.

What does this mean? In traditional Judaism, men are the normative Jews and women "the other" in relation to that standard. In the Talmud women are considered only in so far as they have an impact on the lives of men, *e.g.* at marriage or during ritual states of impurity. There is no comprehensive treatment of a woman's life

---

\* In this paper I have used the words "traditional Judaism" loosely, sometimes referring to orthodox Judaism based on texts, tradition and *halakha* and sometimes referring to the broadly defined category of all male-dominated Judaism, including very non-traditional activity. I also have purposely not defined "Judaism" or "feminism," relying on a common understanding sufficient for my purposes. The "we" in the paper is a general reference to Jewish feminists, but does not represent them all.

I want to thank Shulamith Magnus for helpful editorial comments and Susannah Heschel for a series of exciting conversations. Of course the responsibility for the views expressed is mine alone.

cycle.[1] One classic example of the masculine assumption in Judaism is Moses of Sinai telling the people to purify themselves and to "go not near a woman for three days." Susannah Heschel asks, "Who is being addressed? Am I as a woman not supposed to go near a woman for three days? No, clearly not." Men are the ones making the rules, men are the ones addressed; and the system, even at its most sensitive and humane, is controlled by men to protect and perpetuate their interests, which they see as synonymous with God's and the Jewish people's interests. Even when Jewish men have limited their own rights and protected women, as they have in a limited sense on issues of *get* (divorce) and birth control, their concessions merely reinforce the basic structure of male power, serving to ward off rebellion or chaos.

Feminist Judaism refuses to accept a definition of "other than fully human" for women. We claim the right to be primary, and will not ask permission of the male-dominated tradition in our process of reclamation. What shocks and offends some people about this new claim to primacy is that Jewish feminists are beginning to move beyond any binding mentorship to the literature preserved by men of men's Jewish experience, interpretations and definitions. While non-*halakhic* Jews, male and female, have already assumed some freedom in relation to the texts, textual study is still seen as a priority, inspiring and legitimizing new forms of Judaism. Rabbi Gendler's remark that "Text is the congenital illness of traditional Judaism" would apply equally well to the various movements for Jewish renewal.

For example, well-intentioned New Age Jews have combed traditional texts in pursuit of non-sexist names for God and have generated a list of lovely traditional alternatives. From the Haggadah alone we get *Ha Makom* (the Place), *Ha Makor* (the Source), *Ha Ikar* (the Principle) among others. Yet when feminist Jews choose the name "Elilah" for the Goddess (originated by Jane Litwoman and now used nationally by lesbians and feminists), many New Age Jews disapprove because this word is not found in the texts.[2] But that is exactly the point. Texts are not *the* source for feminist Jews. What matters to us is the outburst of caring, calling, and naming the Goddess, our goddess. Elilah is not the last name we will ever invent; it doesn't even satisfy some of our own criteria in that we are still questioning what deity means to us and how we want to evoke that meaning. But women are choosing a name for God; that is the important thing.

At most, traditional texts represent fifty percent of Judaism, the masculine half. As Heschel points out, "The Talmud is a very important historical document that shaped the lives of our people. But we have to ask *who* was doing that work? History is written by the victors." In a male-dominated social system naturally women were socialized to support the system. As dependents, women learned to use it to promote their own emotional and material survival as well as the survival of the Jewish people. Historically women's relationship to male-defined Judaism was a complicated one of coercion, collusion and creation, just as Jewish survival in an alien world has been.

Today, however, we are able to ask whether there are equally valid approaches to "the other half" of Judaism besides traditional texts. What can history, archaeology, comparative religion and our imaginations tell us about what female Jews were doing and how can that be reconstructed and made relevant today? With a feminist shift in viewpoint, some Jews are beginning to step outside the rabbinic tradition, to question its worth for the tasks ahead of us as Jews and as women. Women occupy a potentially prophetic role at this period of Judaism: the refusal to be the Other forces Jewish Renewal.

Feminist Jews have been criticized for condemning patriarchal Judaism without offering new models. But in fact feminists are engaged in the most revolutionary act, the major theological step of examining traditions from the point of view of disenfranchised Jews. As Heschel says, "We are asking not what did the rabbis tell us about this or that but rather why does it matter what the rabbis are telling us?" Once women are empowered to be full creators of Judaism, we can trust that all the scores of Rosh Khodesh groups, women's *minyans*, Jewish feminist conferences and retreats, political action and study groups, caucuses, publications and projects will result in worthwhile content. After all, the male-dominated tradition took hundreds of years to evolve before being codified. In fact feminists might prefer the current fluid, un-codified situation. But dissemination of ideas and practices would clearly be helpful.

The difficult task is not discovering-inventing-evolving feminist expressions of Judaism—that happens spontaneously when the conditions are right—but taking that liberating leap away from "The" "Jewish" tradition. The misogyny in our tradition cannot be holy. Liberation from that tradition means taking ourselves, our fragmented history as Jewish females, and our imaginations seriously. *It does not mean completely ignoring texts, practices or male-defined history.* We recognize that traditional Judaism is not *only* codification of oppression. In many cases the tradition is all we have to work with as Jews. But the *point of view* in relation to that material will be radically different coming from a feminist perspective. This new point of view is open to both men and women. It sees Jewish women as fully Jewish; anything less than our full participation in creating Judaism is inadequate and unfortunate.

When we re-define the discussion, it becomes apparent that there is nothing contradictory in the term "feminist Jew." Being a feminist Jew might be a contradiction in a male-defined Judaism; but if the feminist is the central actor in the creation of her Judaism, there is no conflict. Feminist criticism of "Judaism" accepts men's right to define Judaism and then condemns it for excluding women. Why assume that Judaism belongs exclusively to men simply because men have had the power to control the definitions for so long? One reason given is the desire to maintain Jewish unity for the sake of survival. But the concept of *klal yisrael*, the unity and continuity of Jewish existence, has in fact been built on the backs of disenfranchised, disempowered women. Women as a class need not be sacrificed to Jewish unity; if Jewish unity is really so valuable, let all Jews work toward liberation with us.

On a practical level the Jewish community consists of men and women who abide, in one way or another, by male-defined Judaism. In struggling with this reality, the Jewish feminist must constantly ask herself the questions: why remain Jewish-identified? why remain a feminist? wouldn't it be easier to avoid these sociological contradictions, to be acceptable, "normal," and included rather than remain a marginal freak?

In answering these questions, many of us keep coming back to some kind of essence of self. We have to live in the world true to ourselves. Just as we can't deny the world beyond a point without killing ourselves, we can't deny our mode of experiencing that world without killing ourselves. Heschel reflects on these issues:

> Why is Judaism important? Maybe we get down to sociological/historical answers. Because my family did it, my people did it. I think about this in terms of what I would want to pass on to Jewish kids. The symbol that is so important you can't act wrongly in relation to it is important. That's something I'd like to give my kids. There's the story of the man holding *tefillin* at the Western Wall yelling at the beggars and then realizing he couldn't don *tefillin*. There are symbols that require respect. My mode of experiencing this is Jewish. If I threw out all the patriarchal manifestations of the world I'd be left with nihilism; I'd commit suicide. I have to pick and choose *something*.

The dramatic shift in viewpoint and the rapidly evolving nature of Judaism have caused a panic among feminist Jews as well as observers. "I have to pick something," says Heschel. But *what* will that something be? Does anything go, and if so, what makes us part of Judaism? What *is* Judaism anyway? Approaches to answering these questions break down along gender lines. Men tend to want a list of what is and isn't Jewish with a list of who is and isn't Jewish. The boundaries are clear; we all know who is in and who is out. Feminists, on the other hand, tend to say, let's work together and see what emerges.

Building on the contributions of Carol Gilligan at Harvard,[3] Heschel summarizes:

> Lawmaking is a masculine way of thinking. Women work out of relationship. I don't assume there is one set of rules, one essence of Judaism, that doesn't change and outside of which you are no longer Jewish. At one time Jews created the Bible, then the Talmud, now what we create will be Judaism for this time. In the past Jews have been willing to make pretty sharp breaks with the past. We weren't so concerned with continuity. For instance, all of a sudden Christianity was no longer idolatry when the economic and social situation required that change.

The assumption of a "bottom line" definition of Judaism stunts the process of discovering Judaism. Instead of searching for a "bottom line," we should ask: "How can a community best live Jewishly?" Focusing on the process of being Jewish, of creating Judaism, rather than on the product, makes the questions look different. Within the context of self-identified Jews acting consciously as Jews, it becomes inappropriate to argue over who is a real or good Jew or about what is or is not Jewish. It *does* make sense to struggle over agreements about both Jewish practice and decision-making within specific communities because the issues are workable agreements, not absolute truth.

Nevertheless, as feminists engaged in this dialogue, we press ourselves and each other, "Is there anything Jewish people could do that would be not-Jewish?" "Are you willing to reconsider monotheism?" "What about making *Asherot* like our Jewish foremothers did?" "What about following in the tradition of the Jewish witches of

197

*Ashkelon?"*

These questions may well make us nervous. But Jewish women need the freedom to ask — and answer for ourselves — every question without being told we're not Jewish. As Heschel states:

> If you are sincerely seeking expression as a Jew, then what you do is Jewish. Converting to another religion and forsaking Judaism is really the only thing that would be outside the bounds of Judaism for me. You have to identify as Jewish in a Jewish context. If you do something as a Jew, then it's Jewish.

It is true that these definitions are somewhat tautological. "A Jew does Jewish things and Jewish things are what Jews do." But is there any better way to define Judaism? *Who* should make the decision about what Judaism is if not Jews broadly and inclusively defined? Women have seen many other forms of Jewish decision-making used at our expense. There may still be unresolved issues and contradictions in a feminist process of defining Judaism, but there is no easy way out.

\* \* \* \* \*

The next step is to ask ourselves what we want to do as feminist Jews. Each feminist Jew and each feminist Jewish community has to decide how to relate to Jewish tradition and how to express feminist Judaism. Even after the shift in viewpoint, the need still remains to do the work of re-creation.

Many groups around the world, of Jewish women only and of Jewish women and men together, are grappling with these issues. There is often a sense of spiritual exhilaration even in the decision-making activities. After one meeting of particularly intense and growthful struggle over issues of feminist language in an egalitarian *khavurah*, one feminist participant said, "I've been *davening* here for a year but this discussion was the first spiritual experience I've had here." The power of liberation is a spiritual force, and feminists tapping into that have discovered an amazing religious potential. Prayer, language and imagery, doctrinal issues, style and form of *davening*, new rituals and the very content of what we choose to transmit as Judaism are all under scrutiny. Emerging conceptions of theology and the nature of community reflect the richness and multiplicity of options open to us as self-creating Jews. We are grounded not by mandates from the past but by a relationship to a four-thousand-year-old history that informs the nature of our questions.

One group that has been working on feminist Jewish community building is the six-year-old Dyke Shabbas Community of Berkeley, CA. Similar communities have developed throughout the U.S. and in Israel. Dyke Shabbas attracts dozens of alienated Jews, most of whom have scanty Jewish education. Every *pesakh*, core Dyke Shabbas members face the dilemma of balancing tradition with liberation. How much of the old Haggadah and traditions should be taught? If the same masculine language and format are taught year after year, aren't feminists perpetuating the very material that has hurt us for so long? But isn't it more empowering to women to know the tradition and then alter it? At least then we have some reference point as Jews.

Dyke Shabbas decided to preserve a thoroughly feminist ritual space, for the most part refusing to teach patriarchal Judaism. The reasoning was that if some group didn't simply insist on new terms, a pernicious allegiance to patriarchal frameworks would be perpetuated. Joanna Katz, reflecting on the same dilemma, suggests that *sidorim* be printed with the traditional prayers on one side of the page and with current versions on the other so that what we are actually teaching is the possibility of transformation.

On a separate, hotly debated question, Dyke Shabbas for the time being chose the one-step-at-a-time approach to creative liturgy, its liturgy consisting of selected traditional prayers translated into the feminine in Hebrew and in English. But how meaningful is it to pray to a Queen of Heaven instead of a King of Heaven? to the mistress rather than master of the universe? Don't we need to totally re-think the very images of God? Then there are questions about Hebrew: if we retain Hebrew language for new images, won't this be an elitist program biased in favor of those with flexible Hebrew skills? Would we lose the sense of mystery and comfort that comes from traditional words and images? Does that sense exist now, or do we just wish it did? Does it depend on not understanding Hebrew? Or on an early childhood of traditional Judaism? Dyke Shabbas hoped that merely changing the gender would be a first step, opening the door to further experimentation.

Another issue that arose for the creators of the Dyke Shabbas liturgy was whether Jewish feminists could call ourselves "Israel," and sons or even children of Israel. Israel, who wrestled with God, who was God's chosen to the exclusion of women, doesn't speak well to the unchosen, Jewish women. But today, as a people, *Am Yisrael* has a meaning of its own. Dyke Shabbas chose to keep the identity of Israel for the sake of Jewish peoplehood. Similar issues have come up in connection to the Torah. Do we as women keep reading the Torah every *shabes*? One feminist developed a ritual honoring the unwritten Torah of the women. This is unresolved and on the agenda for continued deliberation.

In the three examples discussed here concerning feminist relationship to masculine language, to prayer format, and to one doctrinal issue, Dyke Shabbas balanced several different principles: standing firm in the desire to create a truly feminist Jewish community without allegiance to the male-dominated aspects of tradition; being aware that change is a step-by-step matter and that consciousness and knowledge (as well as other scarce resources like time) must be carefully tended along the way; and considering that not everything needs to be changed for the sake of change — there are good reasons to keep some traditions. Jewish groups all over the country are going through similar processes of learning about, evaluating and transforming Judaism.

Feminist Jewish ritual and *midrash* seem to be developing at a fast rate, from the plethora of baby-naming ceremonies to the making of *Asherot* out of menstrual blood and mud. *Davening* in a circle, praying into each other's eyes, bringing movement and touch into the service, are just a few of the directions in which feminist thinking is moving. One beautiful ceremony created by Jane Litwoman calls for a circle of Jews to anoint one another one at a time, saying, "You are the messiah (annointed one)." At Purim a Jerusalem Rosh Khodesh group hung the Hamans of women's lives — sexual harassment, low pay, the beauty industry, etc. Much creativity is visible on the issue of language. The Egalitarian Minyan in Jerusalem keeps quotes from the Torah in masculine Hebrew but changes other prayers to feminine language. Marcia Falk uses first person plural forms such as *Nvarekh et Makor Ha Khaim* (We will bless to the Source of Life) to get away from a gendered God.

A commitment to feminist Judaism pervades our lives as Jews, not only the spiritual elements of our lives. In fact, the freedom to have a spiritual life is integrated with the material organization of our lives. It is hard to reach God in the *davening* circle if, for lack of child care, your babies are distracting and demanding. On the other hand, maybe there is a way for people to come together with God by incorporating babies into the *davening* experience. It is even harder to be part of a spiritual community if the cost of the religious retreat or synagogue membership is prohibitive (and women are the poorest people in a patriarchal system). Feminist challenges for economic justice, for recognition of alternative families and for community responsibility for children could have a major impact on the very shape and standards of progressive Judaism. We discover that the spiritual is political.

\* \* \* \* \*

Feminist Judaism is what feminist Jews create. It is the process of feminist Jews finding answers, perhaps even temporary answers, to the questions posed earlier in this paper. Heschel writes:

> A feminist theology of Judaism must resonate with women's experience, must ground women's lives in a Jewish dimension. The outcome may be new or revised traditions, observances and prayers. But above all, in the future, when a woman looks at Judaism, she should not see only a reflection of the experiences of Jewish men.

Both "women" (in contrast to the biological concept female) and "Judaism" are evolving social constructs, not absolutes; feminist Judaism is the process of Jewish women engaged in self-determination of these constructs. It is clear that this engagement includes a relationship to Jewish people and to Jewish history, but the exact nature of that relationship cannot be imposed from outside the process. Today feminists bring to Judaism the refusal to be seen as less than fully human, and by extension, the refusal to tolerate the treatment of anyone or any group as less than human. In some other historical and social period, the message of Jewish feminists will no doubt be different. The point is that living Jewish women, with commitment to this dual identity, are created by the world and in turn create the world in our image: our lives as Jewish feminists define Jewish feminism.

──────────────── Notes ────────────────

[1] Susannah Heschel has made this point well in her numerous talks to women's and Jewish groups. Also see the book she edited, *On Being A Jewish Feminist* (NY: Schocken Books, 1983). Most of Heschel's quotes in this article come from a series of conversations we had in spring of 1984.

[2] *Elilah* (el-ee-LAH) is a made-up word but it sounds very similar to *elilim*, the Hebrew word for small, foreign gods/idols. Many Jewish men say they don't want us to use a name for God that has these negative connotations. Feminist Jews respond by saying, "What else would the patriarchy have called the goddess? Small, foreign god(dess) is how the goddess was probably seen by the dominant powers." But the main point is that women have the right to choose *whatever* name we want for the deity. Men have had the exclusive right to name God for far too long.

[3] Carol Gilligan, *In A Different Voice: Psychological Theory and Women's Development* (Cambridge, MA: Harvard Univ. Press, 1982).

*ALFA Shabat.*                                    *Photo by JEB*

*Shabat in the open.*                    *Photo by JEB*

*A girls'* kheder. *A rebitsin teaching her pupils to read the prayers. Laskirov, Poland.*
Jewish Daily Forward. *January 16, 1927.*              *YIVO Archives*

*Workshop at Jewish Feminist Conference in San Francisco, May, 1982  Photo by JEB*

# Why I want to be a rabbi

*My family was an observant Jewish family, we celebrated shabes each week, and I began to wait for the light of the shabes candles to fill me each Friday evening. Often I cried when my father sang the kidush . We celebrated each holiday in its fullness: building a sukah , planting trees, lighting candles for lost Jews. I was drawn to these very conscious acts as a young child, and as an adult, I translated my hunger into the idea of becoming a rabbi.*

*It seemed to me that women in Judaism were without spiritual leaders of our own. That we had to look to men for the expression of our Jewishness. I wanted to go directly into the rituals, the prayers, the celebrations myself. So, I applied to rabbinical school last fall, 1984, at the age of thirty.*

*The following piece is what I wrote in response to the question: "Why do you want to become a rabbi?"*

\* \* \* \* \* \* \* \* \* \*

As a young daughter of Zion, I knew that I had stood at the foot of Har Sinai: that the Exodus from Egypt was my exodus, the crisis of faith which became the Golden Calf was my crisis, and that some part of me still wandered in the desert, searching for my Jewish home. Always I participated in the history of my People Israel; with every generation of Jews I lit *shabes* candles and prayed for forgiveness on Yom Kippur. I tell you my childhood fervor because it shaped my relationship to Judaism. For me, being a Jew is living in exile. I inherited the exile of my people beginning with the destruction of the first Temple. I still ask, "How can I sing the Lord's song in a strange land?" But I have come to understand that this sacred song I long to sing is temporal; each Jew must confront the exile of her own generation, for one person's exile is another person's home.

Living in exile is a burden; it forces me to confront who I am and why I am. The exile I face is the exile of the Diaspora Jew. Life in the *galut* means acute psychological fragmentation in the form of separation from the history of my people, my language, and "home" land. Life in the Diaspora means confrontation with my Jewish self. It is a dialogue of pain mixed with moments of celebration when I am able unambivalently to embrace my Jewishness. When I light the *shabes* candles, recite the *shekhekianu* in shul, and when I say *motzi* in the *sukah*, I know such moments.

The exile I speak of is acutely personal and the pain comes in degrees. When I think of Eretz Yisrael, my heart aches. I was so sure as a young daughter of Zion that I could make *aliyah* — that Israel was my home too. Now I ask if Eretz Yisrael can only be my spiritual home rather than my physical homeland. When I am in Israel, I am further alienated from my People Israel. I am a visitor, a distant relative connected by blood, but without a common language: the language of experience, for the Diaspora Jew and the Israeli Jew remain unconnected spiritually and often politically. Historically we are pitted against each other. I long for a reciprocal relationship: I need my brothers and sisters of the Galilee and the Negev. Do they need me? They live in the majority while I live in the minority; where do our experiences meet?

When I think of my grandparents, who came from Russia and Poland to this American Diaspora, again I feel the status of an exile. Their immigrant experience filled them with a different Judaism. My grandparents packed up their Jewishness, carrying it on their backs to new countries. They never expected to rest. Whenever they speak of Nazi Germany, their eyes tell me Jews are never safe. To them this is a fact of life. The exile of my grandparents' generation is physical. While I inherit the exile of immigrant Jews, I experience the exile of my own generation. Ours is an intellectual exile that translates into the lack of first amendment rights, the lack of separation of church and state. I remember being forced to say the Lord's Prayer in public school and staying at home when my fourth grade class went Christmas carolling. I coped with my eyes closed — imagining my mother's white *shabes* tablecloth, her two brass candlesticks protecting my entire family. My American exile is not immediately physically debilitating as was that of my ancestors. But I am not yet free to be the Jew I want to be.

My exile also comes from within myself. As a woman and as a Jew my exile is doubled. I am often exiled from myself, forced to celebrate my Jewish self to the exclusion of my woman self. This is a contemporary, generational burden. I must be able to embrace all of myself simultaneously; I must not have to choose to sit among Jews or to sit among Feminists. I want both. I am representative of my generation; my pain is the collective pain of my peers. If I accept the responsibility of who I am today, then I must go out of my own personal exile and break out of my own isolation.

My experiences as teacher, writer, and lawyer led me to the decision to become a rabbi. When I was in law school, I felt as though what I was studying was too far removed from my own experiences to be personally relevant. Although the laws I studied affected me, they weren't about me, about who I was/am. I wanted Talmud, the original legal questions: it was/is the Jewish questions about justice that I craved. I have waited my whole life to study Torah, Talmud, and the culture and customs of my people in a safe place. I want to contribute to the contemporary interpretation of Judaism, as a woman, as a representative of the post-Holocaust generation and after the establishment of the State of Israel. Each generation requires people who can speak with the authority of experience. My goal is to be a spiritual and intellectual representative of my People Israel by writing, studying, and teaching about the nature of Jewish identity in the late 20th century. Each life choice I made was made as though I was preparing to become a rabbi. My years of self-scrutiny have prepared me for this decision. I am now ready to confront being a Jew directly, within a social context, within the structure of rabbinical school. I am ready for a personal encounter with the sacred that does not exclude my womanhood. And I am ready to challenge my own exile rather than perpetuate it. So that the world of my work is no longer secular, I want to become a rabbi. To work with Jews about being Jews is why I seek to train for the rabbinate.

The consequences of living in exile surround me. My peers struggle with voluntary and involuntary assimilation. On their own they blend in, minimize the importance of being Jews in their daily lives. For some, especially my women friends, being a Jew has meant further second class status and more pain. For them, the burden of what they do not know about Jewish culture and history is overwhelming. Assimilating temporarily soothed the pain of their own alienation. To me, the question becomes one of involuntary assimilation. Constantly I struggle with my own memory. When I was a child I knew the history of the State of Israel backward and forward; I spoke fluent Hebrew; celebrating the holidays rejuvenated me. Today I have cultural amnesia. I fear my right hand must surely have lost its cunning because I live in a world where my identity is not reflected back to me. So I try, with the rest of my generation, to nourish my Jewish soul.

To study with other Jews about Jewishness interrupts the path of my exile and redirects it. My personal quest will become socially accountable. As a rabbinical student, I must ask other rabbinical students, "How to sing the Lord's song in a strange land?" I must ask if Jewish women will always have to sing two separate songs and if Israeli and Diaspora Jews will ever share the same melody? I do not expect concrete answers to my questions. Instead, I expect to assume the responsibility of my own exile in a public environment — to confront and nurture the empty places inside me by studying with other Jews. To go to rabbinical school at this time in my life is to claim my identity as woman and Jew, even though history has taught me that both are despised. The challenge of my generation is to resist alienation from the self. But I want to be whole: woman and Jew together. I want to write, teach and pray within a community of Jews who are not afraid to talk about their own exile.

Jerusalem is my mythic home. Yet that is not enough. Can it ever be my psychological, physical, or spiritual home? Studying to be a rabbi will permit me to ask these questions. I am drawn to the Reconstructionist Movement because it accepts the challenges of time and history and interprets Judaism in relation to the past, present, and future. It is evolving Judaism, not static. I want to contribute to this evolutionary process.

*Savina Teubal*

# The Meaning of the Life of Sarah

from *Sarah the Priestess: The First Matriarch of Genesis*

What is the meaning of Sarah's life? Is Sarah's message different from Abraham's? I believe so.

The legend of Sarah describes an early tradition which the matriarch struggles to preserve a non-patriarchal system involved with the forces of nature and their relevance to the community.

This system is diametrically opposed to patriarchality (as presented in Genesis), which emphasizes individuality and the individual whereas non-patriarchality is concerned with the community at large. Biblical patriarchy is contingent upon the precept of blind faith and obedience. (Abram leaves his homeland because his God tells him to; he is willing to sacrifice his son for the same reason.) As Goddess incarnate, the matriarchs maintained a tradition of self-direction. (Sarah has the authority to banish Hagar but Abram accepts the banishment because his God demands that he do so. Rachel takes the *teraphim*, symbols of her office, because in her eyes she has the authority to do so.)

There is a significant difference between the relationship of Sarah with the deity and that of Abram. Sarah is Goddess incarnate (or directly represents a goddess). Abram is the intermediary between his God and his community, and is rewarded for it: "I give the land you sojourn in to you and your offspring to come, all the land of Canaan, as an everlasting possession" . . . but on condition that "I will be their God." (Gen 17:8) Sarah officiates in the *hieros gamos* to appoint a just ruler of the people and insure the fertility of the land and well-being of its people.

The difference between Sarah and Abram can be understood only in the context of a social period comparable to that of the Jemdet Nasr of Mesopotamia. I think the relief on the Uruk vase of the Goddess/priestess in full regalia at the entrance to her shrine, receiving gifts from a naked ruler/priest, is a perfect illustration of the perception held by the community at Hebron of Sarah and Abram.

Sarah's life as presented in Genesis is indicative of the existence of a social system that was slowly being supplanted by patriarchy. Carol Ochs sees the sacrifice of Isaac as marking the death of the tradition personified by Sarah.[1] I see instead the death of Sarah as marking — not the end of that tradition — but perhaps the beginning of the end. Sarah's separation from her homeland was instrumental in bringing about the change, because it isolated her from the source of her traditions. It took many generations before those traditions were wiped out.

Sarah is symbolic of woman's struggle against a male culture that finally prevailed and eventually subordinated women. How aware was she of the effects of patriarchal encroachment on her own system? We can only imagine what Sarah was thinking and feeling during her interminable years of exile. But we do know that she mustered all her force and energy to banish the offending system (personified by Hagar and

Ishmael) from the area in which she lived, and to ensure the continuation of her own tradition through Isaac.

Sarah's story itself gives us only a glimpse of the social tradition and culture she was defending. We know, for instance, that she was of sufficient stature to be respected by kings in communities outside her own. (The kings reprimand Abram, not Sarah.) In other words, Sarah's position was internationally recognized and was not limited to her own community. The matriarch was also held in high esteem by her husband. Abram is solicitous of her favors before their meetings with the kings; he dutifully heeds her request to provide her with a child and accepts Sarah's decision to treat Hagar harshly when the handmaid is insolent to her. Also, Abram's attitude is deferential and subservient to the three mysterious visitors at Mamre, in contrast to Sarah, who argues with one of them.

It seems to me that the Sarah episodes which include her half-brother Abram cannot form part of the same tradition in which the patriarch is the principal. I would tentatively suggest that there were two distinct personalities: one, Sarah's husband and half-brother, whom we call Abram, and another called Abraham. We have seen the careful, courteous, and respectful Abram in the preceding chapters. Is this the same character as the man who mustered his retainers and pursued and defeated Chedorlaomer and his allies?[2] Is this the same person who fell into a trance and with whom the Lord made a covenant with the promise of giving him all the land from Egypt to the Euphrates? Abraham and not Abram would have reproached Abimelech for seizing the well of water. Abraham resided in the "land of the Philistines" a long time, but did Abram? Did Abraham come back from the south to take Isaac from Sarah and attempt to sacrifice him at the command of his God? When, after that, he returned to Beersheba, what did he do with Isaac? Did Abraham then return to Mamre to bury Sarah? Genesis makes no mention of Abraham's return: the patriarch is there, mourning the death of his wife.

Although this is pure conjecture, I would like to suggest that the *Abraham tradition* was different and distinct from the *Sarah tradition*, in which she had a half-brother/husband named Abram. At some point these two traditions were fused together into what is now our biblical text.

The Abram of the story is, like Isaac, a passive man, easily influenced by the Canaanite patriarchy in which he lived. The name "Abraham," on the other hand, evokes an emotional response built up by centuries of elaboration around the theme of blind monotheistic faith and obedience, of which the patriarch became the symbol.

We get a fuller picture of the *Sarah tradition* with the accounts of the other matriarchs: Rebekah, Rachel, and Leah. The preservation of blood ties was all-important to these women also. Rebekah marries a member of her descent group even though she has to leave her homeland to do so; however, she becomes "disgusted with her life" because her son Esau marries women native to Canaan. She insists that Jacob choose a wife from among her brother's daughters.

On the surface it would seem that blood ties have something to do with inheritance; Sarah banishes Ishmael so that he will not share in the inheritance with her son Isaac. Rebekah's mother and brother are told of Isaac's inheritance, at the time of her betrothal. Rachel and Leah help pry away their inheritance from Laban as though this were the main conflict between them and their father. However, when Laban pursues them, he is after the *teraphim*, the family images; no mention is made of stolen wealth. What inheritance were the matriarchs really concerned with?

Sarah's reason for banishing Ishmael is also unclear. Ishmael had been "mocking" Isaac. What connection did Ishmael's mocking have with inheritance? As explained in Chapter III Ishmael's mocking action must have had a religious connotation. There would have been no necessity for Sarah to banish Ishmael if her purpose was merely to disinherit him from material wealth. (Esau was easily disinherited.) Rather, Sarah did not want Ishmael to influence Isaac culturally, and this is why she banished both the boy and his mother. Sarah was a religious woman and a woman of religion, a priestess. Isaac's religious upbringing must have been Sarah's foremost consideration. I do not believe that Sarah's banishment of Ishmael had anything to do with material wealth; it had to do with religious ethics. The rite of circumcision enforced new rules of conduct unacceptable to the priestess.

Rebekah and Rachel were also preoccupied with religious ethics. Why is Rebekah so intent on having Jacob receive his father's blessing rather than Esau? She is not prepared to allow Esau to succeed in the descent line. Is Rebekah concerned with material wealth?

At Rebekah's betrothal the inheritance discussed had been Isaac's material wealth; later, her son Jacob assured himself of a larger portion of the inheritance, that of the firstborn, which Esau had given him in exchange for a bowl of lentils. Rebekah is not interested in that kind of inheritance for Jacob; she is interested in something else, something that the blessing provides, or represents; she is still "disgusted with her life" even after Jacob has received the blessing. Now she insists on sending him to her brother's house for a wife. Jacob chooses Rachel, who is also concerned with religious culture. Rachel takes the *teraphim* when they leave. Her father Laban would not have chased halfway across the country after some statuettes he could have easily replaced; these particular *teraphim* had some important religious significance, and this is why Rachel took them. So Jacob's choice of a religious woman for a wife followed his mother's ambitions for him. It may have been that without the blessing Jacob would not have been acceptable as the husband of a woman of priestly rank, since it is immediately after the blessing that he is sent to be married. It seems evident that the matriarchs were more involved with the perpetuation of their culture and religion in foreign surroundings than their menfolk were.

Nevertheless, the narratives in Genesis certainly trace the genesis of patriarchal religion and culture. Abraham, Isaac, and Jacob do indeed represent an incipient patriarchal tradition among the Hebrews. The extension of that tradition is what our present civilization is all about.

The narratives illustrate the increasing influence patriarchy had on the lives of women over a period of three generations, until the death of Jacob, or approximately three hundred years if the recorded lifespans are taken into consideration.

Patriarchy's greatest asset in its effort to disrupt the matrifocal establishment was mobility. A man's option to move from one location to another with his women and children forced the family to be dependent on him. Significantly the proto-historical portion of the Old Testament commences with the migration of Terah to Haran. Then, as if to emphasize this crucial event, it is sanctified by El Shaddai, who calls Abram with the significant words *lekh lekha*, "walk, go forth" from your native land. Abram's calling was twofold. Leave your matrifocal home, and go to a new land. Once in the new land the same deity makes a covenant with Abram, saying: To your off-spring I give this land. Although Abram is not a conquering hero he is the follower of a God who leads him away from an established social setting to a new location which promises possessions and power. It is this same mobility which, generations later, allows Jacob/Israel's sons to spread out and take hold of the land Abram was promised.

Ironically, it was Rebekah's decision to break the rule of matrilocality which seal-ed the destiny of her gens or descent group. Rebekah left her matrifocal home to marry Isaac in Canaan. Abram sent his servant to bring a wife from the homeland, but he ad-monished the servant that on no condition must he take Isaac back there. Was this in-tentional on Abram's part? Sarah was dead. Had the matriarch made arrangements for the betrothal of her son? Would Sarah have insisted on a matrilocal marriage for her son as Rebekah did? Rebekah was very young when she made the decision to leave her mother. It is possible that neither she nor her mother realized the implications for the young woman of living in patriarchal Canaan. Is this why Rebekah was so distressed, why she insisted on a matrilocal marriage for Jacob in contrast to the marriages of her husband Isaac and his favorite, Esau?

The wily Jacob did not live up to his mother's expectations. After twenty years of matrilocal marriage, Jacob must convince his wives to return with him to Canaan. Mobility and possession become the characteristics of Jacob's life. His descendants, the twelve tribes of Israel, claim the land promised to their ancestors.

Interestingly, the matriarchs were not totally discounted: a compromise was found. Endogamy was extended to include all circumcised males, but matriliny remained the only authentic path to membership within the group. Thus, circumcision is not the only requirement for Jewish males; they must also be born of Jewish mothers. And whether the man who impregnates a Jewish woman is circumcised or not, her off-spring will automatically be recognized as a Jew, a member of her group.

The narratives of the Sarah tradition represent a non-patriarchal system struggling for survival in isolation in a foreign land. Nevertheless, women of strength emerge from the pages of Genesis, women who are respected by men. Their function in life, though different from that of men, is regarded as equally important to society. Women's participation in society as described in the narratives presupposes a system in which women were able to maintain an elevated professional position into which were incorporated the roles of mother and educator. Just as significantly, these women were in control of their own bodies and their own spiritual heritage.

Sarah, Rebekah, and Rachel, in identification with a goddess, chose to remain childless for decades. They chose to conceive, late in life, because of the circumstances they encountered in exile. They were venerated during their lifetimes as priestesses and as women. It is not clear whether a priestess who became a mother was forced to relinquish her profession. If her progeny was the result of the sexual component in the *hieros gamos*, was her child regarded as the offspring of a goddess, of a mortal woman, or of someone in between represented by a priestess? In other words, did the fact of conception during the ritual of the Sacred Marriage or the fact of birth at a later date establish the status of the mother or the child? In early versions of the ritual the priestess who participated in the *hieros gamos* was thought to be the goddess incarnate; if conception took place the offspring were regarded as part divine. In much later times, a child born of the sacred union was to be exposed to the elements and left to its fate. Sarah's son Isaac, however, was celebrated at a feast given by Abram.[3] Does this mean that Sarah lived at a time when the priestess was regarded as goddess incarnate and her son as semi-divine, as was the case with Gilgamesh? Or was the son's life spared because the priestess was living in safety in exile? What had become of Sarah's status in exile, in the society in which she was living?

How far did Sarah's vision of the society extend? Did she feel that she had been transported to and isolated in a patriarchal future? Did she long for her non-patriarchal homeland? Or did she leave because that social system was changing also? Did she, in fact, have a choice?

These questions and many more can be asked but not answered. But Rebekah's expression of anguish would seem to represent the despair and sorrow experienced by all three matriarchs: "If so, why do I exist?"

Over four thousand years later, this same despair and this same struggle is being experienced by women in both social and religious spheres.

But we are not alone. Sarah is there, standing on the threshold, waiting to be returned to her rightful place in history. Significantly, the title which could qualify the three mothers of Israel, "Priestess," has been totally eradicated from the record. The feminine form of the word for priest (*kohen*) does not appear anywhere in the Hebrew Bible,[4] although it has survived in the form *kahina* in Arabic.

There are still some formidable obstacles to be overcome, but the record of Sarah's life reveals the existence of an alternative system to patriarchy. The social system the three matriarchs defended indicates the presence of a struggle against patriarchy, and of a social structure in which women played a prominent part in religion and culture.

The Sarah tradition gives us an insight into the potential of women's roles to affirm women.

———————————————— NOTES ————————————————

[1]. Carol Ochs, *Behind the Sex of God: Toward a New Consciousness Transcending Matriarchy and Patriarchy* (Boston: Beacon Press, 1977), p. 34.

[2]. D. N. Freedman, "Ebla is a Four Letter Word," LSA (Univ. of Michigan alumni pub., 1977), suggests that the Abraham of Genesis 14 could belong to the third millennium BCE (p. 18). See argument on this point in Chaim Bermant and Michael Weitzman, *Ebla, A Revelation in Archaeology* (NY: Times Books, 1979), pp. 188-189.

[3]. It is significant to the argument that Isaac was not circumcised in infancy, that the great feast given by Abram celebrated the *weaning* of Isaac rather than his circumcision.

[4]. J. H. Otwell, *And Sarah Laughed: The Status of Women in the Old Testament* (Phila.: Westminster Press, 1977), p. 155.

# 5. *Kol Haisha*: Israeli Women Speak

*Two Jewish girls in Palestine.* Jewish Daily Forward. *August 31, 1924.*

# IN MEMORIAM

*January, 1985*

## NAOMI KIES
## 1942-1985

*When we first arrived in Israel in December, 1984, Pnina Putterman Ben-Horin put us in touch with her friend Naomi Kies, because she said Naomi would know how to help us connect with Israeli women to talk about peace, about civil rights activities, about feminism. And Naomi did know how to help. In addition to feeding us, talking with us, spending time answering our foolish as well as our informed questions, Naomi gave us names, places, and introductions to activists, artists, politicians in both Jewish and Arab Jerusalem and on the West Bank as well. Thus Naomi became our guide, and much of what we were able to learn, gather, and achieve in Israel was due directly or indirectly to her help.*

Naomi Kies was born in the US in 1942 to a schoolteacher mother and a lawyer father who worked mostly defending, among others, Italian and Jewish immigrants. He had come from China at age 13.

Growing up in Yonkers, NY in a middle-class Zionist home, Naomi attended Jewish religious school and was part of an Israeli folkdance group. She studied history at Swarthmore College and received a Ph D in political science from M I T , writing her dissertation on voting behavior in Jerusalem. She immigrated to Israel after the '67 War.

In Israel, Naomi taught political science at the School for Preparatory Studies at Hebrew University and at the Open University. She was a frequent commentator and lecturer on Israeli politics and, occasionally, on women in Israel. She never married. She had researched the single-parent family in Israel, and had wanted children of her own.

During the Yom Kippur War (1973), Naomi worked as a volunteer, delivering letters and telegrams, then became an ambulance driver; but in 1982 she refused to serve in Lebanon.

Her political debut had come in the early '70s with the Israeli Black Panther Party. Poor neighborhoods in Jerusalem were protesting the economic plight and discrimination against Oriental Jews, and Naomi became involved. At first the Panthers didn't trust her because she was Ashkenazi. But her dedication earned their trust, and she was able to provide organizational and administrative expertise. After Panther headquarters burned down, headquarters moved into her home. She often responded to emergency calls.

In Israeli politics generally, she was active and well known on the left, along with Uri Avnery, Matti Peled and others in favoring meetings with the PLO in occupied territories and abroad. Throughout her years in Israel she was a peace and civil rights activist, working in the Council Against the War in Lebanon, Committee for Solidarity with Birzeit University (the best known of the Palestinian West Bank Universities), the Council for Palestinian-Israeli Peace. She formed close ties with Arab people in the occupied territories, and developed friendships.

When we met Naomi, she had already been ill for several years and was undergoing treatment. Five months later—May 4, 1985—she was dead of leukemia. In her will she divided the proceeds from the sale of her Jerusalem apartment to be used for peace, civil rights, and feminist projects.

The last time we saw Naomi, she mentioned a recurring image she had of the conflict between the Israelis and Palestinians: two photographs superimposed, so that both occupied the same space, but neither fully. A simpler view would admit just one image; Naomi saw both, knew that any solution had to encompass both.

We honor Naomi Kies not only for the help she gave us, but for her dedication to the causes of peace, justice, and feminism in Israel. And we grieve at the thought of never seeing her again.

*Melanie Kaye/Kantrowitz*
*Irena Klepfisz*

The New Israel Fund has created a project in Naomi Kies' name. Contributions can be directed to NIF—Naomi Kies Project, 111 W. 40 St., NYC 10018.

Melanie Kaye/Kantrowitz and Irena Klepfisz

# An Interview with Chaya Shalom

*Chaya Shalom was born in West Jerusalem in 1944, the fourth generation of Palestinian Sephardic Jews. The youngest of eight children, she got her BA in 1973 from Hebrew University in Jerusalem, where she studied Jewish History and General History. She has held a variety of jobs, including researcher for T.V. programming, producing a puppet show, and teaching Hebrew, and she currently works as a secretary in a high school. She lives in West Jerusalem in the same apartment in which she was raised. She is a feminist activist and organized events for Kol Haisha (Woman's Voice, a women's center and newspaper in Jerusalem).*

*We talked to Chaya on January 16, 1985, in Ein Kerem—an Arab village before 1948—right outside of Jerusalem where we had gone for a picnic. The interview took place in English.*

*Let's begin with some background.*

I was born in '44 here in Jerusalem. I am the youngest of 8, 5 boys and 3 girls, but 2 died in childhood. I was the only one born in a hospital. The others were born at home with a midwife. My parents were born here too. I think we are the 4th or the 5th generation in Jerusalem, in a section called *Zikhron Yosef,* and we are *samakhtet,* which is pure Sephardim, which means we didn't mix with other Jews even. My mother was Rebecca and my father, Itzhak.

*Why do you laugh when you say* samakhtet?

I'm laughing, because there was a time when we were really proud to be *samakhtet,* and I feel I am almost embarrassed to say it now because maybe I am still

214

proud somehow.

*Can you explain what Sephardim means in terms of history, because you said you distinguished yourself from other Jews?*

First there are those Sephardic Jews who keep up Spanish Jewish traditions. They use a language called Ladino. It's the antique Sephardic Spanish language from the time of Cervantes, mixed, of course, with words from the languages of countries they came from like Turkey, Yugoslavia, or Greece. Other Jews who are *now* called Sephardim are from the Mediterranean, Arab countries, and North Africa, like Morocco, Syria, Lebanon, Yemen, and Iraq.

I don't know why they call everybody Sephardim. But once there was a time, now maybe less—when there was discrimination and stereotyping even among the Sephardim. I remember that people didn't like the Kurds, even though the Kurds are very hard workers, good, warm people. I know them. They were the majority in my neighborhood.

*Who didn't like them?*

The other Sephardim. But also the Europeans—the Ashkenazi—and now the Americans. They all came with stereotypes of murderers, bandits, criminals, and I think the Sephardim picked it up. Like the Moroccans were called *Moroccan Sakin*, which means Morocco-knife. I'm not clear where all these stereotypes come from. I know that the Sephardim consider themselves nobles, the high society of the Jews, even when they are lower class economically, like my family.

*What did your parents do? What kind of work?*

My mother was a housewife and a mother. A full-time job. And she was illiterate. She knew a little bit. Here and there she knew some of the alphabet. She could read babies' or kids' books. My father was better educated, like most Jewish men. He went to *kheder,* but I don't think he could read a newspaper. He started working with metal and ended up as a plumber. He was a very good, a very hard worker. He'd get up at five, six o'clock and get home when it was dark. I remember bringing lunch to him at work. He didn't want us kids to be educated. He wanted the first sons to join him at work, and the first one, the least educated, did. The third was the one who broke away. It was because of my mother who wanted her kids to have more education, and she pushed and pushed. She didn't want us to be like her. She wanted us to be better, have better conditions, a better life. So she really had to fight with my father a lot. So the third one was the first to break away and the rest of us followed. So four of us are university-educated.

*Was your family religious at all?*

My mother and father were religious when the kids were growing up, but after the first child, my brother, grew up, they became less religious but remained traditional, like celebrating holidays. When I was a kid, my father took me to synagogue every *shabat* and all the holidays.

*Did you speak Ladino at home?*

At home the adults spoke Ladino among themselves and their guests. So I heard it. I myself didn't speak it, but I could understand it. The person who contributed most to my knowledge is my uncle Bekhor. Every night he would sit and tell us stories, fairy stories. These were like Arab stories, you know like *A Thousand and One Nights.* Most of his stories had a character called Jukha, the village idiot who was always made fun of. Bekhor was an excellent story teller. He kept us in suspense. He was very dramatic. I heard all these popular stories—it was like a ceremony—every night. I really don't know where he got them all. And sometimes he repeated them and we liked him to repeat.

*Your uncle was in your house every night?*

Ken. Every evening. This uncle was also a neighbor. His wife, my aunt, was my mother's sister. She was also our other mother; she also brought us up. And so we had this gathering almost every night.

*So Chaya you were speaking Hebrew then, before '48?*

Yes. I was only four. I spoke to them in Hebrew. They spoke to me in Hebrew. But what dominated was Ladino.

*Were they speaking Hebrew because they were Zionists?*

No, no. Don't forget I had five older brothers and sisters, who were sabras. And in the modern period, they spoke Hebrew at school—it was the national language. Also my father had to use Hebrew at work. No, there was no Zionism there. Who knew what Zionism was? They were born here.

*Did they have feelings about '48?, About the state? Were they happy about that?*

I don't know. I think yes. I don't remember. There is so much idealization in the stories of that time that I don't know what the truth is. I remember my father saying that before '48, Arab people were his best friends, but also that there wasn't complete trust. I'm sure a lot of them were friends because he grew up in the Old City.

*In the Old City was there a lot of mingling of Jews and Arabs? Did they live close together?*

There was a Jewish Quarter and there was a Muslim Quarter, and I think they must have had good relations—in business and personal matters — but I don't know much about it.

*When we were walking through your neighborhood, you were telling us about the women and* Rosh Khodesh.

I have read and heard about it. It was in the Old City in the Jewish Quarter. There was a courtyard (El cortijo) where the Sephardim lived, and it was surrounded by rooms. I don't know who owned it—maybe a rich Jew. And in every room there was a family or two. So the courtyard had quite a social life. Of course, the men went to work and the women stayed home to do housework. The women were together all day and they shared everything. They shared what they had, exchanged what they cooked, and also shared a lot of their personal life and feelings. They were quite open to each other because, as I said, they were together all the time. What they described to me was really a women's community. Especially on *Rosh Khodesh*, the new moon and the first day of each month by the Jewish calendar. It was a holiday when they were free of problems and work.

For example, they decided a certain day would be a laundry day. Laundry day was the hardest day of the week. They didn't let anybody in, no kids, nobody. At that time, of course, they didn't have any electricity or running water. They had to take the water either from the stream outside of Jerusalem or pay an Arab who was passing by to bring it. And they used candles or lamps and it was very hard. Everything was hard to do. Even the laundry water was used afterwards to clean the house or wash the ground or whatever. They had to save it.

So on such a day they'd sit together and to make it easier for themselves, they'd tell stories, personal stories, and they'd sing I think that all these romances—Sephardic and Spanish, the stories and the antique songs—were preserved by women. They were the ones who used them. They sang them on every occasion, at home, at parties, weddings, whatever. And they had a good time. It was a very hard day for them, but they knew how to have a good time.

At the end of the day, a woman would change her clothes. Sometimes she had a *nargillah* [waterpipe used for tobacco] and she relaxed with it. They said it's good for headaches. They usually had a lot of headaches because of the strain of hard work and having so many kids. And they had to manage the house with the little money they had. They really had to be the best financiers in the world to know how to manage the house on nothing. So they had a lot of pressures. And they used the *nargillah* to relax. And then when the husband came home, it was like nothing had happened to her. She smiled and served the food and she didn't complain. Because he had his own *tsores*, his own problems, she couldn't tell him hers. She didn't show what was going on with her. So that's why she shared so much with her women friends. This was part of everyday life, at least before '48.

I am very angry because there were a lot of women there who were like doctors, healers. These women knew all about—how you say—herbs and healing treatments. One was called Tsiporah La Polvera. *Polvera* is a powder. She knew how to heal eyes with a certain powder. Who knows how she made it. There were other women who really did miracles. In the house, you would see planted herbs which were good for a stomach ache or colds and other sicknesses. They also were midwives—like Bolissa Bekhora de Yehiel—and they had to be psychologists too because they prepared women for childbirth and raising children. The tradition was to want the first child to be a boy, and if a girl was born, these midwives helped the parents accept the girl baby. They even lived with the family for a few days and helped her with a lot of jobs. But at the time, nobody thought they were important enough to be remembered. They're not mentioned any place. Only in books by Yakov Yehoshua did I read about them. He talked with old people, not only about the healers but also about the women.

*This was true for your Grandmother — when did it start breaking down?*

After '48. In my neighborhood, you still have these courtyards. Not exactly the same. But those tight neighborhoods still remain here and there for the old women. I don't think there is any of that for the young, but for the old women it's still there.

*Well, what happened in '48 when the State of Israel was established?*

They all moved from the Old City (which was under Jordanian administration) to

217

Jerusalem, the Israeli side. But they assumed it was temporary. And it wasn't. Everyone stayed. Like my family stayed where I live right now. So it changed, the old unity of the people.

*Was it simply the physical move, Chaya, or was it psychological also?*

I think it's the modern times. And, you know, all things change. The new generation doesn't respect the old people at all and are even ashamed of them, ashamed that they're illiterate. The young people think the old ones are not educated, don't have culture. It's only lately—and after pressure from Sephardi leaders—that the culture and history of the Oriental Jews is being uncovered and maybe revived. You can hear it—a famous Yemen singer like Ofra Chaza has started singing Yemenite songs, and Shlomo Bar sings Moroccan songs. And there are others. Now is the time to revive some of the culture.

I remember even in my childhood there was unity, friendship among the neighbors, like baking the *khamin*, the Sephardic name for *tsholent*. Friday you brought it to the bakery to cook. You have to know about the bakery. There wasn't electricity. There was fire. You waited there on *shabat* morning to get your pot. Or you brought your cookies. Not long ago an old friend of mine confessed that she would steal my cookies or my *borekas* on the way home [laugh]. So it was kind of like that. *Pesakh* people made the *matsah shmura* together there in the bakery. It was stamped in the shape of a menorah and other holy symbols. It was very creative. It was really something. Well, nostalgia. So it changed.

*I wonder what else happened in '48 and after. You're talking about a way of life that was disrupted for various reasons. What was it like for you—a Sephardic little girl growing up in the State of Israel?*

I went to this public school called Alliance which was all Sephardic. I don't know the exact history of the school, but it had French support.

*The children and the teachers were all Sephardic?*

No, no. I'm talking about the children. Sephardim — actually Oriental. And most of the teachers were of European background. They were from France and came with this French education which was quite tough. The teachers beat the pupils. There was quite a gap between them and us. I don't know if they understood what all these people were about who were from a poor class, poor status. But you know, my parents, the old people admired the teachers because they were educated. Now the parents are more involved with what's going on in school. Then, they gave all the power to the teachers.

But I want to say that we were quite a proud family. My brother was the only one who married an Ashkenazi, though my mother was pleased with this: he's married to an Ashkenazi woman and she's the daughter of a doctor and she plays a violin. My mother was proud. So things changed when the Europeans, the Ashkenazi came and dominated this country. Even though the Sephardim outnumbered them, the Sephardi image was low. As you know, only lately has the anger come out. I know that when I went to the youth movement Scouts at the age of 10, it was mostly Ashkenazi. And it was religious, supported by the National Religious Party. I went not because I was

*A woman packing* matzoh *in Palestine.* Jewish Daily Forward. *April 21, 1929.*

religious but because my best friend, she was in this movement and so I followed her. I know I felt a difference. There was a difference between the Sephardim and Ashkenazi.

I can't give examples, I just remember feeling different. I had this *bat mitzvah* party and I invited them. And I think, I'm not 100% sure, I wanted to hide some of my Sephardic background—my family, my mother or whatever. I remember some of these feelings. I myself can pass because of how I look. I look Ashkenazi and have a non-Oriental accent. Originally, I had quite an Oriental accent with the *khet* and with the *ayen*. But it changed as soon as I started with this movement. *Reysh*, my *reysh* didn't change. But this accent change did not happen just to me. Most people have adopted an Ashkenazi accent. It really dominates right now. And Sephardim changed their names to more modern Hebrew names; for example, from Mizrakhi to Kedem or Mayraz. *Do most Sephardim try to change their accents?*

Some still have the old, but they're usually not younger than me. Maybe there are some my age. But if you meet my family—my sister and I have Ashkenazi accents. My older brothers, they have really heavy Oriental accents. People who don't know Hebrew would think it's Arabic.

*Were most of your friends Sephardic? Did you have Ashkenazi friends when you were growing up?*

In high school, it was mixed. But I think my best friends were Ashkenazi.

*At what point did you become conscious that you were Sephardic and they were Ashkenazi and that you were ashamed in a way and were trying to change your accent?*

I don't think I was conscious at all. Only lately have I begun to think about it. It's never bothered me because I hated it on the one hand and, on the other, I passed. So I was Ashkenazi. Not that I lied about it. *Khas v'khalila* I was proud to say every time I was asked, "Are you Ashkenazi?" "No, I'm Sephardic." I liked to see the surprise on their faces that I am Sephardic. And not only that I am Sephardic, but that I'm a sabra and not only that I'm a sabra but that I'm also from the city not from a kibbutz, because some people think that I'm from a kibbutz.

*What's happened in the last few years in Israel that your consciousness has been raised?*

I can't say much about this. I can say generally that I think it was Begin's policy to split the people and how you call it—divide and conquer. Yes, that's actually what he did because he himself is Polish—excuse me, Irena—and very Ashkenazi. And for God's sake,how can he talk in my name?

*So Begin's intention wasn't particularly noble?*

No. I'm sure it wasn't. The whole way they deal with it, it's so hypocritical.

*Well, this is totally switching the subject. I want to talk a little bit about feminism. Can you talk about how you got involved with feminism?*

I am quite new to feminism. For me, it occurred together with coming out. From '78-'80 I worked as a secretary for the Organization for Civil Rights. The focus was then on the rights for Palestinians, Bedouins, political prisoners and others. They took up discrimination at the workplace. And there I think my consciousness was raised about the rights of people. Not so much for women—but in general. And then around '80 I met a good friend who was divorced and had two kids. I had conversations with her and it was really the first time I listened to feminist talk. Before it seemed to me more like labels, or something not interesting, not so important. My general political consciousness started only in '75 or '73. Before that I was numbed out. Even after '67. I had been in the army in '62-'65; in '67, during the Yom Kippur War, I was in the reserves. For 10 years since my army service I didn't have any political consciousness.

So conversations with this woman about women started to stimulate me and this happened together with my coming out because I was quite in the closet. I didn't recognize myself as a lesbian. I knew I was, but I never tried to confront it. But this woman knew, even though she was straight. She talked about women, and friendships with women, and how it's different from men, and soon she raised my consciousness as a lesbian.

That was around June, 1980, and *Kol haisha* opened and she pushed me to go there. *Kol haisha* was a women's center, run by a collective; they were feminists. It was quite intimidating for me the first time. I knew only one of the women. We had been in high school together, but we had no connection since then. I started being interested in what was going on. That's why my feminism and coming out happened together. I felt *Kol haisha* was quite a safe place for me. I could be free and act free. Of course, I met a lot of women. And after four months, I started to be active. And within half a year, I joined the collective, which was at that time I think half Israelis, half Americans.

*Can you clarify your terms?*

By Israelis I mean those of us who were born here. At that time we had at *Kol haisha* a lot of activities. Groups, lectures, evening discussions, and many workshops.

A lot of women came and were very active. That collective lasted about two years. And then the women in the first collective burned out. We knew that the most important thing was to reach out to women, but somehow it didn't work. The women that came were more or less educated women, maybe from a higher economic class. But I think our failures was that we couldn't reach women who are most oppressed, those from a lower economic class. The whole political and social situation in Israel, with the religious domination and no support whatsoever from the establishment, made it a mission impossible to reach out to these women. So the collective changed. And it became frozen. There wasn't much activity. Just the place remained. *Kol haisha* magazine which started being published in 1981 every month or two, continued. But in October, 1983, the center closed and publication stopped. The publication of the magazine was one of the big projects. We had 300 subscribers, than less and less. It was the only magazine which had a special column on lesbian issues.

The second collective, which started in the end of 1982, was more dominated by Americans. And *Kol haisha* was labelled a lesbian place. Here feminist means that you are a lesbian. It's a common stereotype. *Kol haisha* became more social and had less political activities. And it was a good place for the women tourists who wanted to get information and meet dykes.

There was always the debate whether we should be political and align ourselves with the left and with Palestinian women. Those who felt we shouldn't do it said we would lose a lot of women and that we had to be less political so maybe more women would come.

In the end it wasn't really very political. A lot of women who maybe wanted to be active probably didn't think this was the right place. So by 1983 the second collective also burned out, and after 3½ years *Kol haisha* closed in October '83.

And since then there has been almost no activity. Sometimes women who work in the rape crisis centers or in battered women's shelters have a feminist activity such as educational work on violence against women. They had a week of activity of street theatre and petition signing. A group of us thought we'd start another center two years ago. We had this women's week and had demonstrations and evening discussions about women's issues. But it's like there's no energy or hope now.

Also—and I haven't touched on this at all—the situation here. Most of the energy for everything is taken away from us by the religious domination and the political issue of security. So there's no place even to deal with women's status. There's very little consciousness. We had an abortion law which allowed women to have abortions for social or economic reasons, but the religious parties pressured to change the law, to restrict abortion. So there was a regression in women's status. Some women think we should put energy into the progressive and peace movements, like *Shalom Akhshav* [Peace Now] or other left activities because they deal with what seems like the main problem.

Other women don't see how the whole situation relates to us as women. And the religion. I don't know, I'm quite in despair about what's happening because this small religious group really dominates us and does whatever it wants. So it's hard. It's hard. I myself don't have energy to fight on all borders.

*If you could control things, what would you like to see happen politically in Israel, particularly with regard to Palestinians and peace? What do you think would be a good solution?*

I believe the Palestinians need their own state, so I hope they will have their own state beside Israel. And I really hope that the Israelis want peace and that the Palestinians want peace. Because you can see what has happened to us as people and human beings in the last 30 years. Since '67 it's worse. Maybe things will calm down and we can finally put our energy into better things than oppressing people and I won't have to watch every place to see if there is a bomb.

I'm very sure that even if the Palestinians have their own state, not everything will be solved. I still think there will be hostility on both sides because it will take time. It will take a lot of time until we trust each other. But at least making peace will be the first step. The other ways only lead us to great disaster. I can see only hope in doing something else. Not only because I think it's the Palestinians' right to have a state. But because the future will be better.

*What do you think is going to happen?*

In the beginning it will be rough. As I said, I don't think there will be trust. But I don't know—with the Arabs, the Russians, the Americans—it's too overwhelming for me to know what will happen. But if I look further—after the first period, I would like to see us put energy into developing this country. Of course, the first thing I would like to see is women's status improved and for it to stop being a religious country as it is now, to have humanistic values and equality for all people.

*Do you think it should be a Jewish country?*

You are asking a hard question because, again, if it is a Jewish country, it means that I discriminate against other people who maybe need a place. But isn't this what happens in every country? I don't know what to say. Ideally why should I care if it is Jewish or something else? So every country should to be open to everyone. It's hard for me to answer.

Certainly—those who were born here—like the Israelis and Palestinians—this country is theirs as well as mine. There's no question about it. I know I would like this country to be open to everyone, but I know that's not realistic.

*Chaya, some people who were born here say that they identify mainly as Israelis rather than Jews. Is that something you've thought about?*

I associate Jew with—I don't know where it comes from—the *galut* [Diaspora] Jew and it's not a good image. It's quite stereotyped—there are two kinds. One is the very orthodox—the black hats and black coats. So this is one stereotype. I really can't, don't identify with them. They are too closed. They are too much in another world. And the other stereotype is the modern Jew who is wealthy, who when he comes here feels—what is it in English?—paternalistic. That's the word. When he comes with his dollars. And, of course, it's an American Jew—with the cars and all that.

*It's mainly American Jews in that stereotype?*

*Ken.* And I think I have it myself, because I remember how they treated me. They came to visit this area, to see the neighborhood or the school. We were the poor ones. And again, this is a Sephardic issue too. We were seen as people who needed to be helped, and they would come and pat our head and take out sugars for treats.

As for anti-Semitism, I don't have the experience. I know it from history. I learned about it. I read about it in the newspapers right now. But I don't have it here. I know other kinds of anti-Semitism. I have the Sephardi-Ashkenazi issue. I have the Arab-Jew issue. I don't geel in Israel I have to be a Jew. What is important for me, what I identify myself as, is Israeli. Of course, I was born here. It's an accident that I am a Jew. I could be Palestinian, Muslim. I don't know. I'm proud of what I am. So if I am a Jew, I'm proud to be an Israeli Jew. *Ken?* This is what I am. But first I am Israeli. Being religious never was an issue for me. It didn't bother me—I mean in my personal life. It bothers me in terms of what is going on in the country.

*Do you feel there's such a thing as the Jewish people? Do you feel connected with Jews outside of Israel?*

Paradoxically I think yes, even after what I've said. I think yes because after all we share a background. There is a history. And when I talk, other Jews know what I'm talking about. Yes, so there is this history, these roots somewhere, thousands of years ago, which sometimes I myself—and, I think, a lot of people—don't want. I'm here in the 20th century. So why should I bother about what happened 2000 years ago? But it seems like it chases you all the time. There is a feeling. I never think about it. But because you're asking me, I answer yes.

*You've been in the States where you obviously met a lot of non-Jews? Was that different for you in some sense?*

In a way. You can't tell Jews by looks. It's only the subject that you pick for conversation that points up the difference between Jews and others. Because as a Jew, Israel and being Jewish comes up a lot. And with others you talk about other issues.

*Is there something you wanted to add about the Israeli lesbians?*

Yes, about feminist lesbians because I don't know much about straight lesbians as we call them. Because as a feminist, I'm quite conscious of what's going on with myself as a woman and as a lesbian.

In Israel, I think, it's like in any other place, I have to be in the closet. What happens is that you have a double life. At work or outside, I myself don't talk about

223

anything in my social life, of course. What should I tell? That I'm with my dyke friends? Maybe I can tell some things about my family or that I saw a movie. But I don't go into detail. To be with women, by the way, to be always with a woman here—maybe it's like that in the States—is shameful. It means you are a poor thing, a poor woman, that you don't have a man. Even when I talk about woman friends, I can see their eyes, how they look at me like I am a poor thing. But sometimes I think the way I talk about these women, maybe they see that it's something else.

Of course, as a dyke I'm angry that I can't hold my lover's or even my woman friend's hand and walk in the streets. It's simple. I can't do it. I know there are some communities in the States—or maybe other cities in the world—where you can do that. Here I can't. Except maybe in Arab villages where women really touch each other and are affectionate. But here, they would know you're a lesbian. You'd attract too much attention. So this makes me angry. At the school where I work, I see a boy and girl almost making out. And *I* can't do anything. Not that I want to make out in front of everybody. But I don't feel free. I have to act quite different.

Right now, because I'm 40, my family has already given up on me. Okay, she won't get married. But it's not only my family. Even the bank clerk asked me when I called a few days ago, "Well, you still have the same family name? Why don't you change it?" He means, of course, that I ought to be married. So you have this pressure all the ..me, all the time because you have to be married. *Married.* Here in Israel, you have to be married.

It's very hard, not only for lesbians, but also for single women to be by themselves. There's this pressure—whether it's verbal or not, you can feel it. It's very odd if women live together after they're students. Up to then it's okay, but afterwards, it's odd. It's risky for a couple to live together. And I'm not even talking about coming out to your family. Very few women I know have come out to their families, and they are very brave. I've come out only to my sister. She was the safest person in my family. *Do you think that's going to change? We've heard some talk about starting a coming out group.*

I don't know. I think as more women come out, the easier it will be for the rest. So the problem is for the first ones. And about dykes and how they look. You know most of the dykes here are feminists and they look like dykes. They're unusual because you are supposed to wear makeup and put all these colors on your face, and wear heels and I don't know what. I know a woman—I won't mention her name—because she asked me not to—in a high position. She dresses well for her job. And the minute she comes home, she changes her clothes. So it's really like having two personalities. I'm glad that at the school where I work, I can look like I look now. There's no problem. But you should see the girls there. My god, what they look like!

What I really miss is Israeli women's culture, like women's songs about women, women's festivals, women's literature in Hebrew and translations of feminist books and, of course, a women's space.

## Update: January, 1988

Today, sitting at home in the cold Jerusalem winter, focusing on the situation of lesbians in Israel, I can say there has been a change in the feminist movement: A lesbian-feminist organization has joined its ranks.

The idea of KLAF—"Card" (acronym for Lesbian Feminist Community) was conceived at the Geneva International Lesbian Conference in the spring of 1986. Being one of the 800 lesbians from many countries, and further, meeting many Third World women, cannot leave you unchanged: the stimulation is so powerful that you ask yourself what action is most crucial for the advancement of lesbians in Israel. The meeting in Geneva made clear to me that we need to foster an Israeli-lesbian culture.

In December 1986 came the opportunity to put this idea forward: I held a workshop on lesbian culture and organizing in Israel. The 17 women who attended voiced the need to continue the discussion and to open it to additional women. About 45 women came to this wider meeting, at which we concluded that before we could organize, we must first crystallize as a community.

We began with a study day about "feminism and lesbianism." Next, women undertook to prepare a series of discussion evenings on various topics, which I organized and which took place all through 1987 at regular meetings in the offices of the Feminist Movement in Tel Aviv. In these evenings we discussed various topics: psychological treatment for lesbians, mass politics, lesbians on kibbutz, lesbian mothers, internalized homophobia, and so on. So far we have published summaries of three discussions: "Feminism and Lesbianism," "Lesbians on Kibbutz," and "Lesbian Mothers." These are the first publications in the country about lesbians in our own voices, as even the first Israeli magazine for homosexuals and lesbians—*Maga'im* (Contacts)—has as editors all men, who have no feminist consciousness.

The regular meetings also gave birth to other ideas like outings into nature, fun days, parties, music, and songs. Creative women in the community have found our meeting place to be safe and supportive, and today we get to enjoy original lesbian singing and poetry, sometimes even outside of exclusively women's circles. The courage to come out in the heterosexual world has undoubtedly been nourished by our lesbian community's support and encouragement.

The nucleus of our community came from women of the Association for the Protection of Personal Rights, the gay and lesbian organization, many of whom had little or no feminist awareness. One of KLAF's successes is that now we all understand the need for a lesbian organization and its connection to feminism. Just recently an activists' meeting decided to work together toward a formal feminist-lesbian organization. Our latest move has been to join the "forum" of feminist organizations in Israel, significant because lesbians' contributions to the Israeli feminist movement have often been denied.

KLAF's activity has brought in more and more women looking for alternatives to the gay bars and discos. From a mailing list of 50 women, we have grown to about 150, aside from the many women who choose to remain anonymous. Everyone on the mailing list receives a regular newsletter about community activities. So what began as a one-woman operation is today an organization with subgroups and committees. I have left the circle of activity for a few months for personal reasons, and today I serve only as spokesperson.

I think that KLAF's goal of crystallizing a community has been accomplished. Perhaps symbolic of the community life is a ceremony of commitment between two women which was held in January, 1988, the first in Israel to the best of my knowledge. Many women were involved in this project, which became a cultural lesbian event. The ceremony was imbued with humor and lesbian-female content, and well grounded in the Israeli-Jewish culture, with much support from the women in the community. Such a ceremony could not have been conceived of one year earlier.

Meanwhile the *intifada* (uprising) and repression against it continue, and I cannot say I feel hopeful about a quick resolution. In fact, many of us are very depressed about the situation. But at least in one area there has been progress. My dream from two years ago, for an independent lesbian organization, is coming true. I hope within the coming years to see an organization that can stand on its own feet and expand its activities beyond the feminist movement to reach women's organizations, universities, educational institutions, and so on. Our numbers will increase, and it will no longer be possible to ignore us.

This is an opportunity to appeal to our sisters to support and help us with any contribution that will further our work. (For KLAF's address, see p. 258.)

*KLAF graphic*

# Lea Majaro-Mintz: Israeli Artist

*Lea Majaro-Mintz was born in Palestine and grew up in Jerusalem, in the Old City where she lives today with her husband and many sculptures of women. She chooses to show her work in a living environment, and, as her creations have taken up more room, she has opened another "home" for her work in Tel Aviv. Hebrew is her native language; our interview, from which her words are excerpted, was conducted in English, in her home, in January, 1985.*

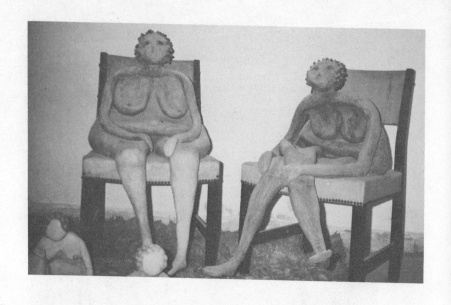

*Excerpted from an interview conducted by Irena Klepfisz and Melanie Kaye/Kantrowitz. Jerusalem January 6, 1985*

I started as a painter and I painted for many years before I went to sculpture. I had my first exhibition 30 years ago. And when the children were born, every painting was connected with them: if I did landscape, there was a little child looking at it. When we went to live in the suburbs, I grew a little garden, so that world of vegetation and insects was the subject of my paintings. When we got a car and went out to the country, the desert attracted me. And I was born here in the Old City, and I painted it from memory many times before we came back to stay.

And then came the Six Day War [in 1967]. My children were still very young, and when I had to take them to shelters, I realized for the first time what war means. And I thought of other mothers who weren't so lucky, whose children were at the front. And that's our great agony — the problem of sending boys to war.

And at the same time, I took my first steps in sculpture. I was working on abstract forms, and one of them I developed into a woman. A human figure. And suddenly I discovered the woman I had in mind—she who has sent her boys to the wars and they didn't come back. A middle-aged woman who has been working on two jobs, one at home and one outside, and raising children and giving all of herself to them.

Well, of course, the drama of the Six Day War was soon over. But the woman's drama went on. She was there. She existed, was part of me. And it was also a time that—at a certain stage of your life, you no longer trust externals, the thing from the outside, and are perhaps less busy giving yourself up to others, and suddenly you discover your own self. So it started with a certain trauma and it went on. . . .

The general subject: first, a person who seems part of the crowd, just as in the world we're not single, we are not by ourselves. We are always surrounded by others. We want to understand what is going on among other people around us. We try situations where we feel we can identify with others. Take a music festival. Everyone can listen to records at home, but we take the trouble to go to distant places to listen to rock music with some 10 or 20 thousand people. The experience is not so much the listening but the listening together.

And since life is like that, I feel I can't make a single sculpture. I have to do them in masses. The crowd is part of life; my sculpture must show this. . . . But even being in a crowd doesn't mean always that we feel together. Sometimes we feel alone. And that ambivalence between being together and being alone is part of the sculpture. . . .

. . .Not every viewer will see the same thing in the sculptures. . . .Some say they are funny and others say they are sad. The truth is that it's sad and at the same time I'm mitigating sadness with humor. Very few see both.

— *Lea Majaro-Mintz*

*Nava Mizrahhi*

# To Be an Arab Jew

To be an Arab Jew.
What is this title?
What does it mean?
Are you Arab? Are you Jewish?
Where you standing?
How can it even be?
You are either Arab,
Or you are Jewish—
Because there is the Arab-Jewish conflict.
But I am an Arab Jew,
Because Farha Abdallah
Came from Iraq
Which is Arab country.
Of course when she came to Jerusalem,
She become Farha Mizrahhi.
She is Jewish.
She been to the synagogue
Every Friday night and Saturday morning.
She keeps kosher.
Her language is Arabic.
The music she listens to is in Arabic.
And her connection to the big world
Is through the Arabic department
Of the Israeli television.
Since she live in Jerusalem,
She could also enjoy some more
Program from the TV station in Amman.
I didn't grow up speaking Arabic.
And through my childhood,
I wasn't able to communicate with my grandmother.
My parents wanted me to speak Hebrew.
Then I went to school and learned English and French.
Arabic never been a priority for them.
In the housing project we lived in,
People     from Persia  Kurdistan  Morocco
Iraq  Egypt  Bukhara  Yemen
Lived one next to other.

And instead of a multi-culture
We heard the national radio play
European and "Israeli" music.
And then was the Arabic department.
But you don't really listen to it
Because in the projects everybody could hear
What you listen to—and you are
Ashamed to be caught
Being an Arab Jew.

## Gevalt Poem

A bath
A big bath
A Turkish bath house
Where an older woman tell you
"Scrub my back."
And when you do
She says: "Scrub harder"
And you say: *"Gevalt!"*

# Bracha Serri

"What excites me most with this business of publishing my book, is the thought of giving it to my mother. My mother is illiterate and I am afraid she will think I am making fun of her by giving her a book. Yet I feel I have written my poems for women like my mother; women who do not have a voice, who can't speak up for themselves. My mother was the first poet I knew. In Yemen she used to sing songs about her problems and feelings, making up phrases and repeating them, making up poems as she went along with the household duties. When we came to Israel, she suddenly became quiet."

This is what Bracha Serri told me a few years ago, when she published her book of poetry, Seventy Wandering Poems. A year of labor and all of Bracha's meager savings were spent on publishing the book. With its publication, Bracha not only turned her back on the publishing houses that had refused her work, but, more important, rejected a culture whose upbringing and inner conditioning had taught her that a woman doesn't need to read and write—and certainly shouldn't speak up in public.

When I first met Bracha, she was publishing poems and short stories under fictitious names. Characteristically, one of the ten sections in Seventy Wandering Poems is called "The Gate of Shame." Each section is dedicated to a different group of people in her life, and "The Gate of Shame" is written for her women students and "all men and women who suffocate in the handcuffs of shame." A graduate in linguistics, Bracha has for many years been teaching illiterate women to read and write.

Bracha was born in Sana, Yemen. At the age of nine, she arrived in Israel with her family (which included twelve children) under the spectacular "Operation Magic Carpet" that brought 50,000 Yemenite Jews to the newly founded Jewish state. From one day to another, these deeply religious, traditional people from a hierarchical, underdeveloped society struggled to adapt to a young, modern, dynamic, secular-socialist framework. The young Zionist state had no time or money for social workers, anthropologists, and psychologists. The cultural disintegration and psychological strain suffered by the immigrants resulted in a bitterness, friction, and sense of loss that lingers today as an undercurrent in the fabric of Israeli society.

According to the cultural standards of her Yemenite society, the nine-year-old Bracha was already a little woman. She had been taught all the household chores and the Jewish laws connected with them. To be a fit bride, she lacked only the skill of baking bread. She could neither read nor write.

Arrival in Israel spelled a new life for Bracha. She attended a religious girls' school and excelled as a student. But at home she had to fight for her right to learn. Her mother thought Bracha was lazy when she poured over books instead of helping out in the house.

"My mother was used to men reading the religious books out loud. In that way she could participate, even though she was illiterate. But I was reading silently and I was a woman. There was never any understanding between my mother and me," says Bracha with a sad smile.

Still, Bracha didn't turn her back on women like her mother. As a graduate student of linguistics at the Hebrew University of Jerusalem, Bracha sought out the Yemenite women in the town of Rosh Ha'ayin. She wanted to record every word and nuance of a language that was dying with its last generation of users. The folktales and songs of the Yemenite women reflected their relationship with their families and the community around them.

Bracha's commitment to apply her knowledge to practical situations led her to spend many years teaching illiterate immigrant women. Through this experience she gained important insights into the world view of Eastern Jewish women. Meanwhile she married, had two children, and worked as a community organizer. Later, after suffering much abuse, she divorced. Overcoming her doubts, fears and anxieties, Bracha began to publish poems in magazines and newspapers and to participate in poetry readings. She knew she was invited as the "token Yemenite," but she was also amazed when women of European background expressed their feelings of recognition and identification.

Bracha's language is close to Biblical Hebrew. In all its simplicity and rhythmic-rhyming style, it has a sophistication and irony that do not come across fully in the English translation.

Bracha Serri, in life and in writing, is expressing and exploring the boundaries and confrontations between traditional values and modern society, between East and West, between female experiences and Jewish values, between women in Israel and the political/social State establishment. She is a woman who has traveled from the feudal world of Yemen to the Israeli peace and women's movements of the eighties. In her writing she tries to hold all these worlds together:

> To hold the world tight
> In the palm of your hand
> Crush it and squeeze it
> As fine as sand
> Toss it to the winds
> Cast it to the deep
> And then in silence
> Lie down to sleep
> (translated by Yaffah Berkovitz)

—Anna Goldman-Amirav

*Bracha Serri*

## Butterfly

When I die
I'll drown in the sea
When I die
I'll scatter like ashes
When I die
I'll be hidden, unseen
When I die
I'll be out of the race
I'll be free to idle
Free to just crawl
Free not to eat
Great life indeed!
No more lovers
No more kids
hanging on
to apron strings
No more duties
shame or honor
No more thoughts
ideas to ponder
Free of disappointment
Free of illusions
Free of clothes, make-up
and religious institutions

No more things to arrange
No more visits to exchange
No more reckonings
No more insults
No more chasing
after results

—You'll bury my body
in a coffin tight
A memorial speech
For me you'll write
That's your blindness
Your illusion
I'll flee the tomb
You've laid for me

Already in life
I've broken all bonds
In spite of my ties
In spite of my loves
Yes, I'll flee your grave
Your heaven and hell
I'll be free of your laws
I'll hold back my feet
From walking your paths

When I die
I'll be
a butterfly
A life's dream
come true.

235

# I Came to You

I came to you beaten
wretched, silent,
You held out your arms,
fists tightly clenched,
to wrap me in your
choking embrace.

I came to you
not wanting to,
led to the slaughter
like a wayward daughter.
You licked poison in my wounds,
leaned against me
till you shattered me,
then gathered the broken pieces
moulded them into shape
to soak up your rage.
Your beatings cut through
to my shame,
touched my defenceless guilt.

And so we clung together
in anguish and
terrible hate.

I hated you with passion,
desire welling up in me,
lust of the mortified flesh
locked in the pit of destruction.
Visions of revenge
my only defence
against powerless feeling,
till I lost all sense!

Then I locked away insult
behind laughter and smiles.
Gave the man compliments awhile.
My tears dried up,
turning into bile.
And so I learnt silence
for each act of violence . . .
till you raised your hand
against the lad.

Then I swore forever
to cut off the hand
that struck the child
—through tears and vomit—
to scar him forever.
Then I vowed to avenge
his stricken terror.

I fled from you
beaten, broken, avenging.
I spread my wings
over my child
and soared above peaks
and dived deeper than water.

I walked away from you,
Strong, sane and
Accusing!

# In My City—Heroes

In my city
heroes walk around,
from the market
to the Kings Hotel.
Children and old people
baskets and women.
Forget suspicious objects!
So what if there are bombs!
from the middle of the night
till half past twelve.

In my city
people laugh
a bomb explodes.
Where are you rushing?
Dynamite and
Kabbalists,
Cars blowing up,
blood and filth.
A woman scrubs the yard.
another shouts and curses.

We search,
how we search,
underneath benches
unearthing rubbish
opening bags and baskets.
It's all a matter of luck.
We'll die,
or live,
and that's that!

The bus is packed,
crammed full
with Arab labourers
we can't manage without.

And should we stop going to the movies?
And who will offer blessings at the Wailing Wall?

The whole city is in love
with the eternal triangle,
The heart of song.
And if I forget thee O Jerusalem . . .
And who will show me the golden path?
And every Jerusalemite
is a hero these days.

## Jerusalem and San'a

Jerusalem on high
and San'a down below
are one.
One is my city
a patchwork of colour,
a Babel of sounds
and smells.
The same openness
the same majesty.
An old woman's blessing
like a neighbour's.
The same yearnings
the same prayers.
G-d has moved
to Jerusalem the capital.
Old Jerusalem
not the young one.

I longed to kiss
these strangers,
our 'enemies',
to whisper my thanks
that they exist
as in days gone by
never to return.

I become a hovering dream
in the lanes of the Old City,
a tiny spirit
from Yemen
which is no more.
Intoxicated with the scents
tipsy with the sounds
the perfumes, the spices,
aromatic coffee
dried figs and almonds
assorted raisins
saffron and myrrh
Sweet incense
from the Temple.

*Translated by Yaffah Berkovits*

## Gavriela Elisha

*Gavriela Elisha was born on November 13, 1954, in Jerusalem, where she has lived all her life except for two brief stays in New York City. Her parents are from the Sephardic communities; her father's family came to Israel from Turkey and her mother's from Iraq. Their apartment rooftopped a building in the teeming market area in Jerusalem, Machaneh Yehuda, which is home to many Sephardic families. Elisha's father is no longer living.*

*Five collections of Gavriela Elisha's poetry have been published. The most recent,* Musika acheret *(Other Music) and* Textim uminitextim *(Texts and Minitexts), came out in 1983 and 1985 respectively. A sixth,* Hashra'a *(Inspiration) was published in 1988. She has also published versions of poetry from China and Japan. Her work appears regularly wherever poetry is printed in Israel—in newspapers, periodicals, and magazines. The Israeli equivalents of* People *magazine have taken note of this hot young star of the Israeli poetry scene. Elisha was awarded the Mati Katz Prize in Literature (1973), the Miriam Talper Prize in Literature (1980), and the Prime Minister's Selection (1980) and has received various artists' grants from the Tel Aviv Fund for Literature and the Arts.*

*In her poems and in her personal life she makes no secret of her sexual orientation, but her preference for women does not encompass her identity in either sphere. Elisha's poems have been translated into Spanish and English.*

—Susan Pensak

### She Had Long Wings and a Small Body

A bird I saved from the claws of the cat
was called "wall swallow" according to the manual.
Bread crumbs and water brought the soft body to life
Her wings did not carry her aloft
She practiced low flying in my room
and in the box that was her temporary home
Today I took her out to the yard
and after a little hesitation she spread her wings
and crossed over the roofs
(She'd been with me a few days
I would listen to the sound of her rushing wings in the box
She had long wings and a small body
I wonder which tree or wall
gives her shelter now
and if she has already found her choir of birds)

*Translated by Karen Alkalay-Gut*

## On the Narrow Lane

I now am on the narrow lane
telling myself
loving is like believing in god

I will go with you everywhere, take me
with you everywhere
I will hear your voice in a dream
and in waking as within a dream

(entering the confusion of the unconscious
in dreams about death and murder
and other illogical.occurences)

now I am on the narrow lane
waiting for deliverance
loving you

in joyous silence, desolate silence
vacuum's silence
a sheet of paper is set out on the table
(and is going) to chart the map of problems

fragment after fragment (used) to spend the night
and early bird song already

my life's brief span, tied hands—
maybe life really isn't worth it
if you don't live like a hero

## (Untitled)

you think you are a queen
who are you
who are you
you think you are a hero
no one can
your brain
what will they say
your
mother father

## (Untitled)

If I were a cut of meat hanging on a hook
At a butcher stall that's in the market
If I were in the butcher's hands
How would he split the meat
What would the homemaker do to me
How would I escape from being
A cut of meat hanging on a hook

*Translated by Susan Pensak*

## Karen Alkalay-Gut

*Karen Alkalay-Gut was born in London in 1945 and grew up in Rochester, New York. She completed her Ph.D. in the U.S., writing her dissertation on Theodore Roethke, and since 1977 has been associated with Tel Aviv University. Her poems have been widely published in Israel. She has translated many plays, stories, and poems from Hebrew to English.*

### A Lithuanian Legacy

The soldiers would come
into my grandmother's yard
pull the head off a chicken
and thrust it into her hand

Cook it woman

The Russian soldier the German
then
the Russian again.

### Reckoning

*(Austria/April Israel/June 1982)*

I

"I do not perceive my individual existence
apart from racial identity,"
I hear myself say—two months after
I've returned to Tel Aviv.

240

## II

The blond Englishman in the beige raincoat
encircles the Jewess with his arm
whilst strolling on cobbled Getreidegasse
between the show windows and the shoppers
and asks her why she lives in Israel.
    She
covers a fierce warmth that wells
with "I have no choice

Born like you in London, but of survivors,
raised with the ghosts of all destroyed
—the aunt beheaded in the forests, the grandmother
you can fit in an ashtray, the whole gallery
—some whose fate remains unsure.
I must live in a land where I make the rules."

The arm
draws tight
protective
"But that
shan't happen again.
How can you
believe it of us?"
Getreidegasse becomes Judengasse,
we enter a shop
where thick-braided salesgirls
disdain to show their wares.
To my question—"Why is this called
'Judengasse' when there are no Jews here?"—they stare blankly.

Back home I warm
to the Englishman
I kept at such a distance
in the twisting alleys
of Salzburg. I clap
a souvenir from him on my car window.
He
does not write.

III

As announcements of funerals drone on
like a class list at the university,
Yoram frowns at the BBC sticker on my windshield:
"Did you hear what those assholes are saying—
'Israeli aggressors'? They defend England
by bombing halfway around the world,
but we can't stop the Katyushas
from destroying our kids."

I think of you, Glynne, in your beige raincoat,
and me, that apologetic, stubborn Jewess at your side.
"I am not against Zionism, you understand, but
a country born in blood
must *expect*
to live in blood."


IV

Near Mozart's birthplace, young Tom,
your urbane colleague from the broadcasting service,
told me: "It doesn't matter now
whether we should be in the Falklands.
Now—
we'd just better win."

You were a boy
when I was born,
both of us
in the Blitz.

V

Now a white-and-blue 707
flies overhead towards Lod, and I think:
What if it brought you here,
what if you could see me
checking people's bags as they enter the school
making packages for soldiers at the front,
calling every friend with a man or boy up north,
spinning the dial or more
more news—

Would I be the romantic Jewess
or the racist one?

## Friend and Foe

*(June 10–12, 1982)*

Skyhawks fly over my city
on the way to bomb yours.
We are awakened by the noise
and I fall asleep restlessly
dreaming of you and your daughters.

"If anything happens to my girls,
I hold you personally responsible."
April 25. Israel is bombing Beirut.
You and I stick to wine with our
lamb casserole in Cyprus
and discuss politics.

Spinning the dial now—from BBC
to the Israel Arm Channel—
I don't know what to believe.
The thin voice of an 18-year-old soldier
telling how a Lebanese
kissed him when he jumped out
of his tank is muddled with the British
accents of the newsmen estimating
half a million homeless
in southern Lebanon.

Minutes after the ceasefire in Beirut,
CBS photographs antiaircraft fire
from a small apartment building.
(Is that where you live? Then
who lives with you?) The Skyhawks
go down on the city again.

Friend! My husband is in civil defense,
and my sons are too small for the army. You
have daughters and are old and alcoholic.
We can't fight this war.
But both of us are in it
and responsible.

## Mechitza

Our portion is a porch—
a side room with two small, curtained windows
opening into the synagogue.
We, who meet at the pool in bikinis,
sit modest and kerchiefed
humbled to our place

And listen. There are no books,
so I cannot review
the chapter of the week
or follow my son's bar mitzvah reading.

Standing around the Torah,
joining in turn in the service—
each man has his honor
as he welcomes a new member.

When my son completes his prayer,
we women will throw handfuls of candies
from behind closed curtains.

I find my place next to a crone
who shares the book she has brought from home,
and, as she points to each work,
cries with joy—"So lovely this chapter
such luck to be able to read this portion."

She compares my boy to hers
killed in the war,
and tears spot the page.
Sitting in the closed-off porch,
candies in both hands,
I weep with her.

## Separation

*Translation by Eyal Megged*

To divide
is difficult.
You close me
and we know
that you are
after all
in your own book,
I in mine.

פרדה

קָשֶׁה
לְהִפָּרֵד. אַתָּה
סוֹגֵר אוֹתִי וַאֲנִי
יוֹדַעַת
שֶׁאַתָּה בְּסַךְ הַכֹּל
בְּסִפְרְךָ,
אֲנִי בְּשֶׁלִּי.

S. *Tall*

# Letter from a Sabra to an American
## on *the Israeli invasion of Lebanon*

It took me a year of thinking, debating and aggravating to get to the point where I can respond. Still, I am doing it with a sense of inadequacy, shame and a fear of exposing myself.

I am an Israeli lesbian,[1] born and living in Israel since 1946. I was born into a world of constant wars between Israel and the Arab and Palestinian nations. I cannot say that I see the end of it yet.

Everything you have read and written about the Israeli invasion of Lebanon is accurate. We, the Israelis who cared to know, had also gotten all the horrendous details of the invasion. Nothing at all can excuse the Israelis for the invasion of Lebanon, for the massacre in the refugee camps and for the interfering in other nations' inner politic; no past suffering of the Jewish people and no present suffering can justify such deeds.

So, as an Israeli woman, I am to be blamed for the deeds of my government: and it is my government even when I condemn it, totally disagree with it and shout it from every street corner.

Well, now that all facts are stated, do I have any right to continue?

But. But how can I tell you (when I am to be condemned) about your government's part in this bloodshed? That you are to be blamed no less? You mention once in a while that these bombs, weapons, etc., are bought with American money and . . . . What next? Aren't there conclusions to be drawn from such facts? Aren't there historical and political analyses to be done?

So, you've been "had," like most American citizens, by the new and more sophisticated politic of the American government. No more "mistakes" like Vietnam, no more troops being sent out to police all over. This—they very well learned—does not appeal any more to the American people. Now the American government is "only" policing through the natives, by giving all the money and the most "developed" weapons to the locals—to do their job for them. And you know what? They get away with it, they really do. If they have "had" you—peace activists, feminists, radicals—why not the others who are less experienced, less informed, who dealt less with past struggles and therefore are less equipped to analyze such changes in politic?

I condemn my government and my people and, no less, I condemn the American government for initiating and supporting the war. And I feel utterly betrayed by you. And who am I to tell you? These were my people's deeds and I will have to live with them for the rest of my life. There is no compensation we can ever make to repay the Palestinian and Lebanese people for our deeds. But, but, who are you to blame us when you are hardly taking any responsibility upon yourself? And what is it that made you so oblivious to your own government's role in that specific invasion?

245

I'll tell you how I feel after reading your letters and articles. I am again the native, the local ignorant who had to be told by you, by the enlightened person from the Super State. I am again the primitive who is causing such bloodshed because I know no better...

I need your camaraderie, but not in telling me how evil I am. I need you to mobilize *your* public to oppose such policy of your own government.

I also need a strong state of my own,[2] the state of Israel, but I certainly don't need your government's support when it encourages and bribes my people into policing the Middle East. It is an easy way out, to forget how much policing the U.S. is doing through local armies, all over the world: the Middle East, Africa, South America, etc. Forgetting is a privilege saved only for you, the people of the U.S. You don't soak your hands in the blood. Why—you have the money to buy others to do the job for you. And yet, it is my people who wet their hands in the blood, and my brothers who fought that war...

It took me a year to gather my courage and write you and you know what? I still feel I am going to be taken as the primitive native who knows nothing. I write and yet I'm very much afraid I am going to be ignored.

S. Tall
Jerusalem

---

[1]Most Palestinian people living in the state of Israel refer to themselves as Palestinians and not Israelis. Therefore, in respect of their demand, I use "Israeli people" only to describe the Jewish citizens of Israel. (I am Jewish.)

[2]Since national struggles of the oppressed are highly encouraged in our time, I am inclined to accept the existence of a state for the Jews as well. I also support the division of the land into two states: a Palestinian state and a Jewish state.

*Melanie Kaye/Kantrowitz and Irena Klepfisz*

# An Interview with Galia Golan

*Galia Golan was born in 1938 in Cincinnati, Ohio, into a non-feminist, non-religious home. She grew up in Cincinnati, Miami Beach, Chicago, Boston, and New York; attended Brandeis University and the University of Paris; she received her Ph.D. in Russian Studies from Hebrew University.*

*In 1966 she immigrated to Israel and has been teaching Soviet and East European studies at Hebrew University from 1969 to the present. She is head of the Department of Political Science, holds the chair in Soviet Studies, and since 1981 she has been founder and coordinator of the first women's studies program in Israel.*

*A founding member of the Israel Women's Network, Galia serves on the Jerusalem Municipality Commission on the Status of Women and the National Council on the Status of Women. She is a spokeswoman and the overseas coordinator for Shalom Akhshav (Peace Now).*

*She is the author of two books on Czechoslovakia, one on the Soviet Union and the Yom Kippur War, one on the Soviet Union and the PLO, and one on the Soviet Union and national liberation movements. She has just begun research on "Women and War: The Political Attitudes of Women in Israel." She is married and the mother of four.*

*We interviewed Galia in Jerusalem in January, 1985. An update follows the interview, but some figures and facts throughout the interview have been updated as well.*

*We'd like to talk about your involvement in the feminist movement and in the peace movement.*

The two are so unconnected it's hard for me to talk about them at the same time. The formal feminist movement was a very small fringe group that was started here probably in the early 70s. It was perceived as a radical, left-wing group, which meant that *they* did have a connection with other issues, especially with war and peace, and with the Arab-Israeli conflict.

247

But that movement was small, and I would say relatively unsuccessful, though they did have some achievements. But they made the feminist cause seem extremist. They took positions on things like legalization of prostitution and drug use, and feminist conferences were dominated by the Palestinian issue and the presentation of Palestinian women. All these are issues which the Israeli public may get to one day, but the minute they all became linked as *the* basic issues of feminism, only a small group of people in the country could be interested in feminism.

This became the image of the feminist movement—that it was extremist. So that when it began to make demands for more basic women's issues—we met a wall of opposition. The Israeli public *was* particularly resistant to feminism, and it used the issue of extremism as an excuse.

The feminists did raise other issues, such as violence against women—battered wives, rape. There's much more awareness today in the Israeli public than there was 10 years ago. And *that* was the work of the feminist movement. They set up centers, they publicized the issue, and with very small means at their disposal, they brought these issues into focus. I think it's enormously to their credit—there are now police units for dealing with rape victims, and while I don't think enough is being done, I certainly would credit the organized feminist groups with what has been accomplished.

Many years after the feminist movement started, more mainstream women became involved. Some of these were women from overseas, but like me—I emigrated long before the women's movement in the U.S.—people like myself who were *not* from the American movement, or Israeli women who had simply gone abroad and been exposed to what had happened in the U.S. And this group began to be active only recently—I'd say since the mid 70s. And when people less extreme in their feminism, certainly less extreme politically, became involved, there began a very slow process of consciousness-raising.

To describe the development of feminist issues—in the late 70s the government set up a commission of inquiry on the status of women. Now the composition of that committee—and it was enormous, 90 people—was very conservative. I don't think any of the feminist movement women were asked to join. But even this group, as conservative as it was, came up with an *extremely* thorough report, several hundred pages long, which was devastating on the status of women in just about every area of Israeli life. And it had very concrete recommendations. But unfortunately, by the time the report was finished, the government had changed. The commission had been set up by the Rabin government [Labor] but presented the results to the Begin government [Likud]. And upon receiving the report, Begin made a comment to the effect that he always liked women, liked his wife and so on. So it just sat collecting dust until now.

Slowly, though, other things did begin to happen. In the university we became more aware of the situation and I organized university women in Jerusalem in the mid 70s and then three years ago opened the first women's studies program in Israel at Hebrew University, which is one of the most conservative institutions here. Then they were able to follow suit in Haifa, and we're hoping that in Tel Aviv and Ber Sheva something will develop.

Then women's councils were set up—twenty-one so far—committees on the status of women in the municipalities. And advisors were appointed, although only in two ministries. And now a national council has been set up on the status of women; and in the kibbutz movement a branch has opened on the status of women. So there are signs of change among the general public, some recognition that there is a problem. There have been many public symposia, and the monthly lecture series in the women's studies program has taken the subject out of the university and to the public. And that series has been progressively better attended to the point where in the past year we were filled to overflow. And it's not an academic audience. And other groups have done similar things, even to the point where NAAMAT, the woman's branch of the Histadrut [national labor union], has launched a campaign to improve the status of women.

*Could you explain what the councils do?*

The National Council was set up by the Likud just before the election and is, therefore, stacked with Likud people. So they got a committee that really can't do very much because it's certainly not feminist or particularly interested in women's affairs. And at the very first meeting it became clear that they didn't know what had been done by the committee under Rabin, and many of them said they didn't know there were problems for women in Israeli society.

So now that there's a new government and a new advisor for women's affairs in the government, we're hoping that will be changed. As envisaged by the original report on the status of women, there would be a public committee which would operate as a watchdog on the government, present proposals for the improvement of the status of women, and generally oversee the implementation of the original recommendations. It remains to be seen whether this will be the case.

As for the committees in the municipalities—the idea was to set up a pressure group in the city to promote the interests of women, more equality for women—whether it be recommending programs to the city and to organizations or actually trying to go out ourselves and raise consciousness. In Jerusalem, one of the first things we're doing is setting up an ombudsman, an office where women can bring complaints. And there's a Women's Lobby (Israel Women's Network) in which I am active. We felt there was a need for a group that wouldn't be hampered by official organizations or government and could go into the street and demonstrate—whatever is necessary to put pressure on the government, on the city, on any group. We had open meetings to try to find out what issues women were interested in—and one of them is, as we assumed it would be, the issue of the religious courts and divorce. We are going to have a press conference at the end of the month, after meeting with the Rabbinate, the Chief Rabbis. And we intend to make this a grass-roots issue with demonstrations and so forth.

*Earlier you said that the Israeli public is particularly resistant to feminism. Could you talk about that, and about some of the issues that the Women's Lobby will be addressing?*

The issues and the resistance are related. The first reason for resistance to feminism is the myth that has existed in Israel since before the founding of the State: a belief that there really wasn't a problem, that because the country was built on egalitarian, socialist ideology, women were equal. And this myth was probably fortified by the War of Independence, in which women *did* take part, in retrospect not as actively as is generally thought, but there is a myth of women participating directly, fighting side by side with the men.

But in fact there never was this equality. There were the ideals, but they were never realized. Then came the War of Independence, which make it *look* like women were taking an active role and reinforced the myth.

The second reason is the security situation, the feeling that whether there was equality or not, everyone has to pull together and put particularistic demands or grievances to the side, be they women's issues or other issues. As a result, Israel is a very macho society, because of the need for, and therefore the glorification of, the army.

And finally, there's the third reason, the fact that we don't have separation of church and state, and the religious establishment has a great deal of political power here. The religious establishment represents the most conservative stream of Judaism, of orthodoxy. There are plenty of religious feminists who argue that Judaism does not have to be chauvinistic or anti-feminist, nor does it have to create a situation for inequality. But the more conservative side of orthodoxy dominates here and *that* side certainly dictates inequality for women and an anti-feminist approach.

All this contributes to a very low consciousness and defensiveness on the part of women. I suspect it's similar to where the American movement was 20 years ago. Whenever you're going to try to raise consciousness, you have to deal first with a certain defensiveness, because what you're doing is saying that what a woman has been until now isn't right. And many women are simply not willing to recognize that.

Our main problems are in part specific to Israel and in part universal. We have all the universal problems: the fear of success, the need to change the image of women, the stereotyping of roles which exists in the media and throughout the educational system, the lack of women in leading positions so there are few role models, the fact that the vast majority of working women are in "women's professions." About everything connected with the psychological side, we're no different from women anywhere else. We have not had any advantage because of our socialist or egalitarian "myth." Women earn less than men. We have a law that calls for equal pay for equal work but it's never been fully implemented. There's inequality in pensions, inequality in retirement age. Also a lot of the protective legislation has been used, of course, against women. We may be better off in some areas; we have certainly better maternity leave than, say, the U.S., and we are better off when it comes to day-care centers.

And we have, as I said, certain specific problems. First of all, we have a short school day. The kids finish at 12 or 1 o'clock. Although we have a fair percentage of women in the work force—38%—a very high percentage of them do part-time work, which means a stigma in terms of earning power, and they're not recognized as heads of households in statistics nor can they file income tax independent from their husbands.

Other problems specific to us: the whole business of marriage and divorce—all family law being exclusively in the hands of the religious courts and women not being able to be judges or witnesses in the religious courts. And general discrimination against women in the religious courts.

And also specific to us is the issue of security and the fact that this reinforces inequality because in war society reverts to stereotypical roles: the woman is the provider who gives warmth and support to her husband coming home from battle.

We're always told, of course, that it's a great achievement that women serve in the army. But in fact only about 70% of our women serve in the army; either they're ineligible or they opt out. And they *can* opt out because the religious party has made it virtually a voluntary issue. About 20% opt out on the religious issue, even though they might not be religious. The 30% who don't serve are mainly ineligible because the education requirement for women is higher than for men. Men are called up to the army with, I believe, fewer than 10 years' education; but 10 years are required for women, so more women are ineligible than men. And then the jobs that women have in the army have tended to be very subordinate. There has been a slight improvement because the head of the women's army is a feminist, so more interesting jobs, including technical jobs, are open to women. Still, women are in a secondary position in the army. Until our pressure, victorious in 1986, the head of the women's army could not be higher than a lieutenant colonel, even though the heads of other branches, even smaller than the women's army, could reach the rank of general. Women conscripts still serve less time than men, do virtually no reserve duty, and cannot serve in combat positions (which denies them the key to status in the army).

All of these are matters we want to bring up, and I haven't even mentioned health. Interestingly enough, as distinct from the U.S., the health issue is not particularly pressing in the consciousness of women. We were able to get an abortion law after a long struggle, and that law itself was not the most positive in the world. But very soon after it was passed, the elections took place, the Likud came in, the religious parties got more power and they threw out the social clause [which expanded greatly the reasons a woman might choose to abort].

Now abortion here is not the problem it was in the U.S. before you got legal abortion. Here abortions are very commonplace. They can be obtained cheaply and perfectly safely. Doctors give abortions because the law is not enforced. It's just that it is still illegal and does still cost money. And, therefore, we would like to have the social clause reinstated. Now the woman who can't afford abortion has to go before a commission to get a legal abortion free within the official health service. Where the religious dominate—as in Jerusalem—you can't get official approval unless you fit the law perfectly.

Since we're talking about feminism and about things that are special to Israel, one of the main differences between Israel and the U.S. is that many feminists in Israel are influenced by or accept the central value of the family in Israeli society. It is a value in Judaism and very central in Israel. And we have not taken up the issue of family *versus* career. What we try to do is family *and* career, find ways the woman can fulfill herself outside the home, trying to change society in such a way that this can be done, so that men will share in the home, there will be a longer school day, there will be even more day-care, so that a woman *can* work outside the home and fulfill herself without giving up the family. We had an evening on single parent families in our public lecture series, and to my surprise we found that the statistics of people choosing the single parent road had not gone up.

*Is there a sense that as women's options increase—better pay, more equal pay, more career options—that they may choose to postpone marriage?*

It's conceivable. But it's really a theoretical question at the moment, and it's not the kind of thing that you hear encouraged a lot. We're demanding the possibility of having a career outside of the home, of taking some of the burden of the dual role off the woman. But *not* by giving up something. There's no reason that the man can't share in the family equally with the woman and that both members can't have dual roles.

*Can you talk about the state of women's studies?*

I started the first program three years ago at the Hebrew University. And now there's an identical program in Haifa. One of the problems the other institutions face that we didn't have is that most of the people working in the area are not tenured. And we were lucky because all the women involved had tenure, which they had gotten by *not* working in Women's Studies. We still don't have a case of somebody in Women's Studies from the beginning getting tenure. So when we came along and proposed women's studies, it was very hard for our male colleagues to say that this wasn't serious, for these were all women with very senior positions. We had static. We had trouble. We call it the Program for Sex Differences in Society, not Women's Studies, because we really did want a gender studies program, and for tactical reasons as well. But basically we got it in fairly easily. All I did was take all people and courses that had anything to do with women's studies or sex differences or gender studies and bring them together. We didn't even try to get a department and we're still not trying. We are all very satisfied with having it as a minor, as a program. And by and large we've made inroads into the regular departments and *that* I think in itself is an achievement. We have a lot of people come to our classes even if they aren't in the program; they take them as electives.

The courses themselves—we have everything. We've got law. We've got religion, women and Judaism, psychology of women, psychology of parenting. Women in politics in Israel. Education for sex roles, informal education of youngsters. Sex differences in public health problems. Communications, linguistics, physiology, biology. We're a bit weak in anthropology and history. We have a course on love and marriage in English Drama. One on women in *Midrash* and folktales. A couple of courses on family planning, which we don't consider women's studies proper, but they're related. We had a course on women in American Literature. Women in China. Last year we had 22 courses; this year, 20.

*Do you teach about women in the Soviet Union?*

No, I don't teach women's studies. I founded the program and I run it, but academically it's not really my field. But I'm considering doing a book with a colleague on women's political attitudes in Israel, or women in war, basically foreign policy - attitudes, because I was asked to give a lecture on the subject last year and I researched it to some degree and found it absolutely fascinating. So that would be the first thing I've done in women's studies.

*Okay, women and war. Is there a connection or bridge between the women's movement and peace activities?*

It's hard for me to make the connection because I've been one of the people who wants to keep partisan politics or the issue of the Arab-Israeli conflict and security out of the women's movement. The movement is composed of people who may be on different sides of these issues: Likud women tend to be right-wing, not feminist, but there still are some in the women's movement. There are others who may not be Likud, but they're not what I would call doves. They're not going to demonstrate with us on the Palestinian issue; in fact, they would completely dissociate themselves from the women's movement if it were to take up these issues. And I feel that the women's issues are simply too fundamental—and too new—to have them risked. This is certainly not the position of the original feminist movement, but I think that was a mistake on their part. In a society which is completely torn asunder on the Arab-Israeli conflict, I think it's a mistake to bring the women's issue into that whole arena, because you're never going to get agreement. I would rather fight the women's battle on one plane, and the peace issue—the Palestinian issue—on another, with different groups and different tactics.

I am *personally* involved with both issues. I'm one of the leaders of *Shalom Akhshav* [Peace Now], which is one of the most significant peace movements in the country. And one of the reasons that Peace Now is by far the largest movement in the country and the one that's been relatively successful—in terms of getting out the public and possibly even influencing policy—is that it's a mainstream movement.

Now our opponents see us as left-wing and extreme left-wing, because they don't want to make any distinction, and that's their problem. But—talk to somebody like Naomi [Kies]—she'll say, "Go see Galia if you want to hear the center position ." [laugh] The movement was started by a group of reserve officers, soldiers from combat units—I mean nothing is more center in terms of the Israeli public than a group like that. And it's not a pacifist movement like the European movements. It's from the mainstream Zionist movement.

*We'd like you to talk about where the peace movement is now, after the election, in relation to Lebanon. What kind of progress do you see? What do you see developing?*

First of all, one result was that we began to shift a great deal of our attention to educational work. We're very upset by the support Kahane got and by support which seems to be predominantly among young people for right-wing, even racist positions. *Were you surprised?*

Well—we certainly were surprised by the support Kahane got—26,000 votes. And the swing to the right among young people. We've been aware of it, but I think it really was driven home in the elections. Peace Now wasn't ready to focus on education until these elections because we thought Labor would do better. If they couldn't do better in these conditions, then clearly something has to be done. In any case, we began focusing a great deal more on getting to youth: setting up a youth movement, groups in the cities, a trip along the peace border over Hanukkah. And we're having a big youth conference next month on the anniversary of the killing of Emil Grunzweig [protester killed in 1982 Peace Now demonstration].

Secondly, we gave the government a certain period of grace on all issues—primarily on the Lebanese issue—because we held a meeting with Rabin right after his government was set up and he convinced us that he really did want to get the army out of Lebanon and was determined to do so. And as you know, two weeks ago we came to the conclusion that nothing was going to happen, there were no signs that the government was going to pull the army out. So we declared an end to the suspension of activities on Lebanon and had the demonstration here in Jerusalem, which was intended to be the opening of a whole round of demonstrations and vigils, building up to a big demonstration in Tel Aviv scheduled for next week.

The issue of the West Bank—we never let up on and we were not satisfied with Rabin's answers on that. We didn't do anything more on the settlements issue mainly because they hadn't set up any new settlements, but now that they have, we've come out with protest against the decision to open six new settlements.

We began as a result of the Palestinian National Council meeting in Amman and Hussein's speech. We called for a meeting with Peres to discuss and to protest basically the government's negative response to what happened, and we began discussions with Palestinians, specifically leaders from the West Bank, pro-PLO people as well as pro-Jordanian. While it couldn't have happened if the Palestinians hadn't been ready for it, we brought about a breakthrough in the sense that we organized a public meeting between the Palestinian leaders from the West Bank identified with PLO, ourselves—a mainstream Israeli Zionist group—and members of the Labor Party. There's never been such a *public* meeting. Because what we're trying to do now is to act as something of a bridge or as a vehicle for bringing Jordan and Israel and the Palestinians in Israel together.

We intend to continue this whole program of bringing Israelis and Palestinians of as high a political level as possible together, not just informal, private talks but publicly, in Arab towns as well as for the Jewish public.

We haven't by any means decided that because Labor is in the government there's nothing left to do. Quite the contrary. We're very concerned about the National Unity Government. Likud could prevent Labor from doing anything, and Labor itself is very divided. We have to continue strengthening the doves in Labor and bringing public pressure.

*When you use the term* Zionist—*there's a lot of confusion at this point in the U.S. about what that term means exactly. Could you explain what you mean when you say that Peace Now is a Zionist group?*

We believe that there is such a thing as a Jewish nation, a Jewish people. We believe that the Jewish people have a right to self-determination. We believe that the Jewish people have a right to a Jewish state. In that sense we're a Zionist movement. We have taken up the whole issue of the Palestinian problem, the Arab-Israel conflict because we believe that without recognition of Palestinian national rights, without a peace settlement between us and the Palestinians, us and the Arab states, Israel will not be able to go on existing. Either there'll be continuing rounds of wars, or we'll be completely torn apart inside. If the Likud has its way and the West Bank is annexed, we may not be a Jewish state much longer because the Jews will become a minority. And as a Zionist movement we oppose this. We don't want Jews to return to the status they had over centuries of being minorities in other lands. We believe that Jews have a right to one place that will be theirs. And that's one of the reasons we took up the whole peace issue as Zionists, for Zionist reasons.

Beyond that though, because we're from the mainstream of Zionism, with a humanitarian interpretation of Zionism, we believe it's morally wrong to have a Jewish state at the expense of another people, by ruling over another people, by occupying other people's lands. And we believe that a solution has to be found that will recognize *both* peoples' rights to the land and *both* peoples' aspirations for self-determination. So we believe a solution can be found on the basis of partition of the land of Israel. Thus the Jews would continue to have a state with security; I think our history is sufficiently traumatic that it should be understandable why we're obsessed with security.

But we believe there's enough room here for Palestinians also—what the exact settlement will be is up to the negotiations. We believe there should be negotiations with all options open and with anybody who is willing to negotiate, and that those negotiations should be based on Israel's right to security and the Palestinians' right to self-determination. And just what that means—if it's demilitarized zones, if it's a Palestinian state, if it's a confederation with Jordan—all that has to be worked out.

*Does* Shalom Akshav *deal with other Israeli foreign policy issues?*

No, we're a one-issue movement. The only other issue we've taken up is poverty and the economic situation, but only from the point of view of money going to settlements on the West Bank instead of to development towns and underprivileged neighborhoods.

One of the reasons we have not become a political party is that were we to take up positions on these other issues, the movement would probably split. This movement unites people on what could be called the dove platform, and even then on the broadest dove platform, so that we don't come out specifically against a Palestinian state, but we don't come out specifically in favor of it. We say all options are open. And in that way we're able to form a broad mass movement. It's why *Shalom Akhshav* exists and has continued to exist.

*What do you think American Jews should be doing in relationship to Israel?*

There have been set up a large number of Friends of Peace Now groups all over the States, southern Latin America, western Europe. We see those groups that identify with us as support groups; mainly we think that they can help us with the pressures we bring on the government, because Israel is sensitive to some degree to what world Jewry thinks. Certainly the government tends to speak in the name of the Jewish people, and has contacts with leaders of Jewish groups abroad. We want to show the government that they're not speaking in the name of the *whole* Jewish people if they take a hard-line position. There are a lot of Jews out there who don't agree with them, a lot of Jews out there who agree with us. So what we try to do is to have people who are in agreement with us express their opinions—particularly here. We're not necessarily keen on their being active publicly overseas. We're mainly interested that they express their views here in Israel, in newspapers, in discussions, when they have meetings with members of the government, to be another part of the pressure group that exists inside Israel.

At the same time, we do want them to some degree to spread our views overseas so that we can reach more Jews and thereby get more Jews involved in pressing the government here. And also we find that—although we didn't intend it this way—we've become a focal point for people who want to continue to support Israel, but who would normally turn their back because of the policies of the Likud government. So now we do make an effort to encourage people—either we send people overseas or people are invited to cooperate with any effort to reach out into the Jewish communities. And I think that's no less important a role than what we originally intended—mobilizing world Jewry behind our positions and pressing the government.

The third thing, of course: we fund-raise overseas and receive money from Jews overseas; we get quite a bit of our support from inside Israel, but the big money is always overseas. So we have a representative in North America who is a liaison between us and all the North American Friends of Peace Now groups. The groups in Europe and Latin America we simply have direct contact with, to help organize them to be part of our lobby here, for support for a different Israel. We don't engage in lobbying non-Jewish groups or the governments abroad; we don't want to try to mobilize opinion or decisions against Israel. We play only in the Jewish scene, although to make our views known we will appear in the media.

*Do you see danger in Jews abroad speaking out critically against Israel abroad?*

I don't think you can tell people not to speak out critically because they don't happen to agree with your view. Criticism has been a legitimate activity that Israeli parties have done since the beginning, and most of them have branches overseas. Everybody has felt it's absolutely legitimate to work among world Jewry to try to sway opinion.

It's true that Jews overseas have been in a very bad position in the past few years, and I understand their concern that if they wash the dirty linen in public, they'll provide ammunition for anti-Semitism or anti-Israeli groups. But our position has basically been that the government's policies have provided the ammunition for anti-Semitism and anti-Zionism, not us. We think that if moderate views are expressed by American Jewry as well, it would help Israel's image.

Of course it depends on how you do it. But if Jews overseas are asked to contribute to Israel—we are, in fact, very dependent upon them—I don't see why they can't express their views. We can't ask them to support us when it's convenient, and then say they have no right to say anything that isn't convenient. And our feeling is that these issues are just too important, vital to Israel's future. They're vital to the Jews abroad because Israel's image *can't* be good for Jews. At some point it's going to affect their lives as well. For all these reasons I think they have a moral obligation to speak up.

## Update: January 1988

Three years later, I can mark progress in two areas and regression in a third. In the personal area, in no small part in response to your questions in 1985, I have indeed merged my feminism and my activities for peace. While I still believe the women's movement must be non-partisan, I do not believe the issues can be fully separated or compartmentalized. My experience in Nairobi in the summer of 1985 and contacts with Palestinian women since then have brought me to a much greater understanding of the role women can plan *as women* in the struggle to end the Arab-Israeli, Jewish-Palestinian conflict. For me personally, I think that feminism and peace-activism are born of the same root, a sense or concern for justice—and that in itself may well be the result of Jewish values embedded deeply somewhere inside me. Nor do I believe that women's rights can be achieved and ensured in this part of the world without the advent of peace.

In the second area, feminism, I think some headway has been made in the past few years. The Israel Women's Network (the Lobby) has become a significant vehicle for the feminist struggle, concentrating during this election year on promoting women in politics. The formal Feminist Movement has been greatly revived and expanded. And the whole cause has enjoyed more adherents and more attention. A number of laws have been amended (though not the abortion law), some women are doing voluntary reserve duty (in an attempt to provide role models and press for equal status in the army), women in various parties are taking collective action, and there are now advisors on the status of women in all government ministries (and some universities).

All of these and other measures are, of course, but a drop in the bucket. Little or no progress had been made toward overcoming the major obstacles to women's rights in Israel. The domination of the military-security "situation" and of the religious establishment—as well as a lack of consciousness and rampant chauvinism (of both kinds)—all still seriously impede our progress. But at least more and more women, and even some men, are joining the effort.

In the third area, that of peace, we are clearly faced with regression, or deterioration. We did finally pull out of Lebanon, but the Palestinian uprising tragically demonstrates what we in Peace Now have been trying to convey for some years: that there is no "status quo" in the territories; that continued occupation and rule over a million and a half Palestinians can only result in bloodshed, violence, aggression, and brutality. Now, as in the past, we are trying to force this new tragic reality into a possibility for progress by demanding a political initiative by the Israeli government—agreement to an international conference, recognition of the Palestinian rights to self-determination, talks with any Palestinians (including the PLO) willing to talk rather than fight or use violence.

We are still convinced that with appropriate measures to ensure Israel's security a peace agreement can be worked out. We are more convinced than ever that the moral corrosion of our own society—wrought by rule over another people, the threat to the democratic nature of our society, and our desire for a Jewish state—coupled with the growth of extremism on both sides and the spread of Islamic fundamentalism, often born of frustration and hopelessness, amongst the Palestinians—all this must move us here in Israel, as well as Jews abroad who care about our future, to act soon.

---

*SHALOM  AKHSHAV* ◇ PEACE NOW

שלום עכשיו

---

# WOMEN'S GROUPS IN ISRAEL

A.L.N. (Organization of Single Mothers). POB 11564, Tel Aviv, 61114. Tel: 03-947925.
Isha Le'Isha (Women's Center). 88 Arlozorov St., Haifa, 33276. Tel: 04-664949.
Israel Childbirth Education Center. POB 3731, Haifa, 31037. Tel: 04-664949.
Israel Feminist Movement. 82 Ben Yehuda St., Tel Aviv, 63435. Tel: 03-234314 or 234114.
Israel Women's Network. 7 Gichon St. Abu Tor, Jerusalem, or POB 2171, Jerusalem 91037. Tel: 02-718922.
KLAF (Lesbian Feminist Community). POB 22997, Tel Aviv, 61228, or POB 4319, Jerusalem, 91042.
L.C.N. (Women's Basketball Organization), C/O Tali Birkan, 6 Giladi St., Jerusalem, 93385. Tel: 02-710385 or 474385.
Municipal Center for Women and the Family. 37 Herzl St., Ramat Gan, 52452. Tel: 03-719697 or 734752.
TAKAM (Division for Equality Between the Sexes—Kibbutz Movement). 10 Dubnov St., Tel Aviv, 64732. Tel: 03-250231, ext. 259.
Women's Awareness Center in Netanya, C/O Dr. Joyce Brenner. Tel: 053-339098.

## Shelters for Battered Women

Ashdod. Tel: 08-558433.
Haifa. Women for Women, POB 4667. Tel: 04-662114.
Herzliya (for Tel Aviv). Tel: 052-551524 or 551022.
Jerusalem. Tel: 02-381587.

## Rape Crisis Centers

Haifa. POB 9308. Tel: 04-660111.
Jerusalem. POB 158. Tel: 02-245554.
Ra'anana. POB 4. Tel: 052-32432.
Tel Aviv. POB 33041. Tel: 03-234819.

## Media

Brerot Publishing House. POB 36448, Tel Aviv 61363. Tel: 03-615470.
Family and Media Research Institute. 10 Abba Hushi St., Haifa. Tel: 04-246950.
Media Watch. 21 Beeri St., Tel Aviv.
Noga (Israel Feminist Magazine). POB 21376, Tel Aviv 61213. Tel: 03-227663.
Second Sex Publishing House. 55 Shenken St., Givatayim. Tel: 03-312349 or 342349.
Women Against Offensive Publicity. POB 8755, Jaffa. Tel: 03-832769.

## Peace Groups

Women in Black, C/O Dai l'kibush (Down with the Occupation), POB 3742, Jerusalem.
Gesher (Bridge), Jewish and Arab Women's Peace Group. 57 Horev St., Haifa. Tel: 04-243230.
Israel Women's Alliance Against the Occupation. POB 4319, Jerusalem.

## Civil Rights

Association for Civil Rights in Israel (ACRI). 2 Turiah St., Abu Tor, Jerusalem, 93511. Tel: 02-718308.
Mitzva (Divorce Assistance for *aqunot*). POB 3186, Jerusalem, 91036. Tel: 02-226339.
Organization for Assistance to *Aqunot*. POB 30953, Tel Aviv, 61316.
Society for Protection of Personal Rights. POB 16151, Tel Aviv, 61160. Tel: 03-246063.

# RESOURCES

*Below is a list of organizations, magazines, and books which could be useful for learning more about the history and current situation in Israel and the Middle East.*

## Organizations

Americans for a Progressive Israel, 150 Fifth Ave., NYC (212) 255-8760
Peace Now Education Fund, 111 W. 40th Street, NYC 10018 (212) 944-2403
New Israel Fund, 111 W. 40th Street, NYC 10018 (212) 302-0066
New Jewish Agenda, 149 Church Street, NYC

## Magazines

*Israleft*, POB 9013, Jerusalem. Bi-weekly in English.
*Israel Horizons*, 150 Fifth Ave., NYC 10011
*Jewish Currents*, 22 E. 17th Street, NYC
*New Outlook: Middle East Monthly*, 9 Gordon Street, Tel Aviv, 63458, Israel
*The Jerusalem Post* (International Edition), POB 81, Jerusalem, Israel

## Books

American Friends Service Committee. *A Compassionate Peace: A Future for the Middle East.* NY: Hill & Wang. 1982.

Avishai, Bernard. *The Tragedy of Zionism.* NY: Farrar, Straus, Giroux, 1985.

Bendt, Ingela and Jim Downing. *We Shall Return: Women of Palestine.* Lawrence Hill, 1982.

Benvenisti, Meron. *Conflicts and Contradictions.* NY: Villard, 1986.

Drew, Jill. *To Go To Berbir—A Journey and a War, Sinister Wisdom,* 26 (1984) + "Editorial Statement," *Sinister Wisdom,* 27 (1984).

Hazelton, Lesley. *Israeli Women: The Reality Behind the Myths.* NY: Simon & Schuster, 1977.

Laqueur, Walter. *The Israel-Arab Reader.* NY: Citadel, 1969.

Memmi, Albert. *Jews and Arabs.* Chicago: J. Philip O'Hara, 1975.

Mendes-Flohr, Paul R. (ed.) *A Land of Two Peoples: Martin Buber on Jews and Arabs.* NY: Oxford Univ., 1983.

Oz, Amos. *In the Land of Israel.* NY: Harcourt, Brace, Jovanovich, 1983.

Saadawi, Nawal E. *The Hidden Face of Eve: Women in the Arab World.* Boston: Beacon, 1982.

Said, Edward. *The Question of Palestine.* NY: Vintage, 1980.

Senesh, Hannah. *The Diary and Letters of Hannah Senesh.* NY: Schocken, 1973.

Shazar, Rachel Katznelson, ed. *The Plough Woman: Memoirs of the Pioneer Women of Palestine,* trans. by Maurice Samuel. NY: Herzl Press, 1975.

Shehadeh, Raja. *Samed: A Journal of Life in the West Bank.* NY: Quartet Books, 1982.

Shipler, David K. *Arab and Jew: Wounded Spirits in a Promised Land.* NY: Times Books, 1986.

Stone, I.F. *Underground to Palestine.* NY: Pantheon, 1978.

Tawil, Raymonda. *My Home, My Prison.* Zed Press (England), 1983.

Timerman, Jacobo. *The Longest War: Israel in Lebanon.* trans. by Miguel Acoca. NY: Alfred A. Knopf, 1982.

World Jewish Congress. *The Implications of Israeli-Arab Peace for World Jewry.* NY: WJC, 1981.

Yermiya, Dov. *My War Diary: Lebanon June 5-July 1, 1982.* Boston: South End Press, 1984 (Israeli Edition by Mifras Pub. House, Jerusalem, 1983).

—MKK
—IK

# 6. Bread and Roses

*What the woman who labors wants is the right to live, not simply exist — the right to life as a rich woman has it, the right to life, and the sun, and music, and art. . . . The worker must have bread, but she must have roses, too.*

—Rose Schneiderman, 1912

*Sarah Schulman*

# When We Were Very Young:

A Walking Tour Through Radical
Jewish Women's History
On the Lower East Side 1879-1919

*This work is dedicated to Stephanie Roth, Beryl Satter, and Maxine Wolf*

I am grateful to the YIVO Institute for Jewish Studies in New York City. I have never had a feeling of community as strong as I have felt at the YIVO. They didn't always agree with me and they didn't always understand me, but they read my work in different stages, provided me with scholarship money, sent me to classes and tutorials and treated me with respect. I am particularly grateful to Adrienne Cooper of the Max Weinreich Center for Advanced Jewish Studies at the YIVO for her wise encouragement, to Jack Kugelmass and Jenna Joselit, and to my Yiddish teachers Mordke Shaechter, Pesach Fishman and Sonia Pinkusowitz. I also want to thank the many Jewish and women scholars and librarians whose work made mine possible; Esther Hyneman for her careful and constructive editing; and the following women who doublechecked my sources: Esther Hyneman again, Melanie Kaye/Kantrowitz, Amy Kesselman, Irena Klepfisz, Rose Perczykow Klepfisz and Linda Vance. Any flaws or inaccuracies that remain are my sole responsibility.

## 1. Fourteenth Street and Broadway—Union Square

Our walking tour begins at Union Square, for decades the site of demonstrations for progressive causes from the Rosenbergs to abortion rights. Here, radical Jewish women joined with the larger American left. Isidore Wisotsky, an anarchist leader, recalls:

> We gathered to make revolution and stayed to talk. And how we talked—anarchism, atheism, against the military, for birth control, against injustice, for socialism and for the rights of workers to organize. . .The right to speak at Union Square was more precious than the bread we sweated to earn. . .Many in the crowd were immigrants, but not all. The square also attracted every kind of radical from Greenwich Village, as well as the dilettanti and just plain spectators and rubbernecks. . .Almost any issue could draw a crowd of 20,000 or more. Our slogans were simple and to the point—"War is Murder," "The Eight Hour Day Today" and "Capitalism is the Cause of All Evil."[1]

## 2. 208 East Thirteenth Street

Anarchist and feminist Emma Goldman lived here on the top floor from 1904-1914.[2] Born in Kovno, Poland in 1869, she moved to St. Petersburg at age 13. In her autobiography, *Living My Life*, she acknowledges the influence of women revolutionary leaders in Russia, especially Sophia Perovskaya, who was executed for the assassination of Czar Alexander II, and Vera Figner, imprisoned for 20 years for the same act.[3]

After threatening to throw herself into the Neva River if she could not emigrate to America with her sister,[4] Emma reached Rochester, NY, married and divorced and moved to NYC by the time she was 20. Within one year, she was elected to the Board of the Anarchist Congress. When Alexander Berkman, her lover and comrade, was imprisoned for 14 years for an assassination attempt, Emma very briefly tried to earn a living at prostitution[5] and studied midwifery.[6] She continued to defend Berkman's name within the left, even jumping on stage to lash one of his detractors with a bullwhip.[7]

When President McKinley was assassinated by the anarchist Leon Czolgosz, Emma was arrested and held for a month. As government repression of anarchists intensified, she assumed the name E.G.Smith and worked as a nurse, seamstress, masseuse, manager; and agent for a Russian acting company.[8] Alix Kates Shulman writes:

> Combative by nature, she always presented the most provocative topics in the most dangerous places, thus feeding her legend. She talked up free love to puritans, atheism to churchmen, revolution to reformers. She denounced the ballot to suffragists, patriotism to soldiers.[9]

Emma was first imprisoned in 1896 and sentenced to seven months on Blackwell Island for inciting riot at a Union Square demonstration in support of a railway strike organized by Eugene Debs. Thereafter, she was arrested so often that she always took a book to public meetings so she'd have something to read if she ended up in jail.[10]

A free thinker who would be considered radical by progressive movements today, Emma lectured in English and Yiddish on unions, feminism, collective living, cooperation and birth control. The latter topic sent her to prison several times. An advocate of tolerance for homosexuals at a time when there was no visible gay rights movement in the US,[11] Emma was "the first and only woman, indeed the first and only American, to take up the defense of homosexual love before the general public."[12]

A tireless organizer, agitator, and publisher of two anarchist papers—*The Blast* and *Mother Earth News*—Emma was dubbed "The Most Dangerous Woman in America" by the FBI, and her deportation hearings were presided over by J. Edgar Hoover. In 1919 she was deported for opposing US military conscription during World War I, and in 1921 she went to the Soviet Union, where she accused Lenin and Trotsky of "the new despotism." Allowed to return to the US, she published *My Disillusionment with Russia* and *My Further Disillusionment with Russia*, which earned her the enmity of the left.

When Berkman committed suicide, Emma joined the anarchists of Spain, who then controlled Barcelona. She lived the rest of her life on $30 a month[13] with no passport until she died in Canada in 1940.

"What I believe," Emma wrote, "is a process rather than a finality. Finalities are for Gods and governments, not for human intellect."[14]

### 3. Twelfth Street and Second Avenue: Cafe Royale

Across the street from Maurice Schwartz's Yiddish Arts Theatre was the Cafe Royale,[15] hang-out of writers, actors, philosophers and kibbitzers. It was also frequented by a new generation of radical, single Jewish women,[16] who drank tea from samovars in the classical Russian style[17]—among them Communist organizers Miriam Zahn and Rose Wartis of the Dress and Cloak Makers' Union, journalist Meta Stein Lilienthal, and Annie Netter, an activist in the Knights of Labor, who roomed with Emma Goldman. You might also see Fannia Cohn, the only woman on the General Executive Board of the International Ladies' Garment Workers'Union (ILGWU),[18] committed to the belief that "the union's activities should influence every possible phase of the worker's life."[19] In the corner, dunking babka in coffee and organizing the shirtwaist strike might be Esther Lobetkin, Bessie Switski, Rena Borky or Yetta Raff.

## 4. 193 First Avenue

One block down from the Cafe Royale lived Lena Meyers, a Polish refugee from Cracow. In 1896, at 28, she committed suicide by drinking carbolic acid. She had been sending her family money earned from prostitution. Two weeks before, Lena

> had received a letter in Hebrew from her mother thanking her for money received and asking, "Lena, why don't you get married? Do you want to be an old maid?"[20]

## 5. Second Avenue and Ninth Street: Cafe Monopole

Now a Ukranian restaurant, Cafe Monopole was a meeting place for activists, actors and community residents. According to one journalist, describing Jewish cafe life:

> Where the cigarette smoke is thickest and denunciation of the present forms of government loudest there you find women!. . .to none would gentle words sound more strange than to the women of the radical coffee "parlour". . .pallid, tired, thin-lipped, flat-chested and angular, wearing men's hats and shoes, without a hint of color or finery.[21]

Although unattractive to this reporter, radical Jewish women were involved in a whirlwind of vibrant and creative activities, among them women's liberation. For example, Manya Mirsky, Katya, Rose Goldberg and others managed to publish birth control information in Yiddish, although Emma Goldman had been imprisoned for attempting this illegal activity. But they found a printer willing to take the risk if he got cash first and if the literature was removed as soon as it was printed. They distributed 10,000 copies from baby carriages in Harlem, the East Side, the Bronx, and Brownsville.[22]

Other women were trying to preserve their experiences on paper. Anzia Yezierska was one of a few Jewish women writing in English about life on the East Side. Then as now, most working-class women writers' work was never published. Born in the early 1800's in Plinsk, a *shtetl* in Russo-Poland, she emigrated in 1892. She married at 17, had the marriage annulled a few months later, remarried almost immediately and divorced three years later, leaving her daughter to be raised by her husband. Historian Alice Kessler-Harris describes her as "fiercely independent."

> Traditional notions of marriage discomfited her, yet she sought out male companions and lovers. Contemptuous of the ordinary and impatient with the unimaginative, she could not conform to social convention for its own sake.[23]

In 1915, she published her first story—"The Free Vacation House"—in *Forum*, and four years later won the Edward O'Brien best short story of the year award for "The Fat of the Land." In 1920 producer Sam Goldwyn bought her book *Hungry Hearts* for $10,000. Moving to Los Angeles, she found she could not write when away from the Lower East Side and returned to NYC. Her fascinating autobiography, *Red Ribbon on a White Horse* (1950), tells of moving from Jewish poverty, of confronting anti-Semitism among the rich and famous, of being marketed as a rags-to-riches girl.

She also describes her experiences in the WPA Writers' Project with other artists like Richard Wright, and exposes the exploitativeness of these much-acclaimed depression recovery programs.[24]

In the 1920's, possibly influenced by her close relationship with John Dewey,[25] Yezierska became interested in the mysticism of Gurdjieff, Krishnamurti and Bahai. She also developed a commitment to what she called "applied Christianity."[26] Anzia's books include *Salome of the Tenements* (1922) a *roman à clef* about the East Side, *Children of Loneliness* (1923) and *The Bread Givers* (1925), the story of a Jewish woman determined to become a writer against the wishes of her religious father. Yezierska died in 1970.

## 6. Astor Place—Cooper Union

Named for multi-millionaire Cornelius Astor, this was the site of a strike organized by Jewish and Italian immigrant working women which affected the history of union organizing in the US. NYC was the center of the American "needle trades," producing half of the country's ready-to-wear clothing. By 1909, there were 600 garment factories and workshops involving over 30,000 workers, three-quarters of whom were women between 16 and 25.[27] Workers had to pay for utilities and equipment in the factories, and garment producers charged them 20% over cost for electricity, needles, and electric belts. They worked with flammable materials, had to pay for their lockers and chairs, and were heavily fined for their mistakes.[28]

Small strikes were first initiated against the Leiserson shop and the Triangle Shirtwaist Factory in September, 1909, by the 100 members of the original union, Local 25, which had $4 in the treasury.[29] Strike benefits were $3 a week for those with dependents and $1.50 for individuals.[30] Both factories hired scabs to break the strike and prostitutes to taunt the picketers. Certain firms specialized in hiring out strikebreakers on a *per diem* basis, and eventually the union also resorted to violence. According to Jenna Joselit, historian of Jewish crime,

> . . .unions relied on their own membership, particularly those well endowed with brawn, to do the "dirty work" of physical intimidation. Eventually, though, professional gangsters replaced the volunteers.[31]

A primary organizer at Leiserson's was 16-year-old Clara Lemlich. Born in Gorodok, on the Austrian-Ukraine border, she emigrated to New York in 1903, after the pogrom and massacre of Jews at Kishinev. Clara was one of the seven women and six men who founded Waistmakers' Local 25 of the ILGWU in 1906. During the 11-week independent strike at Leiserson's, Clara was arrested 17 times and had six ribs broken.[32]

In November, thousands of workers attended a meeting at Cooper Union, where leaders like Samuel Gompers spoke for hours until Lemlich took the floor, saying, in Yiddish: "I am tired of listening to speakers. . .I offer a resolution that a general strike be declared—now."[33] The resolution passed. Lillian Wald supported it. Twenty thousand shirtwaistmakers, mostly women and two-thirds Jewish, went on strike. The 500-member Teachers' Association, headed by Henrietta Rodman, raised funds for it.[34]

The Women's Trade Union League's (WTUL) picket line was the first known volunteer picket line formed outside of the union.[35] Anne Morgan, daughter of J.P., provided bail. Seven hundred and twenty-three women were arrested in the first month.

> The girls, headed by teen-age Clara Lemlich, described by union organizers as "a pint of trouble for the bosses," began singing Italian and Russian working-class songs as they paced in twos before the factory door. Of a sudden, around the corner came a dozen tough-looking customers for whom the union label "gorillas" seemed well chosen.
> "Stand fast, girls," called Clara, and then the thugs rushed the line, knocking Clara to her knees, striking at the pickets, opening the way for a group of frightened scabs to slip through. . .The thugs ran off as the cops pushed Clara and two other badly beaten girls into the wagon.[36]

Picketers, brought to the Jefferson Market Courthouse on 9th Street and 6th Avenue, were either processed and released or sent to the workhouse by judges who berated them with statements like: "You are on strike against God and Nature, whose firm law is that man shall earn his bread by the sweat of his brow."[37] In her *Diary of a Shirtwaist Striker*, Theresa Malkiel wrote about being arrested on a picket line.

> I'm pretty dazed. I've just come back from that living hell called Night Court. . .I'm sure nobody could help cursing the world we're living in after spending a few hours in that place. . .Our girls were all fined from 10 to 25 dollars apiece. I being convicted a second time, was fined 25 dollars and the judge warned me to keep out of his way or he'll send me to the workhouse next time. I listened to him and said "Yes sir" but he needn't think that I'll give up the strike on that account.[38]

Anne Morgan rented Carnegie Hall for a meeting to protest police violence. The "convicts" sat on the stage wearing sashes that said, "I am not a criminal." By March, 354 of the 400 struck shops had signed contracts with the Ladies Waistmakers' Union of New York.[39] Workers won the right to a closed shop, 52-hour work week, and pay raises. Local 25 grew to 10,000 members.[40]

Blacklisted after the strike, Clara Lemlich had to work under assumed names. She was later elected to the executive board of the WTUL and eventually became a paid organizer and speaker for the Suffrage Party and labor. A charter member of the US Communist Party, she worked in shops until 1954.[41]

## 7. Greene and Washington Streets: The Triangle Factory

The largest shirtwaist factory in NYC employed 800 to 900 workers, mostly women. Pauline Newman, who came to America in 1901 from Lithuania, started working in the Triangle Factory as a child.

> We started work at seven-thirty in the morning, and during the busy season we worked until nine in the evening. They didn't pay you any overtime and they didn't give you anything for supper money. . .[O]f course there were [child labor] laws on the books, but no one bothered to enforce them. The employers were always tipped off if there was going to be an inspection. "Quick," they'd say, "into the boxes!". . . .Then some shirts were piled on top of us, and when the inspector came—no children. . .The employers didn't recognize anyone working for them as a human being. You were not allowed to sing. . .My pay was $1.50 a week no matter how many hours I worked. . .[Y]ou got up at five-thirty, took the horse car, then the electric trolley to Greene Street. . . .[42]

In 1911, the factory burst into flames. Because doors and windows were locked to prevent theft, 146 Jewish and Italian women died within 18 minutes. Many jumped out of windows. A giant funeral of 120,000 marchers and 400,000 spectators took place on April 5th. Through drenching rain, a crowd of shop and factory women marched from uptown; a second division of mourners, led by an empty hearse, proceeded silently through the East Side.

> [I]t was not until the marchers reached Washington Square. . .that the women gave vent to their sorrow. It was one long drawn-out, heart-piercing cry, the mingling of thousands of voices, a sort of human thunder in the elemental storm—a cry that was perhaps the most impressive expression of human grief ever heard in this city.[43]

The WTUL held a mass memorial meeting on May 2 at the Metropolitan Opera House, rented by Anne Morgan, where Rose Schneiderman delivered her speech in a whisper.

> This is not the first time girls have been burned alive in the city. Every week I must learn of the untimely death of one of my sister workers. Every year thousands of us are maimed. . . .Too much blood has been spilled. . . .It is up to the working people to save themselves. The only way they can save themselves is by a strong working-class movement.[44]

After the fire, the owners, Harris and Blanck, were acquitted of any wrongdoing and opened a second factory which the Building Department closed as non-fireproof. As in the Triangle, sewing machines blocked the fire escapes. In another factory on 16th Street, Blanck was charged with chaining the doors during work hours and fined $20. Three years after the fire, 23 suits against them were settled at $75 per life lost.[45]

## 8. Eighth Street and Avenue B: Christadora House

Looming over the park is probably the largest abandoned building in Manhattan, slated to be turned into luxury condominiums with the rest of the East Village. Founded in 1897 as a Christian community center called Christadora House, it housed many services for the Jewish community, including English and stenography classes, and provided space for those agitating for women's suffrage. According to historian Elinor Lerner, in the 1915 and 1917 NYC referenda on women's right to vote, "the largest, strongest and most consistent support came from the Jewish community. . .[O]f the top 100 pro-suffrage election districts in 1917, at least 78 were Jewish neighborhoods."[46]

The National Progressive Women's Suffrage Union, whose main support came from Jewish garment workers, pioneered grassroots strategies for suffrage.

> It was the first suffrage group in the city to hold open air meetings, attempt a foot parade and (tried) to approach the urban working class at such public places as ball games, beaches and amusement parks. . .They also distributed leaflets and demonstrated outside of factories and formed alliances with workers on union and labor issues.[47]

One group, The Wage Earners' League, included women from the Henry Street Settlement House and organizers like Clara Lemlich. They canvassed, held mass meetings and rallies, including a joint rally with Black women.[48]

Although Jewish leaders like Rose Schneiderman and Lillian Wald were active in suffrage, and the Socialist Party even opened a suffrage committee headquarters, Lerner points out that the upper-class Christian suffrage movement never recognized

Jewish support. In fact, some leaders actually blamed immigrants for defeats. In a letter to the NY *Times*, Lillian Wald wrote that immigrant voters were more receptive to suffrage than the American born. But the movement continued to view the "foreign born" as a monolith without differentiating between Jews and other groups like the Irish, who were largely anti-suffrage. After the 1917 referendum victory, the suffragists played down the aid they got from radicals, especially pacifists and revolutionaries. They obscured Jewish support because many Jews,together with the Socialist Party,opposed US intervention in World War I.[49]

### 9. 624 East Fifth Street: Hebrew Technical School

Seventy-three percent of unmarried Jewish women were in the labor force at the turn of the century.[50] The Hebrew Technical School, founded in 1879 by the Hebrew Free School Association, was one of the Jewish institutions that trained girls in what the administrators viewed as proper and marketable skills. The school served 125 girls, about 15 years old and graduates of public school.[51]

> The primary object in forming our school was to afford girls. . .an opportunity to become skilled workwomen and to render themselves comparatively independent. The second object was to assist these girls in acquiring such knowledge of cooking, of housekeeping, and of sewing as is requisite for every woman to possess, and which they cannot, as a rule, properly obtain at home.[52]

> Teach a girl to read, to write, and to think, and you make of her a clerk. Teach her to read, write, think, and sew and she is a clerk or a seamstress as the occasion may require. . .Teach her all the foregoing with cooking added and she becomes a clerk, seamstress and housewife.[53]

### 10. 64 East Fourth Street: The Labor Lyceum

On June 3, 1900, 11 delegates of seven unions from four cities, with a combined membership of 2,000,met at the Labor Lyceum to form the ILGWU.[54] For the first 20 years its membership was primarily made up of young Jewish women. Alice Kessler-Harris notes:

> Their rapid organization and faithful tenure was responsible for at least one-quarter of the increased number of unionized women [in the second decade of the twentieth century]. And yet they were unskilled and semiskilled workers, employed in small, scattered shops, theoretically among the least organizable. These women, having unionized at their own initiative, formed the backbone of the ILGWU, which had originally sought to organize the skilled male cutters in the trade. . .The commitment of some women was such that when arrested on picket lines, they offered to spend the night in jail in order to save the union bail costs before returning to the line in the morning.[55]

Pauline Newman, a member of the WTUL, was one of the first ILGWU organizers and participated in the 1909 shirtwaist strike. Looking back at age 86, she said,

> I stopped working at the Triangle Factory during the strike in 1909 and I didn't go back. . We didn't gain very much at the end of the strike. I think the hours were reduced. . .the best thing that the strike did was to lay a foundation on which to build a union. . .Even when things were terrible, I always had that faith. . .Only now, I'm a little discouraged sometimes when I see the workers spending their time watching television—trash. We fought so hard for those hours and they waste them. We used to read Tolstoy, Dickens,

Emma Goldman

uline Newman

Fannia Cohn

Shelley, by candlelight and they watch the "Hollywood Squares." Well, they're free to do what they want. That's what we fought for.[56]

A friend of Fannia Cohn and Rose Schneiderman, Pauline always advocated for women in the unions, despite the sexism of male organizers. Frequently women organized a local, only to be rejected by the male-controlled parent union. In 1910, Pauline organized women candy makers in Philadelphia, but the International Bakery and Confectionary Workers Union delayed issuing them a charter for so long that the organization eventually fell apart.[57] Newman agitated within the ILGWU against sexism, arguing for more women in leadership positions: "Girls are apt to have more confidence in a woman than in a man."[58]

In 1913, Pauline became executive secretary of the Joint Board of Sanitary Control, the bargaining unit between garment labor and management. A long time member of the Socialist Party, she was its nominee for Secretary of State in 1918, and in 1919 she was made director of the Unity Health Center, which provided union members with quality health care.

## 11. First Street and Second Avenue: Women's Trade Union League

This was the East Side office of the WTUL, an organization of upper-class Christian women committed to organizing across class and ethnic lines. Founded in 1888, it sought legislation to regulate women's hours in factories, fought clothing and cigar sweatshops, and forced the appointment of women factory inspectors. In 1903, members adopted the slogan, "An Eight Hour Day—A Living Wage—To Guard the Home" and began cultivating leadership from among working women.[59] According to historian Nancy Dye, League members

> believed that women of all classes, working together, could organize women into trade unions and persuade the labor movement to integrate women into its ranks.[60]

The June 1911 League *Bulletin* noted that:

> The League's representation in the suffrage parade was small. The lack of industrial representation was a source of regret. . .Enfranchisement will strengthen the position of working women and it is the workers who can make the legislators realize, more than any other group, that the demand for enfranchisement of women is a real and vital demand.[61]

The next year they again encouraged their membership to participate in a multi-class parade, emphasizing that the contingents would include women riders on horseback, actresses, architects, waitresses, cashiers and men sympathizers bringing up the rear.[62]

The League provided money, publicity and strategic support to women who wanted to unionize. Photos of affluent society women Anne Morgan and Alva Belmont being arrested on the 1909 shirtwaist strike picket line brought publicity and financial support to the strike.[63]

While the League was theoretically committed to cross-class organizing, anti-Semitism prevailed.

> [Leaders] scheduled a citywide conference of working women on Yom Kippur, despite Jewish members' protests. Only one League ally. . .studied Yiddish. Some allies held stereotypical conceptions of immigrant women. Jewish women were often described as "dark-eyed," "studious," and "revolutionary" in league literature.[64]

Many women affiliated with the League were lesbians and formed lesbian networks. Pauline Newman and her lover had a life-long lesbian relationship and adopted a child together.[65] Mary Dreir lived for many years with Frances Keller and then with organizer Lenora O'Reilly, providing her with a house and life income. Helen Marot lived all her adult life with organizer Caroline Pratt.[66] When Lillian Wald, lesbian founder of the Henry Street Settlement, spearheaded the formation of a child labor committee in 1902, Helen was employed as its chief inspector. In 1905, the League received an anonymous grant to employ Rose Schneiderman as the first full-time working-class Jewish organizer. The donor was later revealed to be Irene Lewisohn, a wealthy German Jew who was part of Lillian Wald's lesbian community.[67]

The community was aware of these women's lesbian relationships as documented in the 1913 novel *Comrade Yetta*. A *roman à clef* about the East Side, it featured Mabel Train, a thinly disguised head of the WTUL, who was "always accompanied by her roommate Eleanor Mead." Mead was

> feared and hated by all Mabel's admirers. It was impossible to call on Miss Train, it was necessary to call on both of them. Without any open discourtesy, with a well-bred effort to hide her jealousy, Eleanor made the courting of her friend a hideous ordeal.[68]

It has taken over 65 years for historians to reacknowledge what the community knew all along, that lesbians were at the center of radical organizing on the East Side, and that their relationships influenced radical politics and strategy.

Rose Schneiderman, who was born in Poland in 1882, emigrated in 1890. After her father's death, United Hebrew Charities placed her in the Hebrew Sheltering Guardian Society. She worked 64 hours a week in a department store for $2.16, and then got a job as a cap liner, for which she had to purchase her own sewing machine. In 1903, anarchist Bessie Braut, her co-worker, influenced Rose and two others to form a local in the United Cloth Hat and Cap Makers' Union. They got the required 23 members and Rose became secretary.

At 21 she organized her first action. On Saturday, when employees worked half a day, the men got paid as they left, but the women had to return at four. They protested and won. A year later she was elected to the executive board of the United Cloth Hat and Cap Makers' Union, the first woman to hold such a position in the trade union movement. When her union struck for 13 weeks, the strike fund paid all married males $6 a week, but women were not eligible.[69]

Sexism within the trade union movement was very high: "The left wing male leaders paid lip service to equality for women but in practice excluded them from positions of importance." Rose Schneiderman was one of the few women to

> succeed in wresting authority from male labor leaders, who zealously guarded their privileges. The garment workers' unions tended only too often to treat women as second-class members; women were not taken very seriously.[70]

After being hired by the WTUL, Schneiderman concentrated on improving the status of women within the trade union movement. The Irene Lewisohn grant of $41 a month enabled her to quit factory work, attend the socialist Rand School on 15th Street, and organize.

In 1917, she became the chair of the industrial section of the Women's Suffrage Party and, three years later, the first Jewish woman to run for US Senate on the Farmer-Labor ticket. Although she had only four years of formal education, she was on the Board of Directors of Brookwood Labor College, Bryn Mawr, and Hudson Shore Summer Schools for Working Women. She served as president of the WTUL from 1926 until 1950 when the organization dissolved. In 1933, FDR appointed her as the only woman on the Labor Advisory Board of the National Recovery Act, and from 1937-43 she served as Secretary of New York State Department of Labor.[71] When she died in 1972, she had a photo of Mary Drier on the mirror in the Jewish Home and Hospital for the Aged.[72]

## 12. Allen Street

Black, White and Hispanic prostitutes still work on Allen Street, which has been a center of prostitution for the East Side since before the turn of the century. But then:

> The pimp was Jewish, the woman was Jewish, the tenement was Jewish and all in a Jewish neighborhood. The prostitute lived with her community and her clientele and boss were also members of that community.[73]

Reformers complained about this integration of prostitutes into the Jewish neighborhood life.

> Frequently these women engage one family in the tenement to do their laundry work, another to do their cooking and still further financial arrangements are made with the housekeepers. The patronage which they distribute is thus utilized to make friends and to purchase the silence of those who might otherwise object to their presence. The children of respectable families are often sent to the prostitutes on various errands and because of the gifts made to the children, these women became important personages in the house and their affairs, the subject of frequent conversation.[74]

The three blocks from Houston to Delancy were full of brothels, dance halls and other places where prostitutes worked, many owned by church corporations and wealthy New York families. Men found Italian girls, as young as 10, in the 50ᶜ brothels on nearby Elizabeth Street, or they could solicit women who worked under the elevated tracks, careful to avoid the cinders and hot oil that fell from passing trains.

Jews have always been reluctant to acknowledge the existence of prostitution in our history, but the myths about our moral past deny the reality of these prostitutes' experience. Jacob Marcus writes: "In the gay atmosphere of the dance hall, smooth-talking and affable young men sought out immigrant women"[76] for prostitution, and the authors of *Jewish Women in America* explain:

> Prostitution among Jewish women in America, no longer the rarity it was in the old country, caused the community great despair. . .Parents. . .were known to sit *shiva*. . .for those who became prostitutes.[77]

Jewish prostitutes were a firm part of Jewish life in America, just as Christian prostitutes were of Christian life. Of women incarcerated in Bedford Hills prison early in the century, Jews (who made up almost 20% of the population of NYC) comprised 18% of imprisoned prostitutes. In a 1912 study of 647 prostitutes, Bedford Hills supervisor Katherine Davis found that most of the Jewish prisoners were American born of immigrant parents, living with their families and contributing most of their money to the family nest-egg. So some families knew they were prostitutes.

Money, of course, was their motive. Davis reported that most women in prison said they earned between $5 and $9 a week before turning to prostitution and from $46 to $72 a week after.[78] This was at a time when high paid male workers earned under $25 per week. Prostitutes were among the highest paid members of the Jewish community, and their money must have contributed substantially to the upward mobility of their families.

## 13. Eldridge and Rivington: University Settlement House

Founded as the Neighborhood Guild in 1886 at 147 Forsythe Street, and moved to its current home in 1903, this settlement provided services, classes, vacation space, meeting rooms, libraries and other programs to improve the quality of daily life on the East Side. It even ran a cooperative dairy and distributed fresh cut flowers.[79]

In 1905, Rose Harriet Pastor, a young English language columnist for the Yiddish newspaper the *Tageblatt* (The Daily Page), interviewed the director of the University Settlement, millionaire socialist James Graham Stokes, a non-Jew.[80] As in the Cindrella tale *Salome of the Tenements*, modelled by Anzia Yezierska on Rose's life, they married, and Rose Stokes became a leader of the Jewish left.

She was born in Poland in 1879, and started working at age 4. Her family emigrated to England, where her mother led a workers' strike in London's East End. Rose wrote poetry in Yiddish, helped translate the work of Morris Rosenfeld into English,[81] and in 1914 started writing a lovelorn column at the *Tageblatt* for $15 a week.[82] When her marriage deteriorated—her increasing sympathy for the Communist cause was one of the reasons for her divorce[83]—she wrote a friend that Stokes had accused her of becoming "unlady-like and hazardous" and "utterly crazy."[84] In 1918 she was convicted under the Espionage Act and sentenced to two years for criticizing the government during World War I. "She had denounced the Wilson administration for its militarism and its tolerance of profiteers."[85] The verdict was later reversed.

Rose ran for Borough President of Manhattan on the Communist ticket in 1921. In 1922, she was a delegate to the 4th Congress of the Communist International in Moscow and began to write for *Pravda* and *The Workers* (later *The Daily Worker*, now *The Daily World*). She was active in all aspects of the labor and birth control movements, as well as most other progressive movements. After her divorce in 1925, Rose experienced severe poverty and married Jerome Isaac Romaine, editor of the communist magazine *Political Affairs*. In 1929, she was severely beaten by the police during a demonstration in support of the people of Haiti. She died of cancer in 1933.

At her trial, Rose spoke of her rags-to-riches life:

> For ten years I have worked and produced things necessary and useful for the people of this country and for all those years I was half starved. . .I worked at doing useful work and never had enough. But the moment I left the useful producing class, and did not have to do any productive work in order to exist — I had all the vacations I wanted, all the clothes I wanted. I had all the leisure I wanted—everything I wanted was mine without my having to do any labor in return for all I had received.[86]

Yezierska described her Rose-inspired heroine as a "blazing comet," an "electric radiance" and a "tragedy queen."[87]

## 14. The Bowery

Currently filled with the homeless and the emotionally ill, the Bowery was once filled with theaters and factories. At 48 Bowery was the Thalia Theatre where the great Bertha Kalish (the "Sappho" of the Yiddish theater) performed. Like the rest of the East Side, it was also an area where women organized. In 1904, 125 girls between ages 14 and 16 walked out of the Cohen Paper Box Factory where their wages of $3 per 1,000 cigarette boxes were cut by 10%. Support came from benefit concerts, from *The Forward*, the United Hebrew Trades and the WTUL.[88]

In the shops women faced sexual harassment from bosses and other workers. According to Baum:

> They suffered their humiliation and fear in private for one did not complain publicly about such matters. Anyway, sexual payoffs for the privilege of holding a job were expected and a common enough practice in cases of advancement within the shop.[89]

> The religious culture of Eastern Europe demanded sexual abstinence before marriage, but regarded women as sexual beings capable of enticing men away from their religious pursuits. Indeed, the culture ensured that the sexes lived very separated existences. . . .[W]ith the loosening of religious taboos in the workplace, the old restraints gave way to what many considered the Americanization of sexual attitudes. . . .While many women may have tried to come to terms with the sexual conditions prevailing in the shops, once they were organized and union grievance committees set up, charges of sexual abuse were among the major complaints made by female workers to union officials.[90]

Despite women's contribution to the trade union movement, and their domination of certain industries like the garment industry, trade unions virtually ignored women's issues. Some labor leaders even wanted to push women out of work to provide jobs for men. In 1879, the president of the International Cigar Makers said,

> We cannot drive the females out of the trade, but we can restrict this daily quota of labor through factory laws (protective legislation).[91]

The 1890 Cloak Operators and Contractors Union strike settlement specified that "No part of this agreement shall refer or apply to females," although 85-90% of the workers were women. In 1913, the ILGWU agreed to the following settlement:

### Terms of Employment and Shop Standards
Wages—The following shall be the minimum rates for week workers:

1. Full fledged cutters (men only) $27.50.
2. Drapers (women only) $15.00.
3. Joiners (women only) $13.00.
4. Sample Makers (women only) $15.00.
5. Examiners (women only) $11.50.
6. Finishers (women only) $9.50.
7. Ironers (women) $14.00.
8. Ironers (men) $17.00.[92]

By union agreement women were slotted into the lower paying jobs, sometimes earning half what men earned, and usually earning less for the same work. Unions also made conscious efforts to exclude women from organizing. They used "such well-known tactics as holding meetings in saloons, scheduling them at late hours, and ridiculing women who dared to speak."[93]

## 15. Grand and Ludlow: P.S. 75, Home of the Women's Literary Club

Of the many radical women on the East Side, women writers appear to have lived especially conflicted lives. Many wrote only in Yiddish, and those who wrote in English had no way to make connections or break into the men's networks. When one did manage to publish a book, it was often destroyed by male critics. Very few works by these women have been collected or translated.

Born in Alexat, a *shtetl* near Kaunas, in 1879, Yente Serdatzky started publishing in 1905 in Warsaw in the journal *Veg* (Path) edited by I.L. Peretz. She came to New York in 1907 and wrote for the *Freie Arbeiter Stime* (The Free Voice of Labor), an anarchist newspaper that was so open to women writers that Jacob Gladstein, the famous Yiddish poet, allegedly submitted work under a woman's name.[94] Because of hostile criticism, Yente stopped writing in 1920 and became a shopkeeper.[95]

Esther Luria was born in Warsaw in 1877 and came to New York in 1912. She wrote for the Yiddish socialist press like the *Forverts*, (Jewish Daily Forward), *Tsunkunft* (Future) and the ILGWU Yiddish paper. Living in terrible poverty, she died alone in the Bronx in the 1920's.

Fradel Schtok, born in 1890 in Galicia wrote for the *Freie Arbeiter Stime*. A cafe literary figure, in 1916 she began to publish short stories in the *Forverts* and *Tog* (Day). Her two books, one in Yiddish and one in English, received negative reviews. She was institutionalized for mental illness in the 1920's.

Celia Dropkin, an avant-garde writer, painter, and the mother of five children, wrote for the socialist and anarchist press. She was also part of the "*In Zikh*" literary circle. These non-aligned radicals who called themselves "introspectivists" wrote experimentally for a very small readership, behaving "as though they were in the mainstream of American political debate when, in fact, they were invisible."[96]

Anna Rappaport was born in 1876, and came to the US from Kaunas in 1897. She made her writing debut in *Die Arbeiter Zeitung* (Workers' Times) with the poem "*A Bild Fun Hungers Noyt in 1893*" (A Picture of the Hardship of Hunger in 1893). Anna, whose poetry captured the living and working conditions of poor women, stopped writing in Yiddish in 1919 when she became a columnist for the socialist English language paper *The Call*.[97]

Norma Fain Pratt has compiled a list of 53 Yiddish women writers whose work appeared in the US in the first part of this century:[98]

| | |
|---|---|
| Pessie Bach | Celia Dropkin |
| Ida Badanes | Sarah Fell-Yellin |
| Sara Barkan | Rivke Gallin |
| Fraydel Belov | Sonia Gerbert |
| Dora Birek | Rayzel Glass-Fenster |
| Minnie Bordo-Rivkin | Eda Glasser |
| Liba Burstin | Bella Goldworth |
| Freidl Charney | Silva Guterman |
| Hasye Cooperman | Rosa Gutman |

275

אױבן: בערטאַ קלינג, אסתר שומיאַטשער, מלכה לי.
אונטן: אידא גלאַזער, שרה רייזן, צילע דראָפקין

Top, from l. to r.: *Malke Lee, Esther Schumiatcher, Bertha Kling.*
Bottom: *Celia Dropkin, Sore Rayzn, Ida Glazer*

*1909 Shirtwaist makers' strike.*

| | |
|---|---|
| Frume Halpern | Kadia Molodowsky |
| Leah Hofman | Rosa Nevadovski |
| Rachel Holtman | Rosa Newman-Wallinsky |
| Malcha Kahan | Bessie Hershfield Pomerantz |
| Pesi Kahana | Anna Rappaport |
| Miriam Karpilove | Chane Safran |
| Esther Katz | Esther Shumiatcher |
| Leah Kaufman | Yente Serdatzky |
| Bertha Kling | Sarah Smith |
| Berta Kudly | Fradel Stock |
| Malke Lee | Deborah Tarant |
| Sarah-Leah Liebert | Malka Heifetz Tussman |
| Shafra-Esther Levy | Chana Vartzel |
| Malka Locker | Rashelle Veprinski |
| Esther Luria | Shifre Weiss |
| Rachel Luria | Hinde Zaretsky |
| Anna Margolin | Miriam Shoner Zunser |
| Esther Miller | |

## 16. Hester and Ludlow: The Laborers' Market

Hester Street, also called *Khazer* (Pig) Market,[99] was full of craftsmen and pushcarts selling every conceivable item.

Bandannas and tin cups at two cents, peaches at a cent a quart, "damaged" eggs for a song, hats for a quarter and spectacles, warranted to suit the eye. . .for thirty-five cents. . . .Here is a woman churning horseradish on a machine she has chained and padlocked to a tree. . . Beside her a butcher's stand with cuts at prices. . .never dreamed of. Old coats are hawked for fifty cents "as good as new," and "pants". . .at anything that can be got.[100]

It was the site of the mothers' riot of 1906. When officials vaccinated pupils in school without explaining their purpose, mothers feared their children were being murdered and converged by the thousands on the school. When the principal locked the doors, women grabbed fruit and vegetables off carts and hurled them at the building. Because of their experience, the mothers believed the murder of their children was a real possibility.[101]

## 17. 7 Orchard Street

A letter came to the *Forverts* on August 1, 1902 from this address.

I am looking for my husband David Silecki, the butcher from Prusani. He is thirty-five years old, blonde, of mediocre height with a round fat face. Whoever knows about him should contact Zuckerman.[102]

Thousands of husbands deserted their families once they got to America. A Jewish National Desertion Bureau published photos of deserters in Jewish newspapers across the nation and in Canada, while United Hebrew Charities gave cash relief to deserted women.[103]

In many cases women were so completely dependent on their husbands for support that they refused to testify against them once the men were apprehended and presented for prosecution. Many took back their chronically deserting husbands time and again.[104]

As a result, United Hebrew Charities decided that no deserted wife would be assisted unless she agreed to prosecute her husband. They noted:

> The growth of the number of deserted women becomes more appalling each year, whether the cause be the inability of the wife to make the home attractive, or whether it be the despair of the husband at his inability to support his family.[105]

These narrow views created an environment in which there was little support for deserted women, and "a striking number of abandoned women turned to prostitution as a means of earning a living."[106] Fourteen and a half percent of the prostitutes at Bedford Hills Reformatory became prostitutes after they were deserted.

Many abandoned women had to place their children in institutions. In 1913, 20% of institutionalized children were from deserted homes.[107] Eighty-five percent of the children in the New York Hebrew Infant Asylum had one living parent. Since Asylum officials wished to Americanize their charges, who were immigrants or children of immigrants, they restricted contact between mothers and children. Some institutions made parents promise to leave their children for at least one year, and 75% stayed more than three years. The German Jewish directors limited parental visits to four days a year, separated siblings, and prohibited food and gifts until the 1890's. They censored all mail and often banned Yiddish. As a result, discharged children, who often could not speak the same language or eat the same food as their parents, became attached to the Asylum: 61% attended High Holy Day services there after their discharge.[108]

Girls were often released earlier than boys because by the age of nine they were deemed ready to care for the children still at home. Girls who grew up in orphanages generally worked in domestic service, not clerical or retail jobs like other Jewish girls.

## 18. Monroe Street Between Pike and Market

The NY *Times*, May 24, 1902:

> It will not do. . .to have a swarm of ignorant and infuriated women going about any part of the city with petroleum destroying goods and trying to set fire to the shops of those against whom they are angry.

In 1902, Jewish retail butchers struck the wholesalers, many of them German Jews, charging them with inflating prices. The strike was settled after two days, but the decreases were not passed on to shoppers. Mrs. Fannie Levy, wife of a cloakmaker and mother of six children under 13, and Sarah Edelson, owner of a restaurant on Monroe and Pike, organized a boycott of thousands of women on the Lower East Side. The strike spread from block to block in one half-hour. Twenty thousand people massed in front of New Irving Hall, and on the first day 70 women and 15 men were arrested for disorderly conduct.[109]

On the second day of rioting, with pickets at every butcher shop, 100 people were arrested and money was raised for bail funds. According to the *Tribune*:

> [T]he main disturbance was caused by the women. Armed with sticks, vocabularies and well sharpened nails, they made life miserable for the policemen.[110]

They also clashed with butchers and dragged meat out of shops to set on fire with kerosene.

That *shabes* "using the traditional communal tactic of interrupting the Torah reading when a matter of justice was at stake," women entered *shuls* and requested support from the rabbis and the men to continue the boycott. When a member complained that women should not speak from the altar, "Mrs. Silver coolly responded that the Torah would pardon her."[111]

The next day, most butcher shops were closed. The boycott had spread to Williamsburg, where meat was burned in the streets. That night 500 attended a meeting of the Ladies Anti-Beef Trust Association,[112] which decided to seek support from Christian women and to consolidate in Harlem, East New York, and the Bronx. In Brooklyn, 400 women patrolled the streets to control the shops. But when rivalry exploded between Mrs. Edelson and Carolyn Schatzburg, male communal leaders, presided over by David Blaustein of the Educational Alliance, took over from the women to "bring order to the great struggle for cheap meat." Joseph Barondess urged "the women to be quiet and leave the fighting to the men." The men founded the Allied Conference for Cheap Kosher Meat with a ten-member steering committee including only three women.[113]

The average woman in the boycott, according to Paula Hyman, was 39 years old, had 4.3 children, and had been in America about 11 years. Most husbands were employed in the garment industry.

> Thus, the women formed not an elite in their community, but a true grassroots leadership. . .
> The initial boycott committee composed of nineteen women, numbered nine neighbors from
> Monroe Street, four from Cherry Street and six from adjacent blocks. . .The neighborhood, a
> form of female network, thus provided the locus of the community for the boycott: all were
> giving up meat together, celebrating dairy *shabbosim* together and contributing together to
> the boycott fund.[114]

## The NY *Times* of August 14, 1902 reported:

> They are very ignorant. . .They do not understand the duties or the rights of Americans.
> They have no inbred or acquired respect for law and order as the basis of the life of the
> society into which they have come. . . .Resistance to authority does not seem to them
> necessarily wrong, only risky. The restraint it can have on their passions is very small.

Perhaps the reporter got this idea from observing the responses of one boycotter when questioned before a judge:

> "Did you throw meat on the streets?" Rosa Peskin was asked.
>
> "Certainly," she replied. "I should have looked it in the teeth?"[115]

The strike ended with a price rollback, and these social networks were used to build rent strikes for the next six years.

## 19. 265 Henry Street: Henry Street Settlement

The Henry Street Settlement House still stands at this spot and still serves the immigrant population of the Lower East Side. Where they previously offered sewing, English, Americanization and literature courses, they now have a Hispanic playwriting program, African dance and special courses for the elderly.

Founded by Lillian Wald, it was originally The Nurses' Settlement. It had 11 full time staff members by 1898 and 27 by 1906. Wald persuaded the Board of Education to put nurses in schools, opposed child labor, agitated for more playgrounds, joined with suffragists, supported the 1909 shirtwaist strike, and was an active pacifist during World War I. She was also president of the American Union Against Militarism, the parent organization of the American Civil Liberties Union, and campaigned for services for battered women and children.

Lesbian/feminist historian Blanche Wiesen Cook writes that Lillian's "basic support group consisted of the long term residents of Henry Street. . .[who] worked, lived and vacationed together for fifty years."[116] One woman with whom she had a very close relationship, Lavinia Dock, wrote to Wald after Wald's meeting with President Wilson:

> What is this terrible burden of responsibility and anxiety now resting on the American men's president? Is it arising from anything women have done or are going to do? Not at all . . .surely there could be no more appropriate moment for women to press forward with their demand for a voice—women who are at this moment going on errands of peace.[117]

Cook writes that "Wald lived in a homosocial world that was also erotic. Her primary emotional needs and desires were fulfilled by women. She was woman-supported and woman-allied."[118]

Irene Lewisohn donated the Neighborhood Playhouse on Grand Street (now the Henry Street Playhouse) to the settlement in 1915. The Lewisohn sisters traveled and corresponded with Lillian. One letter from Irene to Lillian is unmistakably amorous.

> I have some memories that are holier by far than temples or graves or blossoms. A fireside romance and a moonlight night are among the treasures carefully guarded. . .As an offering for such inspirations, I am making a special vow to be and to do. . .Much of my heart to you.[119]

Wald supported the Russian Revolution, prohibition, and pacifism, and visited Russia in 1924 at the revolutionary government's invitation. She supported the League of Nations and founded the National Child Labor Committee, working in public service until her death in 1940.

Of course, social work as a tool for change has always been a controversial issue among radical women. Emma Goldman scoffed:

> Teaching the poor to eat with a fork is all very well. . .but what good does it do if they have not the food? Let them first become the masters of life; they will then know how to eat and how to live. . .[S]incere as settlement workers were, they were doing more harm than good.[120]

## 20. 175 East Broadway: The *Forverts* Building

This building housed the progressive Jewish daily founded by Abe Cahan, the Workmen's Circle, the United Hebrew Trades and the *Folksbiene* Theatre.

The *Forverts* (Jewish Daily Forward) was the most popular Yiddish newspaper in the US. Socialist editor Abe Cahan promoted a wide range of Jewish activities ranging from labor unions to printing selections from the most prominent Yiddish fiction writers. At its height, the paper had eleven local and regional editions with a circulation of 200,000.

Many community and union meetings were held here. At least one event here challenged the union hierarchy. The leadership of most unions stayed male while the rank and file was mostly female. In 1912, the ILGWU started a system of protocols, agreements with management mandating arbitrators instead of strikes. Predictably, arbitrators did not agitate with the same spirit as workers. In 1916, women from the rank and file led a revolt. According to *Solidarity*, February 26, 1916:

> A meeting of shop chairmen at No. 175 East Broadway, ended last night in a general fight. Women became hysterical. . .Miss Ida Grabinski, who has been named chairman of one of the dozen committees of women in the new "equal voice" movement, said. . ."The officers of the union boss us worse than the bosses. . .Now they tell us to work. The next minute they withdraw that order. The women workers comprise more than 65 per cent of the union members throughout the country. . .Why shouldn't we have something to say about what concerns us most?"[121]

────────────────────────── **Notes** ──────────────────────────

[1] Irving Howe, "Oral History of Isidore Wisotsky," Unpublished, YIVO.

[2] Emma Goldman, *Living My Life* (Garden City: Garden City Pub. Co., 1934), p. 349.

[3] Jacob Marcus, *The American Jewish Woman: A Documentary History* (NY: KTAV, 1981), p. 354.

[4] Cecyle Neidle, *America's Immigrant Women* (NY: Hippocrene Books, 1976), p. 169.

[5] Goldman, p. 92.

[6] Greta Fink, *Great Jewish Women: Profiles of Courageous Women from the Maccabean Period to the Present* (NY: Menorah Pub. Co., 1978), p. 115.

[7] Alix Kates Shulman, *Red Emma Speaks* (NY: Schocken Books, 1983), p. 26.

[8] Shulman, p. 29.   [9] Shulman, p. 30.   [10] Shulman, p. 3.

[11] Blanche Wiesen Cook, *Women and Support Networks* (NY: Out & Out Books, 1979).

[12] Magnus Hirschfield, leader of German homosexual movement, cited in *Gay American History: Lesbians and Gay Men in the USA*, ed. by Jonathan Katz (NY: Avon, 1978), p. 570.

[13] Fink, p. 119.   [14] Shulman, p. 49.

[15] *The Book of Trips with Places of Jewish Interest* (NY: Jewish Welfare Board, 1939).

[16] Irving Howe, *World of Our Fathers* (NY: Harcourt and Brace Jovanovich, 1976), p. 237.

[17] Ronald Sanders, *The Lower East Side: A Guide to Its Jewish Past* (NY: Dover, 1979).

[18] Louis Lorwin, *The Women's Garment Workers: A History of the ILGWU* (NY: B.W. Huebsch, 1924), photo insert p. 418.

[19] June Sochen, *Consecrate Every Day: The Public Lives of American Jewish Women, 1880-1980* (Albany: Suny Press, 1981), p. 18.   [20] Howe, *World*, p. 97.

[21] From A.H. Fromerson, "Amusements and Social Life: New York," *The Russian Jew in the United States*, cited in Sochen, *Consecrate*, p. 31.   [22] Howe, "Oral History."

[23] Alice Kessler-Harris, "Introduction," *The Bread Givers* by Anzia Yezierska (NY: Persea Press, 1975), p. ix.

[24] Anzia Yezierska, *Red Ribbon on a White Horse* (NY: Persea Books, 1950), *passim*.

[25] Carol Schoen, *Anzia Yezierska* (Boston: Twayne Publishers, 1982), p. 10.   [26] Schoen, p. 95.

[27] Donna Ippolito, *The Uprising of the 20,000* (Pittsburgh: Motheroot Pub., 1979), pp. 3-4.

[28] Howe, *World*, p. 298.

[29] Nancy Schrom Dye, *As Equals As Sisters: Feminism, The Labor Movement and The Women's Trade*

*Union League of New York* (Columbia: Univ. of Missouri Press, 1980), p. 93.    [30]Ippolito, p. 22.

[31]Jenna Joselit, *Our Gang: Jewish Crime and the New York Jewish Community, 1900-1940* (Bloomington: Indiana Univ. Press, 1983), p. 108.    [32]Marcus, *Documentary*, p. 575.    [33]Howe, *World*, p. 298.

[34]Charlotte Baum, Paula Hyman and Sonya Michel, *The Jewish Woman in America* (NY: Dial Press, 1976), pp. 141 ff.

[35]Phillip Foner, *Women and the American Labor Movement* (NY: Free Press, 1979), p. 327. Also see Ippolito, p. 13, citing Rose Schneiderman, *All For One*, p. 91.

[36]McAlister Coleman, NY *Sun*, quoted in Howe, *World*, pp. 299-300.    [37]Ippolito, p. 21.

[38]Theresa Serber Malkiel, *Diary of a Shirtwaist Striker* (NY: Cooperative Press, 1910), p. 37.

[39]Marcus, *Documentary*, p. 571.

[40]Henry Feingold, *Zion in America* (NY: Twayne Publishers, 1974), p. 174.

[41]Marcus, *Documentary*, pp. 575-579, *passim.*

[42]Joan Morrison and Charlotte Fox Zabusky, *American Mosaic: The Immigrant Experience in the Words of Those Who Lived It* (NY: E.P. Dutton, 1980), pp. 10-11.

[43]From report in the *American*, quoted by Leon Stein, *The Triangle Fire* (Phila.: J.P. Lippincott, 1962), pp. 152-153.    [44]Baum, pp. 152-153.    [45]Stein, pp. 206-207.

[46]Elinor Lerner, "Jewish Involvement in the New York City Woman Suffrage Movement," *American Jewish History*, LXX (1981), 442-461; ref. 443.    [47]Lerner, p. 444.

[48]Lerner, p. 446. I have been unable to find any further information on this occurrence. There are at least two dissertations on the topic of Black/Jewish cooperation in this period: Steven Bloom, "Interactions Between Blacks and Jews in New York City 1900-1930 as Reflected in the Black Press (NYU, 1973); and Isabel Boiko Price, "Black Response to Anti-Semitism: Negroes and Jews in New York, 1880-World War II" (Univ. of New Mexico, 1975).

[49]Lerner, pp. 460-461, *passim.*

[50]Sally Miller, "From Sweatshop Worker to Labor Leader: Theresa Malkiel, a Case Study," *American Jewish History*, LXVIII (1978) 189-205; ref. 191.

[51]Rudolph Glanz, *The Jewsh Woman in America Vol. I: Female Immigrant Generations Jewish* (NY: KTAV, 1978), p. 28.    [52]United Hebrew Charities, 6th Annual Report, 1880.

[53]United Hebrew Charities, 9th Annual Report, 1883.    [54]Lorwin, p. 103.

[55]Kessler-Harris, *Out to Work* (NY: Oxford Univ. Press, 1982), pp. 159-160.

[56]Morrison, pp. 12-14.    [57]Kessler-Harris, p. 157.    [58]Foner, p. 367.

[59]Moses Rischin, *The Promised City: New York Jews 1870-1914* (Cambridge: Harvard Univ. Press, 1962), p. 249.    [60]Dye, p. 2.    [61]Women's Trade Union League Bulletin, June 1911.

[62]Women's Trade Union League Bulletin, May 1912.    [63]Dye, p. 93.

[64]Dye, p. 54. Dye continues: "Italians were [described in league literature as] 'docile,' 'fun-loving,' 'submissive,' and 'superstitious.' "

[65]Alice Kessler-Harris, "Organizing the Unorganizable: Three Jewish Women and Their Union," in Marcus, *Documentary*, p. 85.    [66]Dye, p. 39.    [67]Cook, p. 22.

[68]Arthur Bullard, *Comrade Yetta* (NY: Macmillan, 1913), pp. 99, 100, 103.

[69]Baum, pp. 153-156, *passim.*

[70]Jacob Marcus, *The American Jewish Woman 1654-1980.* (NY: KTAV, 1980), p. 110.

[71]Baum, pp. 152-160, *passim.*    [72]Neidle, p. 147.

[73]April Shour, "Life in the Lower East Side: The Jewish Prostitute," Unpublished, Jewish Theological Seminary.

[74]Robert Weeks Deforest and Lawrence Veillir, *The Tenement House Problem*, Vol. I. (NY: Macmillan & Co., 1903).

[75]J.R. Schwartz, *Orchard Street* (NY: Comet Press Books, 1960), p. 112.     [76]Joselit, p. 51.

[77]Baum, p. 115. For information about Jewish prostitution in Europe, see Edward Bristow, *Prostitution and Prejudice: The Jewish Fight Against White Slavery, 1870-1939* (NY: Schocken, 1984).

[78]Katherine B. Davis and George Kneeland, "A Study of Prostitutes Committed from New York City to the State Reformatory for Women at Bedford Hills," from *Commercialized Prostitution in New York City* (NY: The Century, 1913), *passim*.

[79]University Settlement House *Program*, 1893.

[80]Andre Manners, *Poor Cousins* (NY: Coward, McCann and Geoghegan, 1972), p. 139.

[81]Neidle, p. 174.     [82]Manners, p. 139.     [83]Marcus, *1654-1980*, p. 113.

[84]Neidle, p. 183.     [85]Marcus, *1654-1980*, p. 112.

[86]June Sochen, *Movers and Shakers: American Women Thinkers and Activists, 1990-1970* (NY: NY Times Books, 1973), p. 60.

[87]As cited in Neidle, p. 179.          [88]Howe, *World*, p. 125.

[89]Baum, p. 132.     [90]Baum, pp. 134-35.     [91]Baum, pp. 144-147.     [92]Baum, p. 147.

[93]Kessler-Harris, p. 93.

[94]As reported by Irena Klepfisz from her conversation with the late Arne Thorne, former editor of this anarchist newspaper (Fall, 1984).

[95]Norma Fain Pratt, "Culture and Radical Politics: Yiddish Women Writers 1890-1940," *American Jewish History*, LXX(1981), 68-90; ref. 79-80.

[96]Adrienne Cooper, *"In Zikh"*, lecture at YIVO, December 7, 1983.

[97]Pratt, pp. 77-78.     [98]Pratt, pp. 89-90.     [99]Howe, *World*, p. 69.

[100]Jacob Riis, *How the Other Half Lives* (NY: Hill and Wang, 1962), p. 85.

[101]Gerald Wolfe, Walking Tour of the Lower East Side, offered in 1983.

[102]See also Baum, pp. 116-118, and Howe, *World*, p. 179.

[103]Robert Morris, *Trends and Issues in Jewish Social Welfare in the United States 1899-1958* (Phila.: Jewish Publication Society of America, 1960).

[104]Reena Sigma Friedman, "Send Me My Husband Who Is In New York City: Husband Desertion in the American Immigrant Community 1900-1920," *Jewish Social Studies* (Winter, 1982), p. 7.

[105]United Hebrew Charities, Annual Report, 1896.     [106]Friedman, p. 7.     [107]Friedman, p. 8.

[108]Reena Sigma Friedman, "Jewish Orphanages," lecture at YIVO, October 6, 1983.

[109]Paula Hyman, "Neighborhood Women and Consumer Protest," *American Jewish History*, LXX (1981), 91-105; ref. 94.

[110]NY Daily *Tribune*, cited by Hyman, p. 94.     [111]*Forward*, May 18, 1902, cited by Hyman, p. 100.

[112]Hyman, p. 95.     [113]Hyman, pp. 95-96.     [114]Hyman, pp. 96-99.     [115]Hyman, p. 100.

[116]Cook, p. 27.     [117]Cook, p. 22.     [118]Cook, p. 28.     [119]Cook, p. 23.     [120]Goldman, p. 160.

[121]Meredith Tax, *The Rising of the Women: Feminist Solidarity and Class Conflict, 1880-1917* (NY: Monthly Review Press, 1980), p. 240.

*Enid Dame*

# Ethel Rosenberg: A Sestina

The charges against you never did make sense.
Did you steal a bomb or merely type
a letter? At City College, did you sit at the table
and listen to young men argue about revolution?
Did you say to yourself, being a woman,
"Why do they think it will be easy?"

You were a person who quickly learned what wasn't easy.
The world nagged and withdrew. Only your daydreams made sense.
There, you sang opera. Otherwise, you were a woman
who never could please her mother, who learned to type,
who finally married—a personal revolution!—
the man who (they claimed) filmed documents on his secret table.

You insisted it was really an ordinary table.
You'd bought it at Macy's. That was too easy
for jury and judge, whose image of revolution
was violent, apocalyptic, wholly devoid of sense,
removed from a world of children, dirty dishes, typewriters and the unhappiness of men and women.

I picture you in your three-room apartment, a woman
singing snatches of arias to yourself as you set the table,
loving and hating the house. I know the type.
Scraping and rearranging; refusing to take things easy.
Foreboding washes over you, an extra sense.
Mopping the floor, you dream of revolution.

In those days, there was only one revolution
going, and though it viewed people as workers, not men and women,
you signed its petitions, sens-
ing that freedom begets more freedom. Let's table
the next, obvious discussion: how few things are easy,
how people usually react according to type.

You hardly appeared at your trial, in spite of the type-
face in the headlines distorting your revolution,
mistranslating you. On the other hand, you weren't easy
to understand, or even to kill. A stubborn woman,
you made them do it twice. And somewhere else, at our table,
we—who believed in last-minute miracles—sat quietly, emptied
   of sense.

You've been dead most of my life. I'm the type of woman
who questions what's easy. At night, with crystal and table,
I beg ghosts out of dead revolutions to come to me, to talk sense.

*Ethel Rosenberg's high school graduation photograph, 1934.*

# An Interview with Lil Moed

*Lil Moed was born in 1925 in the Bronx (NYC) to Russian immigrant parents. She grew up in a non-religious, socialist, Yiddish-speaking home among strongly-identified cultural Jews. The mother of two daughters, Toby and Julie, and grandmother of four, Lil has had a career in nursing, mental health, and public health. She has been politically active since the '50s in civil rights, peace and disarmament, and Middle East peace work.*

*We talked to Lil on March 23, 1985 in New York City. She had just finished visiting her mother and daughter in California and was returning to Israel where she had moved in 1984.*

*How did you become involved in Middle East peace work?*

I got involved about five years ago in Los Angeles. My interest stemmed from my oldest daughter, who emigrated to Israel about 10 years ago. I began to visit her every year and realized that I knew very little about the Middle East, very little about Israel.

*Before this did you have a political position on Israel or any feelings about it?*

I can't say I had a highly-developed political position. I grew up as a non-Zionist because I was educated in the Workmen's Circle, which was socialist and anti-Zionist, and I didn't think much about it. I do remember, however, the day Israel was declared a state. I was about twenty-three. I was joyous and I felt proud, which surprised me because I was not consciously political about a Jewish state. In the '50s, I would hear about people going to Israel. A few friends of mine went, but I never felt very involved in their Zionism.

But when my daughter went in '74 and I started visiting yearly, I was drawn to study about the history of the state. I noticed that when I was there, I felt extremely comfortable about being a Jew in the one place in the world where I was part of the majority. That was a very unique experience for me. You know [sigh of relief] I could relax, and that taught me a lot about what kind of oppression I had felt all my life growing up as a Jew. By the way, I'm first generation American, my parents were immigrants. So that more or less started me off on my interest in Israel. I got somewhat familiar with Israeli history and politics.

In the meantime, my daughter had become orthodox about two years later and had decided to live the life of an orthodox Jew — which meant she got married to a man who attends *yeshiva*, she had children and settled in Jerusalem. And I would visit each year. So I started getting more oriented to the orthodox way of life. Now, I've been a socialist all my life and an atheist, and it took a lot to adjust myself during these visits. I was in a very segregated community of orthodox Jews. I didn't get to meet a broad spectrum of Israelis. And even though I traveled in Israel, I didn't make any connections with other groups, like feminist groups or left and peace groups. In '80 I made a decision to throw my political energies into Jewish work.

*Why did you decide that?*

It had to do with going to Israel and with my daughter and my recognition that I had lost touch with Yiddish culture and Jewish groups. When I was growing up in the Workmen's Circle, I learned Jewish history and literature and music. They were an integral part of my life. We spoke Yiddish at home. I went to Yiddish schools—the Workmen's Circle—including *mitl-shul* on weekends on 14th Street near Kleins [N.Y.C.]. I even became a budding Yiddish actress though I was very shy. I was a true cultural Jew. I still speak Yiddish with my mother. I write Yiddish.

But in striving towards a professional career, I began to move out of my immigrant working class background. I dropped my associations with Jewish groups and replaced them with more professional, more mainstream groups. My left politics brought me to progressive international and national organizations in which my Jewishness was only incidental. It's interesting to me now that I ignored liberal Jewish organizations and the Jewish communities they represented because I didn't think they were radical enough. The left seemed a real melting pot.

When my daughter emigrated, I saw how out of touch I'd become and also how ignorant I was about Israel and the Jewish religion. Somehow all of it kind of came together, and I recaptured a strong Jewish identity. I knew then I wanted to start shifting my political activity.

I had been involved in the feminist movement since 1970, and Jewish women were beginning to discuss Jewish identity. I can't really date that, but I remember Jewish women's groups began to form in the mid '70s. In fact, I organized one of the first Jewish C-R groups. We had Passover *seders* with a feminist Haggadah.

My main political interest outside the feminist movement had been peace work. I've always done peace work—from way back in the '50s when I was an active member with Women's International League for Peace and Freedom in Philadelphia. Later in Los Angeles I worked with Women's Strike for Peace and The Committee for a Sane

Nuclear Policy. In 1980—to get a peace and progressive perspective on Israel—I started reading *New Outlook*, a left Israeli journal in English. I wanted to work on Middle East peace. I joined New Jewish Agenda after I and some other people developed a group called Jewish Peace Alliance. For the Los Angeles Jewish community the Alliance seemed far out. They saw it as anti-Israeli which I, of course, think it never was. What we were doing, five, six years ago, was *challenging* the Israeli government: their policies of occupation, their military policies, and foreign policies in South Africa and Central America and the treatment of Arabs in Israel. We challenged these and created an uproar in the L.A. Jewish community. Then, when Agenda was organized, we merged with them and became Agenda's Middle East Task Force. This was in '82.

And from then on, all my active political energy went into that work. We did numerous public forums and radio broadcasts and press conferences about Israel and about our position. We got smeared and attacked, particularly by the Jewish Defense League. But that work developed my consciousness enormously because we started working with Palestinians and other Arabs. Very few Palestinians wanted to work with us, but two or three people came to our meetings and did educationals. I developed a very strong sense about Palestinian self-determination, the need to work on that as an issue, how the lack of a solution really disturbed Israeli society and weakened its moral fiber.

We had many Israelis come and talk about political solutions to the Palestinian-Israeli conflict, so we knew we were supported by the left and by peace groups in Israel. When I was in Israel, I interviewed journalists from *New Outlook* and the Palestinian Press Service and brought back material and information for my group in L. A. I had a very strong feeling that I needed to learn more. I realized that though I was so involved in this issue, I didn't really know Israel and the Middle East and felt I needed to go there. I was about to leave my job. I had been working in health care administration for many years, and I was able to draw my pension. This seemed a perfect time. I was leaving work, my daughter was having her fourth baby. Why not just go? And I did.

So, in '84 I moved to Israel, but I didn't make *aliyah*. I'm still not sure what my position on that is. But I do have the status of a temporary resident, which means I have three years to decide whether or not I'm going to become a permanent resident with dual citizenship.

When I first moved to Jerusalem, I spent most of my time with my family and studied Hebrew. That summer Agenda came through with a tour, and an acquaintance who was doing radio broadcasts on Middle East politics introduced me to a group of feminists. They became my friends and my social group.

*When we talk to American Jews about the issue of Israel, as we did at a conference recently, we find that everybody's going through contortions and pain, but you seem remarkably centered and unconflicted. I wonder how you got there.*

I *am* centered about it, but I've been through a long process on this. For one thing, I had to do a lot of reading in order to speak publicly and deal with the question: how do you criticize Israel without endangering her existence? I didn't start with a strong feeling of Zionism. What I did have, however, was a very strong belief in the right of Jews—like any other nationality—to a state of their own. So I started from that position.

Okay, here's this state: it exists. Now I had to face the fact that the state is militaristic and problematic from my political perspective in terms of socialism, feminism and particularly the rights of Arabs.

*We were talking about how you became so calm.*

I said that it was a long process of educating myself through the Agenda group. At one point I was not exactly fiercely critical of Israel, but very angry at its Palestinian position. And when it invaded Lebanon I think I went berserk. How could a Jewish state attack a civilian population in the name of security? I was angry with every Jew who wasn't doing anything to protest. Agenda went out to the Jewish community. We made every contact possible to talk with Jews, with Jewish groups—such as synagogues and community centers—about our opposition to the Lebanon War. That was a real high point for me. Though we often met anger and opposition, we provided a forum in which Israeli policies were examined. This was unique in the American mainstream Jewish community, which up until then felt unwilling to criticize Israel publicly.

But when I think about that period, it was almost like a test of my "devotion" to the state of Israel. No, not to the state, my devotion to the land, to the people, maybe just say to the people. We had made contact with Israelis who were against the invasion. And all along even before the invasion of Lebanon we had been inviting *Shalom Akhshav* [Peace Now] activists and more radical peace activists to L.A. So I knew that there was another voice in Israel that you didn't hear about as much in our press, and I identified with it. I also read that there were about 38 different kinds of peace groups in that very tiny country of 4½ million.

So when you say I'm centered, it means to me that I have a strong identification with a group of people that share my politics. I don't know if they share my feelings about Jewish survival because Israelis have different feelings about Jewishness. But they are Jews, so I share that. I believe that my politics are the best thing for Israel—the way to ensure Israel's survival.

Now, I'm not the kind of Jew who feels that the center of all Jewishness has to be in Israel. I frankly haven't given that issue enough thought. I'm in the process of reading different opinions about the Diaspora versus Israel.

One big change for me in the past few years is that I've become very tolerant of Jewish religion. I feel tolerant of orthodoxy; that, of course, comes from the fact that my daughter is orthodox. When she and I talk about politics, we differ on some issues, but on the peace issue, which is the most important thing for me, she agrees. She agrees you give up territory for peace, that the way to Jewish safety and security does not rest with the military.

*Did you go through any kind of process about criticizing Israel publicly? I know that's one of the fears of American Jews because it can play into anti-Semitic attitudes.*

In some ways I didn't think too carefully about that because from the day I started Middle East work I had already developed a position of being critical. But I felt secure. I knew I was going to live in Israel some day. I was not the kind of Jew who wanted to disown it. Quite the opposite. I felt I had every right to criticize it. When I gave talks, I would say that for those of us who have integrity and honesty and are concerned about morality, it's a responsibility. When you recognize a reactionary fascistic tendency anywhere in this world, you speak out. Whether or not it's Israeli, whether or not it's Jewish. You need to speak out against it.

*Were you speaking mainly to the Jewish community?*

As I said, we targeted the Jewish community and that was the strategy we developed. Jews were in this emotional bind over how to criticize Israel and be a Jew. That was their dilemma, and I felt that that's where we needed to work—in the Jewish community.

*What did you want the Jewish community to do?*

We wanted them to see the other side of Israel and to start protesting to their congress people to develop a different American policy. Because if you live in America, what do you do? You influence your country's policy towards the Middle East—meaning, you want it to work against an arms race in the Middle East. In other words you don't supply arms to Israelis or Arabs and you don't help build nuclear reactors. You do the same thing you do anywhere in the world. I've worked for disarmament all my life. I want disarmament in the Middle East.

*What do you say to people who say the Soviets are arming the Arabs?*

This is a very difficult issue. But the Middle East is really being torn by two superpowers. My greatest fear is that the U.S. will use Israel as a battleground in the Middle East. If America wants to do something in the Middle East now, it's got Israel to do its fighting. It's got its base. That is frightening. I'm also worried about nuclear war in the area. It's obvious that the issues in the Middle East are interconnected to the larger global issues of disarmament and international economics. These problems must be approached on many levels. There is no easy answer. I understand the fears. I worry about the balance too.

*Are you worried that Israel is going to use nuclear weapons?*

I guess I worry about it, and yet I don't know whether my strong wish that they wouldn't makes me believe that they wouldn't. They couldn't be so crazy. But when you think there's a Sharon, and you think about the military mind, and I don't care where that military mind lives—Israel, the Soviet Union, the U.S.—a hawk is a hawk and I'm scared of those hawks. I've listened to former Israeli army generals speak for peace. Security does not lie in arms. This Middle East question *has to* be negotiated.

*Where do you think the political work is most important—in Israel or here?*

Good question. One of the reasons I'm not convinced I'll make *aliyah* is because for over five years I developed really good skills working with the American Jewish community and doing coalition work, and in some way I feel I should be back in L.A.

I guess my fantasy is to be in both places. I want more knowledge, I need to know what the Israelis are feeling, and I need to know more about Israel to do better work with American Jews. That's why on this trip [to the States] I approached Agenda and said, let's form a chapter in Israel and create a link. Friends of Peace Now here in America have served as a link to the Peace Now movement in Israel, and that's a good way to work too. So part of me thinks I should be here continuing the work.

On the other hand, I think of the new American immigrants in Israel today, and it's scary because very few of them are progressives or peace people. Most of them are strongly nationalistic. I think they're all emotion. Everything is pro-Israel without any

290

discriminating about government or political thought. It scares me that there are very few progressives going to Israel now. I say this to Jews all the time. Come to Israel. Show the Israelis that progressive American Jews want to come to Israel.

By the way, you asked me what I wanted to do with American Jews. It isn't only that I want them to become sophisticated and speak to their senators and congress people just the way we did in Agenda when legislators came into town. I want Jews to think about what they're donating for. It's a very tricky thing. I don't want funds to stop. But I want Jews to write to the United Jewish Appeal (UJA) for it to support work on Arab-Jewish relations, feminist projects, etc. In other words, I want some attention paid to what I call projects with good politics. I don't want that money to develop occupation of the West Bank.

*Isn't there such a fund now?*

Yes, the New Israel Fund (NIF) was developed as an alternative for Jews to give money to Israel without having to go through the UJA, which has been criticized over its distribution of funds. To me the biggest criticism of the UJA is its politics. What are they doing with that money in terms of supporting the takeover of the West Bank? The NIF supports more liberal, progressive projects and it's more direct. The money actually goes directly from here to the project, bypassing a big administrative hierarchy.

*I saw the breakdown of their last budget. They give very specific grants—like $5,000 to a battered women's shelter.*

Yes, and I would love to see more donors give to NIF.

*Within the women's movement there's been an enormous amount of criticism of Judaism and Israel as extremely sexist and patriarchal. In Israel the Rabbinate controls many aspects of women's lives. Can you talk about that in terms of your statement that you feel more comfortable with religion?*

First let's talk about Jewish orthodoxy. It's not a rigid, fixed system. There are orthodox Jews who want to do away with sexism and to change some of the structure and practices. Now, someone like my daughter wants to keep everything the same and this includes political positions—for example, anti-abortion—that I totally disagree with. But I still recognize that there are progressive forces within the orthodox religion. I have friends studying at various *yeshivas* in Jerusalem. There are new kinds of places for people to go to learn about Judaism, where men and women study together. There was an article in, of all places, a Yoga journal—which was called the "New Age Judaism." And the people described were orthodox.

The Americans who practice that now came out of California, I think—where else—and they're '60s people—and they really want to keep the Judaic tradition. They believe in God, keep kosher, observe *shabes* and practice a lot of the rituals. But they want to discard what is oppressive to women, or oppressive period. So we have to recognize that within orthodoxy—when we talk about those terrible orthodox people—there's a movement challenging some of the old patriarchal practices.

Now as for Israel—I would never discount the fact that it's a theocracy. And I believe in the separation of religion and state, and there are organizations in Israel that are working towards that. As long as you have a theocracy, you're going to perpetuate sexism. So a lot of structural changes have to be made. You know, Israel doesn't have a constitution. And some groups are advocating the necessity of having one. And a constitution would be the basis for equal rights and perhaps break up some of the religious power. But that's a hard struggle. The issue is so complex: to think through what it means to have a Jewish state. When you take out all the religion, what does a Jewish state mean? In any case, sexism and patriarchy are embedded in Israeli society as they are in all countries, and they must be exposed and struggled against.

I think we have to be patient. When we're angry or discouraged, we have to remember—it's a new country—only 37 years old. There are a lot of changes that the state will have to go through. And I think that *my* centeredness comes from my feeling that they'll get to it. American Jewish progressives shouldn't turn their back on Israel and say, "Oh forget it!" It's their own anti-Semitism that makes them say that. It's easier to walk away and say, "Forget it, I'll work on Nicaragua." I'd like them to work on both.

*In what way do you think American Jewish progressives can be supportive?*

There are very concrete things to do. You can support Friends of Peace Now. You can support New Israel Fund. You can support New Jewish Agenda or Americans for a Progressive Israel. You become members, you help them with fundraising, which also allows you to do education work and publicity. You speak out for these organizations and help develop a stronger link between Israeli and American Jewish progressives because there isn't a strong link between the two communities.

*It's interesting because progressives in the U.S. and other countries seem to have more contact with each other than they do with Israeli progressives.*

Exactly. I'd like to say to a progressive Jew, how about devoting some of your energy to groups in Israel? For instance, do you know of a direct link with the feminist movement? A great many feminists here in America are Jews. What link do they have with Israeli feminists? I would say practically none, except when they go visiting and call up feminists.

*IF they visit.*

*If* they visit. Right. I'm tired of hearing total condemnation with no recognition that there are Israelis who are struggling with these issues and who need our support.

*We've observed enormous fear among some radical Jews about visiting Israel. They feel deep shame about the reactionary practices of the government and it's real and very difficult to crack through.*

Yes, I agree. It's peculiar that Jewish progressives are willing to struggle here in America, recognize that the struggle is necessary—but when it comes to Israel, they have an all or nothing attitude. If it's not all good, it's all bad. It seems easier for the American Jewish radical to exclude Israel from her sphere of political activity. And yet ideologically, she shares with Israeli radicals many things, such as feminism and socialism.

Which really brings us to another issue: how to work with American Jewish radicals. I believe you must work on an emotional level with them. They must be challenged to examine their self-hatred, and sometimes you can't confront them in those words—it's just too scary. Think of the majority of Jews in the American left. What is emotionally supportive to them? They don't have religion. Most don't have cultural Jewish backgrounds. They don't have and they don't have and they don't have. But—they *do* have left support. Now, if they challenge the left's anti-Semitism, they take out their props. And they're afraid of that, of being isolated. So I think we have to be extremely careful. But it has to be done, and in Agenda we would do this in small groups and very gently.

A couple of years ago Agenda in L.A. did a lot of recruiting in the Jewish community specifically for the Middle East Task Force. There was a man working with us, and we'd be gently talking about Israel to the new people, you know, not bombarding them. Now these new people were leftists but pro-Israel, because the anti-Israel people we couldn't reach at all. But what he did was bombard them with all the horrible things Israel was doing. Well, we never saw them again. They couldn't take it. I used to call it the revolving door of recruitment. We'd draw them in and he'd drive them out. So we have to deal very carefully with people on both sides—those who can't hear about Israel and need gentle prodding to get at their self-hatred and those who are so pro-Israel they can't stand anything critical.

I think it's quite ironic. Many Jewish radicals keep fingering the mainstream Jewish community as having a lot of work to do on changing its attitudes. But the fact is that many Jewish radicals themselves need to do a lot of work on their own attitudes about Jewishness and Israel. They're very conflicted and uncomfortable and they don't really admit it. They cover it with political rhetoric. But I think the heart of every Jewish leftist is waiting to hear, "It's okay to relate to this issue as a Jew. It's okay to be emotionally attached to Israel despite your feelings about the government's actions and policies. Caring won't make you lose your radical perspective or identity, just as you don't lose it when you work as an American against the incredible odds of our system."

Too often radical Jews look at Israel and groan, even though they saw thousands of Israelis on TV protesting the massacres and the invasion. Coverage of Israel in this country *is* bad, but we get *some* information about the divisions there. We know Israel has a government that's split and frequently non-functional and that there's a lot of dissent. And yet many Jewish radicals talk as if Israel is a monolithic country. Why? Why do they discard truth and information? I think it's complicated. I think they have a particular investment in it. Many Jewish radicals don't deal with their Jewishness.

But you know—even though I understand the difficulties since I've experienced them myself—I sometimes get really impatient. There's so much work to be done. There are so many Israelis struggling, really struggling to turn things around and they should be getting help from all of us.

## Update: January 1988

As I reread my interview three years after, I am struck with both continuity and change. I continue to work at urging American Jews to speak out against the occupation of the West Bank and Gaza. But the outstanding difference is my feeling of greater urgency. I write the week of January 24, 1988, the seventh week of the Palestinian uprising, an explosion of despair and frustration that has almost total support of the people living under occupation. You in the U.S. have undoubtedly been horrified by the brutality of the Israeli army and police. We, Israelis and foreign nationals living here, listen to regular updates on Israeli radio, watch TV reports, read news coverage, and wait for the violence to end.

But my Palestinian friends say that despite continuing mass arrests, deportations, beatings, killings and torture under interrogation, this may be a long war: Already it is longer than expected by Prime Minister Shamir and Defense Minister Rabin. This is a battle against people without weapons, against children and young people with a new feeling of empowerment and a willingness to die for their cause. Palestinians both in the occupied territories and within the "green line" (pre-1967 borders) have reacted to their situation with a new unity, across differences in social class and religion.

And how do I fit into the picture? What have I done as an American living here? As an English speaker, I work with like-minded people who have formed a new chapter of the Fellowship (which I wish were called Sisterhood) of Reconciliation, an international organization devoted to peace and justice through nonviolence, following Gandhi's philosophy. This group includes Palestinians, Israelis, and foreign nationals; Christians and Jews. Our chapter grew to about 60 members, and most of our activity concentrated on supporting Palestinians who were losing their land and olive trees to government expropriation. We had planted olive trees to replace those uprooted by the government. We were harrassed by armed settlers who came to protect "their right to the land." Thirteen people— ten Palestinians and three Israelis—were charged with trespassing for taking part in the tree-planting action in the village of Qatana. They have appeared in court, supported by those of us who also participated, and are now awaiting a new hearing. There have been other actions, including a Peace Walk I organized between two villages, to show solidarity with Palestinian villagers who have had thousands of their trees uprooted.

But these actions have more recently been superseded by emergencies such as the deportation of Mubarak Awad, one of our FOR members and the Director of the Palestinian Center for the Study of Nonviolence. Awad, an American citizen like me, is being denied the right to remain here as a resident because he is Palestinian—the right and privilege I have as a Jew. Many American Jews who had made *aliyah* have carried on a strong campaign to allow Dr. Awad to remain and have protested the deportation of other political activists.

Now with the uprising, through a coalition of Israeli leftists, I have moved into emergency activities, helping to collect food, clothing, and medical supplies for the refugee camps that have been under curfew and under siege by soldiers. I have adjusted to moving from one activity or group to another, working where I can contribute best. An important result for me has been contact with Palestinians, both women and men from what had been an unknown culture. Without the personal contact, I could never have understood the uselessness and hopelessness of Israel attempting to hold on to the territories. I have not met one Palestinian who sees any benefit from the occupation; most hate the occupiers, and many are ready to die for their liberation.

I have not been surprised at the universal rejection of the occupation, but I have felt dismayed at the seemingly automatic way in which many Palestinians interchangeably identify the Israeli as oppressor and as Jew. This has been painful. I have remained silent hearing Palestinians speak their minds about the brutality of the Jews. A mother sitting on a pile of rubble, once her home, told how her house had been demolished as a form of collective punishment: Her son had been charged with committing a terrorist act but was never tried in court. Teachers and students have told me about their universities being closed for months; about the shooting of students, sometimes fatal, by Israeli soldiers at demonstrations.

No, I couldn't, in these moments, make my point that there is a distinction between Israeli government policy, the injustices of war and anti-Jewishness. With ongoing relationship I always state that I am a Jew. Often I am met with suspicion. After all, what is a Jew doing on the "other side," working with Palestinians? Given the almost complete segregation of Arabs and Jews in Jerusalem, the boundary line between East and West Jerusalem is thick and hard. Only a few Palestinians and Israelis cross the line regularly to meet for political purposes or, occasionally, for social and cultural events. My efforts to meet with Palestinians make me an oddity among my Jewish friends. Just as I had chosen to live in a Black neighborhood in Los Angeles for 25 years, to live out an ideology of integration, so I have chosen to break barriers and know Palestinians. But the surprise and outrage I sometimes face from other Jews for these attempts threaten me far more deeply than a "similar" disapproval from Los Angeles whites. I am, after all, a Jew and do not want to be isolated from the Jewish community.

On the other hand, the friendships I have formed prove the possibility of sincerity and trust between Palestinians and Jews. And there are Israelis who support such contact, including some Israeli feminists, as in the 1970s many feminists debated and fought for self-determination for Palestinians. Unfortunately that feminist faction has diminished, but I am sure there will now be renewal of that voice within the feminist movement. There are Palestinian women living within the green line, working together with Israelis on the Jerusalem Rape Hotline and on various peace projects. The present emergency has also reawakened those feminists who work with more liberal peace groups to speak out against the occupation. They are organizing to express their outrage and have joined demonstrations, such as the *Shalom Akhshav* march of January 24, where an estimated 50,000 people marched in the streets of Tel Aviv to protest the brutality of the occupation and the need to negotiate a settlement now.

In a few months I shall be in the U.S., where I have arranged to speak to Women's International League for Peace and Freedom, New Jewish Agenda, and other groups about the urgent need to protest Israeli policies. I look forward to meeting American Jews who now have the backing of some traditional Jewish organizations in dissenting from Israeli policy.

Aside from Palestinian/Israeli politics, I have resumed my interest in doing feminist therapy, based on the Radical Therapy model. My professional background—having taught psychology and community mental health—has led me to working with Palestinian mental health workers to develop training programs.

My personal life continues to grow with love and pleasure. My fifth grandchild was born almost two years ago. Part-time life in the orthodox community has sustained my basic belief in avoiding stereotypes and remembering that there are different positions even among the ultra-orthodox on peace issues. I must constantly process my differences with my daughter's beliefs, but so far we have managed a very strong bond based on love and respect, sometimes by avoiding discussion of very "hot" issues.

Perhaps my greatest ambivalence is between living in Israel and returning to the U.S. I miss my daughter Julie and my dear friends so very much. I long for my old feminist community. In the last few years of living in America, I also renewed my interest in Yiddish culture, and—this may be a surprise to some—it is hardly thriving here in Israel. I miss what is familiar to me, the pluralism of America, Black music and art, feminist culture, and even the California "scene." In weighing where to live, I know that a reasonable working knowledge of both Hebrew and Arabic is necessary to be politically effective and socially comfortable. I must learn those languages here. As a Jewish feminist I want to continue with the primary struggle in this area, freedom for the Palestinians, which is ultimately tied to building a just Israeli society. This work must be done on both continents.

# To Be a Radical Jew in the Late 20th Cen

*For Irena K̶...*
*who pushed me*

*To be a Jew in the twentieth century*
*Is to be offered a gift. . . .*
—Muriel Rukeyser, "Letter to the Front, VII," 1944

*So, Melanie, what's with all the Jewish?* This was my father speaking, sometime in 1982, the year he died. I answered him clearly, carefully, the way I did that year because he often got confused, but the answer was not hard to find. I had been away from NY since I was 20—I was then 37—and I had noticed two things: my own hunger for Jewish culture, music, food, language, humor, perspective, Jewish *people*; and, the anti-Semitism palpable—and growing—around me.

Twenty years earlier I had marched on my first demonstration, against nuclear testing. My parents had not pushed me into activism, yet clearly they raised me to do these things. Their parents had come to this country from Eastern Europe, Poland and Russia. None had been political. Yet, as a teenager in the Depression, my father had belonged to the Young Communist League; and, even as an adult, his major hero remained his dead friend Aaron, a Communist who had spoken on street corners and

297

fought in Spain. My mother had circulated petitions against the Korean War, walking up to people on the streets of Flatbush during peak McCarthy period, and she had been spat on. Later she became president of the PTA at Walt Whitman Jr. High, and fought to bring blacklisted performers to sing at the annual PTA meeting.

My mother often says, "When Melanie was 3 years old, I knew it would be Melanie against the world, and I was betting on Melanie." One of her favorite stories of me dates from 1950, when my class and my older sister's had been given dog tags — issued to NYC schoolchildren, as to soldiers — so that in the event of a bomb, our bodies could be identified. My sister, 7 years old, asked what the dog tag was for, and my mother told her. I listened. And had bombs ever been dropped? Roni asked. Imagine the discussion, my mother explaining to a 7-year-old about war, about Hiroshima and Nagasaki. . . And the next time the 5-bell signal rang for a shelter drill and my kindergarten teacher said, "Now, children, it's only a game, remember, under your desk, head down," I, 5 years old, stood up and said it was not a game, it was about dropping bombs on children and they our own government had dropped bombs on children and their eyes had melted and people were burned and killed. The other 5-year-olds began crying and screaming, and the principal summoned my mother to school. "What are you, crazy, telling a kid things like that," the principal is reputed to have said, and my mother to have answered: "I will not lie to my children."

My mother's version of this story emphasizes my role: as class conscience and rebel. But what delights me in the story is *her* courage: though a good student, she had dropped out of high school at 15 and was always convinced that educated people were smarter. Yet she had the political and intellectual backbone to defend me and defy authority.

This was my Jewish upbringing, as much as the candles we lit for Hanukkah, or the seders where bread and matzoh shared the table. My father had been raised observant, my mother, not. But to us breaking religious observance was progressive, the opposite of superstitious; when we ate on Yom Kippur, it never occurred to me that this was un-Jewish. I knew I was a Jew. I knew Hitler had been evil. I knew Negroes—we said then—had been slaves and that was evil too. I knew prejudice was wrong, stupid. I knew Jews believed in freedom and justice. When Eisenhower-Nixon ran in 1952, I noticed Nixon's dark wavy hair, like my father's, and said: "He looks like Daddy." My mother was furious: "Nothing like him!" and went on and on explaining how Nixon had gotten elected to Congress only by smearing Helen Gahagan Douglas (the liberal Congresswoman). I was 7 years old.

Soon we would get our first TV, so my mother (and I) could watch the McCarthy hearings. I knew the whole fate of humanity hinged on these hearings, as surely as I knew the Rosenbergs had been good people, like my parents, with children the same age as my sister and me. I knew government people, like McCarthy, had killed the Rosenbergs, and I was terrified, but it literally did not occur to me that real people, people I might meet, people who had children and went to work, hated the Rosenbergs, thought they should die. Nor did it occur to me that there were people who thought unions were bad, people who did not know you never cross a picket line, did not know prejudice was wrong and stupid.

This is not to say I never heard alternate views, but my parents—though not formally educated or trained in political analysis—had very definite opinions about right and wrong which they passed on to me like the 10 Commandments, ideas I have yet to find wanting.

That this set of principles was Jewish never occurred to me. Around me was Flatbush, a swirling Jewish ghetto/community of first and second generation immigrants, including Holocaust survivors (though they were noted in my mind simply as the parents who brought umbrellas to school when it rained, spoke with my grandparents' accents); there were clerks, trade unionists, salespeople, plumbers; small business people, radio and tv repairmen, people like my parents and their friends; there were teachers and there were even doctors who lived in what we called "private houses" in the outreaches of the neighborhood at the point where not everyone was Jewish.

But where I lived, everyone was, or almost. Jewish was the air I breathed, nothing I articulated, everything I took for granted.

\* \* \*

1963. I was 17, working in the Harlem Education Project.[1] HEP had organized a tutoring project, several rent strikes, an anti-rat campaign;[2] had pressured schools for decent facilities and a Black history curriculum, and helped to create freedom schools for children to attend in protest. A block organization was gradually turning a lot filled with garbage (and once or twice dead bodies) into a park. It was my first experience with a mobilizing proud community and with the possibilities of collective action. I was hooked, though it took me years to recognize how my upbringing had brought me to 133rd St. and Lenox, and primed me for this commitment.

It was also my first experience in a non-Jewish environment. Harlem was the center of Northern Black culture; there were community people, students—some from other cities and communities—some from middle-class homes, some travelling back and forth from the South with stories of Fannie Lou Hamer, James Farmer or of the past: a grandfather lynched in Florida, a great-great-aunt who learned to read in slavery in Mississippi (and Mississippi is still the most frightening word I know). And there were white people, these almost all young, almost all students, some who were my first contact with WASPs; some Jews, though I barely registered that fact since they were not like the Jews I knew. All these students went to colleges like Columbia and Sarah Lawrence, while I went to no-tuition City College, riding the subway 3 hours a day to classes and to Harlem, and would the next year—at 18—move into my own apartment and become financially self-supporting.

At the end of my first summer in Harlem, on the bus returning from the historic March on Washington, a Black man my age flirted with me and I flirted back, and he sang me this song:

> Jew girls from Brooklyn they go wild over me
> and they hold my hand where everyone can see
> O they paint their face like whores
> have me leave them at their doors
> They go wild, simply wild over me

299

Intensely focused on white racism, utterly unaware of racism against Jews, or of the possibility of Jewish danger (the Holocaust was eons ago, irrelevant), I felt only shame at the label—Jew girl from Brooklyn—and at the stereotype—hypocrite, liberal in public but won't bring him home to meet the family. I determined not to be like the others; not to be like myself. . . .

* * *

1966. I was 20, preparing to leave NY for graduate school at Berkeley. I wanted to get away from NY, from my family, my people, to be part of the radical politics developing on the West Coast. At a summer demonstration against the war in Viet Nam, I marched with a slim pale woman from California. She had long straight blond hair, wore some easy cotton shift and sandals; she seemed not to sweat and her voice lilted when she spoke. I had the same body I still have: sturdy, strong legs, heavy black eyebrows, dark hair which in NY's August frizzed and bushed; my skin glistened with oil. I could not imagine how I would fit into the West Coast.

I discovered in Berkeley that the Brooklyn Jewish accent which in NY had always marked me as lower class now marked me as one of those smart Jews from NY. Apart from this observation, passed on by an admiring gentile friend, I have few memories of being a Jew in Berkeley, little consciousness that people's reactions to or assumptions about me had something to do with my particular style of Jewish culture. Jewish political issues moved me not at all, including the 1967 war in the Middle East—I did not identify with Israel—and, when in 1968 I had a minor operation, like Tillie Olsen's Anna I wrote "none" next to *religion* on the hospital registration form because "I didn't want anyone mumbling religion at me if I died."

* * *

1972. I had just moved to Portland, Oregon and was attending a feminist conference, talking with a woman while we waited for the elevator. I have forgotten the context for what she said: that she did not like Jews. They were loud and pushy and aggressive. This was the first time I had heard someone say this outright. I was stunned, didn't know what to say—"no they're not"?—and I couldn't believe she didn't know I was Jewish. I said, loud, flat, "I'm Jewish." I can't remember what happened next or even her face, only the moment by the elevator.

* * *

1975. Yellow Springs, Ohio, at the Feminist Socialist Conference, on the lunch line, the woman in back of me was talking about a Jewish caucus. I didn't ask her anything, didn't even seriously eavesdrop. I couldn't relate to it. I went to a workshop on economics instead. Years later I wonder what they talked about.

* * *

1978. I was working at Rape Relief Hotline in downtown Portland doing counselling, advocacy, community education and organizing. I was talking with my best friend and sister organizer—a middle-class WASP woman—about my sense of awkwardness and ineffectiveness with "straight" women—meaning some combination of middle-aged heterosexual non-movement women; that I seemed to have no social skills, everything I said had the wrong beat. A couple of days later a woman called the hotline to talk about her experience some years back of being battered. She wanted to get involved in hotline activities, and I invited her to stop by. She did. The woman was some 30 years older than I, had raised 2 kids, worked in an office, had never considered herself political. I might have been the first lesbian she'd ever knowingly met. She was everything I was supposed to by my own analysis feel awkward around. We went out for coffee, talked for hours, easy. She was a Jew, an east coast Jew. I realized in some ways I was in the wrong city, the wrong part of the world; I was an alien.

* * *

By the time I left Oregon in 1979, I had developed an interest in Jewish immigrant history and an obsession with the Holocaust. I read avidly, vaguely aware that I needed Jews but feeling as out of place as ever with those who'd received religious education, as with those women in Portland who had started getting together on Friday nights to eat and *shmooz*, to "socialize." I was political. My rejection of these Jewish women's gatherings paralleled closely my pre-feminist contempt for women's consciousness-raising groups. My failure to register this similarity is a tribute to the mind's ability to resist information which threatens.

And then a time of moving, from one *goyish* environment to another. A summer in Maine, Down East, the easternmost point in the US, and if I thought I had seen a Jewish vacuum before, I hadn't. The house we moved into had a swastika smeared on the bedroom door in what looked like blood. A car parked down the road had swastikas and crosses painted on the doors (we spray-painted over them one night). I was becoming very very conscious. Driving out west, passing signs for Greensboro, Atlanta, Birmingham, Montgomery, Jackson, names I knew as sites of struggle and danger, listening to the radio's furious anti-Arab anti-Iranian aggressively fundamentalist christian tirades unleashed by the taking of hostages in the Tehran embassy complex; hearing christian hymn after christian hymn, seeing more crosses, more churches than I had ever imagined: I was afraid.

By the time I got to northern New Mexico—where I lived for the next two years—I knew I needed Jews, nothing vague about it. I sought out a Jewish women's group which met on and off. I was reading and writing about Jewishness. My political work was still not Jewish-related—I helped to organize a women's coffeehouse, and a demonstration against militarism at Los Alamos Science Museum, and at these and other women's events I read work with strong Jewish content. Some women hugged and thanked me, especially Jews and others strongly grounded in their own culture; responses which warmed, emboldened and confirmed me. And some looked blank, perhaps wondering why I was bothering, or why I was being divisive, identifying with a patriarchal religion, or. . . responses which alienated me, pushed me deeper into my Jewishness, sharpened my awareness of difference so that I began to notice and respond to cultural stimuli or casual remarks or jokes or, even, political analysis differently.

* * *

1980. I recognized in Reagan's election that the liberalism I had for years seen as the real danger was being superseded, that the right was gaining power, with all its Jew-hating, racist, sexist, homophobic capitalist thrust. At the same time the anti-Semitism I was encountering in the women's movement and on the left hurt me more, not because it was more threatening but because the feminist left was where I needed to be: this added to my sense of isolation as a Jew.

301

I was also reading analyses of racism and discussions of identity, mostly by Black women, and my proximity to Chicana and Native American cultures allowed me tangible lessons in diversity and in non-mainstream survival. Cultures, people were being defined as Third World or white; where I lived it was Chicana, Indian or Anglo. But none of these categories, none of the descriptive analyses fit me or my culture. I was an English-speaker, my people came from Europe, but we were not Anglo and neither was our culture.

There are many more details, scenes, some I remember and some which still elude me. What is clear to me is this: the more outside of a Jewish ambiance I was, the more conscious I became of Jewishness. For me, it was like Marshall McLuhan's perhaps apocryphal remark: I don't know who discovered water, but I'm sure it wasn't a fish. Inside a Jewish environment, where I could take for granted a somewhat shared culture, an expectation about Jewish survival, where my body type and appearance were familiar, my voice ordinary, my laughter not too loud but hearty and normal, above all, normal. . .in this environment, I did not know what it meant to be a Jew, only what it meant to be a *mentsh*. I did not know that *mentsh* was a Jewish word in a Jewish language.

As I lived longer outside Jewish culture, as I became more fully aware of anti-Semitism, internal as well as external, as I understood my own hunger for home, kin, for *my people*, I was walking further and further along a mostly unconscious, gradual, zig-zag and retrospectively inevitable path.

## I. If I am not for myself. . .

There were many of us on distinct but similarly inevitable paths. What happened as Jewish women began raising Jewish issues inside the women's movement?

Even at the beginning, some of the issues we were raising seemed almost mundane, obvious: issues of direct insult, stereotypes, omission, exclusion, indifference, discrimination, assumptions of sameness, passing, invisibility, cultural difference, concern for cultural survival. . .I—and I think many of us—expected that the groundwork on these issues had been laid, that the heroic and tedious labor undertaken by women of color, with some white and Jewish support, to raise everyone's consciousness about racism would carry over somewhat to inform response to Jewish women.

Not that I thought white—or Jewish—women had always been adequate in their commitment to fight racism. Not that I assumed experience and issues for Jewish women and for gentile women of color were the same; nor did I expect identical experience and issues for all women of color, including Jewish women of color. But I did expect some analogy to be apprehended. I expected that the movement would continue building on general principles, as well as differentiate what was unique.

And this did not happen. I saw resistance, overt rejection, ridicule, a willful ignorance. Not from everyone. From some I saw respect, support and desire to extend themselves. From many I saw hypocritical silence masquerading as respect. From some, hostility. And—most often—I saw a bewilderment, an inability to grasp what was being said about anti-Semitism or Jewish identity, an incapacity to recognize why it mattered. And, of course, the too-polite silence, the bewilderment, the hostility intensified my self-consciousness as a Jew.

Examples are not hard to find. The policy statement that doesn't mention opposition to anti-Semitism.[3] The many courses that include readings by women from a variety of cultures but, somehow, no Jews. The decision that to have a Jew as keynote speaker is too particular, too specialized.[4] The 1984 Women & the Law conference, with its theme *Bread and Roses*, which offered, out of nearly 200 workshops, none on Jews or Jewish issues. (Let me honor those Jewish women who ensured that the 1985 conference would have several Jewish workshops and events.[5]) The flyer for an anti-militarist protest which voiced opposition to misogyny, racism, homophobia, ableism, a number of other -isms, but not anti-Semitism; named a string of identities including "Black, Latina, Asian, Palestinian. . ." but not Jewish.[6] A flyer soliciting material for a feminist journal on issues such as:

> Imperialist Intervention
> Racism, Sexism, Heterosexism, Ageism. . .
> Hunger Education Reproductive Rights
> Disarmament Health Self-Determination Housing[7]

I guess the ". . ." after "Ageism" is supposed to leave room for the inclusion of anti-Semitism, but the general effect is to make Jews feel invisible, unwelcome, or worse.

Why? Why have the basic points been so hard to get? Why have so many radicals been impermeable to a pro-Jewish analysis and activity? Why are we getting the message that many of our erstwhile political comrades and sisters—including some Jews—think it contradictory to be a radical Jew?

The explanation, as I have tried to track it down, is as tangled as the nature of anti-Semitism; as unconscious, as willfully ignorant as an ordinary American's relationship to the rest of the world; as inadequately grasped and developed as the women's movement understanding of race and class and why the movement should oppose racism and class hierarchy.

## Anti-Semitism, Race and Class

I am not one who believes anti-Semitism is inevitable, yet I confess my heart sinks when I consider how resilient this hatred is: Jew as anti-Christ, embodying materialism, money, Shylock's pound of flesh; Marx's analysis of the Jew as irrelevant parasite; shameful victims, who went like sheep to the slaughter; the UN General Assembly's proclamations on Zionism; killer Israelis.

Nor does Jewish oppression fit into previously established analyses. If capitalism is your primary contradiction, the Jewish people is not a class category. If racism, many Jews have light skin, pass as gentile if they wish. If sexism, why should Jewish women identify with Jewish men? If Jewish is an ethnicity, a peoplehood, why don't you live in Israel, or call yourself Israeli? If it's a religion, how are you Jewish if you don't observe?

But not only does Jewish oppression elude conventional categories, Jewish stereotypes prove that anti-Semitism does not exist. Jews are rich, powerful, privileged, control the media, the schools, the business world, international banking: the Zionist conspiracy rides again. How could such powerhouses ever be in trouble? These stereotypes, I've realized, prevent recognition of how we are threatened or demeaned as Jews.

For example: in 1982 when WBAI, NYC progressive radio station, broadcast the disarmament march and interviewed—as the lone voice against the demonstration—an

Orthodox Jew, I was one of several who phoned to complain. "Why pick on an Orthodox Jew as the single representative of conservative politics?" I asked. "Why not?" a man answered. "I've always wanted to pick on an Orthodox Jew." When I expressed shock/tried to explain (obviously I was in shock if I tried to explain), he immediately said, "I'm so sick of hearing about the fucking Holocaust" (which I hadn't mentioned). So I called the station manager, who apologized and proceeded to explain how when someone was making $7000 a year and someone next door was making $15,000 a year (clearly this man knew a lot about neighborhoods) I could understand the resentment.

Sure I could understand. But I had been talking about Jewhatred, not class antagonism. The station manager of NYC's progressive station had leaped from one to the other instantly, automatically. As if all Jews were wealthy. As if all wealth were Jewish. As if anti-Semitism were indulged in only by the poor.

By speaking about anti-Semitism, Jewish women unsettle an unspoken equation in the radical women's movement: in a society like ours, deeply racist and absurdly pretending to classlessness, class comes to be seen as identical to race. People of color are considered the same as working and poor people. Other aspects of racism — cultural erasure, assimilation, self-hate, just to name a few—are simply not heeded, nor are—god forbid—strengths of ethnic or racial minorities acknowledged unless—in a wash of white self-hate—people of color are romanticized as stronger, more authentic, somehow better than whites; but better because they are seen as such victims that mere survival is a miracle.

Meanwhile, these same analyses which ignore class as an independent category, related to but separate from race, ignore the variety of class experience and location of Jews: Jews, you remember, are all rich or at least middle class. Why, then, are we complaining?

Such a non-analysis not only belies the experience of middle-class people of color—the upper middle-class Black families, for example, whose L.A. neighborhood was firebombed in June, 1985; the middle-class Japanese home-land-and-business-owners on the West Coast who had everything confiscated and were imprisoned in camps during the second World War. This perspective also erases the existence of Jews of color and working-class Jews, and the entire white poor and working class; a very substantial group of women.

Related to this unspoken equation: analyses of racism—both on the left and in the feminist movement—have been spearheaded by Black people, and to some extent the experience of Black people in the US provides the model by which we understand racism. And despite the existence and even growth of a Black middle class, the continued grinding poverty of most Black people in this country also suggests an equation of race and class.

And it's true: most immigrant groups have moved up the class ladder, at least to lower middle class or trade union status (which—for men—means pretty good pay), usually pushed up in what has been called "the queuing effect" by a newer group of immigrants against whom prejudice is fresher and stronger.[8] But American Blacks, in their forced passage to this country, in the destruction of many elements of African culture by slavery, in their confrontation with classic American racism against the darkest skin, and in the exploitation of this racism by capitalists to "explain" inequality, have been painfully excluded from the process of queuing. This is evident from the progress of Puerto Ricans and Koreans in NYC, for example, or Cubans in Miami; though more recently arrived than Blacks, these groups have, in effect, cut in ahead of Blacks economically.

But there's another kind of distortion. I have lived outside of NYC for half my 40 years now, and have come to think that the usual explanations of racism and anti-Semitism focus unduly on New York, a focus which has everything to do with location of media and ambitious intellectuals, not to mention a huge Jewish and a huge Black community, each deeply rooted in the city, each a cultural center for their people. And these two communities have often, in the past 20 years, been at odds, not utterly, but noticeably: on community control of schools, in the struggle for the city's limited resources, on affirmative action and quotas. . . And the contrast—between a visible relatively secure Jewish community, mostly (except for the old) employed, and a continuing impoverished Black community with an unequal share of the city's resources, unequally protected and unequally harassed by the police, with an astronomical rate of unemployment among Black teenage males and not much prospect of improvement—the contrast has got to seem stark.

It is this sense of contrast that is drawn upon again and again in people's discussion of anti-Semitism as opposed to racism. But when I look more closely at places other than New York—at Boston, where working class Italians and Blacks have been at odds over school busing; at Detroit, where Iraqi small merchants and Blacks have had racial tension reminiscent of the "Jewish shopkeeper in Harlem"; at northern New Mexico where Chicana/o and Native American communities may have differences, and where Anglos moving to the area are wresting political control from the Chicanas/os; at Miami, where non-Spanish speakers may resent the bilingualism requirement for civil service jobs dealing with the public—my grasp of the complexities of race, Jewishness, ethnicity, class, and culture is greatly enhanced. Instead of being characterized by polarization, in which anti-Semitism is treated as a phenomenon different *in nature* from racism, anti-Semitism can be clearly seen as *a form of racism*.

## The World According to America

There are other factors blocking recognition of the weight of anti-Semitism on Jews. Jewish experience in the US, isolated from the experience of Jews around the world, seems fairly rosy. But Jews are an international people, and the nature of Jewish identity, oppression, fear and danger derive from and connect to experiences outside this country.

Wars between the US and other countries have always been fought *in* other countries; most people in the US live in an extraordinarily protected context. Not only is our country vast and populous and proud of an isolationist spirit (often masking an imperialist reality); but, in addition, the strictly limited immigration during the middle portion of this century has restricted most Americans' knowledge about war, persecution, torture, the experience of refugees. Most Americans seem to believe ourselves peculiarly unaffected by what goes on in the rest of the world. If it didn't happen here, if it isn't happening now, why worry? Nor does a nation busy constructing a California or Texas future over Native American and Chicana/o culture care much about history.

From this vantage point, Jews seem ridiculous when we talk about Jewish danger. We are up against a failure of Americans to take seriously the pitch Jewhating attained so quickly in Europe in the thirties, for example, because Americans think Europe and the thirties so far away. They know about evil Germans, sheeplike Jews, and heroic Americans, but are not taught to see the war against the Jews as a culmination to centuries of Jewhating. Americans are told lies about the base of Nazism, so that we imagine Jewhating goes with a lack of education: working-class people are—as with white racism in this country—blamed. We are not told of the doctors and doctorates trained in Europe's finest universities. For most Americans the Holocaust blurs safely, almost pleasantly, with other terrible events of the past, like Bubonic Plague in the Middle Ages.

Nor have most Americans paid much attention to the persecution of Jews in the Soviet Union, or Argentina, or Ethiopia, unless an ideological point is to be scored against these nations. As for the fact that Jews are *not* in danger in some communities around the world because Jews have been exiled or violently excised from those communities—this is not recognized as a legitimate source of grief and suspicion for Jews to reckon with, a loss—of our people, our culture. Women in the feminist movement, not necessarily educated on these issues, respond pretty much like other Americans.

## The Scarcity Assumption

Then, too, an assumption deeply integral to capitalism has been absorbed by all of us, since it is reflected in so much of what we see. I have called this the Scarcity Theory,[9] not enough to go around: not enough love, not enough time, not enough appointments at the foodstamps office, not enough food stamps, not enough money, not enough seats on the subway. It's pervasive. We learn mistrust of each other, bone deep: everything is skin off somebody's nose.

And in the short run, certain things *are* scarce. To what causes do I apply my limited "free" time? Where do I donate "extra" money? What books do I read, what issues do I follow and become knowledgeable about? Where will my passion be deep and informed, able to make connections and inspire others, and where will it be superficial, giving lip service only? The women's movement has only in the last few years and under considerable pressure begun to face its own racism; class is still addressed in the most minimal ways. Meanwhile, international crises—apartheid in South Africa, intervention in Nicaragua, torture and repression in Salvador and Guatemala—compel attention.

Few of us have learned to trust our own rhetoric, that people will fight harder as they also fight for themselves. So when Jews begin talking about anti-Semitism, it's only "natural" that even the left, which should welcome a people's coming to consciousness, responds as if we're asking for handouts—and whose pocket will they come out of? Ignoring how much political energy can be generated as groups develop a

cohesive identity and analysis, the left accuses Jews of draining the movement
peting for status as victims, of ignoring advantages and options open to us.

Identity politics of all kinds do contain an inherent potential not only for victim-
competition but for splintering movements into 1000 groups whose members at last
feel sufficiently the same: comfy but not a powerful resource.[10] But while the focus of
some Jewish women on identity as a source of personal discovery and support is
hardly unique, criticism of identity politics has been aimed disproportionately at Jews,
sometimes *by* Jews. I'll put this another way: anti-Semitism has sometimes masquerad-
ed as a disdain for identity politics.[11]

**Hurry Hurry**

Some—including some Jews who identify, as I do, with the left—if not disdainful of
our attention to Jewish identity, seem to be rushing us, implying that we are lingering
over what Rosa Luxemburg—a Jewish leftist—called "petty Jewish concerns"; that we
are evading important struggles, being selfish or self-indulgent. Aren't we done
already?

A Jewish lesbian/feminist who has written about racism publishes, as part of a long
essay on anti-Semitism and racism, 5 pages of consciousness-raising questions directed
at Jewish women, prefaced by:

> Since many women have engaged in consciousness-raising about Jewish identity and anti-
> Semitism. . . I have skipped over a basic avenue of inquiry. . .[12]

New Jewish Agenda, a progressive Jewish organization founded six years ago—and to
which I belong—holds its second national convention, Summer '85, inspired by Hillel's
second question: *If we are only for ourselves, what are we?* The question has two
possible takes: an ethical one (the answer is, "less than human"); and a practical one
(the answer is, "a failure," because we are a tiny minority who needs allies.) This is
the question which prompts joining with others, the question of coalition.[13]

But before Hillel asked, "If I am only for myself. . . " he asked, "If I am not for
myself, who will be?" This is the question of separatism, the question that prompts a
gathering of one's people. Literally, who will stick up for me if I don't respect myself
enough to stand up for myself, if I can't articulate my own concerns so that others
understand and care about them? Here is our beginning. Have we been for ourselves
sufficiently already? Do we even know who our selves are?

## II. Jewish Diversity, Assimilation and Identity

Who, what is the Jewish people? This question dazed me when I first voiced it. I
had always known the Jewish people: we lived in Brooklyn, and those whose fathers
made money moved to Long Island. It was simple.

And suddenly it was not simple at all. I began to discover the different experiences,
cultures, languages of Jews. I was 34 when I learned about Ladino, a couple of years
older when I learned of Arab Jews, Kurds, the Beta Israel of Ethiopia, the Colchins of
India. The diversity of the Jewish people shocked me.

Even in this country, I realized, there are vast differences: place of origin, part of the country, class background, religious or secular upbringing and practice, knowledge of and attachment to Jewish culture (which one?!), degree of assimilation.

For some Jews, "passing" seems a choice; for others, passing means total denial and pain; for still others, passing is something they do without even thinking, and for still others, passing —as white/American/normal— is impossible. Some Jews have never felt a moment of Jewish fear; others smell it daily. Some were raised in comfortable suburbs, sheltered from knowledge of anti-Semitism; others came from Europe or the Middle East and relive their own nightmares or those of their families; others grew up in mixed neighborhoods where they were beat up every day after school for being the Jew, and especially on Easter.

To observant Jews, a persistent reluctance by others to take Jewish holidays, *shabes*, dietary customs into account means that they—observant Jews—are not welcome;[14] to others, ignoring these traditions embodies anti-patriarchal struggle. Some Jews are passionately attached to Yiddish culture and want to preserve this; others feel alienated by a Yiddish emphasis: they grew up with Ladino or Arabic, and resent the assumption that Jewish means Ashkenazi roots; some share the rejection of much of the New Left for European anything, and, seeing the future in the Third World and only a moribund or embarrassing past in the remnants of European Jewry, feel no desire to preserve Ashkenazi culture. (Though one might question this last position as self-hating, the people who feel this way do not perceive what they hate as their *selves*.)

Some Jews identify deeply with other Jews; others identify only with white middle-class privilege; some consider themselves people of color. Some invalidate, trivialize or otherwise deny Jewish experience, oppression, and values, say "I'm a Jew" only as a label or a credential, not a perspective. With the diversity of our experience unarticulated in a way that supports all of it, even Jews tend to perceive the needs, complaints, experience of other Jews as extreme, atypical, threatening, not really or not necessarily *Jewish*.[15] Given this lack of agreement about even such basics as the nature of Jewish experience and identity, the parameters of anti-Semitism, how are Jews supposed to work politically *as Jews*?

America is famous for gobbling up cultures, immigrant and native. But in addition, the nature of the Jewish people on the face of this earth has been totally transformed in the past 45 years by three facts:

—The Holocaust: the partial extermination of European Jewry and the virtual destruction of Ashkenazi culture.

—The expulsion of Jews from the Arab countries and destruction of these centers of Judeo-Arab culture.

—The founding of the state of Israel and the ingathering of many Jews.

We have not yet absorbed these transformations. We don't yet know what it means to be a Jew in the late 20th century.

For many North American Jews (in the US and Canada, half the world's Jews) a key issue is assimilation, a seepage of Jewishness out of Diaspora Jewry, except for those who retain or return to religious practice. Assimilation is often treated, by those who would belittle Jewish issues, as privilege, the *ability* to pass, a ticket out of Jewish oppression.

Anyone who has heard—as I have—Jew-hating remarks said to her face because to the speaker she didn't look Jewish knows both the survival value and the knife twist of passing. (And consider how some Jews came to look non-Jewish: Jewish women raped by gentile men during pogroms; Jewish women with lighter skin, hair, more gentile features, considered prettier, more desirable than their darker, more Semitic-looking sisters.)

But assimilation is a much larger issue than who you do or don't look like. Assimilation is the blurring or erasure of identity and culture. As I have come to recognize Jewish identity and culture not as givens, there for the taking, but as profoundly valuable *and vulnerable*, assimilation has become a source of pain: loss, some of which I can retrieve, some not: gone.

The point is that Jewish identity is not just about oppression, about anti-Semitism and survival, though clearly this is part of our history and we need our history. We also need our culture, need to know *where we grew*. We need *not* to disappear into the vague flesh of America, even if this disappearance were possible.

Those who call resistance to assimilation a luxury might do well to think about calling "sexual preference" a luxury, or reproductive rights, or access to education or creative expression. None of these is *bread*, but "Bread *and* Roses" was a demand voiced by Rose Schneiderman, a union organizer and a Jew.

What are the roses? As Jews we need our peoplehood, our culture, history, languages, music, calendar, tradition, literature. . . We need these things because they are beautiful and ours, and because the point of struggle is not bare survival but lives full of possibility.

But Rose Schneiderman's metaphor flounders. Our culture is not a rose, it is our backbone. To say it matters that we're Jews; to bond with our people; for a tiny minority, these acts trigger intense fear—fear of being boxed into a perspective that is assumed to be narrow and selfish, fear of being isolated, as we have often historically been isolated.

And the only thing that counters this fear is love for our people, pride in our culture.

*If I am not for myself, who will be?* Hillel could not have predicted the need American Jews in the late 20th century would bring to his first question: the need to know the self, the people, the culture. For several years I have given workshops across the country on anti-Semitism, racism, and more recently, Jewish identity. I have heard Jews talk about gathering as a group, loving the comfort, the opportunity to discuss anti-Semitism, offer support, eat wonderful food, laugh . . .but then? uncertain what to do next, as Jews. I have watched Jews sob as they grappled for the first time with the meaning of Jewish resistance, of violence and non-violence in the context of the Holocaust. Jewish radicals are just beginning to tangle with Jewish identity and its relationship to Jewish culture, tradition and politics.

So it's not surprising that we are still, many of us, uncertain in our responses. What *is* a good radical Jewish response? How do we take positions that won't be used against us or where we won't be invisible as Jews? How, for example, do we support the struggle against apartheid, confront the anti-Semitic emphasis on Israel as well as the assumption that as Jews we support the Israeli government's position, do all of this without getting crazed or isolated? What is our position on arms sales to Israel? What's our position on Israel generally? Why do we, as Jews, need a position on Israel—on another country's foreign and domestic policy? What is our relationship to the mainstream Jewish community? How do we look clearly at the strength we have, as a people, without worrying that they'll see us as running the world again?

These questions need to be answered by Jews talking with one another, developing political and emotional clarity and cohesion. And this requires Jewish space in which to piece together a deeply felt Jewish identity and perspective inch by inch from the various threads of tradition, literature, ritual, religion, culture, values, politics, language. Some of us will spend our lives building Jewish identity; others will draw on this work as a strong foundation from which to live our politics. Particularly for those of us who are not religiously observant, much confusion attends our grasping — through anti-Semitism and often prodded by anti-Semitism — for something beyond common danger. We need to figure out how to undo assimilation without being nostalgic or xenophobic: how to reach in and out at the same time.

## III. Guilt vs. Solidarity

Most feminist theory on identity was developed by women of color and focused on fighting racism.[16] I have come to think that had white women fully grasped the nature of this fight and *their own reasons for joining it,* they would now be grasping what Jewish women are trying to do. For the suspicion which greets a developing Jewish identity—from some Jews as well as gentiles—is only partly explained by anti-Semitism (the sense that Jewish identity *in particular* has no value) and by scarcity (the fear that focus on Jews will detract from other pressing issues). The way Jews have been met with "not you too," the way anti-Semitism becomes the one issue too many, suggest that many white women are angry and resistant to dealing with racism but are too frightened to express that anger openly;[17] suggest further how little our movement has taught us to see struggles against racism as life-giving, nourishing; as our own.

Most white women have learned, instead, guilt: to oppose racism because it's their—I am tempted to say christian—duty, for they seem to offer two models: the missionary and the crusader.

### Guilt: How Not To Build a Movement

If you join a struggle because you know your life depends on it—even if remotely: because you identify with the people, because people you love are involved—you have one attitude toward the people and their struggle.

But if you join because lucky you, you should help out those less fortunate—you have a different attitude: you consider those you deign to help pathetic victims. (It's no wonder Jews remain outside the paradigm, because Jews are pegged as overprivileged powerhouses: gentiles don't feel guilty about Jews.) The missionary in some way sees herself stooping to pick up the white woman's burden, a dangerous attitude, reeking of condescension, of failure to believe in the value or capacity of other people. Besides, "the white man's burden" was a polite name for imperialism. I don't imagine that white women in the women's movement are the British Empire, but people who take this attitude are—at best—focused on themselves. They want that rosy do-gooder glow.

They can be harmless. And sometimes they *do* good. Guilt has prompted some white women to act against racism: white teachers who make sure to include books by Third World writers; white women with access to funds, grants, etc., who make sure that women of color get heard, solicited, funded. These acts are not negligible, whatever their motives. And though people acting from guilt may not be reliable allies, they will do in the short run. Sometimes they're all the allies there are.

The crusader, another sort of frail ally, plays on white guilt. She attacks white women whose racism has showed, isolating and shaming them. I have seen her in women's communities all over the US: in crisis centers, in print, in women's studies programs. . . Sometimes, I confess, I have been her. And just as crusaders were supposed to gather souls but really killed, so the white knight, I have come to call her, destroys more than she saves.[18]

By doing so, she gains power in her own community—white women are afraid of her—and, besides, she is on to something. The white knight often does useful work: were this not true she would have no credibility—people aren't fools. But instead of enlarging the circle of women doing anti-racist work, fostering an atmosphere in which people believe they can change—by struggling compassionately with other white women, by communicating a vision of why one struggles—the white knight banishes most potential allies, leaving herself and a few others as the only decent white women in town.

Her power thus depends on racism, making her, in the end, no more reliable as an ally than the guilt-responsive missionary, since she has, objectively speaking, a stake in maintaining racism. She can, of course, function overtly as a christian knight and attack other christians who exhibit anti-Semitic behavior, etc.; but since the guilt quotient on Jewish issues is low, she's less likely to get response.

Sometimes acts inspired by guilt or by fear of acting wrong have a positive impact. And, for the most cockamamie reasons, people land in situations from which they change and wisen. I did not take the D-train to Harlem when I was 17 with my present consciousness, yet I would not have developed my present consciousness without those formative experiences.

But guilt itself, as a motivating factor, is rooted in a way of thinking which does not promote change. Guilt asks: am I bad or am I good? guilty or innocent? racist or not? Very different from asking "is this a racist *act*?" which allows me not to commit it, or to do the work that ensures I never commit it again. For in order to change you have to be willing to expose yourself—at least to yourself—and observe and examine and understand. This takes time, patience, and a respect for process. Guilt prompts a longing to purge all impure impulses quickly, get it over and done with once and for all.

Impulses which seem impure are not examined or transformed; they are stifled while you keep busy trying to act as though you have the right impulses.

We've all seen white women act like corpses around women of color, so afraid of doing the wrong thing: meaning, anything natural, treating a person like a person. For guilt is a freeze emotion: you can't think, you can't feel, you can only knee jerk. This is the infantilizing function of guilt: you lose faith in your own responses because the risk of their being wrong is more than you can handle.

In addition to militating against real change, guilt exercises an uneasy influence over the real difference in resources and options which women may enjoy, leading to downward mobility, pretending to have less, gleefully selecting the most oppressed possible identity: *office worker*, not *daughter of a lawyer and dropout from a prestigious college most office workers never get near (as students).*

And why does someone embrace an identity of oppression? Because it's groovy? The insult of this must be apparent. Because she feels guilty about what she's got? Are money, power, privilege worthless resources to ignore, bury, pretend away? The insult of this ought to be apparent too.

And besides: behind the guilt, the desire to belong, be one with the people, etc., the resources remain, quietly drawn on or untouched by anyone, but ready to be picked up and used at some future date. So guilt helps people hoard what they've got, because they never come to terms with how to use resources productively.

The thing is: anyone who really wants to hoard her money, power and privilege sooner or later will. She can be targeted for guilt trips—to let go of some of what she wishes no one knew she had—but beneath the guilt had better be fear: fear of exposure, fear of conflict, so she'll stay in line and act right. And how does any sane person react after a while to fear, guilt? Is this a way to build a movement?

Nor can guilt mobilize those who don't feel guilty. Try telling a white working-class woman, for example, to fight racism because of how privileged she is. She may think racism is wrong and may be committed to fight it; she may also think that movement analyses of racism are ridiculous because she is not living the easy life her white skin is supposed to guarantee her. Whatever privilege she may have, she clings to—things are tough—but she hardly feels guilty. Only recognition of a common goal, the possibilities and—I want to say—the joys of solidarity will inspire women who don't feel guilty to join another struggle as their own.

## Solidarity: How To Build a Movement

Solidarity requires the bonding together of a people engaged in common struggle. But solidarity also means standing alongside another struggle, not because you feel guilty but because you recognize it as your own; it means using what you have on behalf of the struggle.

Angela Davis notes, for example, Prudence Crandall, a white woman who risked her life in defense of education for Black girls.[19] Or the strategy suggested by Maria Chapman Weston, a white leader of the Boston Female Anti-Slavery Society; when a white pro-slavery mob burst into a meeting chaired by Weston, she realized that the mob sought to isolate and perhaps violently attack the Black women in attendance, and thus insisted that each white woman leave the building with a Black woman at her side.[20] Or, at the world anti-slavery convention in London, at which the notorious decision was made to bar women from the floor, there were a few men who refused to join the floor but stood with the women in the gallery, silent. Among them was the Black abolitionist Charles Remond,and the white abolitionists William Lloyd Garrison and Nathaniel Rogers.[21] Black leader Frederick A. Douglass, too, at least initially supported the then-radical demand of women's suffrage and used his male privilege on behalf of the emerging women's rights movement.[22] Or, the women workers in the stockyards (mostly Irish and Poles) and in the garment industry (mostly Jews and Italians) who deliberately—and contrary to the practice of the AFL and most of their peers—sought to include and organize with Black women.[23] Or the Women's Trade Union League, upper middle-class college-educated white suffragists who worked in support of immigrant women's unions.[24] Or the Black and white college students—including many Jews—who went south to challenge segregation.

All these actions are examples of informed coalition work. None is a passive giving something up; they are all an aggressive wrapping of two peoples in a cloak only one has. These are acts which build trust between peoples.

But those who performed these acts which build and justify trust—I can't believe that they did not understand that these acts were *also* in defense of *their own freedom,* a freedom without which they, the actors, could not breathe.

*If I am only for myself, what am I?* Lonely. Hungry for sisters, comrades. Listen to the words of the fiery Grimke sisters, white abolitionists who recognized "the special bond, linking them with Black women who suffered the pain of slavery. . .'They are our countrywomen—they are our sisters.'"[25] Or the slogan displayed at the April '85 march in Paris to protest increasing violence against Jews and Arabs (many of whom are also Jews) and to protest increasing racist propaganda about purifying France for the French: *Ne touche pas à mon pote.* "Keep your hands off my buddy."

None of the passionless rhetoric which has come to dominate our movement's discussions of race, class. Obviously if your friends, if your sisters are suffering you put everything you have into the struggle to free them *because you need their freedom as your own.*

Your privilege, insofar as it divides you from others, is *in your way,* unless you resolve how to use it for others, as well as for yourself. This is a non-guilt approach: drawing on what is best in people, not suppressing what is worst.

And let me say something which in this (christian) culture may come as a surprise: what is best in people is not self-abnegation. What is best in people is a sturdy connection between respect for the self and respect for the other: reaching in and out at the same time:

> *If I am not for myself, who will be?*
> *If I am only for myself, what am I?*

## IV. Some Strategies for Action

As we come into our Jewish identity, we feel somehow that to be justified in asserting it, in opposing anti-Semitism, we must be innocent victims, trying to make our oppression palpable to those who don't understand it. My beginning search for Jewish identity focused on the Holocaust and on the immigrant experience only partly because such a search must. So did a number of poems we received for this anthology—not because of direct knowledge, but for some other reason. The only other subjects which appeared in such profusion were "grandmothers" and the "Triangle Shirtwaist Factory Fire."

We need our history/herstory, and these are our handles, what we know. These are also all images of greater persecution than most American Jews are subject to today. As Jews, afraid of the myth of Jewish power; as (white?) feminists, guilty about our skin privilege, we are so hungry for innocence that images of oppression come almost as a relief. Innocence, even suffering, seems the only alternative to guilt.

But innocence has its price: while it relieves us of responsibility, it also denies us our strength. The assumption is: since we have been victims, we cannot ever be anything else. Witness Begin, invoking the Holocaust to justify the invasion of Lebanon. *How could Jews be oppressive after all we've suffered?* From this perspective, class hostility, for example, has no basis in class distinctions but is only a front for Jewhating. We have to recognize that Jews are relatively well-off economically compared with most people of color in this country, as with the rural white poor; and that Jews endure about the same level of poverty as other ethnic groups who immigrated around the same time. Our job is to untangle class hostility from anti-Semitism, not to pretend the Jewish people still works in the sweatshop.

Non-Jews rely on this innocence too, including people of color. Witness how some excused Farrakhan's description of Hitler as a great German. Was it because support for Jackson's presidential candidacy transcended Jewish danger (which, given Jewish wealth and power, could not possibly be *real* danger)? Or was it because Farrakhan is Black, and a cry of hatred against Jews carries no threat when the speaker is, by definition, powerless? (Need it be said that this racist as well as anti-Semitic?) From this perspective, the fears of elderly Jews in racially mixed neighborhoods that they will be mugged and robbed are merely a front for racism, instead of reflecting the reality of urban violence: old people are marks, especially when living in communities no longer theirs. Our job here is to untangle concern for safety from racism, not to come up with justifications for mugging.

How this need for innocence translates politically is a disaster. The attitude that claims we—of any group— are essentially victims and so can't be charged with our behavior is destructive to all of us. If we can't do anything wrong, the fact is we can't do *anything* at all — and how in that state of powerlessness are we to build a vast movement sufficient to transform the exceedingly powerful state we live in? Defensive, protective of that dubious privilege of having our suffering acknowledged, we are at something of a standstill. Can't we look at each other and begin to see what we might build? Can't we extend towards each other so that we can draw on each other's strengths, learn to trust that we can use our power in positive ways?

## Working Alone/Working Together

True coalition is not a smattering of tokens. True coalition forms between groups;

the premise is that each group has a strong base in a larger community. Thus Jews who want to work in coalition need not only to know who we are but to be bonded with other Jews.

For feminists, for lesbians, this presents its own complications. Some of us won't work with men. This is not a flawed choice. Some of us will have to be separatist—as Jews, as women, as lesbians, as whoever we are. Separatism gives strength, a base from which coalition is possible. Some of us—because of desire or need— will choose to be with our own. There are different forms of struggle, and separatists often are in the vanguard, creating a strong identity and consciousness for the whole community, including those who are not themselves separatist.

Those of us who choose to work in coalitions can assert that identity and consciousness to others. I know many Jewish women, myself among them, have participated in anti-racist, anti-apartheid, anti-intervention work, but not visibly as Jews. It is time we became visible as Jews, as some are doing.

Yet we need at the same time strategies for combatting anti-Semitism, for Jewish visibility fans the coals of indifference and passive contempt. An individual visible as a Jew simply attracts, like a magnet, all available anti-Jewish prejudice, or gets written off as an exception. And sometimes we even need strategies to ensure visibility. A Jew who travelled to Nicaragua recently tells of her attempts to be visible as a Jew to the Nicaraguan Press, attempts frustrated by her travel group's leader, whose job it was to inform the press about the group members and who kept "forgetting" to mention the Jewish member. Just as women, as lesbians, need our own groups—for support and as bases for coalitions, a Jewish group travelling to Nicaragua might have had the desired impact, built Jewish pride *and* Jewish-Nicaraguan solidarity. To reach in and out at the same time.

The particular example of Nicaragua offers another possibility for solidarity and coalition. Progressive Jews have something in common with progressive Native Americans who oppose US intervention in Nicaragua, yet are concerned about the status of the Miskito Indians. We might learn from each other ways to express concern about our people without having this concern either used by the right or discredited by the left.

Again, focusing on Nicaragua, there is work to do in the Jewish community, to make sure the justified fear of anti-Semitism is not exploited by the US government, that Jews have access to the facts. There's a need for community education by strongly-identified Jews; there is also a need for honest discussion of liberation theology, of its potential for anti-Semitism (if the revolutionary impulse is christian, where does that leave us?), and of ways we can support the revolution without supporting an unexamined christianity.

## Fears

But there are fears. Mine are that non-Jews won't care about working with us. Who are *we* that they should bother? Our numbers so small, we are so disposable, a liability almost; dislike of us a point of unity among everyone else. And as women, as lesbians, as underemployed professionals or workers at traditional women's jobs, most of us

*Jewish women at the South African Embassy, Washington, DC.
Last day of Hanukkah and Christmas Day. 1984.*     *Photo by JEB*

don't even have money to contribute. Sometimes I am simply afraid that radical Jews are on the wrong side of history, trapped between self-respect, love for our people and culture and what we, politically, ideologically would support were it not tangled with Jewhating. I know I am not the only radical Jew whose stomach ties in knots reading the radical press or attending a rally.

Non-Jews, especially people of color, may fear that Jews will deny differences in experience, will aim for the great white American marshmallow of you're oppressed/I'm oppressed.

No doubt on every side there is prejudice, ignorance and mistrust. I think of the Jew who uses the names Palestinian and Lebanese interchangeably, has not bothered to distinguish between the two peoples; the Arab who blames Leon Klinghoffer's death on "the fact that the whole country of Palestine has been hijacked by the . . .Zionist Jews of Europe, America and elsewhere," not only condoning the brutal death of an old man in a wheelchair, but also hiding—with the words "and elsewhere"—the thousands of Jews forced to leave *their* homes in Arab countries.[26] The Jew who says "We made it, why can't they?" or "Who cares, they're all *goyim*!" The Black who says *"They* made it on my back." The Chicana/o who says *"They're* all landlords." There is work to do on all sides.

James Baldwin, in 1967, wrote: "A genuinely candid confrontation between

Negroes and American Jews would certainly prove of inestimable value. But the aspirations of the country are wretchedly middle-class and the middle class can never afford candor."[27] A genuinely candid confrontation amongst all of us—a genuinely *specific* and candid confrontation — is much needed; and Baldwin is precise, as ever, in indicating that we must be prepared to go further than liberal acceptance, further than maneuvering for our own (larger) slice of the pie. The theme re-emerges: we must *want* equality, and we must grasp that equality does not coexist with class structure.

As a feminist and a Jew, I am asking women of color not to abandon us as we assert our Jewishness, not to hear this assertion as a lowered vigilance against racism.

And I am asking Jews not to withdraw into self-righteousness, not to insist that gentiles understand everything immediately, yesterday. We are not without dignity if we explain our issues. I am also asking Jews not to be so afraid of being trapped with other Jews—including, perhaps, some whose politics or attitudes offend us—that we forget that people can change, including our own people; including ourselves.

## Commonality

I am saying there have got to be many points of unity among us. Even in my fear that non-Jews won't care because we are a small—useless—minority I find a connection—with Native Americans who express the same fear, of irrelevance; and another similar fear, genocide —historical and cultural. And I see difference: the grinding poverty in which most Native American people live.

And in my recognition that Jews are better off economically than most people of color, I find connection with some Asian Americans, not the recent immigrants, from Southeast Asia, who tend to be very poor, but with many Japanese Americans. Looking specifically at the situation of Japanese Americans I see a people also traumatized by events of the past 40 years—internment in camps; the atomic bombs dropped on civilian cities of Hiroshima and Nagasaki; a fear of cultural loss and assimilation; and continued economic discrimination, despite their apparent integration into professional and business life. And I see differences: Japanese—and other Asian-Americans—pressed into the sciences, engineering, computers, pushed away from the humanities, the arts, where much Jewish talent has been channeled.[28]

I could go on. And if I am doing my work, I *will* go on, understanding the ways in which Jewish history and experience are like and unlike the experience of other groups, the ways in which the light skin of some Jews has and has not protected them, the issues *as defined by Jews* and the issues *as defined by other groups*.

We might then, as Jews, offer support to Japanese Americans seeking restitution from the US government for their internment and confiscation of property during World War II, and to those still fighting their convictions for refusing to report for "relocation."

We might express—in unison with Japanese American women—our disgust at the stereotype and acronym JAP—a racist name for Japanese people as well as a sexist scapegoating of Jewish middle-class women for the crimes of capitalism.

We might, as Jews, press our religious and community institutions to offer sanc-

317

tuary to refugees, from El Salvador and other countries, as some are doing, recognizing our own history as refugees. We might, as Jews, support attempts of women garment workers—jobs once held by Jewish and Italian women—to organize for better conditions and pay. We might support bilingual efforts of Chicana, Latina and Francophone communities, grasping through our own linguistic losses the importance of retaining one's language.

We might decide that even in the midst of vitriolic disagreement about peace in the Middle East, we must never accept or leave unchallenged instances of racism against Arabs, remembering our own history of prejudice and stereotypes.

We might even, as Jews, offer support to people whose struggles and issues are different from ours now and in the past simply because we care about justice; because we know that while nothing guarantees allies, callousness guarantees callousness.

Of late, there are positive instances of coalition. An event in NYC of Jews and Latinas/os (including some who are both) reading and performing their work, much of which is bilingual (Spring, 1984). Prior to several of Farrakhan's most recent appearances, coalitions of Black and Jewish leaders joined to denounce him. (In Baltimore, the same group joined to condemn Kahane prior to his appearance there.)[29] In the feminist movement, a Jewish-Arab-Black coalition which prepared for the International Women's Conference at Nairobi has been speaking about this gathering, including information on Jewish-Palestinian dialogue.[30] A workshop for Black-Jewish dialogue is being offered at the 1986 Women and the Law conference for the second year. It seems that many of us may have learned something from drawing close to the precipice of total withdrawal and isolation.

If we could start working together *before* we trust, understand, or like each other, we might learn to. Black activist and performer Bernice Reagon says we are stumbling because we have to take the next step.[31] We have gotten entirely too theoretical about these issues, expecting that with words, with ideas, we can work it all out in advance. Perhaps we need to engage, even in uncertainty, and work out issues as they arise. Maulana Karenga, a theorist for the Black movement, has pointed out that a coalition on a specific issue does not create reliable allies: he is critical of what he calls the reliance of middle-class Black movement leaders on alliances with Jews.[32]

But the positive side to Karenga's depressing analysis is that you don't need to be reliable allies to form a coalition. Having formed one, it may be possible to overcome mistrust and establish a larger common ground. It is impossible to do this without some concrete basis of unity, and focusing on the task at hand can help reveal commonality.

The problem is not a lack of common issues, not a lack of desperate need. The problem for us, as Jews, is that we are often afraid, afraid to gather with other Jews, afraid to be visibly Jewish, afraid—too often with reason—to know the extent of anti-Semitism in our comrades, neighbors, co-workers, friends. We are afraid of being or of seeming racist; afraid of our own ignorance of Jewish culture and tradition.

And because, as radicals, we have been taught to see dignity in resistance, in the struggle against oppression, we sometimes idealize oppression. We must remember to respect the struggles Jews have waged on behalf of their children, who are, sometimes, us. We must remember: what is beautiful is the resistance, and that people can—and must—resist from their own authentic place in the world.

This means we must reach out to Israelis fighting for peace, civil rights, and feminism without secretly feeling the Palestinians are more beautiful, because more besieged. One of the hardest acts of self-love for American radical Jews is to identify in this way with Israelis, and I have come to believe it is a crucial stretch, for the alternative is denial of the Jewish connection. It is from this solid, self-knowing place that we can work towards peace and justice in the Middle East.

It is also from this place of valuing resistance that we are able to reach out to those in the Jewish community who have themselves been fighters for justice, or supporters of this fight, to ask them to continue this tradition; to ask them for what is best in themselves too.

Last Rosh Hashonah I stood with my friend Mitzi Lichtman at the edge of the Atlantic performing (in our own way) the ancient ritual of *tashlekh* –casting our sins into the water, in the form of stones. And among all the sins we hurled into the ocean, the sin of self-hate and the sin of failing to feel compassion for others mingled, as indeed they should, for they are the same sin.

And Hillel had a third question: *If not now, when?*

---

Portions of this essay were first developed as talks given in Mankato and Minneapolis, MN, on "Anti-Semitism, Racism, and Coalitions" (1984); a workshop given at the 1985 Women & the Law Conference on "Dealing with Racism as Jewish Women"; and as a review of Yours In Struggle which appeared in off our backs (10/85). I thank the women who attended these events and talked with me about these issues. Much of the essay was also developed in conversation with Irena Klepfisz. I thank Linda Vance for her critical acumen, generous editorial attention, humor and patience. Responsibility for the opinions and analysis is mine alone.

---

### Notes

[1] The Harlem Education Project (HEP) was a branch of the Northern Student Movement (NSM), founded in New Haven as the northern arm of the Student Non-Violent Coordinating Committee (SNCC), the most militant of the southern civil rights activist organizations.

[2] The anti-rat campaign consisted of a number of young Black people armed with rifles very visibly hunting rats in Harlem apartment buildings. The sluggish city health department responded immediately to combat the rats.

[3] The National Women's Studies Association, pressed by angry Jewish women, agreed to mention opposition "to anti-Semitism against Arabs and Jews." Since hatred and discrimination against Arabs are regularly included by the term "racism"—and since, oddly enough, these same phenomena directed against Jews are often excluded—I wonder why Jews are not allowed to use "anti-Semitism" to mean anti-Jewish racism, its historic meaning.

[4] I have heard this a number of times from women who attended conference planning sessions.

[5] Cynthia Kern deserves particular credit for her work. Let me mention that these Jewish events were mostly open to gentiles but were attended almost exclusively by Jews.

[6] Flyer for *Not In Our Name*/Women's Resistance Action, Boston Office. See exchange of letters—a critical letter by me and Mitzi Lichtman, and a self-critical response by several *Not In Our Name* women—in *Gay Community News* (11/17/84).

[7] *Heresies.*

[8] For a discussion of the queuing effect, see Stanley Lieberson, *A Piece of the Pie: Blacks and White Immigrants Since 1880* (Berkeley, Univ. of Calif., 1980), pp. 296-326; 377-81.

[9] See my earlier discussion, "Anti-Semitism, Homophobia, and the Good White Knight," *off our backs* (5/82).

[10] Cf. Black activist Bernice Johnson Reagon, on the *discomfort* of working in coalitions: "[Coalition is] a monster. It never gets enough. It always wants more. So you better be sure you got your home someplace for you to go to so that you will not become a martyr to the coalition." See Reagon's fine discussion, "Coalition Politics: Turning the Century," *Home Girls*, ed. Barbara Smith (NY: Kitchen Table/Women of Color Press, 1983), p. 361.

[11] The felicitous wording is Linda Vance's.

[12] Elly Bulkin, Appendix to "Hard Ground: Jewish Identity, Racism, and Anti-Semitism," *Yours In Struggle* (Brooklyn: Long Haul Press, 1984), pp. 194-98. See my review in *off our backs* (10/85).

[13] Adrienne Rich, speaking at the NJA Convention, added another question—"If not with others, how?"—showing a peculiar failure to note that Hillel's second question already confronts the need for coalition. Her question also places the burden on Jews, as if *we* have refused to work in alliance with Gentiles, whereas in fact the opposite has often been true. The history of Jews engaged in political activity hardly suggests a people unwilling to work with others; what this history reveals, rather is *erasure* of Jewish participation, Jews drummed out of movements by anti-Semitism, as well as substantial Jewish contributions to revolutionary activity. See, for example, Elinor Lerner, "Jewish Involvement in the New York City Woman Suffrage Movement," *American Jewish History*, LXX (1981), 442-61.

[14] See below for Susie Gaynes' moving statement about recognizing how some Jewish women were made to feel unwelcome by just such a reluctance.

[15] In this discussion I am drawing heavily on Irena Klepfisz, "When Jewish Women Disagree," unpublished (1983).

[16] For an early clear statement of identity politics, see the Combahee River Collective, "A Black Feminist Statement," reprinted in *Capitalist Patriarchy and the Case for Socialist Feminism*, ed. Zillah R. Eisenstein (NY: Monthly Review Press, 1979).

[17] See Susanna Sturgis' analysis of feminist resistance to dealing with fat oppression, "Is this the new thing I'm going to have to be p c about?" *Sinister Wisdom* 28 (1985).

[18] See Kaye/Kantrowitz, ". . .the Good White Knight."

[19] Angela Davis, *Women, Race & Class* (NY: Random House, 1981), pp. 34 ff.

[20] Davis, p. 38.

[21] Davis, p. 48.

[22] Davis, pp. 50 ff.

[23] See Eleanor Flexner, *Century of Struggle: A History of the Women's Rights Movement in the US* (Cambridge, MA: Belknap/Harvard Univ., 1978). But also see Rosalyn Terborg-Penn, "Survival strategies among African-American women workers: A continuing process," *Women, Work & Protest: A Century of US Women's Labor History*, ed. Ruth Milkman (Boston: Routledge & Kegan Paul, 1985). Terbourg-Penn cites the occasional interest of mostly white CIO Unions in organizing with Black women, but the more common lack of interest.

[24] Nancy Schrom Dye, *As Equals As Sisters: Feminism, The Labor Movement and The Women's Trade Union League of New York* (Columbia: Univ. of Missouri Press, 1980), p. 93.

[25] Quoted in Davis, p. 44.

[26] M.T. Mehdi, letter, NY *Times* (10/17/85).

[27] James Baldwin, "Negroes Are Anti-Semitic Because They're Anti-White," 1st pub. NY *Times Magazine* (1967); reprinted in *Black Anti-Semitism and Jewish Racism* (NY: Schocken, 1972), p. 11.

[28] See Prof. Ronald Takaki's remarks, quoted in the NY *Times* (9/4/85).

[29] See Earl Raab, "Poisoned Good: Understanding the Farrakhan Factor," *Moment*, vol. 11, no. 2 (Jan.-Feb. 1986), 13-17.

[30] The dialogue was organized by New Jewish Agenda.

[31] Reagon, p. 368.

[32] Maulana Karenga, "The Crisis of Black Middle-Class Leadership: A Critical Analysis," *The Black Scholar* (Fall '82), pp. 16-32.

*Susie Gaynes*

# Rosh Hashonah 5743

The following statement was made by Susie Gaynes to open a women's concert given in upstate NY.

*from the New Women's Times—December 1982.*

*My name is Susie Gaynes. I am a member of the production crew. Before we begin tonight, I would like to make a statement about the scheduling of this concert. As some of you may know, tonight is Rosh Hashonah.*

*When this concert was first being scheduled, months ago, the producers consulted me and several other Jewish women about the advisability of having the concert on the Jewish New Year. I told them that I was a Jew but it really didn't matter to me and I doubted it would be a problem.*

*Earlier this week I found out that some women in the community were very upset about the conflict and had sent out angry letters and were even considering picketing the concert. My reaction was—Oh God, what's the big deal. Troublemakers are such a drag! But that night I couldn't sleep and when I told a Jewish friend, who's from out of town, about the whole mess the next day she was shocked that the concert had been scheduled and was very supportive of these women.*

*We talked for a long time and when we discussed responsibility and blame she said the real women at fault were those Jewish women who had advised the producers in the first place.*

*Her words hit me like a brick between the eyes.*

*I'm not saying she's right—we all must take responsibility—but what she said helped crystallize a lot of things for me.*

*The issue for me is not just whether I'm a "religious" Jew or not and might want to attend Synagogue tonight but my insensitivity to my own identity and how an anti-Semitic world has made me, a Jew, indifferent to the meaning of tonight .*

*This concert never would have been scheduled on Christmas or Easter or the Christian New Year celebrating 1900 and 80 some odd years since Jesus. We as Jews tonight celebrate the year 5743. And although probably most of us no longer attend the religious services of the particular faith in which we were raised, holidays are a time when family is important and tradition can be comforting.*

*You are my family. And women's music is an important tradition in my life—in all our lives. What a wonderful way to bring in the New Year.*

*The good that comes from tonight's mistake is that you, as an audience, will hopefully come away with more awareness and I, as a Jew, have, as a result of my own responsibility in this mistake, gained new insight into my relationship with my Jewishness.*

*I am looking with new eyes at my own pride—and lack of it. My discomfort, my indifference and my outright fear of being a Jew.*

*Meg, who will be here shortly, has a beautiful song about reclaiming one's roots called Southern Home. So, thanks to my friend whose words, as the song says, "opened the door to a love I'd been trying so hard to ignore—a longing so deep and so strong—for my home."*

*I would like now to light the traditional candle and bring in the New Year. It is a time for meditation, contemplation and new beginnings. I'll light the candle and then recite the Hebrew prayer that accompanies the making of light.*

*Amen, Blessed Be, Happy New Year.*

## —An Interview with
## ———Grace Paley

*Grace Paley was born in 1922 in the Bronx. A mother of two, grandmother of one, she has been active in the anti-militarist and women's movement for many years. She is the author of three collections of short stories—*The Little Disturbances of Man *(Viking/Penguin),* Enormous Changes at the Last Minute *and* Later the Same Day *(both, Farrar, Straus & Giroux), and a book of poetry,* Leaning Forward *(Granite Press). She teaches at Sarah Lawrence and at City College, CUNY, and lives sometimes in New York City and sometimes in Vermont, where we interviewed her in September, 1985.*

*When we talked on the phone the other day, you said you were going to go to Synagogue for Yom Kippur. Have you always gone?*

No, I haven't. I used to take my grandmother. We lived in the Bronx. And the *shul* was about two doors away. It was the same kind of little private house—we used to call them private houses in the Bronx—the same kind of house as ours. The *shul* eventually, when the neighborhood changed, became an Iglesia Penticostal. I used to take my grandmother, but I never attended services and my parents were very anti-religious. They laughed at religion. I mean they wanted me to take my grandmother because they wanted me to take *her*, but if I had become serious, they would have been amused. And I can't say lightly amused. My father came here in 1905. He was already a young man of 20, so he must have been born in '84. And he hated religiousness. And so did my mother. My mother even more maybe. My grandmother was not orthodox. She did not insist on a kosher home. But we didn't insult her. I don't think she was very insistent either. She wanted Passover. She wanted the holidays. She wanted Saturday. She wanted to go to synagogue and she did. But my parents obviously had made their rebellion against all that in their youth. And this grandmother—whom my father loved deeply, by the way—was the person they rebelled against and they won. And she was in their house. So that's the way it was.

*When you go now, why do you go?*

Well, I have gone to services *here* [in Vermont] the last 3-4 years. And I think probably part of the reason is that when I'm in New York I feel I'm *in* a continuous Jewish community. So for me there's a communitarian reason really. And I think if the rabbis were impossible, you know I might not. But they've been Hillel rabbis related to the school, which means they need to be kind of open, receptive, you know. They're sometimes willing to stick their necks out politically and at the same time they're deeply religious. At least Rabbi Michael Paley is—no relative. And I'm interested in what the community is here.

When I talk about the religious attitude of my family, people like to say words about Jewish self-hatred. But there was *none* of that. There was *no* wish not to be Jewish. There was *no* desire to pretend we were something else. In fact, along with his opposition to religion, my father had biblical feeling and knowledge which he shared with me. And this was true to such a degree that I just grew up liking things Jewish, kind of pleased with myself for having had the sense to be born into this family instead of some other. When I left home and lived in the Midwest, it would be one of the first things I would tell people, really—at least in the beginning.

*Then what happened?*

Well, what happened is I learned more about anti-Semitism in a very real sense. But I still did it. Announced who I was—I mean. I liked it.

*What was your sense of what it meant to be Jewish when you were growing up?*

Well, it meant to be a socialist. Well, not really. But it meant to have social consciousness. It also meant that we were related to those generations of the Jewish Bible. We had common history. Our neighborhood was solidly Jewish. Next door there could be somebody who wasn't. That would be a very exotic person. The whole block didn't have more than two people who weren't Jewish. So my idea of the world was that it was totally Jewish. And the people to be worried about and pitied are the ones outside. So there is a sense that the stranger is the one to be remembered. The reason that it's repeated in the Bible so many times that we were strangers in Egypt is really to make us behave decently. This seemed to me very much a part of being Jewish. And it wasn't a matter of hospitality, which is as American as apple pie, so to speak. It wasn't hospitality; it was a normal sense of outrage when others were treated badly, and along with that the idea that injustice not be allowed to continue. Blacks, for example. When I was a little kid, I said the word "nigger," my big sister hauled off and socked me. When I tell her this, she's absolutely amazed. She really doesn't remember it. But those are the feelings that seemed to me very important, that seemed to me for some peculiar reason related to being Jewish.

*Was it connected with anything specifically Jewish?*

No, just that all the Jews I knew were people who were concerned about the fate of the world and what to do about it. And not that they weren't upwardly mobile. They were, surely. I mean, my father came here when he was 20 without a word of English, and he became a doctor within the next 6 to 10 years. He learned English. Actually he also learned Italian. And they liked to do well, and they didn't do much politics. They read the paper. They talked at every meal about the world, but they didn't do much. They *had* been active in Russia in their youth, been dangerously active, imprisoned. But not here. And my uncle, a young anarchist in his 20s, was deported in Palmer Raid days. But it just seemed to be related to this business of your attitude towards others, how you were to deal with the other. I learned that expression recently: "the other." How to deal with the other.

*You've been an activist for a long time. Did that seem to you like a Jewish thing to be also?*

I have to give a talk which I'm nervous about in Houston, Texas at the Jewish Y. And I'm going to call it "Thinking Globally, Acting Jewish." And yet I've learned a lot from other groups. I learned a lot from Christian pacifists. But it seemed to me they had learned a lot from Jews without knowing it. I mean they do walk around saying everything out of Isaiah even putting lots of it into Jesus' mouth. Like it's theirs alone. *Really. Like they invented ploughshares.*

Right. Right. They started the ploughshare movement. And, of course, we're the ones who till just recently haven't had much army or too many weapons either. Well I think a lot about that. I don't know to what degree this is Jewish or not Jewish. I mean there are other influences in one's life, like being born female.

*At the conference in Greenfield a year ago on Non-Violence and the Jewish Tradition you were saying you had thought more about being Jewish lately.*

I never *didn't* think about it. I wrote stories about Jews and I still do. But this business of going to temple here in Vermont—which isn't even a temple, it's the chapel of the school—has to do really with being in an entirely different community. My present husband—Bob's not Jewish. Very few people around here are. So, my going comes from a very simple longing to see my own people. I made Vera [Williams] go with me. She was visiting me. I said, you'll really be surprised. I know if I'm interested, she'll probably be interested. So we went. And the Rabbi kept trying to say humankind instead of mankind. He really was working on it. We both felt a kind of softness towards him. Every now and then he slipped. And the Cantor was a woman and she sang absolutely beautifully. She sang so beautifully that people didn't want to sing with her. They really wanted to hear her, to receive her. So I think that's it, just a real longing to be with your own people and to be with them at a very profound point in their year, in their life, in their thinking.

*A lot of people we've talked to said that Israel's invasion of Lebanon in '82 was a real jolt. People who for years hadn't thought about their Jewishness were sort of forced to start thinking about it in relationship to Israel. Did that have an effect on you?*

Well, since I think a lot about politics, it had an effect on me. But it didn't have a jolting or a changing effect. It wasn't so much a surprise as a new reason for sorrow and disgust. I was pleased at the services that year that this young fellow really spoke out very strongly.

Sometimes I think that the Left has really made some terrible mistakes. I was talking about it the other day—the way the people in Nicaragua can separate the *people* of this US from the *government*. And that is partly a result of a decision by the Left. It's not just a strategy decision, it's true.

It's a decision which the Left made in Vietnam, which was to divide the country. A very sensible, simple thing to do, to see us as opposed to the government. True too. It did not weaken the people of Nicaragua or Vietnam. So, I've never understood why my sisters and brothers on the Left haven't been able to do the same in relation to Israel. And if they'd done it a long time ago, I think things could have been different. If they had pointed out again and again: the people and the government, I mean, the difference at that time. A big majority of the American people were not yet against the war in Vietnam when the Vietnamese said, "We know you're not the government." There were maybe nine people on assorted street corners in '62, '63, '64 and the Vietnamese were already talking like that, right? So it's not as if you would have had to say the *majority* of the people in Israel are against this. Enough of them were in opposition. Why it wasn't done I—I know why it wasn't done.

*Why?*

Anti-Semitism. [all laugh knowingly]

*Has that changed at all with the Left? Gotten worse? Or do you think it's the same?*

No, I think in some ways it's better. In the women's movement press, too. You were really both very useful and really strong and influential. And I think a lot of women began to think seriously about anti-Semitism. Just because women started to stand up, others suddenly realized they had legs. The work the two of you did perked up a lot of people I talked to. I was really surprised in some cases by a new understanding in certain women that certain attitudes were plain anti-Semitism. Some suddenly said *uh huh*. On the other hand there were quite a lot of people that didn't see it at all.

*For a lot of Jewish women, Israel was sort of like a relative that you felt embarrassed by, that everybody was always going to identify you with.*

Right.

*That was sort of the level at which the understanding operated—just embarrassment and shame. Have you ever worked politically on Israel?*

No, I haven't done that, directly. As an anti-war worker, I've included Middle East concerns.

*You just came back from Nicaragua fairly recently and you were talking about the connection between religion and the government.*

Well, it's a Catholic country, seriously so. The people believe. I went to one of the liberation churches. It was very lovely and wild; they did a lot of wild singing and Indian music with flutes and drums, and guitars. And the priest spoke beautifully. He compared Nicaragua to Jesus. He said Jesus was killed because he refused to abandon the poor. And that's what Nicaragua's enemies wanted her to do on pain of death. Like Christ, Nicaragua would never abandon the poor. In Nicaragua, religion is connected to local work, the life of the oppressed. The Pope, though, has to convert the whole world. That's his job. In doing that, he has to behave a certain way to the powerful. But in a poor country, people can just believe. They have the moral ideas of the religion which are perfectly good, nothing wrong with them. Christian ideas, the basic ones. It's just that most Christians never use them.

*Do you think it was a mistake to link politics with religion?*

Oh, you know the Communist Party in Nicaragua is absolutely opposed to giving in to the religious groups. They think the Sandinistas are far too deferential to the religious groups. And they speak up about it. And I became aware of that because one the women in our group was obviously a Communist Party person, and she talked at length about this. And I saw why. I mean, in the same sense that my father. She was born and raised a Catholic and she hated every bit of it. She despised the religion as oppressive, just as my father and mother thought Judaism was. I was just looking at this article in the *New Yorker* on Hasidic Jews. And there's this general sentimentalization of them, and they really were what my father hated, ran away from.

*This is switching the topic. But do you remember in Greenfield we were sitting at a table with a bunch of young women, who said they wanted to get together as Jewish women to talk about racism. And yet they had never talked about themselves as Jews.*

You know in my lifetime, Jews have been very close to Blacks, really have had very close relations, and I just happen to be reading this book *When and Where I Enter* [by Paula Giddings]. Anyway, I noticed it's full of these Jewish names of people who were working in that movement. Well, some of these kids missed those years. A lot of us have thought about racism. In a sense, I've thought about it since I was 5 years old when my sister smacked me. And my thinking about it was Jewish thinking. So that in a way I think these Jewish women are "thinking Jewish" when they say that they want to think about racism. And I think it's a good thing. They feel they're talking from that Jewish base. They don't think they've skipped. They're in it. But I know what you're talking about. It's natural because they're young that they assume that nobody has thought about it yet. And it's also weird. In some groups I've worked with, a couple of young women would come in and say: "Start talking about racism. We're all racist because we're not talking constantly about racism." It probably never entered their minds that many of us *had* been talking about it for years, acting on it for years, and that it was not a new subject for many of us at all, had always been one of deep concern. But it *was* new to them.

I just got this letter from the American Jewish Committee, which is helping to start up group meetings of Blacks and Jews. I think for most Jews who live in New York there's a real sadness about this terrible split that's happened. This craziness, you know, this nasty anti-Jewishness among Blacks and anti-Blackism among Jews. It's so painful, I think that a lot of people feel that. I went to a few meetings of Jewish and Black women. And it's interesting that *women* really wanted those meetings and initiated them.

I knew a lot of those kids [in Greenfield] because I've worked with them in the Women's Pentagon Action and in Not In Our Name. I was interested to see them in Greenfield. One of these women from here in New England was a really great, stubborn, inspiring war tax resister. And not only was she there, she knew all the prayers before supper, prayers after supper, etc. That's what I found surprising.

*That they knew so much about the tradition?*

That I didn't even know they were Jewish. And that I had worked with them. I figured they were kids mostly of middle-class families that had retained some of the ritual and been raised to be *bat mitzvah*, to go to Hebrew Sunday School, and learn the prayers. So they had learned those forms and maybe rebelled against them a little, stored them away for a few years to do other political work. And that's where I met them. And they had moved towards feminism because of their disappointment maybe with sexism, which would be very natural for young women of the late '70s. I mean they would have been really angry if they'd walked into a *shul* and had seen how women prayed. So I think they were re-evaluating their Jewishness. And trying to think of it in these new terms. They certainly knew more than I knew.

*Both the women and the men at that conference talked about having worked with people in the movement for years—mostly the peace movement—and not having known they were Jews. Do you think people were afraid to say they were Jews—or it just didn't come up?*

Well, it does come up, it can if you want it to.

*But now, suddenly, they were all at this conference because they somehow wanted to be.*

The push may have come from Lebanon. It may have come from the sense that something's going wrong, the tradition was not meant to be like that. I mean there was one woman there who had really worked hard with the Women's Pentagon Action, was seriously non-violent, active in the lesbian-feminist peace movement and fiercely, very fiercely. And with a few Yiddish words thrown in. But there she was at the conference. If you live long enough you really become patient. People improve. If they're already wonderful, they become slowly more wonderful.

*Grace, did you speak Yiddish at home?*

We spoke mostly Russian. My mother and father talked Russian. My grandmother talked only Yiddish. I was able to talk a little Yiddish.

*But you spoke to them in English?*

Mostly. I understood Yiddish, street talk Yiddish.

*Where did your parents come from in Russia?*

South Russia. It used to be called Donetz. It was also called Stalino and before that it was called Usovka. It was named by an Englishman named Hughes who owned a steel mill.

*Was your background, your Jewishness an influence on your writing?*

I think that a lot of my writing has a kind of Jewish Russian accent. I think its language and its feeling is. But when I first began writing people said I was being influenced by Isaac Babel. Well, I'd never read him. But I realized what the influences might be—that he probably had the same grandfather I had and the same great-grandmother. And what I'm influenced by is sound and feeling which has nothing to do with literature—in the beginning. It's just ordinary speech, ordinary stories, inflections and tunes. A tune is a language, so to speak. So I think it was more like that. I felt the power of Russian writers because we read them at home. And then Jewish storytelling through my parents, through my father, a certain kind of storytelling you know, and that's not literary. But it becomes finally literature.

*A kind of parenthetical style where you sort of get everything in.*

Yes, you don't omit anything. I mean it really is a way of talking about everything at once, while making some absolutely trite remark. You can't talk about anything without bringing in the world. It's out there.

*How old were you when you started becoming active politically?*

Well, I guess I always was a little bit. I have this memory—I just remember in junior high school or high school—very early. Something came up about a pledge not to go to war or something like that. I was right there, right away. And so I began to do that very early.

*Were the first people you did that with in your neighborhood? Were they also Jews?*

Oh yes.

*This is in the Bronx?*

Yes. In high school, I would say almost all. I had a very good friend in junior high who wasn't Jewish, now that I think of it. But almost everybody was, and in high school kids were either Jews or Italians.

*When did you first start working with non-Jews? When did you go out of the neighborhood?*

Oh, well I tell you, I learned a lot from non-Jews. And that happened during the Vietnam War really. I'm just trying to think. In school, most of my friends were Jewish. All the boys. If a boy wasn't, he'd be so interesting everybody would fall all over the place. So exotic. I remember calling my best friend, Evi, on the phone and telling her that these two guys had just come over to the house, and I didn't think they were Jewish. She came down right away. It turned out they both were, and I married one of them.

Actually during the war [World War II] I left New York, and I got married young when I was nineteen and I lived in army camps, and most of the boys were not Jewish—Jesse's friends you know. They were very interesting to me. I got to know them little by little. You know it was another world, so I was interested in it. But politically I began—[working with non-Jews] around the time of the Vietnam War. The PTA—that was a good organization. As soon as I began to work locally, I worked with non-Jews. Since I lived in the Village, the people were very mixed. And the non-Jews were politically active too, at least the ones I knew. We Jews were kind of global, but the Christians had a better local sense. Many came from small towns. They believed you could fight City Hall and they did. And I learned from them. And then I got to know people in the pacifist movement. And those ideas were brand new to me. I think I was always basically opposed to war, militarism. But I didn't know there were real ideas about those things, political philosophies that were in opposition to my old socialist-centered self. And I would say that this began to happen around '60 and '61. But then again later, one of the first women's consciousness-raising groups—a very early one that I joined, I'd say three quarters of the women were Jewish. Again in the beginning of any movement there always seemed a preponderance of Jewish women. *You said you're talking more with Jewish groups right now. Do you feel that you need to talk more to Jewish groups or that there's a special thing you want to convey to American Jews?*

Well, I feel both those things, I feel that I haven't worked among Jews enough in a sense. I feel that I've lived among them all my life and that I've fought with them and so forth. But I haven't worked with them in any organized kind of way. I mean if I've joined an organization, it hasn't been usually a Jewish organization. I'm a member of New Jewish Agenda, but I don't really work with it specifically. So I feel a little—I feel I have a bad conscience.

*Grace, is there anything else that you want to say about Jewish women and Jewish identity?*

That word identity has been hard for many women who live secular lives and maybe harder for religious women and also feminists. But the women's movement has made a big difference. I don't know who it hasn't helped in this world. It's given a lot of Jewish women courage to stay Jewish and fight. And fight for those ordinary rights. R-i-t-e-s. Rights to have rites. That really seems important. It meant a lot to us to have those young women at the conference [in Greenfield]. I haven't yet said that it's very possible that I'm able to come back to this, to go to the *shul*, to do it whole heartedly, to feel I have a natural place in that community—it's possible I'm able to do all of this because of the women's movement and its influence. Because of the way a lot of Jewish women took hold, women much more religious than I. Without their courage and what they did, I might not have begun to go to this temple. I might not have done that. *It's ironic because when you think about women who are religious, they're usually labelled conservative. Yet, they're the ones that made the push.*

They're the ones that did it.

*So that the "progressives" could come in and feel comfortable.*

That's really true. I hadn't thought of it that way either.

*Often when we think about Jewishness and the women's movement, we feel anger for the anti-Semitism. We don't speak much about the Jewish women who are feminists, who pushed and fought in the Jewish community.*

Yes, who make those changes for *us*. For *me* certainly. I certainly would never have persuaded my daughter to go to services, or Vera. The connections are always surprising.

*Bernice Mennis*

# Jewish and Working Class

*A Talk at the 1987 National Women's Studies Association
Plenary Session on Working-Class Women*

When I was called to speak at this conference about working-class experience, my immediate reaction was: "No, get someone else." One voice said: "I have nothing worthwhile to say." A second voice said: "I was not born poor. I always ate well. I never felt deprived. I have not suffered enough to be on this panel." Both voices silenced me. The first came from my class background—a diminished sense of competence, ability, control, power. ("Who are you anyway? You have nothing to say. No one cares or will listen.") The second, the guilt voice, comes from a strange combination of my Jewishness, my fear of anti-Semitism, my own psychological reaction to my own deprivations: a denial of my own pain if someone else seems to suffer more.

Economic class has been a matter of both shame and pride for me, depending on the value judgments of the community with which I identified. The economic class reality has always remained the same: My father had a very small outdoor tomato and banana stand and a small cellar for ripening the fruit. Until he was 68, he worked twelve hours a day, six days a week, with one week vacation. Although he worked hard and supported our family well, my father did not feel proud of his work, did not affirm his strength. Instead, he was ashamed to have me visit his fruit stand; he saw his work as dirty, himself as an "ignorant greenhorn." The legacy of class.

And I accepted and echoed back his shame. In elementary school, when we had to go around and say what work our parents did, I repeated my father's euphemistic words: "My father sells wholesale and retail fruits and vegetables." It's interesting that later, when I was involved in political actions, my shame turned to pride of that same class background. The poorer one was born, the better, the more credit.

Both reactions—shame and pride—are based on a false assumption that one has control and responsibility for what one is born into. (Society—those in power, institutions—is responsible for people being born into conditions of economic limitation and suffering, for racism and classism. But as individuals we do not choose our birth.) That blame/credit often prevents us from seeing clearly the actual effects of growing up in a certain class: what it allows, what it inhibits, blocks, destroys. Also, if we take credit for what is out of our control, we sometimes do not take sufficient credit and responsibility for what is in our control: our consciousness, our actions, how we shape our lives.

What becomes difficult immediately in trying to understand class background is how it becomes hopelessly entangled with other issues: the fact that my father was an immigrant who spoke with a strong accent, never felt competent to write in English, always felt a great sense of self-shame that he projected onto his children; that my father had witnessed pogroms and daily anti-Semitism in his tiny *shtetl* in Russia, that we were Jewish, that the Holocaust occurred; that neither of my parents went to school beyond junior high school; that I was the younger daughter, the "good" child who accepted almost everything

330

without complaining or acknowledging pain; that my sister and I experienced our worlds very differently and responded in almost opposite ways. It's difficult to sort out class, to see clearly. . . .

Feelings of poverty or wealth are based on one's experiences and where one falls on the economic spectrum. The economic class and the conditions we grow up under are very real, objective, but how we label and see those circumstances is relative, shaped by what we see outside ourselves. Growing up in the Pelham Parkway–Lydig Avenue area of the Bronx, I heard my circumstances echoed everywhere: Everyone's parents spoke Yiddish and had accents; they all spoke loudly and with their hands; few were educated beyond junior high school; no one dressed stylishly or went to restaurants (except for special occasions) or had fancy cars or dishwashers or clothes washers. (Our apartment building had, and still has, only one washing machine for 48 apartments. The lineup of baskets began early in the morning. My mother and I hung the clothes on the roof.) We ate good kosher food and fresh fruits and vegetables (from my uncle's stand). My mother sewed our clothes or we would shop in Alexander's and look for bargains (clothes with the manufacturers' tags removed). Clothes were passed between sisters, cousins, neighbors. I never felt poor or deprived. I had no other perspective, no other reality from which to judge our life.

When I went to the World's Fair and watched the G.E. exhibit of "Our Changing World," I remember being surprised that what I believed was a modern-day kitchen—an exact duplicate of our kitchen at home—was the kitchen of the '40s. When I received a fellowship for graduate school, I was surprised to discover I was eligible for the maximum grant because my parents' income fell in the lowest income category. I was surprised when I met friends whose parents talked about books and psychology and art, when I met people who noticed labels and brand names and talked about clothes and cars (but never mentioned costs and money).

What I also didn't see or appreciate was all the work and struggle of my parents to maintain and nourish us, work done silently and without any credit for many years. A few years ago I wrote a poem called "The Miracle" about my mother and her skilled unacknowledged work. (This poem appears on p. 189.)

Clearly our assumptions, expectations, and hopes are unconsciously shaped by our class backgrounds. At a very young age I learned to want only what my parents could afford. It was a good survival mechanism that allowed me never to feel deprived or denied. At a later age, when I would read in natural history books about the "immortal species," the lesson was reaffirmed: The key to survival was always to become smaller, to minimize needs. Those species that had become dependent on more luxuriant conditions perished during hard times. Those used to less survived.

There is something powerful about surviving by adapting to little. The power comes from an independence of need, an instinct that allows us to get by. But it is a defense, and, like any defense, its main fault was that it never allowed me to feel the edge of my own desires, pains, deprivations. I defined my needs by what was available. Even now I tend to minimize my needs, to never feel deprived—a legacy of my class background.

Class background reveals itself in little ways. Around food, for example. My family would sip their soup loudly, putting mouth close to bowl. We would put containers directly on the table and never use a butter dish. We would suck bone marrow with gusto, pick up chicken bones with our hands, crunch them with our teeth, and leave little slivers on our otherwise empty plates. We would talk loudly and argue politics over supper. Only later did I become conscious of the judgment of others about certain behavior, ways of eating, talking, walking, dressing, being. Polite etiquette struck me as a bit absurd, as if hunger were uncivilized: the delicate portions, the morsels left on the plate, the proper use of knife and fork, the spoon seeming to go in the opposite direction of the mouth. The more remote one was from basic needs, the higher one's class status. I usually was unconscious of the "proper behavior": I did not notice. But if I ever felt the eye of judgment, my first tendency would be to exaggerate my "grossness" in order to show the absurdity of others' snobbish judgments. I would deny that that judgment had any effect other than anger. But I now realize that all judgment has effect. Some of my negative self-image as *kluts, nebish*, ugly, unsophisticated is a direct result of the reflection I saw in the judging, sophisticated eye of the upper class.

Lack of education and lack of money made for an insecurity and fear of doing almost anything, a fear tremendously compounded by anti-Semitism and World War II. My parents were afraid to take any risks—both from a conviction of their own incompetence and a fear that doing anything big, having any visibility, would place them in danger. From them I inherited a fear that if I touched something, did anything, I would make matters worse. There was an incredible nervousness in my home around fixing anything, buying anything big, filling out any forms. My mother still calls me to complete forms for her. When my father was sick, my parents needed me to translate everything the doctor said, not because they did not understand him, but because their fear stopped them from listening when anyone very educated or in authority spoke.

I did not inherit the fear of those in authority. In fact, my observation of people's condescension, use of authority, and misuse of power helped shape my politics at a young age. I identified with the underdog, was angry at the bully, fought against the misuse of power. But I did inherit their fear of taking risks, of doing anything big, of trying anything new. I have trouble with paper forms; I've never been able to write a grant proposal; I have no credit cards. I sometimes seek invisibility as a form of safety.

For poorer people, for people who experience prejudice, there is a strong feeling that one has no power, no ability to affect or control one's environment. For nine years my family and I lived in a very small three-room apartment; my sister and I had no bedroom of our own. When we moved from the fifth floor to the sixth, we got a tiny room just big enough for two beds and a cabinet. I never thought to put up a picture, to choose a room color or a bedspread. I had no notion of control over private space, of shaping my environment.

That feeling of lack of control over one's environment, of no right to one's own space, was psychologically intensified by my parents' experiences of anti-Semitism and by the Holocaust. These fostered a deep sense of powerlessness and vulnerability and, on an even more basic level, a doubt whether we really had a right to exist on this earth.

In college I took a modern dance class. A group of us began "dancing" by caving in on ourselves, slinking around the side walls of the gym. I remember the teacher saying that to dance one needed to be able to open one's arms and declare the beauty of one's being, to take up one's space on the dance floor: to say "I am here." For many women who experience poverty and prejudice this kind of self-assertion feels foreign, impossible, dangerous. One of the unconscious effects of being born wealthy is a natural sense of one's right to be here on this earth, an essential grace that comes from the feeling of belonging. (The danger, of course, is that wealthier people often take up too much space. They do not see the others crushed under their wide flinging steps.) Where the poorer person's danger is the self-consciousness that shrinks us into invisibility, the wealthier one's is the unconscious arrogance that inflates.

But what happens when one feels self-conscious and small and is seen as large, wealthy, powerful, controlling? At a young age, I knew the anti-Semitic portrait of the wealthy, exploitative Jew. I also knew that I did not feel powerful or controlling. My parents and I felt powerless, fearful, vulnerable. We owned nothing. All my parents saved, after working fifty years, would not equal the cost of one year of college today. What does it mean to have others' definition of one's reality so vastly different from one's experience of it? The effects are confusion, anger, entrapment. I lost touch with what was real, what my own experiences really were.

As a political person I felt particularly vulnerable to the hated image of "the Jew." I knew it was a stereotype and not my experience or the experience of any of the Jews I grew up with—but it still made me feel guilt, not pride, for any success I did have, for any rise in status. If the stereotype said "Jews have everything," the only way I could avoid that stereotype would be to have nothing. If you are poor, you are not a Jew. If you are successful, you are a bad Jew. The trap.

The economic and professional success of many second-generation Jews became tinged for me, as if we had done something wrong. To feel bad about achievement, to hold back one's power, is very destructive. My aunts and uncles, my parents, my friends' parents all had little education and little money. Yet we—my cousins, my sister, my friends—not only went to college but even to graduate school and law school. I was speaking the other day with my aunt, who was saying what a miracle it was that her four children were all professionals and she was poor and uneducated. But the miracle was not really a miracle at all. It was the result of parents who saw education as very, very important—as a way out of the entrapment of class and prejudice. It was the result of parents who worked desperately hard so that their children could have that way out. It was a City College system in New York City that provided completely free education while we worked and lived at home.

In one generation we created an incredible economic, class, professional, and educational distance between ourselves and our parents. The danger of this success is that we forget the material soil that nourished us, the hard work that propped us up; that we lose our consciousness of the harm and evil of condescension, exploitation, oppression, the pain of being made to feel inferior and invisible. Anzia Yezierska, a Jewish immigrant writer, says "Education without a heart is a curse." But to keep that consciousness and that heart and to be able to step onto the dance floor of life and say "I am here," reflecting back to our parents the beauty and strength we inherited from them, that would be a very real "miracle" indeed.

Melanie Kaye/Kantrowitz and Irena Klepfisz
with Bernice Mennis

## *In Gerangl*/In Struggle

### A Handbook
### For Recognizing and Resisting Anti-Semitism
### and for Building Jewish Identity and Pride

*The following outline was begun in 1982 and developed over the past three years as we led workshops and continued our own consciousness-raising. It is incomplete, is meant not to be read and absorbed, but used and discussed, ideally by Jews in groups or in correspondence with other Jews. A good procedure might be to take one or several paragraphs to talk about at a given gathering. Each section also has suggested exercises for discussion. Some of the topics naturally overlap. We expect this outline to require revision and hope to hear from those who use and change it.*

## Strategies of Anti-Semitism

Anti-Semitism operates through ordinary avenues of prejudice and hatred, in individuals and in institutions. In addition there are gambits particular to anti-Semitism, widely used in situations like mainstream US culture—or the women's movement—which are not overtly rabidly Jewhating (vs. Hitler's Germany or the Ku Klux Klan). Recognizing these strategies, we are ourselves less vulnerable to their manipulation; we can expose them to others, and develop strategies of resistance.

In this handbook, we have organized strategies of anti-Semitism into three major categories according to how they affect Jews: Fostering Silence; Preventing Jewish Solidarity; and Isolating Jews from Other Groups. (Strategies for resistance have also been organized into parallel categories: Breaking Silence; Building Jewish Identity, Pride and Solidarity; Creating Coalitions.)

### I. FOSTERING SILENCE
#### A. The Christian Assumption
Because the US (and most other western societies) are ostensibly secular, yet Christianity is the assumed underpinning, Jews and Jewishness are often invisible. Jewishness just "doesn't come up." To bring it up seems impolite or disruptive. Thus Jews remain invisible even to each other, unable to bond.

#### B. The Myth of the Powerful Jew
Because Jews are assumed to be rich, privileged and running the world, prejudice against us is made to seem trivial, not potentially dangerous. What's the point of mentioning it? How can we be so selfish as to expect others to pay attention to something so insignificant (like an elephant complaining about a flea)?

## C. The Complexity Argument

Often when we point to an instance of anti-Semitism we're told that the issue is very complex, subtle, unclear. This is a strategy to make us apologetic, unsure (and to excuse gentile inaction). In fact, the *majority* of instances of anti-Semitism are pretty clear. The sense that an oppressive behavior is "subtle" often reflects an early stage of consciousness, as in the early phases of feminism we found instances of sexism "subtle." Similar instances we now consider blatant and outrageous, a result of growing confidence in our perception.

## D. Jewish Disagreement

Defining anti-Semitism is a task for Jews. But Jews don't always agree—due to assimilation, denial, fear, ignorance of each other's Jewish experience and just plain diversity. Often these differences are used to silence and invalidate us when we speak about anti-Semitism: "But so-and-so doesn't think it's anti-Semitic and she's a Jew. . ."

## E. The Demand for Perfection

Jewish women articulating issues and problems of Jewish identity, seeking strategies against anti-Semitism, will make mistakes—because we are beginning. Some people will criticize not just the mistakes but the fact that we speak before we have every detail worked out. As women, as lesbians, as political thinkers, we have all at one time or another been told to keep quiet until we could formulate a fool-proof theory, until we had resolved or named every complexity. Such a demand for perfection is stifling, nothing more than a convoluted, covert strategy to shut us up.

## F. The Myth of Jewish Paranoia

The charge of anti-Semitism is frequently countered by the accusation that Jews are paranoid and overly sensitive. Jews are not paranoid. Rather, we are fearful. And rightly so, given our long history of expulsions, pogroms and massacres, given that 6,000,000—one-third—of our people were exterminated just over forty years ago.

## G. Resistance Makes It Worse

We are told it is better not to make a fuss, not to draw attention to ourselves. We are told that if we point out anti-Semitism, it will get worse, and, in the end, we will be responsible for it. (Often, it's Jews who say this, out of fear.) We are told that unless anti-Semitism is outrageous—killing us—we should let it go, not focus on it. This strategy allows anti-Semitic forces to gain strength and momentum without any Jewish opposition or resistance.

### Exercises

*1. Read Anzia Yezierska's story "Bread and Wine in the Wilderness," in* The Open Cage. *Discuss Christian assumptions, Jewish invisibility.*
*2. Make a list of subjects, issues related to Jewish identity and anti-Semitism that you have been afraid to bring up because you felt you did not have a perfect answer or analysis.*

3. List instances of anti-Semitism that you witnessed and that you did not confront. Analyze them in terms of your own feelings during these episodes; your fantasies of what would happen if you had a confrontation; what you achieved/did not achieve by remaining silent.

4. List and analyze situations in which you have wanted your perceptions confirmed and validated by someone else.

5. Analyze instances of your "disbelief" or "denial" of anti-Semitism, by yourself, by others. What attitudes in your past (family) and in your present (friends, etc.) reinforce your disbelief and denial?

6. Describe instances in which your perception of anti-Semitism was challenged by "You're being paranoid" or "overly sensitive." Discuss fears you might have about being called paranoid. How does this fear reinforce the strategy that anti-Semitism is complex and not easily recognizable?

7. What is lost and what is gained by breaking silence?

## II. PREVENTING JEWISH SOLIDARITY

### A. Jewish Stereotypes

Jewish stereotypes are plentiful and often contradictory. A few examples should suffice: Jews are dark, small, hairy, have big noses; are loud, pushy, paranoid, neurotic, hypocritical, callous, clannish, intellectual, artistic, materialistic, rich or middle class, nouveau riche and tasteless; business-people, capitalists, landlords; all educated; Jewish mothers, Jewish American Princesses; revolutionaries, commies, atheists; liberals; imperialists, bourgeois, subversive to revolutions, etc.

Stereotypes embarrass us, make us ashamed of ourselves and of other Jews. By attempting to avoid the stereotypes, we may well avoid identifying as Jews or may even avoid contact with other Jews.

### B. The Promise of Assimilation

Assimilation promises that if Jews give up their Jewishness, we can belong to the dominant culture, escape anti-Semitism, be safe. The Jew becomes afraid of associating with identified Jews, of defending other Jews. This "promise" is based on: 1) anti-Semitism is perpetual and impossible to resist or overcome; 2) there is nothing of value in Jewishness to make Jewhating worth resisting; 3) assimilation is possible. But complete assimilation takes generations, involves a complete rejection of Jewishness; and one is then left bland and rootless.

### C. Self-Hate

Assimilation is a continuum, with self-hate at the extreme edge. Jewish self-hate manifests itself as overt hostility, indifference to Jewish history and culture—considering Jewish issues trivial and irrelevant in comparison with more "universal" concerns. A self-hating Jew generally believes, consciously or unconsciously, that we must transcend our Jewishness if we are to be full participants in a just society, that Jewishness is too limiting.

## D. Jewish Identity as Limitation

Jews have frequently been pressured to give up a strong Jewish identity by being charged with narrowness, exclusivity. We are told we should have no loyalty or attachment to Jews living in other countries, or, in more contemporary terms, to Jews who are not radicals or feminists, for example. We are reminded of something "higher" or "more important" than our Jewishness. To affirm Jewish identity strongly is frequently to be told that we are being unpatriotic, unfeminist, unradical, a strategy that keeps Jews divided, indifferent to our fate as a people.

## E. Good Jew/Bad Jew

The premise of this strategy is that Jews are bad, with a few exceptions (good Jews). "Good" and "bad" are defined in a variety of ways, along political, cultural, religious, class, etc. lines. What doesn't vary is the pressure to separate from the bad Jews in order to demonstrate that you're one of the good ones.

### Exercises

1. *Stereotypes:—What stereotypical traits do you think you embody? How do you feel about them?*
*—What is not stereotypical about you? How do you feel about it?*
*—What stereotypes are most repugnant/frightening to you? Discuss your feelings about someone you know who you think embodies these.*
2. *Assimilation:—In what ways did your family encourage assimilation? In what ways did you benefit from it?*
*—In what ways did your family struggle against assimilation? In what ways did it work against you?*
*—In what ways does your current circle or life encourage assimilation?*
*—Discuss the differences between secularization and assimilation. What kind of assimilation do you find acceptable? unacceptable?*
*—Discuss the differences between self-hate and assimilation.*
3. *Limits:—Describe what you know of the circumstances of Jews living outside of the US. What are your feelings about these Jews? Outline strategies and a course of study that will fill in gaps in your knowledge.*
*—Consider your feelings about a strong Jewish identity and loyalty to other identities or perspectives. Are there conflicts? What are they?*
4. *Good Jew/Bad Jew:—What Jewish groups did your family look down on? admire?*
*—What groups in the Jewish community do you identify with? Are they connected to your family?*
*—What Jewish groups do you dislike? are afraid to be associated with? are ashamed of? (a) How much contact have you had with these groups? (b) To what extent are your feelings based on first-hand/second-hand knowledge?*

## III. ISOLATING JEWS FROM OTHER PEOPLE

### A. Scapegoating

Historically Jews have often been blamed for problems inherent in the society as a whole (e.g., racism in the US, unemployment under capitalism). Scapegoating assumes that Jews have a lot of power, have control over gentile environments (e.g., the "Israel Lobby," rather than US economic and military interests, being blamed for US Middle East policy). Jews' traditional roles as middle "men"—in business, education, media—make Jews visible and apparently responsible for policies we didn't make, but sometimes represent. Thus Jews are separated from potential allies.

## B. Polarization

Polarization occurs when two oppressed groups are pushed apart and hostility encouraged between them. Commonality is minimized. Differences and extremes in both groups are stressed and labelled representative. Both groups are viewed as monolithic, automatically pitted against each other. E.g., some Jews oppose affirmative action; most Blacks support it (many Jews only oppose quotas). This is a difference. But the Jewish community is not monolithic. Jewish women and radicals tend to support affirmative action. And on most other political issues (with the possible exception of US policy in Israel), Jewish and Black opinion is very close. Yet what we hear most about is the Jewish-Black split.

## C. Using the Holocaust Against Us: Competition and Denial of Commonality

Some people deny that the Holocaust took place, or deny that it is as bad as genocides against other people, or claim it is cancelled out by events since 1945, especially those involving Israel. Another strategy glorifies the Holocaust: we please as victims, morally pure when we are being slaughtered. The Holocaust has also become a measure of oppression: "if we're not being marched to the showers, how bad can it be?" So we should shut up about it. The lack of understanding about the Holocaust and its true effect on the Jewish people separates us from other peoples who have suffered genocide, or are now struggling against it. It erases common experience and common concerns over loss of culture, language, etc.

## D. Applying a Double Standard

Jews are frequently subjected to a double standard. Our suffering should have made us morally better; and since it hasn't we do not deserve support or compassion. The double standard is seen also in the contempt with which Jewish success is treated, the condemnation of Israel as the worst imperialist offender of the 20th century.

Jews adopt this double standard themselves and frequently expect more of other Jews than of gentiles. When Jews do not meet those expectations, there is fear and shame. Like other minorities, we worry about our wrongdoers and how their actions will reflect upon the community as a whole.

### Exercises

1. Discuss and analyze historical instances of scapegoating (e.g., the Dreyfus case, the Rosenbergs).

2. Discuss and analyze instances of scapegoating in your experience.

3. Describe a situation in which you saw Jews and another group polarized against each other. Example: Jackson's campaign. How could this have been turned around? Brainstorm strategies.

*4. Remember a situation in which you felt yourself being polarized as a Jew in relationship to another group. How could this have been turned around? Again, brainstorm strategies.*

*5. Discuss the uses and limits of comparing oppressions. Pick three groups in the US. Compare each with Jews and with each other in the following areas: cultural security, economic status, physical safety, communal solidarity. Make a chart. Leave blank areas you don't know. What have you learned? Discuss.*

*6. In what ways is the Holocaust similar to other genocides? In what ways is it different? Should the Holocaust have made us "better"? Has it?*

*7. Discuss/analyze instances in which you have seen a double standard in operation.*

*8. In what ways do you have a double standard for Jews and gentiles? Where does it come from?*

*9. Is the double standard you have for Jews and gentiles different than the ones you have for men and women? gays and straights?*

## Strategies for Resistance

That Jews, as a people, still exist is proof that we have always resisted anti-Semitism. We have resisted directly, in a variety of legal, illegal, physical, intellectual ways; and we have resisted by our adherence to a sense of ourselves as a people with cultures (religious and/or secular) we cherish. Sometimes we have had to resist utterly on our own; sometimes others have joined with us or welcomed us—or been willing for us—to join with them.

### I. BREAKING SILENCE

### A. Gather With Other Jews

Form CR/Study groups with other Jews to create community and connection, exchange experiences, validate perceptions. Especially Jews living or working in isolated situations need to come together. Jews in strongly Jewish environments may still need a focused time to discuss and learn with other Jews.

### Exercises

*1. Collect oral family histories, identifying areas of silence and shame and breaking taboos. Consider topics that emerge from these histories such as self-image, blame, guilt, powerlessness.*

*2. "No Jew is ever completely assimilated." Discuss.*

*3. Recall your family traditions and rituals, religious and ethnic customs, political and ethical values. Discuss the relationship to Jewishness.*

*4. Discuss the neighborhood where you grew up in terms of how it influenced your image of yourself as a Jew.*

*5. Compare your attitude towards Jewishness now with your attitude when you were growing up. If you have children, or if there are children in your family, compare the family's attitude towards the children's Jewishness; compare the children's attitude, insofar as you know this, with your attitude as a child.*

6. *Keep and share journals recording your observations and changing feelings about Jewishness.*

7. *Define areas of Jewishness (culture, religion) which you feel ignorant about and would like to know more. Make a list of books (be realistic about numbers), read and discuss.*

8. *Try to identify areas in which members have special knowledge: language, religion, food, history, assimilation, passing. Exchange information.*

9. *Start reading about the Jewish community on a regular basis.*

10. *Organize a Jewish cultural event—invite Jews and gentiles.*

## B. Develop Visibility

As Jewish invisibility can make us feel isolated and timid, Jewish visibility can strengthen us, allowing us to find each other, encouraging us to articulate Jewish perspectives, concerns, etc., when working in non-Jewish environments and movements. But visibility can also bring anti-Semitism to the surface, making us feel like targets. We should expect some of this and prepare responses.

### Exercises

1. *Describe two episodes, one when you identified yourself as a Jew and one when you didn't. What occurred? What did you feel? How could you have behaved differently in each?*

2. *Describe situations in your current life in which you have remained invisible as a Jew. Are you the only Jew or are there others?*

3. *Role play how you might bring up Jewish issues in these groups. Imagine responses from other Jews and from gentiles.*

4. *Review books, cultural events, forums, conferences, workshops from a Jewish perspective. Examine assumptions.*

5. *Write letters to mainstream, feminist publications and organizations on Jewish issues that concern you.*

6. *In colleges, community centers, request Jewish courses, Jewish lectures and events.*

7. *Organize events open to the community around Jewish holidays.*

8. *Organize an evening of discussion on a Jewish topic that's of concern.*

9. *List groups you're in that are non-Jewish identified and examine their concern/awareness of anti-Semitism.*

10. *Strategize ways to raise Jewish issues. Consider how to get other Jews in these groups to express concern.*

## II. BUILDING JEWISH IDENTITY, PRIDE AND COMMUNITY

To combat polarization within the Jewish community, to withstand the forces which keep us separated from this community—our own self-hate and assimilation, or the community's elements of sexism or homophobia—we need to build our sense of identity, our pride in being Jews, and solidify our sense of being a people, the Jewish people. We need something with which to identify beyond danger. We need to take joy in our Jewishness. Here we need our culture as well as our history.

## A. Examine your Attitudes About Being Jewish

### Exercises

1. *Make lists of things you associate with being Jewish; share with your group.*
2. *Make lists of things you are proud of about being Jewish; share with group. Talk about how many of these "pride" items showed up on the general list of No. 1.*
3. *Make lists of stereotypes. Share them with your group; discuss them using the criteria developed by the feminists Redstockings, to ask about statements or beliefs about women. Ask: is this true? is it a result of our oppression? is it true and valuable, something looked down on by the mainstream culture, but something we want to maintain? For example: Myth: All Jews go to college. Is it true? No. Is it a result of our oppression? Many Jews do go to college or look towards education to escape poverty or oppression. Is it true and something we want to keep? Our tradition values education: this isn't a bad thing for a culture to value. (The Myth's barb relates back to the anti-Semitic strategy of erasing Jewish oppression: How can college graduates be oppressed?)*

## B. Study Jewish Culture and History

Go out and read! Familiarize yourself with the history of the Jewish people and the history of anti-Semitism; with the various Jewish cultures; with the conditions of contemporary Jews outside the US; with Israel and the Middle East. Read different Jewish journals and papers. Subscribe to Jewish publications. Read mainstream publications, focusing on their coverage of Jewish issues. Examine the diversity of Jewish experience in your own group.

### Exercises

1. *Familiarize yourself with Jewish music, art, literature, from both the Ashkenazi and Sephardic traditions. Familiarize yourself with the local Jewish community resources. Share with others.*
2. *Learn about the Jewish calendar, the holidays; find ways—feminist, traditional, radical—to celebrate them.*
3. *Talk to Jews of your mother's generation; or your grandmother's; collect their stories. Learn about Jewish folklore, esp. the female traditions.*
4. *Talk to children, your own or others, about Jewish culture. Find out what Jewishness means for them, share what it means for you.*
5. *Study Jewish history. Get at least an outline sense of Jewish developments and wanderings.*

## C. Develop a Jewish Perspective

Had assimilation not been a central experience for so many American Jews, we would not need to develop a Jewish perspective. We would have this perspective. To undo assimilation, we need to construct consciously a way of seeing that incorporates the meaning of a given event, etc. for Jews, as well as for others.

## Exercises

*1. Know where Jewish communities are in the US and in the world. Read the news, consciously assessing it from a Jewish perspective.*
*2. Know who's Jewish; notice who (among public figures) is identified as Jewish and who isn't.*
*3. Look at analogies with the experience of other peoples: women; gays; Blacks; Native Americans. . . Notice differences as well as similarities.*

## D. Participate in Jewish Community

Some of us already do participate in Jewish community; but many feminists and lesbians, alienated by the focus on the traditional nuclear family or by religion—and a lot of organized Jewish community life seems to happen around the nuclear family or religion—have stayed away. Yet there are Jewish communities where we might feel comfortable, at least on occasion, events which can nurture our Jewishness and reacquaint us. Where appropriate raise feminist, lesbian, anti-racist. . .issues. Learn and struggle.

### Exercises

*1. Read some Jewish publications, such as* Jewish Currents, Sh'ma, Shmate, The Book-Peddler.
*2. Attend relevant events: lectures, films, exhibits, political forums, etc.*
*3. Make a list of Jewish groups and activities in your area. Think of (at least) one "thing" you might get from them.*

## E. Israel

Jews outside Israel cannot help but be affected by what happens in Israel. Often we have family or friends there; and, in any case, avoiding the connection is much like avoiding connection with one's Jewishness. As feminists, as progressive people, we need to have a positive relationship with Israel. We should know what's happening, and we should recognize the variety of opinion among Jews inside and outside Israel, including in our group. Beware of splits: tolerate differences.

### Exercises

*1. How do you feel when you hear the word Israel, Israeli?*
*2. What was your first knowledge of Israel? your feelings about it? Have your feelings changed? How?*
*3. Do the words "Jew" and "Israeli" mean the same thing? Discuss.*
*4. "Israel is like a crazy relative. You don't know what they'll do next but you're somehow connected and responsible." Do you agree? Discuss.*
*5. How do you feel when you hear the word Palestinian, Palestine? Arab?*
*6. How do you feel when you hear Israel has been attacked? of an Israeli being killed by terrorists? How do you feel when you hear about Israeli terrorists?*
*7. How did you feel when Israel invaded Lebanon? about the Sabra and Shatilla massacres? about the huge demonstration of Israelis against the war? about the killing of Emil Grunzweig, a peace protestor, by Jewish extremists?*

8. *Have you ever visited Israel? When? What were your reactions? If no, have you ever thought about it? What were/are your thoughts? Did/do you feel connected to the Israelis? How or how not?*
9. *What do you feel proud of about Israel?*
10. *Read Amos Oz's* In the Land of Israel. *Discuss; maybe role-play different characters (or female versions. . .).*
11. *Stay informed. Read a publication like* Jerusalem Post, New Outlook, Israeleft.
12. *Contact and support Israeli feminists and peace activists.*

## F. Class

Americans are especially unaccustomed to thinking in class terms. This fact, coupled with stereotypes about Jews—all rich—confuse class issues for us, making it difficult to discuss issues surrounding money. We frequently experience guilt, avoidance. Issues of class are potentially volatile. Avoid polarization, but be honest.

### Exercises

1. *What to you constitutes poverty? working class? middle class? upper middle? upper? Define/describe. What did your grandparents do? parents? you?*
2. *What parental and familiar messages were you given about class? What were you taught to do?*
3. *What do you assume about someone else's background or status if you know she's a Jew? if he's a Jew? Has anyone ever made assumptions about your class because you're a Jew? How did you feel? Were these assumptions correct?*
4. *Have you ever chosen to disguise your class origins or class status? Have you ever wanted to? Discuss. Was there a relationship to your Jewishness?*
5. *Develop a Jewish-centered analysis of Jews and class. Where are Jews in the economy? How does this break down between women and men? What is the relationship of Jews to (other) working-class peoples? to other primarily immigrant groups?*
6. *Learn the proud tradition of Jewish unionism, radicalism, Jews in the Left.*

## G. Solidarity and Critical Thinking

Perhaps one of the most difficult issues for Jews is how to bond as a people and still admit differences, criticism. There's an old joke: two Jews, three opinions. Humorous, yet painful, and sometimes self-destructive. How can we act on our principles, yet not divorce ourselves from other Jews when we disagree? This is particularly difficult when we disagree in predominantly non-Jewish identified groups or environments.

### Exercises

1. *Identify antagonisms and tensions among Jews you were aware of when growing up. What were the roots? Do you maintain some of these attitudes today?*
2. *Analyze splits in the past—political, religious, cultural. In each case, what were the benefits? What was the damage? Was the split inevitable?*

3. Look at an incident where a community/family/movement you were part of split. Why did it happen? What was the effect? Was the split essential?

4. Discuss the difference between solidarity and conformity.

5. What are the difficulties of criticizing another Jew publicly?

6. Remember an instance in which one Jew publicly criticized another. Describe and discuss implications.

7. What are some ways to criticize other Jews without feeling anti-Semitism, undermining solidarity, or creating a good Jew/bad Jew dynamic? criticism for sexism, racism, elitism. . .? for anti-Semitism?

8. When should criticism be public? when inside a group?

9. Think of a Jewish group that you consider furthest from your experience and values. Then consider if there is any common ground between you. If not, how must the question of solidarity among us be dealt with?

## H. Real Jew/Inadequate Jew

Jews are a highly diverse people. Although this diversity is a resource, sometimes our differences also make it hard for us to feel—or to stay—connected, to grant validity to one another or to ourselves. Some of us may ascribe all power and wisdom to Jews who seem like the "real" Jews, the ones who know about Jewishness; some deny validity to the experience and perceptions of Jews who seem insufficiently—or differently—grounded or schooled, to assimilated Jews, for example, or converts, or secular Jews; some—defensively or ignorantly minimize the expertise, commitment and insight of those who've spent years grappling with Jewish issues. But solidarity can only be built through acknowledging our differences and willing to find some common ground and interest as Jews.

### Exercises

*To discuss in a Jewish group:*

1. What is one way in which your form of Jewishness marks you off from all the other Jews in your group?

2. Who in the group are you furthest from in terms of Jewish experience? Do you have anything in common? If not, what does this mean? Is it possible for Jews to have nothing in common?

3. "We are all goyim to each other." (Klepfisz, p. 45). Discuss.

4. Do you fulfill/disappoint your image of the Jewish group you come from? Describe someone who fulfills this image; someone who disappoints it.

5. Who do you think are the real Jews? Are you one?

6. Does your sense of Jewish validity or adequacy change depending on context? With observant Jews? Sephardim? Ashkenazim? Hebrew speakers? Yiddish speakers? Ladino speakers? Lesbians? Heterosexuals?

7. Do you consider converts Jews? a child of a Jewish father? a Jewish mother? an assimilated Jew? a non-observant Jew? Why? WHAT'S JEWISH?

## III. CREATING COALITIONS

Because we are a small minority, Jewish self-interest demands that we draw strength from each other and ally ourselves with other groups. We need to recognize and support diverse expressions of Judaism and Jewishness. As a people committed to ethical values, we need to support the struggles for freedom, dignity and self-determination of other peoples.

## A. Coalitions Among Jews

Building solidarity among Jews is *also* coalition work. The Jewish community is diverse and antagonisms frequently have historical roots. Yet we need to bridge our differences. As feminists, lesbians, mothers, workers, anti-racists. . . we want to reach as many branches of the Jewish community as possible, and muster support for women's issues, gay rights, anti-apartheid, etc., in addition to work against anti-Semitism and in support of Jewish cultures. We need to connect Sephardic and Ashkenazi Jews, observant and secular, gay and heterosexual, on issues of concern to some or all of us.

### Exercises

*List different Jewish communities you can think of.*
*1. Looking at several issues which concern you, identify where each community would (in your opinion) line up.*
*2. How would you verify the position of each group?*
*3. Pick one issue where several different, perhaps antagonistic groups might agree, and design a strategy to connect them. What are possible blocks to coalition? How might these be overcome?*
*4. Design a cultural event in which diverse Jewish identities are represented. Imagine the work group that successfully pulls off such an event. How would you form such a group?*

## B. Coalitions with Gentiles

We might choose to work with other groups on common issues—e.g., pro-choice, nuclear disarmament, anti-violence against women; on issues of obvious concern to Jews—e.g., anti-Klan work; or in support of particular struggles—e.g., the Sanctuary movement, anti-apartheid. In all cases we need to participate clearly and visibly as Jews. In this way, we bridge the distance between other groups and Jews, especially if at the same time we have or form ties with Jewish communities.

Working with non-Jews will probably mean at some point having to deal with anti-Semitism. We will also need to be knowledgeable about other groups, dealing with our own class, race, and other biases. We shouldn't let imperfect knowledge be a reason to refrain from acting. We learn more from acting than any other way.

### Exercises

*1. List a dozen political issues you are concerned about. For each discuss:*
*—Is there a Jewish perspective?*
*—What groups that you know of share your concern? Don't forget to include categories you may belong to. What other groups do you think might share your concern?*

—*Strategize ways to connect as a Jewish group with each of these groups on this issue.*
—*Imagine different events you'd like to see happen (e.g., community meetings, direct action, civil disobedience, referendum. . .) Pick one and list the steps required to make it happen.*
*2. For those issues where Jews are not directly involved but might offer support:*
—*Discuss how the Jewish community might help. Which Jewish community?*
—*Design a plan to motivate Jewish support.*
*3. What are particular demands of support politics?*
*4. Discuss the issue of planning and leadership. To ensure participation from other groups, representatives from those groups must be included in the initial planning stages. How can you make sure this happens?*

## C. Working with Gentiles on Jewish Issues

For Jews, this is the scariest part. We are afraid no one will join us if it's "just" our issue; that no one else will care. We are not fools to be afraid. But from a place of inaction and fear, we can do nothing. We must organize ourselves on our issues and look for the common thread/threats. Send speakers, representatives to other groups to stimulate interest. Think of how to broaden the base on a Jewish issue.

### Exercises

*1. List some issues which are ours: "only" Jewish (international; national; local). What groups can you imagine supporting these? opposing? being indifferent? How can you find out?*
*2. Strategize ways to connect with sympathetic groups; to move an indifferent group to care.*
*3. Discuss the fear that no one will join us. How can you assess how realistic the fear is?*
*4. Discuss experience with non-Jews (individual and groups) being supportive; indifferent; hostile. What happened? What did you say, do? Imagine replaying the situation. Have you ever been surprised?*

## D. The Trap of the "Right" Issue

There are a great many issues and problems which demand attention. There may be reasons for focusing on one or another at a given time—to counter an embargo against Nicaragua, for example—but in a more extended time frame, working in any number of areas is crucial. Jews in large cities may be able to pick and choose from a variety of issues and active movements. Jews in smaller communities may have to create a movement to be active in. Try to cultivate a sense of possibility, about ways to express political opinion, to make change. Think of the changes we have seen and helped create in our lives as women, as lesbians, as Jews. . . .

### Why stop?

# Glossary

Words from other languages are indicated as (Y) Yiddish, (H) Hebrew, (S) Spanish, (G) German, (GK) Greek, (A) Arabic.

**a dank** (Y) Thank you.

**Alliance Israelite Universelle** (F) Established by Adolphe Crémieux, a French Jewish statesman, in the last quarter of the 19th century, it focused primarily on circumstances of Sephardim and Oriental Jews.

**aliyah** (Y,H) Emigration to Palestine or Israel.

**am yisrael** (H) "The people of Israel" or the Jewish people.

**asherot** (H) Tiny female figurines found throughout the Middle East. Probably used in women's religious practice in some way, by Israelite and non-Israelite women. They are in characteristic "Asherah prayer posture"—hands holding breasts. Male-dominated Hebrew establishment considered asherah worship in any form to be pagan idolatry.

**Ashkenazim** Jews of German and Eastern European descent.

**ayen** (H,Y) Letter of the alphabet.

**bar mitzvah** (Y,H) Ceremony marking a Jewish boy's assuming the responsibilities of an adult at the age of thirteen.

**bas mitzvah** (Y) Ceremony marking a Jewish girl's assuming the responsibilities of an adult at the age of thirteen.

**bat mitzvah** (H) See **bas mitzvah.**

**bobes** (Y) Grandmothers.

**borekas** (H,S) Pastry filled with eggplant, potato or cheese.

**borukh ato** (H) Beginning of a blessing.

**bubba, bube**(Y) See **bobe.**

**Chedorlaomer** One of the kings "of the North" mentioned in Genesis 14 who invaded Sodom and Gomorrah and took Lot captive. Abraham joined in the pursuit and saved his kinsman.

**Converso** (S) Jews of Spain and Portugal forced to convert to Catholicism, but who retained their Jewish identity in secret; commonly known as Marranos.

**Damascas Gate** A gate into Old Jerusalem.

**davening** (Y) Anglicized version of *davenen*, to pray.

**Der forverts** (Y) *The Jewish Daily Forward*, American Yiddish newspaper.

**Diaspora** See **galut**.

**Di Yunge** (Y) "The Young" A Yiddish literary movement begun in 1907 in NYC. They rebelled against "political" or "national" content in literature and emphasized aesthetic considerations. Influenced by the French Symbolists, the group included Mani Leib, Reuben Iceland, Moshe Leib Halpern, among others.

**dreydl** (Y) Top, traditionally played on Hanukkah.

**El Shaddai** Deity of the mountain or breast. Traditionally the personal God of Abram. Rendered "Almighty" in English.

**Expulsion** The expulsion of the Jews from Spain in 1492 by the Inquisition.

**galut** (H) Diaspora. The meaning goes back to the destruction of the Temple, first in 586 BCE and then in 70 CE; the dispersion of the Jewish people outside of the state of Israel or Biblical Palestine. It is any place of exile, i.e. outside of Israel.

**gefulte fish** (Y) Ground cod or white fish mixed with matzoh meal, boiled, and served chilled; traditionally eaten on *shabes*.

**Gemora** Part of the Talmud.

**gevalt** (Y) Help! emergency!

**goles** (Y) See **galut.**

**gotenyu** (Y) Dear God!

**goyim** (Y) Non-Jews; usually derogatory.

**graytser** (G) Austrian monetary unit.

**Haggadah** Collection of hymns, tales, psalms, etc. read during the *seder* on the first two nights of Passover.

**halakhah** (Y,H) Jewish law, both written and oral.

**Haman** See **Purim.**

**Har Sinai** (H) Mount Sinai, where Moses received the Ten Commandments.

**hasid** (Y,H) Adherent of Hasidism, a religious movement founded in the 19th century by the Baal Shem Tov; originally based on rebellion against Talmudic expertise.

**Havurah** (H) Lit. group, society. A movement in the US to bring Jews together to celebrate holidays, study, share common Jewish interests, organize around diverse political issues. Egalitarian usually between the sexes and in sharing rabbinical functions.

**hieros gamos** (GK) Usually translated Sacred Marriage. Part of a ritual mystic union between divinities, royalty or clergy.

**Histadrut** General federation of labor in Israel and one of the most powerful organizations in the country.

**hummous** A dip made out of chick peas and sesame paste.

**Ima** (H) Mother.

**In zikh** movement (Y) "Introspectivist Movement" of Yiddish writers in the US right after World War I. Led by poet Jacob Glatstein it advocated experimentation in modern Yiddish poetry, individualism, anti-didacticism.

**Jemdet Nasr** Represents Late Protoliterate Period ca. 3000 BCE. Named for archeological site of that period in Mesopotamia.

**Judeo-Español** (S) Judeo-Spanish; see **Ladino.**

**Kaddish** (H) Prayer for the dead recited for a year from date of burial and then on each anniversary.

**kaffiyeh** (A) Headdress worn by Arab men.

**Kahane, Meir** American Jew who founded the right-wing militant Jewish Defense League (JDL). Now member of Israeli Knesset (Parliament) and *Kach*, political party dedicated to keeping the West Bank and expelling Israeli and Palestinian Arabs.

**ken** (H) Yes.

**khas v'khalila** (H,Y) God forbid! perish the thought!

**kheder** (Y,H) Room ; traditional religious school.

**khet** (H,Y) Letter of the alphabet.

**kibbitzer** (Y) Joker.

**kibbutz** (H) Collective farms in Israel where work, food, and child rearing is shared.

**kipot** (H) See **yarmulke.**

**Kiryat Arba** A Jewish settlement in Hebron, the West Bank.

**klal yisrael** (H) "The whole of Israel"; a concept referring to the unity of the Jewish people.

**klezmer** (Y) Musician(s) who played at weddings and holidays.

**klotz** (Y) Someone who is clumsy.

**kol haisha** (H) A woman's voice.

**kosher** (Y,H) According to Jewish dietary laws separating meat from milk and milk products and abstaining from shellfish and certain kinds of meat.

**Ladino** Jewish language developed by Jews in Spain, combines Spanish and Hebrew and other language of countries where Spanish Jews (Sephardim) lived. Also called Judezmo or Judeo-Spanish.

**lantsman** (Y) Someone from the same town in the old country.

**latkes** (Y) Potato pancakes traditionally eaten on Hanukkah.

**Likud** Right wing party (est. 1973) led by Menachem Begin as Prime Minister.

**Lilith** Adam's first wife; because she was rebellious she was cast aside and "replaced" by Eve.

**Litani** River in Lebanon; Israelis are diverting its waters into Israel.

**Lot's wife** Biblical figure; turned into a pillar of salt when she looked back to see the destruction of Sodom and Gomorrah.

**manger** (G) Austrian monetary unit.

**manna** Food miraculously provided to the Jews when they wandered in the desert after having escaped from Egypt (Exodus 16:14-36).

**matzoh shmura** (H) Matzoh which is strictly supervised while being made.

**mekhaye** (Y) Delight, pleasure.

**menorah** (Y,H) Candelabra, used at Hanukkah.

**mentsh** (Y) Literally, person; but used to mean decent, adult, responsible, humane—depending on the context.

**meshuge** (Y) Crazy.

**Midrash** (H) Story-type interpretation of Bible in regard to Jewish practices, ideas, history, ethics.

**minyan** (Y,H) The quorum of 10 men required to be present for a religious service.

**mitl-shul** (Y) Secular Yiddish high school.

**motzi** (H) Blessing over the challah on Sabbath.

**NAAMAT** Women's branch of the Histadrut; see **Histadrut**.

**National Unity Government** The current coalition government in Israel between Likud and Labor parties.

**nebish** (Y) A nobody, a wishy-washy person.

**omeyn** (Y,H) Amen.

**Oriental Jews** Jews from the Middle East—the Arab countries, North Africa, Asia Minor; in Israel, they are often referred to as **Sephardim**.

**pesakh** (Y) Passover, the holiday celebrating Jews' liberation from slavery and exodus from Egypt. It lasts for 7 days; on the first two nights it is traditional to hold *seders*.

**Peres, Shimon** Former Minister of Defense; currently Prime Minister in the National Unity Government as head of Labor.

**Purim** (Y,H) Holiday celebrating the saving of the Jews from persecution in Persia by the Persian Haman.

**Rabbinate** Rabbinical Court in Israel; it has sole jurisdiction over marriage and divorce.

**Rabin, Itzkhak** Former head of Israel Defense Forces during Six Day War (1967) and ambassador to US. Served as Prime Minister (Labor) from 1974-77.

**ranish** (G) Austrian monetary unit.

**rebitsin** (Y) Rabbi's wife.

**rechov** (H) Street.

**reysh** (H,Y) Letter of the alphabet.

**Rosh Hashonah** (Y,H) The Jewish New Year.

**Rosh Khodesh** (H) Beginning of Jewish month, new moon.

**sabra** (H) Jews born in Israel; like a cactus they are said to be tough on the outside and soft on the inside.

**salaam** (A) Hello; peace.

**seder** (Y,H) The traditional meal eaten on the first two nights of Passover.

**Sha, shtil!** (Y) Ssh, be quiet!

**shabat** (H) See **shabes**.

**shabes** pl. **shabosim** (Y) Sabbath.

**shalom** (H) Hello; peace.

**Shalom Akhshav** (H) "Peace Now"—Israeli peace movement founded in 1977. Unaligned with any political parties.

**Sharon, Ariel** Former Minister of Defense; headed Israel Defense Forces in invasion of Lebanon in 1982; forced to resign following the massacres of Palestinians at Sabra and Shatilla.

**shaytl,** dim. **shaytele** (Y) Wig worn by women after they marry.

**Shekhekianu** (H) Prayer said in honor of a joyous occasion.

**Shekhinah** (H) Divine Presence in the world; according to Jewish mysticism, the feminine principle of God.

**Shema** (H) "Hear"—Opening word of Hebrew prayer said twice daily (Deuteronomy 6:4).

**sheyne meydele** (Y) Pretty girl.

**shiva** (Y,H) Traditional seven days of mourning after the death of a close relative.

**shmaltz** (Y) Rendered chicken fat.

**shmooz** From the Yiddish *shmuesn*, to chat and talk intimately with someone familiar.

**shtetl** (Y) Small Jewish town.

**shule** (Y) Secular Yiddish school.

**shuls** (Y) Anglicized pl. of *shul*, synagoguges.

**sidur,** pl. **sidorim** (Y,H) Prayer book.

**Sixty-Seven War** The Six-Day War between Israel and Egypt, Syria and Jordan, won quickly by Israel and resulting in the Israeli occupation of the West Bank and reunification of Jerusalem; often spoken of by Israelis as a turning point in Israeli history/politics.

**suka** Booth built during holiday of *Sukkes* to commemorate the wanderings of the Jews in the desert after their exodus from Egypt.

**talises** (Y,H) Anglicized pl. of *talis*, prayer shawl.

**Talmud** Body of literture interpreting the Torah, containing the Mishnah and the Gemorah.

**tantes** (Y) Aunts.

**tashlekh** (Y) Ritual performed on Rosh Hashonah; men gather at a stream and shake out their pockets over the water as a symbolic gesture of washing away their sins.

**teraphim** Sacred statuary of goddesses and gods, of various sizes. Customary part of Israelite households. Also used for the purpose of divination.

**tfilin** (Y,H) Phylactaries containing Biblical quotations strapped to the head and arms of Jewish men during their weekday morning prayers.

**Theresienstadt** Concentration camp in Czechoslovakia used by Germans as a "model" camp to show the Red Cross; nearly 34,000 Jews died there.

**Torah** The first five books of the Old Testament; the Pentateuch.

**tsholent** (Y) A baked dish of meat, potatoes and vegetables made for Sabbath; it was cooked the day before and kept warm so as to obey the prohibition against cooking on *shabes*.

**tsimes** (Y) Vegetable or fruit stew.

**tsores** (Y) Troubles, distress, woes, miseries.

**Ulpan** Centers in Israel which teach immigrants Hebrew.

**Uruk Vase** Alabaster, from Uruk (biblical Erech) ca. 3500 BCE with relief of Inanna at the entrance to her sanctuary. Believed to represent a phase of the *hieros gamos.*

**West Bank** Refers to the territories invaded and occupied by Israel in 1967 on the West Bank of the Jordan River; area of continuous struggle between Palestinians and right-wing Jewish settlers, the latter wanting the territories annexed to Israel.

**yarmulke** (Y,H) Traditional skull cap worn by Jewish males.

**Yerushalayim** (H) Jerusalem.

**yeshiva** (Y,H) Jewish academy devoted to religious study.

**yikhes** (Y) Parentage, lineage.

**yids** American slang for Jews, derogatory.

**Yom Kippur** (Y,H) The Day of Atonement; a solemn day of fasting and repentance.

**zeydes** (Y) Grandfathers.

Esther Hyneman

Joan E. Biren (JEB)

Tania Kravath

Adrienne Cooper

Raquel Partnoy

Judith Wachs

Susie Gaynes

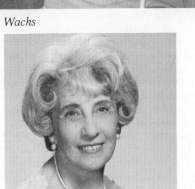

Rose Magyar

Teya Schaffer[r] with Jackie Winnow

Marilyn Zuckerman

# Contributors' Notes

**Karen Alkalay-Gut** was born in London. She lives and writes in Tel Aviv.

**Raquel Rita Arditti:** I was born and grew up in Argentina, in a Turkish Jewish family. I studied in Italy, where I got a doctorate degree in Biology. I came to the United States in 1965. I am one of the founders of New Words, a feminist bookstore in Cambridge, MA, and I teach at the Union Graduate School. I am one of the editors of *Reproductive and Genetic Engineering: A Journal of International Feminist Analysis.*

**Aishe Berger:** I am a 25-year-old lesbian wandering Jew searching for her roots; for now I've found them in San Francisco, where I write poetry and study social work. This past year, I've been teaching poetry to Jewish Elders, doing comedy improvisations and singing *nigunim* with my *rosh-khodesh* group when the new moon comes along with all of its promises.

**JEB (Joan E. Biren)** was born in 1944 in Washington, D.C., where she still lives in an effort to balance the political energy through activism with other progressive people. She is a photographer who tours with multi-image shows, most recently *For Love and For Life: The 1987 March on Washington for Lesbian and Gay Rights.* JEB has published two books: *Making a Way: Lesbians Out Front* and *Eye to Eye: Portraits of Lesbians.*

**Sandra Butler** is a writer and community organizer who uses language to shape and heal her world.

**Adrienne Cooper:** Live in New York City with my daughter, Sarah. Born and raised in Oakland, CA, lived for 5 years in Israel. Brought up in a "Conservadox" Jewish household. Live with a more or less constant internal experience, reevaluation and reconstruction of my Jewishness. Associate Director of the YIVO Institute for Jewish Research.

**Enid Dame:** I was born in Beaver Falls, PA, where most classmates and neighbors were not Jewish. My parents eventually moved to Pittsburgh, partly in search of a Jewish community. Jewishness for me has always been cultural, ethical, social, and political. Today I live in Brooklyn. For the last year, I've been working on a novel about (among other things) Jewish radicals of the '30s and '60s trying to live intelligently in the present time.

**Elana Dykewomon** is the current (1989) editor of *Sinister Wisdom* magazine, author of *Riverfinger Woman* (among other books), a lesbian separatist, descendant of the Baal Shem Tov, typesetter, poet and, after many wanderings, now lives in Oakland, CA. This story was written as an exercise in her Jewish Lesbian Writers' Group. She has a lot of dykes to thank for many things and hopes they know who they are.

**Irene Eber:** My father's family hails from Mielec, a small Polish town. I came to the U.S. in 1947 and now live in Jerusalem, where I teach Chinese history and literature at the Hebrew University. I write on Chinese intellectual history, literature, and European literature in Chinese translation. "Choices" is one of a series of short stories about the Holocaust, its aftermath, and Jerusalem.

**Eliel (Gavriela) Elisha** was born in 1954 in Jerusalem. Her mother is from Iraq, her father from Turkey. She has published six poetry books, the most recent (1988) is called *Inspiration.* One of her books is a translation of the Japanese poet Ryo Kan, and she is translating Ilda Gidlo, a Native American poet, into Hebrew.

**Jyl Lynn Felman:** I grew up in Dayton, OH. For kosher meat mother had to phone her month-long order into the kosher butcher in Cincinnati and we would drive there to pick it up. I had a full Jewish education: Hebrew school, a Bat Mitzvah, then Israel and Kibbutz at 17. I have always been in confusion about my Jewish identity, living in *galut*, being gay and searching for a Jewish community that is home. Some of my work is in *Tikkun, Genesis 2, Sojourner, Sinister Wisdom*, and an essay "Accept The Stranger in Your Midst" is included in a book about gay Jews to be published by Beacon Press in Fall, 1989. A collection of short fiction, *Chicken Wings*, is ready for an editor.

**Judy Freespirit:** I was born in Detroit in 1936. Both my parents were non-observant, first-generation American Jews. Our family had a strong Jewish identity that I experienced as tribal membership more than religious affiliation. My background is working class and I am employed as a secretary at U.C. Berkeley. I love the sound of Yiddish words and Yiddish music. These days I find a special comfort in my relationships with other Jewish lesbians.

**Ellen Gruber Garvey:** I grew up in New York City, where I absorbed whatever Jewish education I have from storybooks and eavesdropping. My writing has most recently appeared in *Feminist Studies, Sinister Wisdom*, and the *Minnesota Review*. I'm currently a graduate student and teacher at the University of Pennsylvania.

**Susie Gaynes** is the associate director of Syracuse Cultural Workers, publisher of the "Peace Calendar" and other progressive artwork. Frequently surrounded by recovering Catholics and fallen WASPS, she never tires of telling the stories of Chanukah and Passover as patiently and lovingly as she did in her grade school days, when the teacher always called on her for this honor because she was "the only one."

**Galia Golan** is an Israeli feminist, peace activist, and scholar.

**Julie Greenberg** is a lesbian/feminist activist, finishing her sixth year of rabbinical school. She is mother of one-year-old Rosie Greenberg and is working on expanding the family.

**Ellen Hawley** is a writer, editor, and teacher. She is a New Yorker in exile in Minnesota and her last name started out as Gurievich.

**Tryna Hope** is a social worker, a writer, and a lesbian living in western Massachusetts. Her *yikhes* includes her father, an Orthodox Rabbi, and her mother, a Russian Socialist.

**Esther F. Hyneman** is the product of a mixed background: her maternal grandparents were impoverished Russian Jewish immigrants, while her paternal grandparents, both born in Boston in the mid-19th century, were wealthy assimilated German Jews. While her Jewish identity comes from both sides, it was her father's family that instilled in her pride in Jewishness. Esther teaches literature at Long Island University in Brooklyn. A skilled carpenter and builder for the past 25 years, she recently, in middle age, began a new life as a painter.

**Melanie Kaye/Kantrowitz** was born in 1945 in Brooklyn, raised to be an activist and a teacher, grew up in the Civil Rights Movement of the early '60s and the Antiwar and Women's Liberation Movements of the late '60s. Graduated from CCNY, earned a Ph.D. from the University of California, Berkeley. Her fiction, essays, poetry and reviews appear in such diverse places as *Nice Jewish Girls, Lesbian Love Stories, Women's Review of Books, Jewish Currents, Sojourner, Fight Back! Feminist Resistance to Male Violence*, the *Barre-Montpelier Times-Argus*, and the *Village Voice*. She has published a book of poems, *We Speak In Code* (Motheroot, 1980), and is completing a collection of stories. From 1983 to 1987 she edited and published *Sinister Wisdom* Magazine. She teaches Writing and Women's Studies at Vermont College.

**Gloria L. Kirchheimer** grew up in a Sephardic household where Ladino was spoken and has recorded an album of Sephardic folksongs for Folkways Records. A number of her short stories have been published in literary magazines, including *New Letters, Kansas Quarterly, North American Review, Carolina Quarterly*, and others.

**Irena Klepfisz** was born in Warsaw, Poland, in 1941 and came to the United States at the age of 8. She is a poet and author of *Keeper of Accounts* (Sinister Wisdom Books, 1983) and *Different Enclosures: The Poetry and Prose of Irena Klepfisz* (Onlywomen Press, 1985). An activist in both the Jewish and lesbian feminist communities, she has lectured, written, and led workshops on feminism, office work and class, homophobia, Jewish identity, Yiddish culture, anti-Semitism, and the Middle East. She is currently teaching creative writing and women's studies in the Adult Degree Program of Vermont College and translating Yiddish women writers. In 1988 she received an NEA Fellowship Grant in poetry and is working as translator-in-residence at YIVO Institute for Jewish Research.

**Tania Kravath:** I was born in 1943 in the Bronx. My mother, an immigrant from Poland, encouraged me to attend Yiddish and Hebrew schools and helped me develop a strong cultural Jewish identity. I live and teach in New York City and am currently working in clay.

**Jennifer Krebs** was born in 1957 and grew up in the only Jewish family in Spencerport, NY. She received many years of Hebrew and Jewish education in Rochester, NY and was Bat Mitzvahed. She now lives in Berkeley, CA, and writes as much as she can.

**Beatrice Ilana Lieberman:** Born 1951—raised in San Francisco—daughter of the late Estelle—strong, enduring—and Gershon—poet, aphasic—recently returned to Bay Area after years in Israel with lover—daughter Maayan is eight and blooming—wrote poems and played folk music since childhood—currently teaching first grade and loving it.

**Rose Magyar:** Born in Hungary, 1901. Deported to Auschwitz-Birkenau July 1944. From that transport of 5000, I am the only survivor of my age. Mother, husband, four brothers, all peers, most of my large family perished. My sister and I are the sole survivors. My daughter—retired Dean of Bates College. I give poetry readings in many colleges and universities. My poems are read to classes on the Holocaust at Southern Connecticut State University.

**Anna Margolin** (1887-1952), Yiddish poet.

**Lea Majaro-Mintz** graduated from the Bezalel Academy of Art in Israel, and earned degrees in Law (Jerusalem Law School) and English Literature (Cambridge). She has taught art, written criticism and a textbook published by the Israel Ministry of Education and Culture. Her sculpture and wall reliefs are shown in museums and galleries throughout Israel and elsewhere, and have won many prizes. *Conversations in Clay* (1981) and *More Conversations in Clay* (1984) are exhibitions of her work in book form. "'Together and Alone"—a group of six figures—is in the permanent collection of the National Museum of Women in the Arts in Washington, D.C.

**Isabelle Maynard** supervises a child abuse unit in a California agency and has an M.S.W. from the University of California, Berkeley. She has been writing short stories for the past eight years and has had them published in *Present Tense, Kaleidescope, San Francisco Short Story Review,* and *Across the Generations*; her poetry has been published in *Agada* and *Shmate*. A recent play, *The Ace,* was produced in San Francisco. She is currently involved in an oral history project about social workers and collaborating on a movie script about her childhood days in China.

**Bernice Mennis:** I live in the Adirondacks, sharing land and building a home with close women friends; writing; and teaching (in Vermont College's Adult Degree Program and Skidmore's University Without Walls program in the prisons).

**Nava Mizrahhi** was born in Jerusalem in 1955 to a working-class religious Jewish family. She is half Iraqi, part Persian and Spanish. She was one of the founders of *Kol Haisha,* women's center/bookstore in Jerusalem, and was also active in the civil rights and feminist movements there. Currently resides in Oakland, CA.

**Kadia Molodowsky** (1894–1975) Yiddish poet and novelist.

**Grace Paley** is a writer, teacher, peace activist and troublemaker.

**Raquel Partnoy** lives in Bahia Blanca, Argentina. She presented her first one-woman exhibit in 1963.She paints still lifes and landscapes, with preference for Bahia Blanca's port, though her later work incorporates the human figure. Her daughter Alicia was imprisoned during the junta years, and has written about this experience in *The Little Schoolhouse* (Cleis Press).

**Susan Pensak**'s translations of poetry and prose by Argentine poet Alejandra Pizarnik appear in anthologies and literary magazines that include *Sulfur, The Poetry Miscellany, 13th Moon, Sinister Wisdom*, and *Woman Who Has Sprouted Wings* (edited by Mary Crow). She has translated a novella, *Chiliagony*, by Puerto Rican poet, critic, and historian of ideas Iris M. Zavala. Theories of salvation and the practices of redemption are her concern. She lives in Manhattan.

**Barbara Rosenblum** died of breast cancer on February 14, 1988. The form of alternating voices developed in "Reverberations" became the basis for a book entitled *Cancer in Two Voices*, which Sandra Butler is completing. It is a document of the psychological, relational, political, and social dimensions of her life with cancer.

**Rochelle G. Ruthchild** is Director of the Russian School and Core Faculty in the Graduate Program of Norwich University in Vermont. Twice an exchange scholar to the USSR, for a total of nineteen months, she has written and lectured with a focus on the status of women in pre- and post-revolutionary Russia. Active in the women's movement since the late 60s, she enjoys gardening (organic, of course) in her spare time.

**Teya Schaffer:** I am a secular/cultural Jew, a lesbian of the feminist persuasion; born 1948; raised middle class on Long Island. My father was born in Russia, my mother in Brooklyn; my Bronx-born lover and I are raising a California son who thinks of New York as the "Old Country."

**Fradel Schtok** (1890–1930) Yiddish/English poet and fiction writer.

**Sarah Schulman** is the author of four books: *The Sophie Horowitz Story* (Naiad Press, 1984), *Girls, Visions and Everything* (Seal Press, 1986), *After Delores* (E.P. Dutton, 1988), and *People in Trouble* (E.P. Dutton, 1989), a novel about AIDS activism. She has written for theatre, performance, and video and has published extensively in the progressive press. Sarah is currently at work on an operative libretto.

**Bracha Serri** was born in Yemen. She lives and writes in Jerusalem.

**Chaya Shalom** is an Israeli sabra and activist.

**Jayne Sorkin:** I was born in Austria in 1946 and grew up in Israel. My family and I immigrated to the U.S. in 1961. Currently, I'm a psychiatric nurse working in Manhattan and am the mother of two boys, ages 14 and 12. I enjoy writing both prose and poetry.

**Elinor Spielberg** was born on Long Island in 1951 and moved to Vermont on her own in 1969. She now spends her time between Vermont and Brooklyn and is completing her first novel, to be published by Doubleday. "In childhood Judaism meant stories, jokes, synagogue and women lighting candles. The Rabbi told stories in the daytime, but the best stories were told at night by the women. Not only stories, but dreams, too. I can recite two of my great-grandmother's most significant dreams."

**Elza Frydrych Shatzkin** (1936–1962) was a child survivor born in Poland.

**S. Tall** is an Israeli sabra.

**Susan Talve** is a rabbi and mother in St. Louis.

**Savina J. Teubal** is a Sephardic Jew born in Manchester, England, of Syrian parents. Savina has lived in the U.S. since 1959, where she has published many essays and articles regarding the ancient Near East and its relation to the events in the *Genesis* narratives. The second printing of *Sarah the Priestess* was published by Swallow Press in 1986. Savina is now working on *Hagar the Egyptian and the First Martriach of Islam*, to be published by Harper & Row in 1990.

**Judith Wachs** was born in Brooklyn in 1938 into an Ashkenazi Orthodox environment. She earned an M.A. from Columbia University, taught in New York City public schools, wrote on women's and antiwar issues, and joined her 11-year-old daughter Cindy in initiating the historic first suit against Little League. For the past 15 years she has studied, taught, and performed Medieval, Renaissance, and Sephardic music. She is the founder and artistic director of Voice of the Turtle, a 10-year-old quartet that specializes in Sephardic musical traditions. She is currently researching the significant role that Sephardic women have played in the preservation of their musical heritage.

**Ruth Whitman** is the author of seven books of poetry, including *The Testing of Hanna Senesh* (Wayne State University Press, 1986) and three books of translation from Yiddish poetry. The recipient of a Fulbright Writer-in-Residence Fellowship in Jerusalem, a Bunting Institute Fellowship, a Rhode Island Council on the Arts Grant, and a National Endowment for the Arts Grant, she teaches poetry at Radcliffe College and the Massachusetts Institute of Technology.

**Vera Williams:** Born 1/28/27, I grew up mostly in the Bronx with radical non-religious parents. I've been active in intentional communities (including Black Mt. College) and the Free School, Peace and Feminism movements, along with parenting (three children), writing for both adults and children, and graphic arts. My children's books include *A Chair for My Mother* (1983 Caldecott Honor book) and *Stringbean's Trip to the Shining Sea* (with Jennifer Williams, 1988 Globe Horn honor book). This year I did the paintings that accompany Grace Paley's writings to create the War Resister's League 1989 calendar.

**Marilyn Zuckerman:** Born in Brooklyn, 1925, now living in Arlington, MA, where I write and teach poetry and fiction writing. Published two books of poetry: *Personal Effects*, (Alice James Books, 1976) (along with two other poets) and *Monday Morning Movie* (Street Editions, 1981). I am working on a collection of autobiographical fiction. The story in *Dina* is from this series; another won a 1985 PEN Syndicated Fiction Award.

*A generation goes.*

Drawing by Raquel Partnoy

358

*A generation comes. . .*

Drawing by Raquel Partnoy

──────────── Credits for work published elsewhere ────────────

Joan E. Biren (JEB), "ALFA Shabat," *Sojourner: Jewish Women's Issue,* "Shabat in the Open," *The Jewish Calendar 5746,* "Workshop at the Jewish Feminist Conference," *Jewish and Female* by Susan Weidman Schneider, Simon and Schuster (1984); Enid Dame, "Lilith's Sestina," *13th Moon* (Spring, '86), "Lot's Wife Revisited," *The Little Magazine,* "Ms. Lot Makes. . ." *Pulp* (1982), "Vildeh Chaya," *Conditions* (1978), "Ethel Rosenberg Sestina," *Conditions* (1984); Ellen Gruber Garvey, "How This Week is Different," *Shmate: A Journal of Progressive Jewish Thought* (Fall 1985); Susie Gaynes, "Statement to the audience . . .," letter in *New Women's Times* (Dec. 1982); Irena Klepfisz, *"Di rayze aheym,"* Lilith, *"Etlekhe verter,"* Women's Review of Books, *"Fradel Schtok,"* Moment; Gloria Kirchheimer, "Food of Love," *Shmate* (Dec. 1983); Isabelle Maynard, "We Must Return the Hospitality," (retitled "Let's Have Fun"), *Across the Generations;* Grace Paley, "In This Country, But In Another Language. . . .," *Later the Same Day,* Farrar, Straus & Giroux (1985); Teya Schaffer, "With Love, Lena," *Shmate* (June/July, 1982), *Common Lives/Lesbian Lives* (Aug. 1984), *Center Voice,* Pub. of Berkeley/Richmond Jewish Community Center (July/Aug. 1982); Ellie Spielberg, "Straight and Tall" . . ., NY *Times;* Savina Teubal, "The Meaning of the Life of Sarah," excerpt from *Sarah the Priestess: The First Matriarch of Genesis,* Swallow Press, (1984); Ruth Whitman, "Bubba Esther, 1888," *Permanent Address: New Poems 1973–1980,* Alice James Books (1980).


──────────── Credits for Contributors' Photographs ────────────

Rita Arditti by Estelle Disch; Joan E. Biren by JEB; Enid Dame by S. Litvak; Elana Dykewoman by JEB; Jyl Felman by Susan D. Fleischmann; Judy Freespirit by Cathy Cade; Susie Gaynes by Linda Dederman; Julie Greenberg by Roz Mandel; Melanie Kaye/Kantrowitz by Judy Waterman; Irena Klepfisz by JEB; MKK and IK by Linda Vance; Tania Kravath by Yonah; Jennifer Krebs by Deborah Trontz; Bernice Mennis by Margaret Blanchard; Grace Paley by Dorothy Marder; Teya Schaffer by Peggy Hughes; Savina Teubal by Miriam Black; Ruth Whitman by Morton Sacks; Bracha Serri by Debbie Cooper; Gavriella Elisha by Lisa Cohen; Marilyn Zucker by Sardi Klein; Chaya Shalom by Julie London.